Johann Martin Lappenberg, Elise C Otté, Benjamin Thorpe

A History of England under the Anglo-Saxon Kings

Vol. I

Johann Martin Lappenberg, Elise C Otté, Benjamin Thorpe

A History of England under the Anglo-Saxon Kings
Vol. I

ISBN/EAN: 9783337077884

Printed in Europe, USA, Canada, Australia, Japan

Cover: Foto ©ninafisch / pixelio.de

More available books at **www.hansebooks.com**

HISTORY OF ENGLAND

UNDER THE

ANGLO-SAXON KINGS

Translated from the German of

J. M. LAPPENBERG, F.S.A.,
FORMERLY KEEPER OF THE ARCHIVES OF THE CITY OF HAMBURG

BY THE LATE

BENJAMIN THORPE, F.S.A.,
EDITOR OF THE 'ANGLO-SAXON CHRONICLE,' 'ANCIENT LAWS AND INSTITUTES OF ENGLAND,' ETC.

NEW EDITION

REVISED BY E. C. OTTÉ

TWO VOLUMES.

VOL. I.

LONDON:
GEORGE BELL & SONS, YORK ST., COVENT GARDEN,
AND NEW YORK.
1894.

NOTE.

Mr. THORPE's Translation of Dr. Lappenberg's History of the Anglo-Saxons having been for some years out of print, it has been thought expedient to republish it in the cheaper and more convenient form of the Standard Library. A thorough revision of the Translation has been made for the present edition, while a few of the passages, originally omitted with the full concurrence of the Author, have been restored. These and other alterations, including the division of the matter into chapters, together with the addition of an Index, and occasional notes, giving the more recent dates of the publication of works referred to in the text, will, it is hoped, be found to have increased the value of Mr. Thorpe's Translation.

E. C. O.

LONDON, 1880.

*** The reader is cautioned in respect to various statements in the first volume which rest only upon the authority of the itinerary *De Situ Britanniae*, formerly attributed to Richard of Cirencester, but now proved to be a forgery of the last century. The same remark is applicable to statements ascribed to Ingulph in the second volume. See Literary Introd., p. lii.

CONTENTS OF VOL. I.

Author's Preface . . . . *Page* xi
Translator's Preface xvii
Literary Introduction xxi

PART I.
BRITAIN UNDER THE ROMANS, B.C. 54.

CHAPTER I.

Earliest Knowledge of Britain—Descent and Traditions—Language—Religion—Government—Customs—Tribes—First Appearance of Romans—Julius Cæsar; his Account of Britain—Departure of Roman Legions. . . *Page* 1

CHAPTER II.

A.D. 43-120.

Invasion by Claudius—Caractacus—Conquest of Mona—Boudicea—Agricola—Mode of Government—Guilds—Celtic Tongue—Princes—Laws—State of Country . . . 28

CHAPTER III.

A.D. 120-350.

Picts and Scots; their Resistance against the Romans—Conflicts between Roman Commanders—Emperor Severus brings Reinforcements to Britain—Roman Losses—Truce with Northern Tribes—Romans build Wall of Defence in the North—Tranquillity restored; but disturbed again by arrival of Saxon Pirates—History of Saxon Tribes—Carausius; his Influence on the Settlement of Saxons along the Frankish and British Shores—Constantius and his wife Helena in Britain—Their Son, Constantine the Great, proclaimed Emperor in Britain—Spread of Christianity in Britain—Agreement of the British with the Eastern or Byzantine Church—Persecutions—Civilizing Influence of Romans—Roads—Churches—Picts and Scots—Princely Families—Tyranny of Roman Officials . . . *Page* 50

CHAPTER IV.

A.D. 350-446.

Roman Generals—British Settlements in Armorica—Roman Legions retire—St. Germain—Christianity in Britain—Pelagius—Miserable Condition of the Country . . . 73

PART II.

FROM THE LANDING OF HENGEST AND HORSA TO THE ACCESSION OF ECGBERHT, A.D. 449-800.

CHAPTER V.

Vortigern—Northern Auxiliaries—Hengest and Horsa—British Traditions—Chronology of Anglo-Saxons—Their Races—Modes of Reckoning 86

CONTENTS OF VOL. I. vii

CHAPTER VI.

MIDDLE OF THE FIFTH CENTURY.

English Language—Saxons—Angles—Jutes—Frisians—The various Tribes in Britain—Resistance of the Lloegrians or Britons—Success of Saxons . . . . . *Page* 107

CHAPTER VII.

Arrival of fresh Hordes of Northmen—Resistance of Britons—Ællie—Various Sections of Saxons—Cerdic—Angles—Their History—Northumbria—Britons—Their Territorial Divisions—Germanizing Influence 132

CHAPTER VIII.

MIDDLE OF THE FIFTH TO CLOSE OF THE SIXTH CENTURY.

Condition of Britain—The Dignity of Bretwalda—Kingship among Germans and Northmen—Ceawlin of Wessex—Marriage of Æthelberht with Berhta—Conversion of Men of Kent—British Churches—Gregory—Augustine—Interview between King and Augustine—Baptism of King—Conference between Augustine and British Bishops—Arrogance and want of Conciliation on both sides . . . 157

CHAPTER IX.

THE SEVENTH CENTURY.

Conversion of Essex—Rædwald of East Anglia a Convert—Æthelfrith of Northumbria's Opposition to Christianity—Eadwine's Marriage—His Influence on the Destinies of the People—Conversion of Eadwine and his Ealdormen—Paulinas becomes Archbishop of York—Peace and Prosperity of Northumbria—Eadwine resigns his Crown—Calamities of Northumbria—Penda of Mercia—Death of Eadwine—Murder of his Son Eadfrith—Oswald acknowledged as Bretwalda—His Valour and Piety—His Warfare with the British—His Conflicts with Penda—Conversion of Wessex—Coolwulf of Wessex—He falls in Battle . . 181

CHAPTER X.

MIDDLE OF THE SEVENTH CENTURY.

Successors of Oswald—Oswiu—Overthrow of Penda—Progress of Christianity—Oswiu's Efforts to reconcile the British Church with the Papal See—Synod of Whitby—Archbishop Theodore—His Influence in asserting the Supremacy of the Romish Church — Bishop Wilfrith — His Character and Conduct—Introduces the Roman Ritual and Rule of St. Benedict . . . . *Page* 207

CHAPTER XI.

LATTER HALF OF THE SEVENTH CENTURY.

The Arts in England—Mercia—The Mercian King—Wulfhere's Efforts to spread Christianity—Northumbria—Increasing Power of Clergy—Anglo-Saxon Missions Abroad—Scottish Foundations—Ceadwalla—His successive Conquests—Abdication—Wilfrith's Influence in Converting the Anglo-Saxon States to Roman Catholic Christianity—Ecclesiastical Institutions—Bishoprics—Disputes with the Scottish and Welsh Clergy of the British Church—Anglo-Saxon Churches and Monasteries 224

CHAPTER XII.

THE EIGHTH CENTURY.

Anglo-Saxon Clergy—Canon Law—Church Discipline—Use of Mother-tongue—Pilgrimages—Tithes—Saxon School in Rome—Superstitions—Venerable Beda—Decline of Northumbria—Its Kings and Chieftains—Disturbed Condition of the Kingdom—Pestilence and Wars—First Landing of Northmen on Lindisfarne—Their Ravages—Burning of Wearmouth Monastery—Defeat of Northmen—Continued Convulsions in Northumbria—King Eadwulf seeks help from Charles the Great—Is succeeded by his Son Eanred, who reigns 33 years amid great Dissensions . . . 253

CONTENTS OF VOL. I. ix

CHAPTER XIII.

THE EIGHTH CENTURY.

State of Mercia—People Warlike, Illiterate—Laws of Succession—Penda and his Sons—Æthelbald's Reign—His Successes—Offa—His Expeditions against the Saxons—Charles the Great—Offa's Dyke—London—Archbishopric of Lichfield—Offa's Learning—His Power—His Treachery to young Æthelberht of East-Anglia—Cenwulf—His Successes in Kent and Wales — Disputes with Wulfred his Primate . . . . *Page* 280

CHAPTER XIV.

FROM THE SEVENTH TO THE NINTH CENTURY.

The so-called Heptarchy—East-Anglia—East Saxons—Kent —Its Rulers— Sussex—The Smaller States— Gradual Preponderance of Wessex—Its Rulers—The Britons and Armoricans—Ceadwealla; his Baptism, Abdication, and Death 304

CHAPTER XV.

FROM THE SEVENTH TO THE NINTH CENTURY.

Ine—His Wars against East-Anglia—His Long Reign—His Laws—Boniface—Abdication and Pilgrimage of Ine—Oswald—Æthelheard—Cuthred—War with the Mercian King Æthelbald—Mercians Defeated—Wessex Freed—Cuthred's Successors—First Landing of Northmen—Queen Eadburh—Her evil Influence—Her Flight and ultimate Fate 329

NOTES 345
GENEALOGICAL TABLES:
   Sons of Woden 352
   Kings of Kent 353

GENEALOGICAL TABLES (*continued*):
 Kings of Wessex, from Woden to Ecgberht . . *Page* 354
 Kings of East-Anglia 355
 Kings of Essex 356
 Kings of Bernicia 357
 Kings of Deira 358
 Kings of Mercia 359
 Princes of the Lindisfaras 360
INDEX 361

AUTHOR'S PREFACE.

BY many it will, without doubt, be thought singular that the history of a State which has always been of prominent, and often of paramount, importance in the affairs of the world, should have been undertaken by one who cannot, in the position of a professor, have found an excuse for venturing on a task of such difficult execution, by the possession of any superior means of accomplishing it. Doubly unfit, too, must appear the individual, who, in addition to the above-mentioned objections, lacks the necessary leisure to bestow on so great a theme, in consequence of having for many years been attached to a practical calling, which, though favourable to particular historical and legal investigations, and the elaboration of his native history, is not so conducive to the grasping of general views, or to a conception of the more strictly poetic and moral elements of history; and at the same time may be regarded as adverse to any attempt at vivid description of independent events, or of individual feeling. These considerations seem to render a few words necessary regarding the personal circumstances of the Author in reference to his work.

AUTHOR'S PREFACE.

The editors of 'The History of the European States'[1] had for some years been seeking for a person willing and qualified to undertake the History of England, but had generally found that the external as well as internal difficulties attending that study had held German scholars aloof. The first historical inquirer of our time, to whom the affairs of England were familiar from his youth, and whose premature loss we have never ceased to deplore, had, it is said, at an early period cherished the hope of being one day enabled to undertake such a work. The most acute also of living historians had, at a later period, actually undertaken it, when another direction given to his investigations withdrew him from all thoughts of England.[2] When the question was put to me, What is to be done? I could at the time answer only by naming certain German scholars, whose limited leisure proved however unfavourable to the undertaking; while the Englishmen to whom application was made, preferred to devote themselves to the later centuries only of English history. Under these circumstances, and considering that some resolution had to be taken—several volumes of 'The History of the European States' having already appeared—I accepted the honourable invitation to compose the history of a country rendered estimable to me by long residence there in early days. Having completed the arrangement of the archives of

[1] Geschichte der europäischen Staaten, herausgegeben von A. H. L. Heeren und F. A. Ukert.
[2] The literary reader will hardly fail to recognise in the one the celebrated historian of Rome, BARTHOLD GEORGE NIEBUHR, and in the other, the learned and enlightened LEOPOLD RANKE.—T

this city,[1] and having consequently a larger share of leisure, I had commenced several historical and legal works, of which some are either complete, or are in part in the hands of the friends of German history; but I did not sufficiently take into account the time consumed in the elaboration of records and other ancient documents, while I placed too much reliance on a bodily frame no longer possessing the vigour of youth. And it was only the consciousness of what England and many of its sons had been to me, together with the magic of numerous delightful recollections, that inspired me with sentiments befitting one who was to recount to his native land the advantages and defects,—as well as much that appeared to Germans as extraordinary phenomena, —in the political existence of the English people.

The Author's residence in the city of his birth, the libraries of which, in works relating to the Insular Kingdom are richer than most others of Germany; the valuable knowledge to be obtained there relative to the commerce, the industry, and other circumstances of the present England; its proximity to that country, which is alike favourable to literary intercourse and personal observation; the illustrations of the Anglo-Saxon tongue which in common life offer themselves even at this day to the Lower Saxon—these were the points that could be urged against the doubts of the Author as to whether he should, or should not, devote himself to the undertaking. In addition to these, it

---

[1] They perished in the calamitous fire in May 1842.—T.

might be urged, that various occupations connected with the history of the commerce of the Middle Ages, and the use of valuable records of which some are [1] preserved at Hamburg,—a city which, previously to the great elevation of England in the latter years of Queen Elizabeth, was frequently in intimate connection with the English court—seemed to justify the hope that the work might be made useful even to the English student.

When, however, the wished-for leisure for forming the plan of the new undertaking arrived, greater difficulties than had been anticipated presented themselves, more particularly with reference to the earlier part of the history. The defects of the edited authorities are not unknown in England,[2] and the conviction of the necessity of their thorough revisal had been expressed by Gibbon, who, in his great work, was only able to apply a very partial remedy to the evil. Of modern writers, the greater number, though industrious, were wanting both in criticism and in knowledge of general history; while to the German it could not be difficult to gather new views with regard to old English history, on the paths opened to him by countrymen of his own; but for the confirmation and establishment even of views which could be proved indisputably just, all authorities and preliminary labours were wanting.

[1] For *are* we may now substitute, *were before the conflagration.*—T.

[2] It must be borne in mind that Dr. Lappenberg wrote in 1833.—E. C. O.

Even the simple work of procuring the most important original authors demanded much time, which should rather have been devoted to the work itself. Alike welcome and encouraging, therefore, was the appearance, while my volume was in progress, of the work of SIR FRANCIS PALGRAVE,[1] which, by the novelty of its views, and the variety and abundance of its matter, both imparted instruction and invited to a more complete establishment of the opinions it set forth. Not less propitious to my undertaking was a correspondence accidentally established with CHARLES PURTON COOPER, ESQ., the Secretary of the Parliamentary Commission on the Public Records, who not only made me acquainted with some new sources, but afforded me an opportunity of applying more conformably to the objects of that Commission many historic and literary notices, which must otherwise have found a place in my work only as a sort of literary ballast.

That the progress of my labour has been less rapid than could be wished, is partly to be ascribed to the necessity of a new verification and reference of the accounts to their first sources, which will henceforth, in consequence of the better materials at hand, be more rarely requisite; and partly also to the interest, never yet sufficiently considered, which the history of the unmixed German race in Britain, before their Romanising by the Normans, must possess for their Continental brethren. I have therefore deemed it right not

[1] 'Rise and Progress of the English Commonwealth.' See Literary Introduction, p. lxiii.—T.

to be sparing of anything that could contribute to the groundwork of a history of the Anglo-Saxon period, and that admitted of historic proof. The genealogical tables [1] which I have drawn up, of the Anglo-Saxon royal houses, will be found at the end[s] of the volume[s].

My earnest endeavour to know and make known those sources of old English history which are at present accessible would have been even more unsuccessful, had not the chiefs of the libraries at Göttingen, Hanover, Kiel, and Wolfenbüttel most kindly favoured me with the long and uninterrupted use of many rare works and manuscripts necessary for such investigations. While feeling it my duty to express to these estimable friends my sincerest gratitude for the confidence and kindness shown me, I feel myself called on again to mention my valued friend MR. COOPER, to whose influential mediation I am indebted not only for many highly interesting and important works for the Norman and later portions of English history, but also for the communication, before the completion of the present work, of several valuable materials, prepared under the Record Commission, for Anglo-Saxon history.

J. M. LAPPENBERG.

HAMBURG, 16th September, 1833.

[1] These, in the present Translation, have not only been revised by me throughout, but also augmented by—(1) a table of the ancestors of Woden, showing also the descents from his several sons ; (2) the ancestors up to Woden of the founders of the Germanic States in Britain ; (3) the genealogy of the princes or ealdormen of Lindisse (Lindsey).—T.

TRANSLATOR'S PREFACE.

FOLLOWING the example of my worthy and learned friend the Author, and in compliance with the general usage on such occasions, I will endeavour, as briefly as possible, to lay before the few who will honour this History with a perusal, an account of the part I have taken in it beyond that of a mere translator.

Having been presented by Dr. Lappenberg with a copy of his work immediately on its publication at Hamburg in 1834, the interest excited in me by its perusal was such that I resolved on attempting a version of it into English. For although histories of the same period in the mother-tongue and of good repute were not wanting, yet it appeared to me that in this were contained many particulars, especially with reference to chronological criticism, and to what may be called the German portion of Anglo-Saxon history, not elsewhere to be found in a condensed form, as well as much other information, which the Author's pursuits in the field of old Teutonic literature had enabled him to introduce almost as a matter of course, at a time when that field was a sort of *terra incognita* to most lovers of historic literature in England.

My resolve was partly executed; a translation to the end of the so-called Heptarchy was completed, when, to my mortification, I found that not one of the booksellers to whom it was offered would risk anything in its publication. Nor indeed were they to blame, for it seemed at the time that few persons in this country interested themselves much about old history—a study which, from some unknown cause, had unfortunately never found that favour among us with which it has for ages been regarded in Italy, France, and Germany—though the fruits of the Record Commission, and more especially the hope of the immediate publication of a volume of the late Mr. Petrie's 'CORPUS HISTORICUM,' certainly justified the expectation of better days. Discouraged by this somewhat discreditable state of things, and far from satisfied with my translation (which was a translation in the strictest sense of the word, without the slightest attempt at addition or rectification by reference to the sources of our early history), I destroyed the labour of many months; and it was not till the winter of 1842 that circumstances induced me again to think of a translation of Lappenberg's Anglo-Saxon History.

During the intermediate time I had laboured sedulously in the field of Anglo-Saxon literature, and having, while editing for the Government the 'ANCIENT LAWS AND INSTITUTES OF ENGLAND,' been put in possession of Mr. Petrie's unfinished volume and other authorities, I could not withstand the temptation thus thrown in my way to test and enlarge the text of Dr. Lappenberg's History by the help of the original writers so fortunately placed within my reach. This task led ultimately to a new translation of the whole, with many alterations and corrections, and such additions as appeared indispensable to the original, in which the narrative had been abridged and several facts unnoticed, in compliance with the necessity of conciseness imposed on the Author by the circumstance that his volume, forming one of a collection, could not be extended beyond a certain limit.

On the first notice of my intention to translate his work, Dr. Lappenberg most kindly supplied me with a considerable quantity of matter, both as additions to and corrections of the original, the substance of which will be found in the text, in new annotations, or embodied with the old ones; while my own additions and modifications have more especial reference to the text, though a few notes by me[1] will be met with occasionally scattered throughout the volumes. In fulfilling this part of my task it has been my endeavour to give our early story as faithfully as possible, and as fully as the bounds of good taste would allow. The passages from the ancient historians, occasionally interwoven into the text, I have rendered, not from the Author's German version, but directly from the originals.

Should it be objected by any one, that unnecessary pains have sometimes been bestowed in recording, from charters and other sources, the names of petty kings (subreguli), of whom little or nothing, beyond the fact

---

[1] These are distinguished by the initial T.

that they once existed, is known to us, an answer is at hand, that the knowledge of a name, especially if in combination with a date, may, in the progress of inquiry, lead to the knowledge of a fact; and, for numismatic pursuits, such notices are often of the highest utility. Even legends are not to be indiscriminately rejected, as void of value, in recording the history of times of which it may be said that the germ of many an important event connected with the establishment and progress of religion, as well as many a mainspring of action, may sometimes be found in a legend.

B. THORPE.

LONDON, 1845.

LITERARY INTRODUCTION.[1]

As all our knowledge of ancient times necessarily depends on an acquaintance with the original sources of history, it is only when such sources are supposed to be already sufficiently known, that an accurate specification of them can be dispensed with. The want of such a specification for the History of England is felt even in the literature of England itself,[1] but is more particularly disadvantageous to the natives of other countries, where the most extensive libraries are too often only sparingly supplied with these original authorities. But if it be the object of an historic work to promote a critical knowledge of history, and to aid the solitary student in his researches, mere literary or bibliographic notices will be found wholly inadequate;

[1] [This Introduction was written more than forty years ago, and consequently some of its statements have lost their original significance. This is especially the case in regard to the Author's remarks on the absence of certain printed authorities for English history; and as the deficiencies which he deplores no longer exist, it has been deemed advisable to abridge, and even in some instances to expunge, the various passages in which comments were made on the condition of historic literature in England, which the lapse of time had rendered not merely irrelevant, but misleading. And it may here be observed that the publication of the fine series of historical authorities under the official superintendence of the Master of the Rolls, and the labours of Mr. E. A. Freeman, Professor Stubbs, and other historians, have gone far towards making good deficiencies which were criticised reasonably enough by Lappenberg.—E. C. O.]

and, as a basis for such researches, an accurate review of the several authorities, and of their peculiarities and deviations from each other, must be set forth.

The following notices and critical remarks are given with due regard to brevity, and have reference solely to the most important sources of Anglo-Saxon history, to the exclusion of Greek, Roman, Northern, and German authorities, as well as of separate biographies, which will be found cited under the several periods with which they are connected.

The earlier printed collections of English chroniclers belong for the most part to the seventeenth, and some even to the sixteenth century. The earliest is that of Dr. Matthew Parker, archbishop of Canterbury,[1] containing the British History of Geoffrey of Monmouth, his epitomiser Ponticus Virunnius, Beda's Ecclesiastical History, Gildas, William of Newburgh, and an extract translated into Latin from Froissart. Besides the above, Parker, as early as 1570, had caused Matthew of Westminster, and, in the following year, Matthew Paris, to be printed; and, in 1574, Walsingham, and Asser's Life of Ælfred, the latter with Anglo-Saxon types. This collection was followed by that of Sir Henry Savile, under the title of 'Rerum Anglicarum Scriptores post Bedam Præcipui,'[2] containing the three principal works of William of Malmesbury, Henry of Huntingdon, Roger of Hoveden, Ethelwerd and Ingulf—a great acquisition for history, though so uncritically edited that a considerable portion of Henry of Huntingdon is reprinted verbatim in Hoveden. The chronicles of Matthew of Westminster and Florence of Worcester were printed separately in the same year. A few years later that unrivalled antiquary William Camden (ob. 1623) in-

[1] Rerum Britannicarum Scriptores Vetustiores et Præcipui. Lugd. 1587, fol. [2] Londini 1596. Francofurti 1601. fol.

creased the number of collections, with his 'Anglica, Normannica, Hibernica, Cambrica, a Veteribus Scripta,'[1] containing a new but faulty edition of Asser's Life of Ælfred, William of Jumièges, Walsingham (to which is needlessly appended an extract from the same work, the Hypodigma Neustriæ), Giraldi Cambrensis Itinerarium, Descriptio Cambriæ, Topographia Hiberniæ, and Hibernia Expugnata. As a proof of the little interest taken in England in fundamental historic knowledge, it may be mentioned, that so far from other and more careful editions being there produced, these collections were reprinted only in Germany; nor was an edition of the Saxon Chronicle brought out for half a century, though next after Beda this is the most important source of Anglo-Saxon history, and the basis of all that relates to this period in the principal of the before-mentioned Latin chronicles.

The 'Historiæ Anglicanæ Scriptores Decem,' edited by Sir Roger Twysden,[2] is chiefly useful for the Anglo-Saxon period, as it contains Simeon of Durham (who not only frequently supplies the deficiencies of Florence, but also gives many particulars not to be found elsewhere), as well as the abbot of Rievaulx, 'De Genealogia Regum Anglorum,' and his Life of Eadward the Confessor. Of greater interest for the ante-Norman period are the collections printed at Oxford, of which that by Dr. Fell, bishop of that city, contains the best edition of Ingulf, the History of Peter of Blois, and the Chronicle of the Abbey of Melrose.[3] In the other,

[1] Francofurti 1603. fol.   [2] Londini 1652. fol.
[3] Rerum Anglicarum Scriptorum Veterum, t. i. Oxon. 1684. fol. Of this collection no more appeared. As Fell's name is not mentioned in the volume, the work is frequently confounded with the similarly printed one of Gale.

edited by Dr. Gale, are comprised Gildas, Nennius, Ædde's Life of Wilfrith, John Wallingford, the valuable Chronicles or Histories of the Abbeys of Ely and Ramsey, besides other works of importance for the Anglo-Saxon period of English history.[1] Since this time no similar collection has appeared. Next we may mention the collection of Sparke, known as 'Historiæ Anglicanæ Scriptores varii,'[2] the chief portion of which has reference to the abbey of Peterborough, or to the Life of Thomas á Becket. Of greater interest for us, though exclusively confined to church history, is the 'Anglia Sacra' of Wharton,[3] a valuable collection of the chronicles of various dioceses and monasteries, and Lives of celebrated ecclesiastics. Many English chroniclers were, in the beginning of the last century, edited by the indefatigable Thomas Hearne, though less critically and carefully than could be wished; and as his publications are detached and independent of each other, they are consequently not easily available.[4] For our present purpose the Scottish chronicle of Fordun[5] is perhaps the only one of them possessing any interest.

The wish for a complete collection of the English historians of the Middle Ages was first publicly expressed by Gibbon, who had a more comprehensive knowledge of that period than Hume, or any of his contemporaries. It can, however, scarcely be a matter

[1] Historiæ Britannicæ, Saxonicæ, Anglo-Danicæ Scriptores xv. opera Thomæ Gale. Oxon. 1691. This volume, containing the earlier writers, is usually regarded as the first, though the second, containing some writers of the Norman period, is dated 1687.
[2] Londini 1723, in two small folios.
[3] Londini 1691, ii. tom. folio.
[4] [Gale's ed. of Gildas, as also Joscelin's (1568), are from a Cottonian MS. now lost. The extant MSS. are later and of less value—E.C.O.]
[5] Johannis de Fordun Scotichronicon genuinum, edit. Th. Hearne, v. tom. 8vo. Oxon. 1722. [6] See his 'Miscellaneous Works.'

of regret that his proposed scheme was not carried out, since it comprised the selection of John Pinkerton as the director of the undertaking.

The hope once fostered by the historic inquirer, of deriving considerable information respecting the earliest history of Britain from Welsh sources, has not been realised. The history of Wales and Cornwall has undoubtedly received some elucidation, and it is also highly interesting to have determined the very great antiquity of the poems of the bards Aneurin, Taliesin, Llywarch Hên and Merddyn, some of which may probably be assigned to the sixth century.[1]

The historic Triads of the Welsh contain considerable information, but require much illustration for their complete elucidation. Adherence to an originally perhaps well-adapted form, can, in its later wholly unfitting application, only counteract the object of the composition, and cause it to degenerate into insipidity.[2]

The oldest known British historian—if his work, 'Liber querulus de Excidio Britanniæ,' called also 'Historia,' can give him any pretension to that title —is Gildas,[3] born A.D. 516, a scholar of St. Iltut and monk of Bangor, who, after a life spent partly in travel or pilgrimages, partly in solitude, is said to have died

[1] This estimable treasure of old British literature is, with other relics, published in the Myvyrian Archaiology of Wales, a collection of historical documents from ancient MSS. 3 voll. 8vo. Lond. 1801-7. Compare Turner's Dissertation on the age of those poems in his 'History of the Anglo-Saxons.'

[2] See, besides the Myvyrian Archaiology, Edw. Lloyd, Archæologia Britannica. Oxon. 1707. Davies, 'Celtic Researches.' Lond. 1804. 8vo. Edw. Williams, 'Lyrical and Pastoral Poems.' Lond, 1794. 12mo. vol. ii.

[3] See p. 129. He was born in the year of the battle of Bath, which Beda, from a misconception of the text of Gildas, places in 493.

at the age of fifty-four, and to have been buried in the abbey of Glastonbury. To Gildas is also ascribed an 'Epistola,' wherein he pours forth the bitterest lamentations over the corruption and general wickedness of his time. The History must have been composed in the year 560, the Epistle before 547,[1] in which year Maglocun, king of Gwynedd, mentioned in it, died.[2] Beda, Alcwine, and Lupus cite Gildas, surnamed the Wise.[3] Geoffrey of Monmouth refers to a larger historical work of Gildas, which is no longer extant, unless it be the 'Historia Britonum,' which bears the name of Nennius.[4]

This last-mentioned work, entitled also 'Eulogium Britanniæ,' is usually ascribed to Nennius, abbot of Bangor, a pupil of Elbod, archbishop of Gwynedd.[5] The year 688, assigned as that of its composition, can, therefore, have reference only to the work in its original form; that which has reached our time having many additions and interpolations. The preface to the ordinary manuscripts places its composition in the year 858, a date reconcileable with 809, that of the death of Elbod. A valuable manuscript of this work in the Vatican, of the tenth century, in which the

[1] Both works are printed in Gale, t. i.; the first also in C. Bertrami Britannicarum Gentium Historiæ antiquæ Scriptores III. Havniæ. 1758. 8vo. Since the first edition by Polydore Vergil (Lond. 1526. 8vo.), Gildas has been frequently printed.

[2] Annales Cambriæ h. a. King Constantine, who is likewise mentioned by Gildas, was living in the year 589. See Annal. Camb.

[3] See also Will. Malmesb. de Antiq. Glaston. ap. Gale, t. i. p. 296. A 'Life of Gildas,' "scripta a monacho Ruyensi," is printed in the Bibliotheca Floriacensis,' Lugd. 1645. 8vo. [See Stevenson's edition, printed uniformly with Gildas, for the English Historical Society. —T.]

[4] This is Turner's opinion. History of the Anglo-Saxons, vol. i. p. 201.   [5] See Stevenson's edit. pref. p. viii.

greater part of these additions are wanting, names Mark the Hermit as the author, or, perhaps, the copier only, in the year 945. An edition from this manuscript, with learned and excellent remarks, was published by the Rev. W. Gunn.[1] Nennius names as his authorities the Annales Romanorum, Chronica S. S. Patrum, and Scripta Scotorum Anglorumque et Traditio Veterum. The Welsh Triads are undoubtedly comprised in the last, as his work abounds in trilogies.[2] An important circumstance for criticism seems to have been overlooked, viz. that a considerable portion of this work has been inserted, and often verbatim, by Henry of Huntingdon in his Chronicle, though without mention of the name either of Nennius or of Mark the Hermit. Thus (p. 695, edit. Petrie), "apud quondam auctorem (Nenn. ix.) reperi." (Ib. p. 707) "dicitur a quibusdam" (Nenn. xxxviii. xxxix.). In one place (p. 712) he quotes him under the name of "Gildas historiographus."[3] The chronology followed by Nennius is that of Eusebius, though, in the manuscripts, particularly in that of Mark, it is much corrupted.

Geoffrey ap Arthur, born at Monmouth in 1152, bishop of St. Asaph, is the English foster-brother of the Danish Saxo Grammaticus. In the choicest Latin

[1] Historia Britonum, by Mark the Hermit. Lond. 1819. 8vo.
[2] Cap. vii. "Venerunt tres filii cujusdam militis Hispaniæ cum xxx. chiulis apud illos, cum xxx. mulieribus in unaquaque chiula;" Cap. xxv. "Nonus (3 × 3) fuit Constantinus;" Cap. xxvii. "Tribus vicibus occisi sunt duces Romanorum a Britannis;" Cap. xxviii. "tres chiulæ;" Cap. xlvii. three battles with the Saxons; Cap. xlviii. "Hengistus elegit ccc. milites," etc.
[3] The passages from Nennius to be found in Henry of Huntingdon are particularly from cc. 2-4, 9, 10, 16, 23, 28, 36, 38, 47-49, 51, 54, 61, 62. Some passages in Huntingdon accord most closely with the Vatican MS., e.g. p. 712, ed. Petrie, "Arthurus belliger."

of his time he has composed a history of the Britons,[1] consisting of the grossest fables, interpersed with some historic traditions. In later times authors seem to have unanimously agreed in an unqualified rejection of the entire work, and have therefore failed to observe that many of his statements are supported by narratives to be found in writers wholly unconnected with and independent of Geoffrey. He professes to have merely translated his work from a chronicle in the British tongue, called 'Brut y Brenhined,' or 'History of the Kings of Britain,' found in Brittany and communicated to him by Walter, archdeacon of Oxford.[2] The 'Brut' of Tysilio[3] has, with some probability, been regarded as the original of Geoffrey's work, though it is doubtful whether it may not itself be rather an extract from Geoffrey.[4] The Latin elaboration of the British original seems to have been completed about the year 1128. That the whole is not a translation, appears from passages interpolated, in many places verbatim, from the existing work of Gildas,[5] of whom (lib. iv. 20, vi. 13, xii. 6) he cites another work, 'De Victoria Ambrosii,' no longer extant. From Beda, of whom he speaks (lib. xii. 14), Geoffrey has rarely

[1] Editio princeps ab Ascensio, 1508, 4to, from three Parisian MSS.
[2] Not Walter Mapes, as is generally supposed, but an early Walter Calenius. See Douce in Warton, H. E. P. vol. i. p. 60, edit. 1840.
[3] Translated by P. Roberts, and printed in the Welsh Archaiology, vol. ii., under the title of 'A Chronicle of British Kings.' See Dissertation on the origin of Romantic fiction in Europe, in Warton, H. E. P.
[4] Turner, H. of the A.-SS. vol. i. p. 159.
[5] All doubt will vanish on comparing Geoffrey vi. 3, with Gildas cc. xiv-xvi. Cf. also Geoffrey v. 5. with Gildas viii.; Geoffrey v. 3, 14, with Gildas x.; and xii. 6. with Gildas xix.

LITERARY INTRODUCTION.   xxix

extracted verbatim, though he seems, in many places, to have had before him either Nennius or his original,[1] since the similarity of thought and style and the identity of several Latin expressions can hardly be accidental.[2]

Among the writers who copy from Geoffrey of Monmouth, we must not reckon either William of Malmesbury or Henry of Huntingdon, both of whom he mentions at the end of his own work. Ordericus Vitalis is probably the first who (though without naming him) has excerpted from him, viz. lib. xii., in the prophecy of Merlin (Geoff. bk. vii. 3). After him comes Alfred of Beverley, who cites the 'Historia Britonum,' without mention of the author, and does not conceal his doubts as to its credibility. The 'Historia Britonum,' cited in the Chronicle of Albericus, is probably that of Geoffrey.[3] Gervase of Tilbury gives copious extracts from him, and is said to have written four books of Illustrations of his work; and Ponticus Virunnius of Treviso,[4] who lived at the close of the fifteenth century, made an epitome of it in six books.

Several writers, even contemporaries of Geoffrey, have expressed themselves strongly against his propagation of the legends concerning Arthur,[5] under the

[1] Compare particularly Geoffrey vi. 12-15, 17, 40-42, with Nennius xxxvi., xlv., xlvii., l.-lii.
[2] The edition of Geoffrey of Monmouth in Parker's collection is extremely faulty. An edition from the excellent MS. in the library of the Prince of Schaumburg-Lippe at Bückeburg would remove many critical doubts.
[3] See p. 5, and an. 434, 442, etc.; also concerning Merlin's prophecies, aa. 717, 1136, 1139.
[4] In Parker's collection.
[5] Giraldus Cambrensis (vols. i. ii. iii. iv. edited by J. S. Brewer; vols. v. vi. vii., edited by J. F. Dimock), 1861-1877.—E. C. O.

guise of authentic history. Among these William of Newburgh and Giraldus are the most conspicious; and at an earlier period William of Malmesbury had also declared himself against the British traditions of Arthur. On the other hand, the welcome reception given to this clothing and embellishment of the old favourite traditions was greatly promoted by the policy of Henry the First: which may even have given occasion to the composition of Geoffrey's work.[1]

'Le Brut d'Angleterre' of Robert Wace appears to be a French imitation of Geoffrey,[2] an old English translation of which, made in the thirteenth century by Layamon, a priest dwelling on the banks of the Severn,[3] proves the delight taken by the people in these traditions. In his preface, Layamon informs us that he did not merely translate Wace, but made use of other historic sources.

The Chronicle of Caradoc, a monk of Llancarvan, has been estimated too highly with reference to English history. This work, which reaches to the year 1156, has been translated and edited, first in 1584 by H. Llwyd and Dr. Powell, and secondly in 1697 by H. Wynne. Its chief basis is the Anglo-Saxon Chronicle and a Welsh chronicle, into which the author has interwoven many British traditions, though very uncritically and unchronologically. It is believed to have

---

[1] This supposition is rendered very probable by Turner. See 'History of England,' vol. iv. pp. 339-355.

[2] Cf. Warton, H. E. P. vol. i. p. 58, edit. 1840; also the Abbé de la Rue's papers in the Archæologia, voll. xii.-xiv.

[3] [This translation, so important for the old language of England, has been edited with a prose version in modern English, by Sir F. Madden, for the Society of Antiquaries (London, 3 vols. 1847). —E. C. O.]

been composed in the monastery of Strata Florida. Some manuscripts are as early as the year 1410.[1] The Welsh chronicle used by Caradoc is probably the 'Chronicon Walliæ,' from the year 444 to 954, together with the beginning of the continuation of the same, or the 'Chronicon Cambriæ,' to the year 1286. An edition of both is given in the ' Corpus Historicum ' under the title of 'Annales Cambriæ.'[2] The chronology followed in these Annals is not reckoned from the birth of Christ, but begins with a year which may possibly be intended for that of the coming of the Saxons, but which would indicate an adherence to the Anglo-Saxon chronology, while among the Welsh we might rather expect to find a continuation of the Roman annals. The uncertainty arising from this mode of calculating is the more to be regretted, as these few pages, notwithstanding their brevity of detail, contain valuable notices of the rulers and of the military history of all the British tribes; and the general history of the Britons, as it has hitherto been known to us from Caradoc, acquires from them numerous as well as important additions and rectifications. ' The Chronicle of the Princes of Wales,' written in Welsh, entitled ' Brut y Tywysogion,' begins with the abdication of Cadwaladyr, in the year 681, in which Tysilio and Geoffrey of Monmouth terminate, and is continued to the conquest of Wales by Edward the First.[3] This work (which, to the end of the ninth century, appears to have been translated from the ' Annales Cambriæ')

[1] See Cooper on the Public Records, vol. ii. p. 457.
[2] Annales Cambriæ, edited by the Rev. John Williams ab Ithel. 1860.—E. C. O.
[3] ' Brut y Tywysogion,' or the Chronicles of the Princes of Wales, edited by the Rev. John Williams ab Ithel. 1860.—E. C. O.

has been erroneously attributed to Caradoc of Llancarvan. The 'Brut y Sacson' is merely a manuscript, somewhat varying from the 'Brut y Tywysogion,' interpolated with passages from the Annals of Winchester (ascribed without sufficient reason to Richard of Devizes) and other chronicles.

The oldest Irish chronicles, written partly in Irish and partly in Latin, contain but little useful matter for Anglo-Saxon history, though they report some circumstances illustrative of the battles of the inhabitants of Scotland and Wales with the Anglo-Saxons, with a few otherwise unknown particulars and some variations, which cannot, however, shake our faith in Beda and the Anglo-Saxon chroniclers, but deserve attention as originating from other records of history. Dr. Charles O'Connor published a collection of these Annals under the auspices of the late duke of Buckingham and Chandos, entitled 'Rerum Hibernicarum Scriptores Veteres, auctore Carolo O'Connor, S.T.D. Buckinghamiæ,' 1814–1826. iv. tom. The first volume contains introductions, giving very instructive accounts of Irish manuscripts, the chronology of the Irish kings, the oldest proofs of the history of Ireland from the Greek and Roman authors, as well as from native historians and poets. The second contains—I. Annales Tigernachi ab anno 305 a. C. ad 1088 p. C. II. Annales Inisfalenses ab anno 428 ad 1088. III. Annales Buelliani ab anno 420 ad 1245. The third volume contains the Quatuor Magistrorum Annales Hibernici usque ad annum 1172, collected about the year 1634 by Michael O'Clery, a Franciscan friar, and other learned Irishmen. In the fourth volume is given a complete edition of the Annales Ultonienses ab anno 431 ad 1131, previously known only from some printed fragments.

LITERARY INTRODUCTION.   xxxiii

The General Index to the whole, which closes the last volume, can hardly be said to correspond to the industry displayed in the work itself.

Beda's great work, 'The Ecclesiastical History of the Angles,' must be reckoned among the most complete, and, for posterity, as one of the most important works of that age. The first twenty-two chapters of the first book are chiefly verbatim extracts from Orosius, Gildas, a legend of St. Germanus, with a few others, the sources of which cannot with certainty be indicated. In the greater and more important portion of his history, Beda confirms the credibility of his narrative by naming the various archbishops, bishops and abbots among his countrymen and contemporaries, who had supplied him with all necessary information from their own archives and even from those of the papal see. Many other individuals were also questioned by him, the substance of whose testimony, with regard to contemporary events and credible tradition, is embodied in his admirable work.[1]

The other historical writings of Beda are — two Lives of St. Cuthberht (one in hexameters), and the interesting History of the Abbots of Wearmouth, viz. Benedict, Ceolfrith, Eosterwine, Sigefrith and Hwætberht. His Chronicon also contains some historic notices,

[1] Cf. Schmid, l. cit., and his 'Introduction to the Laws of the Anglo-Saxons.' See also p. 265 of this volume. The best edition of the Latin text, and of the A.-S. version of Beda's History, as well as of the smaller historical pieces, is that of John Smith, Cantab. 1722, folio. Regarding a MS. of the church history of the eighth century, and a projected edition by the Archivarius de Ram at Mechlin, see Mone, 'Quellen und Forschungen,' Th. i. [An excellent edition of Beda's historical works has been published by Mr. Stevenson, in 2 voll. 8vo, for the English Historical Society. An edition of all Beda's works has also been recently published by the Rev. Dr. Giles.—T.]

VOL. I.

which have been used by Paul Warnefrid in his History of the Lombards, and at a later period have been transferred into the numerous works to which Beda's Chronicle has served as a basis.

Meritorious and comprehensive works have often been prejudicial to historic research, by casting into oblivion the materials out of which they have been formed. This observation applies particularly to the History of Beda, and we feel its truth the more acutely, as it is evident that he must have found much recorded matter relative to the history of his country, which the plan of his work did not permit him to insert: hence our information with regard to Wessex, the most important of the Anglo-Saxon States, is extremely scanty. Among such records may be enumerated, Genealogies of the royal races, Lists of the successions of kings and eminent ecclesiastics, Necrologies or Obituaries, and Dionysian tables.

Of the oldest genealogies, there is one that deserves especial notice, which is given at the end of a manuscript of Nennius, written in a British hand, and containing some important matter relating to the eastern and northern kingdoms of England. Others, hitherto incompletely printed, are inserted into the texts of the Saxon Chronicle and Florence of Worcester, whence they have passed into other chronicles.[1] With reference to Northumbria, much matter of this kind is to be found in Simeon of Durham.

Many regal tables are blended with the genealogies. Such a table of the West Saxon kings has been repeatedly printed,[2] and because it concludes with Ælfred, it

[1] See Textus Roffensis, cc. xxxvi. xxxvii.
[2] Prefixed to Wheelocke's edit. of Beda, p. 5; after Spelman's Vita Ælfredi, p. 199. Inserted by Gibson and Ingram in the Sax. Chron. a. 495.

has, without sufficient ground, been attributed to that monarch. It not only deviates materially from the common accounts, with respect to the regnal years of the West Saxon kings, in assigning to Cerdic a reign of sixteen years only instead of thirty-six, but is also inconsistent with itself, by placing the accession of Ælfred 396 years after the year 494, *i.e.* in 890, instead of A.D. 871. The primitive custom of dating public documents from the regnal years of the kings must have made an accurate knowledge of those years a matter of general necessity, as Beda also testifies, when speaking of many recorders of royal reigns, who, by a judicial sentence, blotted from their list the names of two unworthy kings,[1] adding the year of their reign to those of their worthier successor.

The Necrologies contain, besides the day of the death of these for whose souls masses were to be celebrated, an account of the donations whereby they rendered themselves worthy of that benefit, also the names of the kindred with whom the patronage of the foundations remained, and other particulars often of general interest.[2] The old English Calendar is a large necrology, consisting for the most part of the names of Anglo-Saxon saints and pious benefactors, bearing evident signs of its origin from the obituaries of several churches.

From what we are able to ascertain, small chronicles were composed before the time of Beda, though probably not founded on the Dionysian nineteen-yearly Easter tables, but rather on the regnal years.[3]

[1] Osric of Deira and Eanfrith of Bernicia.
[2] See such a necrology from the cathedral of Canterbury in 'Anglia Sacra,' t. i. p. 52 sq.
[3] It has already been remarked by others, that the Annales

Although the very probable origin of the oldest German annals, to be found written on the margins of the Dionysian tables in the Scottish cloisters of Ger-

Majores Juvaviensis (or Annals of Salzburg, printed in Mon. Germ. Histor. t. i.) bear on their face signs of their Anglo-Saxon origin. Their real or presumed errors will be discussed in another place; here we shall merely remark, that they alone supply us with the day of the death of Eadbald, king of Kent, viz. xiii. Kal. Feb. a. 640. More important, however, in a similar respect are the Annales Lauresham, Alamannici et Nazariani, though for their just appreciation requiring illustration; we must, therefore, in the first place, observe, that "a. 713 mors Alfrede et A'dulfi regis," is not an erroneous memorial of the death of king Ealdfrith (Aldfrith), who died in 705, but of Alflæd, the daughter of Oswiu of Northumbria, born in 654, who died in her 59th year as abbess of Whitby, consequently in 713 (see Beda, iii. 24), and of Ealdwulf or Aldulf, king of the E. Angles, who succeeded to the crown in 664, the year of whose death was hitherto unknown. In the 'Annales Petav.' also his death is recorded in 713, under the name of Agledulfus. Under the name of the abbot Domnanus, whose death is placed in 705, hardly any other can be meant than the celebrated abbot of Hii or Iona, Adamnan, who, as we know from Beda, v. 1, 15, died about that time. The year 702 adopted by the editors is, as Smith himself confesses, arbitrary. Tigernach, Annal. and Fabricius (Bibl. Med. Ævi) nearly approximate to the above date, viz. ix. Kal. Oct. 704. Disguised as this name is, as well as those of other bishops and abbots, yet their sound enables us to recognise their Irish origin. Anno. 729, Macflatheus is probably the same name as the abbot of Bangor's, Machlaisreus, in the ancient antiphoner of that cloister (Muratori Anect. t. iv. p. 159). In Dubdecris abbas, ob. 726, may perhaps be concealed a successor of Adamnan at Hii, who lived between 716 and 729, by Beda (v. 22) named Duunchadus. Anno 707, " Dormitio Tigermal," probably Tigernoth or Tigernach, bishop and confessor, whose death-day was celebrated in the Anglo-Saxon church on the 5th April. Anno 705, " Canani episcopi" we must not seek in Caman, abbot of Bangor, or the later Cronan, but, perhaps, in bishop Colman, who had left Lindisfarne in 664 and returned to Hii. An abbot is mentioned as having died in 716 in Tigernach, Annal. h. a. Also in the ancient 'Annales breves Fuldenses' (Monum. Germ. Hist. ii. 237) are

many, may tend to show that this usage was carried thither from Britain, still the practice of Scottish monks would prove nothing for the Anglo-Saxons, and sufficient traces are, moreover, to be found, that among the latter an era was in use dating from their coming into Britain, which, at least in secular matters, they had not laid aside in the time of Beda. This chronology, combined with the record of the regnal years, has, to the exclusion of the Christian era, been used by Henry of Huntingdon and other later chroniclers, and justifies the inference of sources no longer in existence.

The oldest of these small chronicles known is a Northumbrian one, ending shortly after the death of Beda.[1] Of some others, mentioned in catalogues of manuscripts in the libraries of England, we are without the means of judging whether they are earlier than Beda and the Saxon Chronicle, or epitomes of them. Some larger ancient chronicles also still exist in manuscript in the English libraries; among them may possibly one day be found the 'Gesta Anglorum,' cited by Adam of Bremen,[2] which work I am unable to recognise in any of the known authorities.

An important work for a most interesting period of English history is the Life of King Ælfred by his friend Asser, bishop of Sherborne. Though this biography itself has not reached our times in any good

given, besides the years of the death of the Northumbrian kings Ecgfrith and Osred, those of the Scottish bishops of Lindisfarne, Aidan, Finan and Colman: the year of the last is, however, to be referred to that of his above-mentioned departure. In the 'Fasti sive Annales Corbeienses' (ap. Pertz. Monum. t. iii.) are likewise to be found notices of Finan, Colman and Ecgfrith.

[1] Printed in Wanley's Catalogue, p. 288; in Smith's preface to Beda; and in Petrie, Corpus Historicum, p. 290.
[2] Lib. i. c. 35, and ii. 15.

manuscript, we are fortunately enabled to restore it in many places from Florence of Worcester, who has inserted a considerable portion of it verbatim into his chronicle. In the Cottonian library there was a manuscript of Asser of the tenth century, which was slighted because it was wanting in several passages to be found in the other manuscripts, though they were also wanting in Florence. It was, consequently, pronounced defective, though the genuineness of the greater number of these passages is extremely questionable: as an instance may be cited the celebrated one relative to the antiquity of the University of Oxford, which first appeared in Camden's edition, and the non-appearance of which in the best manuscripts has, in the judgment of party-spirit, rendered them obnoxious to suspicion.[1] These passages have at a later period been inserted into Asser's Life of Ælfred from a work to which the name of Asser's Annals has erroneously been given,[2] although it is a compilation from the Saxon Chronicle, Dudo's Norman History, several legends, Asser's Life of Ælfred, and other sources, and can hardly be earlier than the eleventh century. To these Annals the title of 'Chronicon Fani Sancti Neoti' was given by Leland, from his having found them in that place.[3]

After Beda, the chief source of the early history of England, and one of the most important in the whole historiography of Northern Europe, is the Anglo-Saxon Chronicle, composed in the language of the country, and

[1] Edit. Parker, 1570. Camden, 1600 and 1603. Annales Rerum Gestarum Ælfredi, auct. Asserio, rec. F. Wise. Oxon. 1722. 8vo, containing a collation with the Cottonian MS. Printed also in the Corpus Historicum.
[2] In Gale's collection, t. i.
[3] See Wise's preface to his edit. of Asser.

in the later centuries, abounding in contemporaneous narratives. A thorough critical examination of its authorities, manuscripts, and versions would be a work of the highest utility for English history, but this has hitherto been but very partially attempted, and without any great result. Such an examination is the more difficult, as the texts of the manuscripts, or rather the elaborations of them, which have been written in various monasteries, often differ from each other, and have, in the printed editions, been by their editors blended together without regard either to dialect or locality.[1]

The oldest known manuscript of the Saxon Chronicle is that in the library of Corpus Christi College, Cambridge, written to the year 891 in the same hand, and not of later date than the tenth century.[2] The dialect in which it is composed seems to be the Mercian,[3] while the other copies are in that of Wessex. It is continued in Anglo-Saxon to the year 1070, and in Latin to 1071. This manuscript, which should serve as the basis of a text, has hitherto been only partially used by the editors.[4]

The other manuscripts are—1. One formerly belonging to the abbey of St. Augustine at Canterbury, now in the Cottonian library, where it is marked, Tiberius A. vi. It extends to the year 997. Another copy

[1] This want has been supplied through the labours of the Translator of the present work. See the 'Anglo-Saxon Chronicle, according to the several Original Authorities,' edited, with a translation, by B. Thorpe, and published by the authority and under the direction of the Master of the Rolls, 1861.—E. C. O.

[2] Accounts of the several MSS. are given in Ingram's edition, and in Cooper on the Public Records, ii. p. 167.

[3] [Earle disputes this fact; see his edition of 'Two of the Saxon Chronicles Parallel,' p. viii.—E. C. O.]

[4] For a full account of the MSS. of the Chronicle, see Preface to Thorpe's 'Anglo-Saxon Chronicle,' 1861.—E. C. O.

(Otho, B. xi.), continued to the year 1001, perished in the fire at Ashburnham House in 1731. This was the basis of Wheelocke's edition.[1] 2. A manuscript presented to the Bodleian library by archbishop Laud, marked Laud 636 [formerly E. 80].[2] This manuscript, originally brought down to the year 1122, has been continued (with many Normanisms in language and orthography) to 1154. It was written in the abbey of Medeshamstede (Peterborough), and contains many demonstrably false documents relative to that foundation. From which circumstance—though its text indisputably belongs to the more recent ones—it has sometimes, though rather rashly, been concluded, that the monks of Peterborough were the original authors of the Saxon Chronicle. 3. Greatly abridged and Normanised, though enriched with some accounts wanting in the other copies, is a manuscript originally perhaps from Canterbury, but now in the Cottonian library (Domitian A. viii.). Both this manuscript and the one last mentioned have been particularly used in Gibson's edition.[3] Gibson used also a Peterborough manuscript, brought down to the year 1016, and thence continued beyond 1080, but now lost. 4. Of greater importance are two manuscripts used by Ingram in his edition of the Chronicle, one containing the annals of the abbey of Abing-

[1] Cantab. 1643. folio, printed at the end of his edition of Beda's History.
[2] Literal translations into Latin from the Laudian MS. are contained in the Annales Waverleienses (ap. Gale, t. ii.), which we know, however, only from the year 1066. Less exact, but not to be mistaken, is the use made of this MS. by Henry of Huntingdon.
[3] London, 1823. 4to, with an English translation and critical remarks. An English translation also by Miss Gurney was printed but not published; it is highly commended.

don to the year 1066, the other those of the cathedral of Worcester to the year 1079, both in the Cottonian library (Tiber. B. i. and B. iv.). These are nearly allied to each other, and in the later years have many valuable accounts, which in the other more strictly Saxon Chronicles are given more briefly or differently. 5. A transcript from an unknown original, made by Lambarde in 1563, containing the history from A.D. 1043 to 1079. It is printed in the Appendix to Lye's Dictionary, and agrees verbatim with what Ingram gives from the Worcester copy.

This slight review may serve to call the attention of everyone familiar with such studies, and desirous of using in its original form the Anglo-Saxon Chronicle— on the several copies of which the oldest Latin chronicles of England are based—to the difficulties attending an exact critical examination of that estimable relic.

As from the time of Beda to that of William of Malmesbury—a space of nearly four hundred years—England possessed no chronicler who recorded the history of the whole country, independently of the Saxon Chronicle, an inquiry into the sources and authors of that work is the more desirable.

For the earliest centuries of the Christian era to the year 449, Beda 'De sex hujus mundi ætatibus,' and his Church History, Gildas, and some others are regarded as the authoritative sources. I find, however, that it is only in the accounts of the ancient inhabitants of Britain and Ireland that Beda (H. E. lib. i. c. 1) is used. For all the rest, Eusebius and some unimportant ecclesiastical history have been excerpted, Beda being tacitly used only where the Chronicle coincides with, or deviates from his narrative. (Compare Sax. Chron. aa. 189, 435, 443, with Beda, lib. i. cc. 4, 11, 13.) The calculation of the years from the creation is according to that of Eusebius and Orosius, who from that epoch to the birth of Christ reckon 5198 years.

From the year 449 to 597 the Chronicle contains, with some Kentish accounts, matter almost exclusively relating to Wessex, in which Beda is unfortunately so deficient. In confirmation of the general veracity of the Chronicle is the correct notice of two eclipses of the sun, in the years 538 and 540, and again in 664 and 733, though of the two last mentioned the day and the hour, which are given by Florence, are omitted in the Chronicle. From the first-named period to the year 731, when Beda's History terminates, the events are probably for the most part derived from that source; the accounts which are not to be found in Beda being but few, and chiefly derived from the late Laudian manuscript (as in the years 603, 616, 617), though the better manuscripts have also some additions, with the sources of which we are unacquainted (as in the years 693 and 710), together with some accounts which, as Florence has remarked, deviate from Beda. From 732 to 845 the Chronicle is the primary source, though during this period unquestionable errors are observable in the manuscripts; for instance, the eclipse of the moon in 796, correctly given by Simeon of Durham, is in the Chronicle placed under the year 795. From 851 to 887 extracts from Asser's Life of Ælfred, with a few variations, are faithfully transferred into the Chronicle.

The year 977 forms a break in the Anglo-Saxon Chronicle, as with this year two ancient manuscripts conclude, together with the latest record of their oldest Latin copier Ethelwerd. From this time, but more particularly from the year 1001, which is also remarkable for the ending of some manuscripts, the deviations become more considerable, particularly in the Abingdon[1] and Worcester Chronicles; and even these, though agreeing together much more closely than with other manuscripts, yet in some places differ considerably from each other, as in the years 1046, 1048, 1049, 1053, the former has Mercian records which are wanting in the latter.

With respect to the origin of these Chronicles, the first question to be decided seems to be, whether they, like so many other chronicles of other nations, written in the language of the country, have not been originally composed by ecclesiastics in Latin, as the ordinary language of the church, and afterwards translated into Anglo-Saxon. When we call to mind that Ælfred translated, or caused to be translated, into Anglo-Saxon the Church History of Beda, the History of Orosius, etc., and that before Beda's time the language possessed the poetry of Cædmon, little doubt can be entertained of the probability that these annals, which till Ælfred's time are written with extreme simplicity, and may even be pronounced meagre, were also composed in the Latin tongue. Florence of Worcester repeatedly cites the 'Chronica Saxonica' (aa. 672, 674, 734), by which it appears on comparison that he means our Saxon Chronicle. Whether, besides the well-known Latin elements of the Chronicle, a West Saxon one, written in the language of the country, may have contributed to form its basis, it is now impossible either to assert or contradict: luckily the credibility of its scanty notices is not affected by our ignorance of that point. The continuations of the Chronicle are often written by contemporaries, to identify whom, however

[1] ['Chronicon Monasterii de Abingdon,' edited by Rev. J. Stevenson, 1858 (printed for the first time).—E. C. O.]

desirable for criticism, would with our present means be a difficult if not an impracticable task. Even in such a research, the question might not be unimportant whether it really was or was not first written in the language of the country. On comparing Florence with the Chronicle, we find that the former bears the nearest resemblance to the Worcester manuscript; though Florence has many details wanting in the latter, as in the years 1040, 1041 and 1049; while *vice versâ*, the former has some notices, viz. under the years 693 and 710, and even 1044, relative to king Eadward's marriage, which are wanting in the latter.

Notwithstanding the variations existing among the several manuscripts, their general resemblance, particularly a striking agreement in many chronological errors, both in the Anglo-Saxon and Latin texts, must appear very remarkable. In explanation of this, Gibson refers to an account, that in the monasteries of royal foundation in England, whatever worthy of remembrance occurred in the neighbourhood was committed to writing; that such records were at the next synod compared with each other, and that from them the Chronicles were composed. It must, however, be remarked, that this account, given by Walter Bower, the continuator of Fordun's Scotichronicon,[1] who wrote in the beginning of the fifteenth century, cannot, without further authority, be applied to the portion of the Anglo-Saxon Chronicles in which we are at present interested.

Till the year 1036 poetical fragments are occasionally inserted into the Chronicle, viz. in the years 937, 941, 958, 973, 975, 1011, 1036, and 1065. That these verses were not composed in the years under which they stand

[1] Edit. Hearne, t. iv. p. 1348.

is sometimes manifest from their words, as in the year 958, on the accession of Eadgar, where allusion is made to his conduct and character; and under 975, where the year of his death is spoken of, which it is said took place, according to the calculation of those skilled in numbers, in the month of July.[1]

Of the Latin elaborations of the Saxon Chronicle the oldest is that of Ethelwerd, in four books, to the year 975, in which, as we have observed, some manuscripts of the Chronicle itself also terminate. With the pompousness characteristic of the Anglo-Saxons he gives (and often incorrectly[1]) an epitomised version of the Chronicle, and would without the aid of the original be the more difficult to understand, as the only ancient manuscript of the work perished in the fire at the Cottonian library, and is made known to us solely through the printed text in Savile's collection. The fourth book, however, contains some valuable information relative to the reigns of Æthelred and Ælfred, not to be found in Asser and the other chroniclers, and not to be ascribed to some lost manuscript of the Saxon Chronicle, but rather to Ethelwerd himself, whose adherence to the Chronicle is, nevertheless, to be continually recognised; and even the verses inserted in that record under the year 975 are very indifferently imitated by him in Latin.

Ethelwerd was not an ecclesiastic, but an ealdorman descended from king Æthelred the First. He calls himself, in true Anglo-Saxon style, Patricius Consul Fabius Quæstor Ethelwerdus. He is generally sup-

---

[1] Sax. Chron. a 710. "gefuhton wið Gerente" he renders "bellum gesserunt contra Uuthgirente." Malmesbury (lib. i.) severely blames his style.

posed to have been the ealdorman of that name[1] who died in the year 1090, a supposition which appears even more erroneous than that which makes him a son of king Ælfred, who died in 922. Ethelwerd dedicates his work to a relation (consobrina) named Mathilda, who was descended from king Ælfred, the brother of his ancestor (abavus) Æthelred, through his granddaughter Eadgyth, the wife of the emperor Otto the First. Some, on the strength of the words, "Eadgyde, ex qua tu principium tenes nativitatis," and "vera Christi ancilla,"[2] have supposed this Mathilda to have been the daughter of Otto, who became abbess of Quedlinburg; but this abbess was not his daughter by Eadgyth, who died in 947, but by his second wife Adelheid, born in 955;[3] nor can the relationship intimated be by a daughter, but only by a granddaughter of Eadgyth, as Ælfred is called not the *abavus*, but the *atavus* of Mathilda.[4] Now this person I find in the daughter of Liudolf,[5] the son of Otto and Eadgyth, by Ida, a daughter of Hermann duke of Allemannia, born in 949, and married to Obizzone of Milan, the ancestor of the Visconti family; a conjecture which finds corroboration in the request of Ethelwerd to Mathilda that she would inform him to what the king in the neighbourhood of the Great St. Bernard (juxta Jupitereos montes) the sister of Eadgyth had been given in marriage, and what offspring they had; which

[1] Nicolson, Engl. Hist. Library, p. 48.   [2] Prolog. lib. i.
[3] She died in 999. Cf. Annal. Quedlinburg, a. 955 sq. ap. Leibnitz, Script. Rer. Brunsvic. t. i., and Pertz, t. iii.
[4] Lib. iv. c. 2 f.
[5] She also became abbess of Quedlinburg, and died in 1011. Annal. Quedl. "Abstulit (sæva mors · et de regali stemmate gemmam Machtildam abbatissam, Liudolfi filiam." Her birth is registered by Annalista Saxo, a. 949.

it would be easy for her to learn, both by reason of her influence,[1] and of the proximity of her abode. Mathilda's place of habitation would also appear to explain why a layman came to render such a work into Latin for a lady. According to our hypothesis, the period when Ethelwerd lived is also determined, since he must have composed his work about the year 1000. Which, however, of the two sons of Æthelred, whether Æthelm or Æthelwold,—who married a nun whom he had carried off, and in 905 fell in an insurrection in East Anglia, against Eadward,—was the great-grandfather of Ethelwerd, appears no longer ascertainable. Three eminent men of his name died about that time—in 1001 the heah-gerefa of the king, in 1016 the son of Æthelwine, and in 1017 the son of Æthelmære the Great. Of Æthelwine's mother, Ælfwen, the wife of the under-king Æthelstan of East Anglia, we know that she was of royal lineage, and that the education of king Eadgar was entrusted to her: she may possibly be the link wanting in the descent of Ethelwerd from king Æthelred.[2]

Soon after the establishment of the Norman dynasty on the throne of England the Anglo-Saxon tongue rapidly became corrupt, and fell into disuse among the clergy, who, not from any parade of learning, but from necessity, wrote the annals of the kingdom in the language of the Church, the only one intelligible to them. Of their works, several composed in the first half of the twelfth century or earlier have reached our time.

The most estimable translator of the Saxon Chronicle is Florence, a monk of Worcester, called also Bavonius,

[1] Prolog. lib. i. "Quæ non solum affinitate, sed et potestate videris obpleta, nulla intercapedine prohibente."
[2] [The question of Ethelwerd's identification is discussed by Mr. Riley in the 'Gentleman's Magazine' for July 1857.—E. C. O.]

who has inserted into the Universal Chronicle of Marianus Scotus, an Irishman, who passed his life in the abbey of Fulda (ob. 1086), besides a translation either of a manuscript of the Saxon Chronicle resembling the existing Worcester manuscript, or of a text emended and enlarged by himself,[1] extracts from Beda, the greater part of Asser's Life of Ælfred, and many valuable genealogical and other notices down to 1118, the year of his death. Florence had not only excellent manuscripts before him, but has translated the Anglo-Saxon more correctly than the other chroniclers. That he made use of the Historia Eliensis or its sources seems highly probable, from the close agreement of his account of the murder of the ætheling Ælfred at Ely with that in the History (lib. ii. c. 32), which deviates from that in the Saxon Chronicle (a. 1036).[2] Florence's Chronicle is continued by another monk of his monastery to the year 1141. His work was printed at London in 1592 in 4to, and at Frankfort-o.-M. in 1601 in folio, after the 'Flores Historiarum' of Matthew of Westminster.[3]

Marianus himself has but few special accounts relative to Britain, and these refer chiefly to Scotland and to certain ecclesiastics. Florence had apparently a much more complete manuscript of Marianus than that from which Pistorius printed; hence we find in him many accounts relating to Germany, even to the abbey of Fulda, by Marianus, an examination into

[1] Cf. both under the year 988.
[2] Cf. Florence a. 1070 with the Hist. Eliensis, lib. ii. c. 44. [Mr. Freeman regards the 'Historia Eliensis' as a later work, compiled from Florence and William of Poictiers.—E. C. O.]
[3] [Florence of Worcester was edited by the Translator for the English Historical Society, 1848-9.—E. C. O.]

LITERARY INTRODUCTION. xlix

which would be an indispensable preliminary labour to a better edition of this chronicle.

The work of Florence forms in great measure, word for word, the basis of a chronicle of events from the year 848 to 1129, compiled about the last-mentioned year by Simeon, precentor of St. Cuthberht's at Durham, but which contains also some special Northumbrian and Scottish accounts.[1] Of such, however, more are to be found in another work of the same author, entitled ' Historia de Gestis Regum Anglorum,' from the year 616 to 957. In the latter he makes use of Beda, the ' Historia vel Chronica hujus patriæ,' and some legends of saints. The narrative of Harold's visit to duke William, inserted in his chronicle under the year 1066, is also given in Eadmer's ' Historia Novorum,' lib. i., though somewhat abridged; whence it is evident that the latter cannot have been Simeon's source. The ' Historia Dunelmensis Ecclesiæ,' also under the name of Simeon, in three books, contains much interesting matter for the history of the North of England. Of this work it is supposed that Simeon, to the year 1097, was only the transcriber, and that the author was the prior Turgot,[2] who after 1108 became bishop of St. Andrew's.

The Chronicle of the abbey of Melrose (Mailros),[3] from the year 735 to 1270, is for the Anglo-Saxon period merely an extract, with a few unimportant additions, from Simeon of Durham.

[1] The notices relative to Normandy, aa. 876 and 906, agree literally with the Chronicle of Rouen (Chronicon Rothomagense), which deserves to be noticed on account of the chronology.
[2] Simeon is printed in Twysden's collection, and to 1066 in Petrie, C. H. Respecting Turgot see Twysden's preface.
[3] Printed in Fell's collection, t. i.

LITERARY INTRODUCTION.

Henry, archdeacon of Huntingdon, compiled an 'Historia Anglorum' from the year of Julius Cæsar's landing to 1135, which is continued to 1154. The first six books embrace the period in which we are concerned, for which, besides the usual sources, Henry has availed himself of many traditions; while for the later period he has recorded either what he had witnessed himself or received from eye-witnesses.[1] Some of his few principal sources are still undiscovered: the more important of the known ones, exclusive of Eutropius, Paulus Diaconus, etc., are Beda's Chronicon and Ecclesiastical History, Nennius (whom he calls Gildas), and the Saxon Chronicle, which he sometimes misinterprets, though perhaps less often than has been supposed. His chronology is extremely confused and frequently inaccurate, as are also his genealogical notices. Particularly attractive, however, are his accounts of battles, which often appear to be borrowed from old poems.[2] A very close agreement with the more copious Ailred of Rievaulx, which leads to the conclusion of a common, though to us unknown, source, is manifest in his account of Eadmund Ironside. A striking contrast to the other monastic chroniclers, who cannot bestow sufficient praises on Dunstan, appears in his commendation of king Eadwy: and in general, throughout all that this author relates or suppresses may be recognised the patriotic Anglo-Saxon, equally averse both to temporal and ecclesiastical oppressors. That he availed himself of Norman sources may, perhaps, be inferred from his narrative of the sons of Emma, which agrees so closely with the Roman de Rou; as well as

[1] See 'Historia Anglorum Henrici Huntendunensis,' edited by Thomas Arnold, 1879.—E. C. O.
[2] e.g. The battle of Brunanburh.—T.

from accounts strictly Norman given by him alone of all the English chroniclers, as A.D. 1047, of the battle of Val des Dunes, and William's speech before the battle of Hastings. From similar works he has probably derived his old British stories, as that of the princess Helena and others, which are not to be traced either to Nennius or Geoffrey of Monmouth, according to our manuscripts.[1] Henry's work is dedicated to the same Alexander bishop of Lincoln whom Geoffrey addresses in his 'Historia Britonum.' A continuation of Henry of Huntingdon from 1042 to 1275 is extant.[2]

Roger of Hoveden in Yorkshire, chaplain to king Henry the Second, a jurist and professor of divinity at Oxford, was living in the year 1204. This writer has been much too often quoted, as, even to the last year of his Annals, he has (excepting a few trifling additions) copied from chronicles known to us, and, for the Anglo-Saxon period, from Simeon of Durham and Henry of Huntingdon. The beginning of his work, including the 'Prologus,' to the year 803 (edit. Frankf. pp. 401-407), is from Simeon (pp. 90-119); the following to the year 849 (p. 414) is from Huntingdon (pp. 341-348); hence to the year 1122 (pp. 414-477) is from Simeon's second work (pp. 137-245); after which, from 1122 to 1148 (p. 490), Roger returns to Henry of Huntingdon.[3]

Alured, or Ælfred, treasurer of the monastery of Beverley, has in his Annals excerpted from Beda,

[1] He is copied literally by Rob. du Mont, John of Wallingford, Hoveden, the Waverl. Annals, R. de Diceto, Matt. Paris, Bromton, Gervasius, Robert of Gloucester, etc.
[2] Cooper on the Public Records, ii. p. 165. See Historia Anglor. Henr. Huntend. edited by T. Arnold, 1879.—E. O. O.
[3] See Chronica Magistri Rogeri de Houedene, vols. i., ii., iii., iv., edited by William Stubbs, M.A., 1868-71.—E. O. O.

d 2

Geoffrey of Monmouth, and Simeon of Durham. He ends with the year in which the last mentioned terminates; but we are not thence justified in concluding that he wrote in that year, or in inferring that the work of Geoffrey, which is known to have followed those of Henry of Huntingdon and William of Malmesbury, had already appeared in 1128. Traces of an immediate use of the Saxon Chronicle are occasionally discernible in Alured, as a. 879 (883), relative to king Ælfred's mission to India. The lists of Anglo-Saxon kings, contained in the sixth book, are, with the exception of the introduction, from the appendix to Florence of Worcester: the author's own additions are very short and unimportant.[1]

These are the principal works which, on account of their close adherence to the earliest sources of Anglo-Saxon history, must here be cited. In the first centuries after the Norman Conquest several other English historic writers appeared, who, devoted to the new dynasty, excite our attention chiefly by reason of the baneful influence which, through their Norman prejudices and false criticism, they have exercised on the early history.

The work ascribed to Ingulf, an Englishman, born about the year 1030, secretary to William of Normandy, and afterwards abbot of Crowland (ob. 1109), is the first to be noticed.[2] In this composition almost all the charters are forgeries,[3] a circumstance which of itself, perhaps, might not invalidate the general credibility of the rest of the work—which consists of a history of Crowland abbey, interspersed with matter relating to

[1] Alured was edited by Thomas Hearne, Oxon. 1716.
[2] Cf. Ingulf, a. 1075, where an account of his life is inserted.
[3] See Hickes, t. iii. p. 73.

LITERARY INTRODUCTION. liii

the kingdom of Mercia, and, at a later period, to all England, to the year 1091;—but the narrative of Ingulf not only abounds in gross errors and anachronisms with regard to contemporary events, but contains matter demonstrably fabulous; such is the account of his having studied Aristotle at Oxford.[1] Even in the Life of abbot Thurketul, which, though composed by his relative, the younger abbot Egelric, is said to have been continued by Ingulf, it is stated that Constantine king of Scotland (erroneously for that king's son) fell in the battle of Brunanburh, in 938, by the hand of Thurketul, and that the emperor Henry the First (who it is well known died in 936), after that battle sought the hand of Æthelstan's daughter for his son Otto. In the accounts of Ælfred and Eadward the Elder, the so-called Ingulf agrees so frequently, both in erroneous matter and words, in chronology and facts, with William of Malmesbury, that it will be difficult not to regard this part of his chronicle as an interpolation from that author, since a source common to both cannot be indicated. The account, too, of the interment of two cousins of Aethelstan in the abbey of Malmesbury is to be found in both writers,[2] for which the latter cites as his authority an historic work in Latin hexameters. A charter also of Malmesbury of the year 974 is given more fully in Ingulf than in the printed work of the monk of that cloister. Even in that part of his chronicle in which contemporary

[1] "Primum Westmonasterio, postmodum Oxoniensi studio traditus eram. Cumque in Aristotele arripiendo," etc. For a judicious and interesting notice of Ingulf see Biographia Britannica Literaria, vol. ii., composed by Mr. Wright for the Royal Society of Literature. —T.

[2] Ingulf, p. 39; W. Malm. lib. ii. 6. Cf. also in both the passages about Eadwine.

events are recorded, Ingulf, as we have already observed, is not trustworthy: as in the years 1056 and 1062, where he calls count Radulf, the husband, instead of the son of Goda. The contemporary abbots of Crowland are confounded by him. He seems to have made use of Ailred of Rievaulx. At the same time it must be allowed that the continuation of Ingulf's work by Peter of Blois seems to impress it with a stamp of genuineness. From the foundation of his abbey till its destruction by the Danes in 870, Ingulf appeals to five older chroniclers, viz. Aio, Thurgar, Swetman, etc.[1] By whom the history from 871 to 948 has been supplied we are not informed. . Hence it seems not unreasonable to suppose that the true history of Ingulf has not reached us, but that in the work before us we possess a compilation made at an early period, into which portions of the real Ingulf are interwoven, and in the use of which the utmost caution is to be observed. It is printed in Savile's collection, and in that of Fell; no manuscript is known to exist.

Ailred (Æthelred), abbot of Rievaulx in Yorkshire, has collected genealogical notices of the Anglo-Saxon kings. Of his other writings, none need be mentioned except his Life, or rather Legend, of Eadward the Confessor.[2] His praise of Eadgar and account of Godwine's death remind us strongly of Alured of Beverley.

The works of William, a monk and librarian of Malmesbury[3] abbey (ob. about 1142), are remarkably

[1] Ingulf, a. 974, and at the close of the work.
[2] Printed in Twysden's collection.
[3] Printed in Savile's collection, excepting the fifth book, 'De Gestis Pontificum,' which is to be found in Gale and Wharton. [Of the two first-mentioned works, an excellent edition with English notes, etc., has been published by T. D. Hardy, Esq. for the English Historical Society.—T.]

attractive, both from the manner in which he treats his subject and from his arrangement, which deviates from the usual chronological order. These are, 'De Gestis Regum Anglorum,' lib. v.; 'Historiæ Novellæ,' lib. ii.; 'De Gestis Pontificum Anglorum,' lib. v.[1] From the 'Prologus' to the first book of his principal work it appears, that Malmesbury was unacquainted with the invaluable historic productions of his contemporaries. The authors named by him are Beda, Ethelwerd, and Eadmer. In the words, "quædam vetustatis indicia chronico more et patrio sermone, per annos Domini ordinata," he evidently alludes to the Saxon Chronicle. Together with many interesting narratives preserved by Malmesbury, is to be found an abundance of insipid tales quite irrelevant to his subject, but to which his work is mainly indebted for much of the approbation which it has received; for after Beda and Geoffrey of Monmouth, no old English historic writer has been more resorted to by chroniclers, both of his own country and of the Continent, than William of Malmesbury. Among the more ancient of the latter may be named Alberic des Troisfontaines and Vincent of Beauvais.

To Matthew, a monk of Westminster abbey, is ascribed an historic work, compiled in the fourteenth century from various chronicles, entitled 'Flores Historiarum.'[2] From a kind of inadvertence this chronicle has been much used, because it has not been noticed that almost all his sources (for the Anglo-Saxon period)

[1] [See Wilhelmi Malmesbirensis Monachi de Gestis Pontificum Anglorum. Libri quinque. Edited from William of Malmesbury's autograph MS., by N. E. G. A. Hamilton, of the Department of MSS. British Museum, 1870.—E. C. O.]
[2] Francofurti, 1601. fol.

have been preserved, extracts from which have by him only been abridged and often unskilfully brought together, and, when dates were wanting, not unfrequently inserted under wrong years. Of his sources with which we are concerned may be mentioned Nennius, Beda, Asser, the Saxon Chronicle, Florence of Worcester, Geoffrey of Monmouth, William of Jumièges, (e.g. a. 887, from lib. i. cc. 6-11, relative to Hæsting, and later about Rollo), Marianus Scotus, and William of Malmesbury, whom he occasionally mentions by name (as aa. 979, 1035). To the foregoing Henry of Huntingdon might perhaps be added, though some passages in his work, chiefly concerning the North of England, on which that supposition is founded, are more fully given in Matthew, and may therefore have been more circumstantially taken from a source common to both. The account of the single combat between Eadmund Ironside and Cnut seems to have been extracted from Ailred of Rievaulx. Many legends and narratives from monastic chronicles are inserted by Matthew; hence several notices are to be found scattered throughout his work which the future gatherer of materials for English history may deem it worth his while to collect.

To John Wallingford, abbot of St. Albans (ob. 1214), Gale ascribes a chronicle published by him of events from the year 449 to 1036.[1] This author makes some attempts at historic criticism, in which, however, he is eminently unsuccessful. For the history of the northern Anglo-Saxon provinces, he gives us some accounts not to be found elsewhere. He makes great use of the first six books of William of Jumièges, and also, though not immediately, of Dudo of St. Quentin; as we find in

[1] Printed in Gale's collection, t. i.

Wallingford the narratives of the latter, together with the additions and continuations of the former of these two writers (as pp. 532 and 533, from Guil. Gemet. lib. i. cc. 3–5; also p. 548, from lib. v. c. 8; pp. 549, 550, from lib. vi. cc. 10–13). He also makes mention of Geoffrey of Monmouth, Henry of Huntingdon, and William of Malmesbury, and excerpts the Lives of the saints Guthlac, Cuthberht, Neot and Eadward, also Britferth's Life of St. Dunstan. His quotation from the 'Historia Gothorum' is copied from William of Jumièges.

We have now to mention, in a few words, those Norman writers who have touched on this portion of English history. In this respect Dudo, dean of St. Quentin, is but rarely of immediate interest, though, for the history of the ancestors of king William the Conqueror, he is not only the source of several chronicles generally more noticed, but is also, notwithstanding his many poetical ornaments and chronological errors, much richer in undoubted facts than the learned editors of the 'Materials for French History' have been aware of.[1]

More immediately interesting to us is William, a monk of Jumièges, whose 'Historia Normannorum' reaches to the conquest of England by the Normans. His work being dedicated to the Conqueror, it follows that what forms the end of the seventh and the eighth book, which is continued to the year 1137, cannot have been written by him.[2] He has, as we have seen, been excerpted by many English chroniclers. Both these writers are contained in Du Chesne's collection of

[1] See Bouquet, t. x. Preface, and p. 141. The proofs of my assertion cannot be given here, but will appear in a chapter on the history of Normandy before the year 1066, prefixed to the 'History of England under the Norman Kings.'

[2] Bouquet, t. xi. Pref. No. xii., and t. xii. Pref. No. xlix.

'Scriptores Rerum Normannicarum;' the latter also in Camden's 'Anglica Normannica,' etc., an edition much inferior to that of Du Chesne, which is founded on two manuscripts from the library of De Thou.

Of much importance for historic research, notwithstanding its poetic garb, is the 'Roman de Rou,'[1] a history of the dukes of Normandy, interwoven with many traditions, by Robert Wace, a native of Jersey, bred at Caen, and afterwards, by appointment of Henry the Second, a prebendary of Bayeux. Of his 'Brut,' written about the year 1155, mention has already been made. In the 'Roman de Rou' is to be found much exclusive and credible matter for the history of the eleventh century, in the use of which, however, due allowance is to be made for the national prejudices of the Norman. This work also seems to have served as a source to some of the English chroniclers. It has for the first time been printed by M. Pluquet.[2]

Anterior to Wace was Bénoît de Ste More, or, as he is styled by Wace, Maistre Beneit, who wrote in French a metrical chronicle of the dukes of Normandy, consisting of 48,000 verses. The only ancient manuscript known of this work is in the British Museum (Harl. 1717).

In the language of the Gallo-Normans, but written

[1] Written after 1170. See *v.* 16538 sq.
[2] Rouen, 1827. 2 vols. 8vo. And 'Remarques' by Le Prevost and Raynouard, 1829. [For a very able prose version of the portion of the Roman de Rou relating to the conquest of England, with highly valuable and interesting illustrations, the public are indebted to a most worthy and amiable man and excellent scholar lately deceased, under the title: 'Master Wace, his Chronicle of the Norman Conquest from the Roman de Rou; translated, with notes and illustrations, by Edgar Taylor, Esq., F.S.A.' London 1837. 8vo. —T.]

in England for the lords of the land a century after the Conquest, is 'L'Estorie des Engles solum la translation Maistre Geffrei Gaimar,' a metrical chronicle of England from the landing of Cerdic in the year 495 to the death of William Rufus in 1099.[1] It seems to have been composed about the middle of the twelfth century, and follows the Saxon Chronicle, which the author frequently misunderstands. It contains, however, many, though not always historic, additions, by which Gaimar as the oldest known authority—though he refers to an earlier—is rendered of importance. This work, to the year 1066, appears for the first time in the 'Corpus Historicum.'[2]

Of great moment for the illustration of the downfall of the Anglo-Saxon dynasty in England is the biography of William the Conqueror by William of Poitiers, archdeacon of Lisieux. Though valuable for his matter, this author is objectionable on account of his style, in which he is an imitator of the Roman classics, particularly Sallust, and not only inserts fabricated speeches into his narrative, but not unfrequently sacrifices a part of the truth for the sake of sparkling antitheses and oratorical pomp. He is sometimes copied by William of Jumièges, but more copiously by Ordericus Vitalis; so much so indeed, that some defective passages in our manuscript of William of Poitiers can be supplied from Ordericus with tolerable security. His work

[1] L'Estorie des Engles solum Geffrei Gaimar, edited by Sir Thomas Duffus Hardy, late Deputy Keeper of the Public Records.—E. C. O.

[2] See also extracts in Depping, Histoire des expéditions maritimes des Normands, and Monumenta Historica Britannica, p. 764 note; and Michel, Chron. Anglo-Norm., t. i. Cf. also Wiener Jahrb. Th. 76. p. 259 sq.

is printed in Du Chesne's collection, and in a separate edition by Baron Maseres.[1]

Of English metrical chronicles, that of Robert of Gloucester, written about the year 1280, is one of the most valuable.[2] It begins with the tales of Geoffrey of Monmouth, but in the Anglo-Saxon portion follows chiefly William of Malmesbury, and sometimes Henry of Huntingdon, as in the story of Cnut on the seashore, and the speech of William before the battle of Hastings. His relation of the single combat between Eadmund and Cnut, with the prolix speech, is apparently an imitation of Ailred of Rievaulx.

A similar chronicle, written in French verse,[3] by Peter Langtoft, a canon regular of the order of St. Augustine, at Bridlington in Yorkshire, whence he is also called Pers of Bridlynton, though extant in manuscript, is known to us only through the English metrical version of Robert Mannyng, or, as he is more usually called, Robert de Brunne.[4] The editor has omitted the part copied from 'Le Brut.' This chronicle, which ends with the death of Edward the First in 1307, was without doubt composed and translated not long after that time. The little contained in it of Anglo-Saxon history, for which Gildas, Beda, Henry of Huntingdon, and William of Malmesbury are

[1] Historiæ Anglicanæ circa tempus Conquestus Angliæ a Gulielmo Notho, Normannorum Duce, Selecta Monumenta, etc. London, 1807. 4to.
[2] Edited by Thomas Hearne. Oxon. 1724. 2 vols. 8vo.
[3] Extracts from the French text are printed in the Chron. Anglo-Norm. t. i.
[4] Edited by Thomas Hearne. Oxon. 1725. 2 vols. 8vo. [The Chronicle of Pierre de Langtoft, vols. i. and ii., edited by Thomas Wright, is now to be found in the Rolls Series; as is also the Metrical Chronicle of Robert of Gloucester—E. C. O.]

cited, are old English legends inserted by Robert de Brunne, of which that of Havelok, king Gunter's son, he says expressly is not to be found in Pers of Bridlynton.

It is a remarkable circumstance that the majority of the later chroniclers are from Yorkshire or the neighbouring counties, which may, perhaps, be attributed to a longer preserved nationality in those parts. Their chief sources are rarely the Saxon Chronicle and Florence, but rather Henry of Huntingdon and William of Malmesbury, whose traditions and fables they have generally transcribed at greater length. This remark is particularly applicable to the work, too often appealed to, ascribed to John Bromton, abbot of Jervaulx in Yorkshire, who lived towards the end of the fourteenth century. It comprises the period from the year 588 to 1198, whence it might be suspected to be the production of some earlier writer, did it not contain mention of the marriage-contract of Johanna, sister of Edward the Third, with David, afterwards king of Scotland. Besides the chroniclers just enumerated, Bromton also copies Florence and the Flores Historiarum: he likewise mentions the chronicle of Walter of Giseborne. Norman anecdotes he relates in the same order as Wace in the Roman de Rou.

The only merit, with reference to Anglo-Saxon history, hitherto possessed by Bromton,—that of being the earliest source of many interesting legends,—is now effaced, as we find the same in Gaimar; and they are also to be found, though in an abridged form, in the unprinted chronicle of Douglas of Glastonbury, the Hamburg vellum manuscript of which reaches to the time of Edward the Third, in which the names, disguised like those in Gaimar, sufficiently betray the use of a Norman source.[1] In the earlier part of his chronicle Douglas follows Geoffrey of Monmouth; in the later portion he has accounts exclusively his own, relating to the wars between England and Scotland in the thirteenth and fourteenth centuries, which are valuable through the communication of contemporary ballads.

We have occasionally, in the course of our researches, made use of smaller historic works, of which many monastic histories and Lives of Saints are still in manuscript only. Letters also, homilies, and other documents, have been but partially brought to light, of which several, connected with later times, will be noticed hereafter.

Of other helps to Anglo-Saxon history, the first to be mentioned are the Charters, a complete collection of which is now in course of publication by the English Historical Society. Of these important documents two volumes have already appeared,[2] containing charters of Anglo-Saxon kings, ealdormen and prelates to the year 966. To the first volume is prefixed an Introduction by the learned editor, embracing an ample fund of information illustrative of the use and nature of those instruments, their dates, tests of their genuineness, etc., indispensable to those who have not made such monuments a particular branch of study. Older collections, which are in great measure superseded by this highly useful publication, are—the Textus Roffensis, belonging

[1] Thus, cap. iii. Renaude for Reginald; cap. cxii. Estrilde for Ælfthryth, the queen of Eadgar; cap. cvii. in "Alured that Dolphynes was called" it is not *Dauphin*, but Gaimar's (v. 3023 sq.)
"Elueret, Edelwolfing ert apelez;" also, cap. cvii. "a Dane that me called Roynt," from Gaimar, v. 3016, "un Daneis, uu tyrant, ki Sumerlede out nun le *grant*."

[2] Codex Diplomaticus Ævi Saxonici. Opera Johannis M. Kemble, tom. i. and ii.

to the cathedral of Rochester, containing, besides many valuable charters, etc., the only copy extant of the Laws of the Kentish kings. This manuscript, compiled by bishop Ernulphus in the twelfth century, was communicated to the world by that laborious and meritorious antiquary Thomas Hearne: also Hemming's Chartulary of the church of Worcester. Many charters are also to be found dispersed in Hickes's Thesaurus, Smith's edition of the historic works of Beda, the monastic histories of Ely and Glastonbury, etc. The greater number, however, of these documents having reference to churches and convents, those of the latter description are consequently collected in the 'Monasticon Anglicanum,' originally edited by William Dugdale and Roger Dodsworth, in 3 vols. folio, 1682, continued by J. Stevens in 2 vols. folio, and lastly edited anew by John Cayley, Esq., Henry Ellis, Esq., and the Rev. B. Bandinel.[1]

The edition of the Anglo-Saxon Laws and Institutes commenced by the late Mr. Price, under the authority of the Commission on the Public Records, but continued and completed by Mr. Thorpe,[2] exhibits a purer text, accompanied by collations from every known manuscript, than that of the earlier editions In

[1] London, 1817–1830. 8 vols. folio.
[2] Ancient Laws and Institutes of England; comprising Laws enacted under the Anglo-Saxon Kings from Æthelbirht to Cnut, with an English Translation of the Saxon; the Laws called Edward the Confessor's; the Laws of William the Conqueror, and those ascribed to Henry the First: also Monumenta Ecclesiastica Anglicana, from the seventh to the tenth century; and the Ancient Latin Version of the Anglo-Saxon Laws. With a compendious Glossary, &c. Printed by command of His late Majesty King William IV., under the direction of the Commissioners on the Public Records of the Kingdom. MDCCCXL. 1 vol. fol., or 2 vols. royal 8vo.

the ecclesiastical portion of the work is printed for the first time the Penitential of archbishop Theodore, the prototype of most of the later penitentials, particularly that of archbishop Ecgberht. In this work also some interesting secular documents are given for the first time in print. Before the appearance of this edition, that of Dr. Wilkins was the most complete, though abounding in errors of no trivial character. An edition of much merit, and highly useful to the German scholar, was begun by Dr. Reinhold Schmid, of which the first volume only has hitherto appeared.[1] The Anglo-Saxon ecclesiastical laws, the councils, and other church documents, are also contained in the collection of Sir Henry Spelman, though more completely in the later one of Dr. Wilkins.

The Welsh Laws, viz. those of Howel Dha and other princes, have also been recently communicated to the world under the same authority, in an excellent edition by Aneurin Owen, Esq.,[2] containing the original text, founded on several manuscripts, with an English translation. The Welsh Laws had been previously edited by Dr. Wotton, with a Latin translation, and subsequently by Probert with an English one.[3]

[1] Die Gesetze der Angelsachsen. In der Ursprache mit Uebersetzung und Erläuterungen herausgegeben von Dr. Reinhold Schmid, Professor der Rechte zu Jena. Leipzig, 1832. 8vo.

[2] Ancient Laws and Institutes of Wales; comprising Laws supposed to be enacted by Howel the Good, modified by subsequent regulations under the native Princes prior to the Conquest by Edward the First: and Anomalous Laws, consisting principally of Institutions which, by the Statute of Ruddlan, were admitted to continue in force : with an English Translation of the Welsh Text. To which are added a few Latin transcripts, containing Digests of the Welsh Laws, principally of the Dimetian Code. With Indexes and Glossary. Printed by command, etc. MDCCCXLI.

[3] The Ancient Laws of Cambria, translated from the Welsh

LITERARY INTRODUCTION.　　　lxv

For the study of Anglo-Saxon numismatics, the work of Ruding on the coinage[1] is to be recommended, as containing much useful information on that ample sudject; also the valuable works of Mr. Akerman,[2] and several papers in the Archæologia.

On casting a glance at the labours of later historic writers since the introduction of printing, we are carried back to Douglas of Glastonbury, whose work forms the basis of the oldest printed chronicle of England,— that by the printer William Caxton, in the year 1480.

But it was not until the fall of the Stuarts and the rise of the commons of England that the country first gained a tolerable history of the Anglo-Saxons in the mother-tongue, by the hand of the illustrious John Milton[3] who, above all others, successfully employed the Germanic element of his native tongue.

Unimportant as Milton's work may appear at the present day, we must, nevertheless, praise the careful examination it evinces of the genuine sources of early history, which was so highly laudable in one who was blind—verging on his seventieth year—a poet of the highest order—and an energetic statesman, to whom the dryness of the chronicles was so distasteful, that he could not withhold the public expression of his sentiments to

by William Probert. London, 1823, 8vo. From a MS. of the year 1685.

[1] Annals of the Coinage. 4 vols. 4to.

[2] Particularly 'Coins of the Romans relating to Britain.' 8vo, 2nd edit. enlarged.

[3] First printed in 1671. It is reprinted in the several editions of his Prose Works, and also in Kennet's Complete History of England, vol. i.

VOL. I.　　　　　　　　　　　　　　e

that effect. The 'Chronicon Regum Angliæ' of David Langhorne [1] is a very useful work, evincing considerable critical judgment in its compilation from numerous and the best authorities known at the time for the history of kings and wars to the reign of Ælfred. The Life also of that king by Spelman forms an epoch in the historic literature of England. In 1724 appeared the work of Rapin de Thoyras, who, however, did very little for the Anglo-Saxon period, and even seems to have been ignorant of the existence of many sources then already in print. In the notes of his translator, Tindal, many rectifications and additions are to be found. A considerable advance is manifest in the portion dedicated to the Anglo-Saxon period of Carte's History of England,[2] the earlier part of which has served as a storehouse to David Hume, who was lamentably deficient in fundamental knowledge of the early Middle Ages. Hume is justly praised for his lively picture of the history of the Stuarts, and for some portions of that of the Tudors, and as being the most acute of modern investigators, and an unrivalled model for historic composition, in whom was united with English strength and Scottish perspicuity, the grace of the land of his mental cultivation. But in this very praise is implied the cause why Hume, who at first had occupied himself only on the history of the Revolution (from which, not till a later period, he carried back his work to the beginning of the history [3]), could not evince in his account of the Middle Ages either the enthusiasm or even the industry of Milton. It is not, therefore, surprising that

[1] London, 1679, 8vo.
[2] London, 1747-1755, 4 vols. folio.
[3] The History of the Stuarts appeared in 1755, that of the Tudors in 1759, that of the earlier period some years later.

Gibbon,—with his widely comprehensive studies,—who in acuteness and powers of combination was the equal of his great contemporary,—is, in the notices of the Anglo-Saxons contained in his immortal work, more instructive than Hume. After these another star of the first magnitude in the British horizon remains to be named, Edmund Burke,—though, as in the case of Milton, as the author of a work of no great estimation, an Abridgment of English History to the year 1216, in which the part relating to the jurisprudence of the Anglo-Saxons has, however, considerable merit. From this specimen, which, though not printed until after his death, was probably the labour of his earlier years,[1] we may regret that this most talented of British statesmen did not seriously devote himself to the subject.

It might almost appear as if it were intended to be shown that the greatest geniuses among a people devoted to freedom have felt themselves irresistibly drawn to the study of their native history, when we yet mention the History of England by Sir James Mackintosh, the apparent antagonist, though in fact the intellectual son, of Edmund Burke.

Failing health and the pressure of unwelcome age induced Mackintosh to contract the plan of his undertaking, and death interrupted that which he had still hoped to achieve. Mention will hereafter be made of the excellence of that which he has accomplished : for the short section on Anglo-Saxon history, the praise of spirited and just conception, as well as of worthy representation, may here suffice.

[1] It was written in his twenty-seventh year, and appears in the collection of his works. Eight sheets of it were printed by Dodsley in 4to, in 1757, which with the author's corrections are now in the British Museum.

A few respected investigators of old English history remain yet to be noticed, and first Whitaker, who, under the title of a History of the Town of Manchester, has given a very learned account of the country under the Romans.[1] A similar work is his Genuine History of the Britons asserted against J. Macpherson.[2] In the highly esteemed work of Dr. Robert Henry,[3] the Roman period is treated with predilection and success; but it can only be by a comparison with his predecessors that we extend our commendation to the Anglo-Saxon portion of his history.

To Sharon Turner, for his labours on the history of the Anglo-Saxons,[4] students are under a lasting obligation, particularly for his profounder investigation of their state of culture, his unprejudiced application of Welsh literature, and the use which he has made of many unprinted sources. At the same time it must be acknowledged that this meritorious collection of materials is charged with many unnecessary digressions, and that the author has often sacrificed critical discrimination to his predilection for superabundant details.

Lingard's representation of Anglo-Saxon history[5] is distinguished for its just arrangement, as well as for the clearness and solidity of its style; though he has generally confined himself to a repetition of the facts related by his latest predecessors, and only in

[1] Second edition, corrected. London, 1773. 2 vols. 8vo.
[2] Second edit. Lond. 1773.
[3] 'History of Great Britain.' 6 vols. Edinb. 1771-1793. 4to, often reprinted.
[4] 'History of the Anglo-Saxons.' 1799-1805. 2 vols. 4to, frequently reprinted in 3 vols. 8vo. The 6th edit. is the last that has appeared.
[5] The last edit., in 13 vols. 12mo, with corrections.

rare cases, where Catholicism prompted him to a refutation of some narrow views of English Protestantism, has he given us the result of independent and new investigations.

Sir Francis Palgrave has, in an elaborate work,[1] endeavoured, and not unsuccesfully, to supply the existing want. The political institutions of the Anglo-Saxons are examined by him with much acuteness; he has also given, in great part from sources hitherto but little used for the purpose, a very valuable chronological view of the larger states, as well as of the provinces dependent on them; though in the application of some modern hypotheses, chiefly with regard to the derivation of several historical phenomena in the institutions of the Anglo-Saxons from Roman elements, he probably goes too far. While the present work bears evident proof for how much multifarious information its Author is indebted to this learned inquirer, yet several of his principal notions cannot be acknowledged by us as new, but as an ancient common property of the Continental investigators of the history of nations and laws. Palgrave has likewise published, in a small volume,[2] principally designed for youth, and embellished with maps and other engravings, a History of the Anglo-Saxons, containing some of the results of his inquiries.

[1] 'The Rise and Progress of the English Commonwealth.' Anglo-Saxon Period. II. Parts. London, 1832, 4to.
[2] 'History of England,' vol. i. Anglo-Saxon Period. London, 1831, 12mo, forming volume xxi. of the 'Family Library.'

A
HISTORY OF ENGLAND

UNDER THE

ANGLO-SAXON KINGS.

PART I.
BRITAIN UNDER THE ROMANS, B.C. 54.

CHAPTER I.

Earliest Knowledge of Britain—Descent and Traditions—Language—Religion—Government—Customs—Tribes—First Appearance of Romans—Julius Cæsar; his Account of Britain—Departure of Roman Legions.

FOR the earliest notice of its existence among nations, Britain is indebted to that spirit of commerce, through which it was itself one day to become so great. More than a thousand years before the birth of our Saviour, Gades and Tartessus had been founded by the Phœnicians, whose fearless traders we behold, in our dim vision of those remote times when tin was brought in less abundance from the ports of Spain, after a tedious coasting-voyage of four months, fetching that metal from the islands which Herodotus[1] denominates the Cassiterides, or islands producing tin (κασσίτερος), and which now bear the name of the Scilly islands.[2] Herodotus was

[1] Lib. iii. § 115.
[2] Camden's 'Britannia,' p. 1112. Cf. Heeren's 'Ideen,' ii. 191. Beckmann's Hist. of Inventions, vol. iv.

unable to ascertain the position of these islands, nor does he even mention the name of Britain. It is probable that the Phœnicians never sailed thither direct from their own coast,[1] though Midacritus,[2] the individual who is recorded as having first brought tin from the Cassiterides, seems by his name to have been a Phœnician. The earliest mention of the British islands by name is made by Aristotle,[3] who describes them as consisting of Albion and Ierne. The Carthaginian Himilco, who, between the years 362 and 350 A.C., had been sent by his government on a voyage of discovery, also found the tin islands, which he calls Oestrymnides, near Albion, and two days' sail from Ierne,[4] in Mount's Bay.[5] His example was some years after followed by a citizen of the celebrated colony of the Phocæans, the Massilian Pytheas, to the scanty fragments of whose journal, preserved by Strabo and other ancient authors, we are indebted for the oldest accounts concerning the inhabitants of these islands.[6] The Massilians and Nar-

[1] Strabo, lib. iii., relates that a Phœnician shipmaster, being chased by some Roman vessels, ran his ship upon a shoal, leading his pursuers into destruction, while he escaped on a fragment of the wreck, and received from the state the value of the cargo he had sacrificed.—T.

[2] Plin. Hist. Nat., lib. vii. c. 57.

[3] 'De Mundo,' c. iii. Ireland, under the name of Iernis, is mentioned by the author of the 'Argonautica,' v. 1179.

[4] On this geographic conclusion see the 'Metropolitan' for January 1832.

[5] Of his diary, which was extant in the fifth century, we possess fragments in the poem of Festus Avienus, 'Ora Maritima.' If, with Ukert and Lelewel ('Entdeckungen der Carthager und Griechen auf dem atlantischen Ocean'), we place Himilco in the middle of the fifth century A.C., the honour of having discovered Britain must be denied to the Phœnicians and given to the Carthaginians.

[6] Murray de Pythea Massiliensi, in Nov. Comment. Götting. tom. vi.

bonnese traded at an early period (by land-journeys to the northern coast of Gaul)[1] with the island Ictis (Wight, or St. Michael's Mount)[2] and with the coasts of Britain. This early commerce was carried on both for the sake of the tin—an article of great importance to the ancients—and of lead; though these navigators extended their commerce to other productions of the country, such as slaves, skins, and a superior breed of hunting-dogs, which the Celts made use of in war.[3] British timber was employed by Archimedes for the mast of the largest ship of war which he had caused to be built at Syracuse.[4] Gold and silver are said to have been found there; also an inferior sort of pearl, which is still to be met with.[5] This country and its metals soon became an object of scientific inquiry to the Greeks, as is proved by a work upon the subject by Polybius, the loss of which must be painfully felt by every one acquainted with the acuteness and sound judgment of that historian.[6]

The Romans first became acquainted with Britain through their thirst after universal dominion. Scipio, to his inquiries concerning it among the merchants of the

[1] Diod. Sic. lib. v. c. 38.

[2] The near resemblance between the names is in favour of the first supposition; while to the second the account of Diodorus, lib. v. c. 22, is alone applicable, who, describing this island, says, that at flood-tide it appears as an island, and at ebb as a peninsula. The proximity to Cornwall, the British tin country, likewise favours this interpretation.

[3] Strabo, lib. iii. Oppiani Cyneg. lib. i. v. 468. Nemesian Cyneg. v. 123 sq.

[4] Athen. Deipn. lib. v. c. 10.

[5] Cf. Strabo, lib. iv. Tac. de Vita Agric. c. xii. Pomp. Mela, lib. iii. c. 6. Sol. Polyh. c. liii. Suet. lib. i. c. 46. Plin. H. N. ix. c. 57, and the contrary testimony of Cicero, ad Fam. vii. 7, ad Att. iv. 16. [6] Polyb. lib. iii. c. 37.

three most distinguished Celtic cities, Massilia, Narbo, and Corbolo, had received no satisfactory answer;[1] and Publius Crassus is named as the first Roman who visited the Cassiterides, and who observing that the metals were dug out from too low a depth, pointed out a better method of extracting the ore to those who were willing to follow it.[2] This was probably the officer of that name who, by Cæsar's command, had achieved the conquest of the Gaulish nations inhabiting the shores of the British Channel.[3]

Through Cæsar's conquest of the South of England, and the later sway held over it by the Roman emperors, we are first enabled to form an idea of the country. Well might the goddess of science and of war appear to the Greeks and Romans under one form (for it was the Macedonian and Roman swords that fixed for antiquity the limits both of the earth and of historic knowledge), though their idea of Britain is, it must be confessed, a very obscure one, and stands much in need of the reflecting light of modern scientific research. To Strabo, as well as to Cæsar and Ptolemy, even the figure and relative position of the British islands were uncertain. According to Strabo, Ireland lies to the north of Britain;[4] while to Ptolemy, the northern coasts of Ireland and Scotland appear in the same latitude.[5] These errors must necessarily occasion numberless mistakes with regard to the positions of tribes and territories, when given according to the

[1] Strabo, lib. iv.
[2] Strabo, lib. iii.
[3] Cæsar, B. G. ii. 34.
[4] Geogr. lib. ii.
[5] B. G. v. 13. Geogr. lib. ii. c. 2. See also the excellent disquisitions of Mannert in his 'Geographie der Griechen und Römer,' Abth. 'Britannia.' The Nuremberg Globe of 1520 has still the map of Ptolemy. In Edit. Überlin. of Ptolemy Britain first appears in an upright position.

degrees of longitude and latitude. Our knowledge too with regard to the inhabitants is rendered extremely unsatisfactory by the circumstance, that in the islands and their several districts very different degrees of civilization were met with, to which different authors have attached an opposite and often too general significance. The inhabitants of the Cassiterides, whose position even Strabo seeks off Gallicia,[1] are described by Pytheas in almost the same words as the Iberians are in other passages. Besides mining of a very simple description, they applied themselves to the rearing of cattle, and exchanged tin, lead, and hides with the traders, against salt, pottery, and brass wares. They appeared rambling about their ten islands leaning upon staves,[2] with long beards like goats, and clad in dark garments reaching to their heels and fastened over their chests. It is not improbable that these accounts are also applicable to the neighbouring coast of Cornwall, perhaps even to the tribe of the Silures in South Wales ; but it is uncertain whether in these mountaineers we are to recognise Iberian settlers,[3] or an original native

---

[1] Geogr. lib. ii. If the existence of these islands were not a fiction invented by the traders of Gades for the purpose of misleading their commercial rivals, and inducing them to undertake fruitless expeditions, they must be looked for only on the coast of Cornwall. The ignorance, or silence, of later writers concerning them may perhaps be explained by the supposition that the hazardous passage by sea was forgotten after the way by land through Gaul became the usual route.   [2] Strabo, lib. iii.

[3] Tac. Agric. c. xi. The opinion of Tacitus is much contested from having been made to apply to all Britain. Dionysius Periegetes, v. 563, also declares the inhabitants of the Cassiterides, descendants of the Iberians. On the difference between the Iberian and the old British languages, see W. v. Humboldt's 'Prüfung der Untersuchungen über die Urbewohner Hispaniens vermittelst der vaskischen Sprache,' p. 163.

population identical with that of the rest of South Britain. Navigation along the coasts, though only in small boats of twisted osier covered with leather, had, for a length of time, been very active.[1] The tin, formed into square blocks, was brought to the Isle of Wight, where it was purchased by merchants and carried over to Gaul, and then, in a journey of about thirty days, conveyed on horses to Marseilles, Narbonne, and the mouths of the Rhone.[2] A commerce of this kind, by exciting individual industry, had long rendered the inhabitants of the southern coast of Britain active, docile, and friendly to strangers. Yet was their spirit sunk in a slumber which held them to their native soil, until, through the calamity of a most unjust hostile invasion,—from being a country not reckoned among the nations of Europe,[3]—the land of British barbarians, known only to a few daring mariners, became a province closely connected with imperial Rome, and has finally grown to be the one among European states which more than any other has impressed the stamp of its character and institutions, not only upon this portion of the globe, but also upon lands and regions not discovered till after a long course of ages.

The inhabitants of Britain, with the exception, perhaps, of those above mentioned as Iberian colonists, belonged to the same great national family which we find in Gaul and in Belgium, and which commonly

---

[1] Lucani Phar. lib. iv. v. 134. Plin. H. N. lib. iv. c. 30, vii. 57. Sol. Polyh. c. xxii. F. Avien. v. 104 sq. We find vessels of the same description in use at a later period among the Saxon pirates. Isid. Orig. lib. xix. c. 1.

[2] Diod. lib. v. 22. Strabo, lib. iii.

[3] Even Diodorus speaks of the neighbouring islands lying between *Europa* and Britain.

bears the name of Celts. The supposition of Tacitus [1] that a difference existed between the northern and the southern race, and that the former, from its strong bodily structure and red hair, was of Germanic origin, is by other accounts shown to be groundless. The language still living, particularly in Wales and Brittany, as well as the druidic worship, which, though blended with Christianity, survived to a late period in the former country, and for a thousand years, gave the people energy to withstand the English invaders, form the leading characteristics of this once great race, and these, being its intellectual portion, have been preserved the longest. There is no channel, therefore, through which we may hope to acquire a more intimate knowledge of these people than that afforded by the scientific endeavours of Welsh scholars to elucidate their primitive national literature, although, unfortunately, the results of these efforts have not yet led to any definite results.

In treating of the primitive history of the Britons, a writer must use their native traditions with great caution. Like those of the other European nations, they appear only in that Romanized garb which was fashioned in the modern world under the last rays of the setting Roman sun. Though at every step in the region of British tradition we meet with traces of an eastern origin, yet the tales of the destruction of Troy, and of the flight to Britain [2] of Brutus, a great-grand-

---

[1] Vita Agric. c. xi.
[2] The oldest authority for this tradition is Nennius, who professes to have derived his information "partim majorum traditionibus, partim scriptis, partim etiam monumentis veterum Britanniæ incolarum." Geoffrey of Monmouth is several centuries later, as is also the poem of Robert Wace, 'Le Brut d'Angleterre.'

son of Æneas, are, in the unnational travestie in which alone they have been transmitted to us, wholly devoid of historic value, and the simple truth seems lost to us beyond recovery. The vain Britons gratified their pride in adorning themselves with the faded tinsel, and appropriating to themselves the fabulous national tradition of Rome.

The name of Kymry or Cumry, by which the Welsh still distinguish themselves, as well as that of the north-west county of England, Cumberland; the similarity to the Welsh of the words that have been preserved of the language of the old Kimmerians or Cimbrians; the traditions of the Welsh Triads, as well as the Roman narratives,—all justify the assumption, that the race existing in Britain in the time of Cæsar belonged to those Kimmerians who had gradually moved forward out of Western Asia. Though the obscurity attending the name of that people envelopes also the epoch of their immigration, yet we may conclude, from Cæsar's own account, that it took place long before the time of that conqueror. Hw Cadarn, or Hu the Powerful, as the Triads relate, led the nation of the Kymry from Deffrobany, or the Land of Summer, where Constantinople now is, over the misty ocean, to the uninhabited island Britain, and to Llydaw (Armorica, or Brittany), where they established themselves. They delivered the country, which had previously been called Clas Merddin (the land of sea-cliffs), and afterwards Fel Theis (the island of honey), from the dominion of bears, wolves, and bisons. Prydain, son of Ædd the Great, became ruler of the land, which, through the wisdom of his government, enjoyed a Saturnian age, and retained his name; but later expeditions of Lloegrwys from Gwasgwy or Gascony, and of Brythones from Llydaw, are said to have joined their kindred on the island, and to have settled in the south-east parts.[1]

A language resembling that of the Britons was, according to Tacitus,[2] in use among the Æstii on the shores of the Baltic, the inhabitants on the western coast of which long retained the name of Cimri. The Britannic Moorland on the Ems[3] seems to owe this ancient appellation to the same Cimbric race. In Belgic Gaul, between Boulogne and Amiens, dwelt a people bearing the name of Britanni;[4] an early example of the constant intercourse between both shores, and a striking proof how little even the greatest separation by water, however convenient a boundary for objects of state, avails in dividing nations; whilst a low mountain may form the line of division between barrenness and verdure, and may maintain intact the most dissimilar languages and customs. That the Belgæ inhabiting the British coasts came hither from the Belgium of the continent we know from Cæsar,[5] who speaks of the aboriginal inhabitants, that is the Albiones (whose name we recognise in the Scottish Alpin, Albany), as dwelling in the interior of the country. We have here the first definite indication of the immigrations of the northern nations, and we are thus able in Britain to detect the first step in that long course of invasion, which closed more than a thousand years later in the battle of Hastings, and the victory of the Normans. But, besides the Belgæ, there dwelt also in the thickly-peopled island of Britain, the Atrebates on the Thames, the Cenimagni on the Stour,

[1] Archæology of Wales.   [2] Germania, c. xlv.
[3] In Groningen, now called the Bourtanger Moor.
[4] Plinii H. N. iv. 17.   [5] B. G. v. 12.

and the Parisi on the Humber, whose relationship to the Gaulish tribes of the same name seems unquestionable. The names of places also, particularly those with the Celtic termination *dunum*, equally prove the identity of these peoples.

This state of the population plainly shows us to what class of nations Britain belonged when the foot of Cæsar first trod its shores; by which event the tales of mariners about the tin islands soon fell into oblivion, the veil was withdrawn from Britain, and the land, won for civilization by Roman arms, had the rare fortune to find her first historian in one, for whose thirst of knowledge, penetration, and ambition, neither science nor the world were too extensive.

The continental Gauls, to whom the Channel formed no intellectual barrier, were yet more closely united with the natives of Britain by the common religion of druidism. The important information given us by Cæsar, that the Gauls, though in general possessing a higher degree of culture than the Britons, were, nevertheless, accustomed to seek their more profound knowledge among the druids of the latter,[1] together with the account of the same observer respecting the density of the British population, leads to the inference that migrations had taken place from the north to the southern lands, which had slowly and by piecemeal been conquered by their countrymen. The several mysteries of the druidic doctrines are the more obscure to us, as the transmission of them is not from the most ancient sources, but from times in which the severe

[1] B. G. vi. 13. "Disciplina in Britannia reperta atque inde in Galliam translata esse existimatur: et nunc, qui diligentius eam rem cognoscere volunt, plerumque illo discendi caussa proficiscuntur."—T.

religious spirit of druidism had yielded to the purer doctrines of Christianity, and the desecrated, secret lore of the druids been made subservient to scientific, patriotic, and often impure purposes. The accounts of the bardic oxstall, the mystic cauldron, and similar traditions of the Welsh, are to us either unintelligible, or devoid of historic value. The simple old monuments of British faith,—the cromlechs, huge stones set perpendicularly with a transverse stone; cairs, or concentric circles of stones; rocking stones: cairns, or mounds of stone covered with earth, &c.; numbers of which, in the West of England, and in the other British islands, offer themselves at the present day to the contemplation of the antiquary—while they indicate but a rude state of external worship, yet prove that a vast exertion of physical and mechanical power was applied to the purposes of religion.[1] To a later age those places of old religious veneration were often rendered of importance by being dedicated to Christian worship,[2] a case which in Britain may have happened the more frequently, as no obstinate resistance appears to have been made by druidism to the introduction of Christianity. We find no trace of idol worship among the druids. The oak and mistletoe were objects of their profound veneration, and they adorned their sacrifices with oak

[1] An appeal to Hecatæus (Diod. lib. ii.) cannot, it is true, prove that Stonehenge (Chorea gigantum, *Brit.* Cor Gawr) is there alluded to, but it is mentioned by the bards of the sixth century, and may with confidence from this be applied to older heathen monuments and customs. Regarding such monuments, see Mone's 'Geschichte des nordischen Heidenthumes,' Th. ii. pp. 435–454, where also the religious tenets of the Britons are treated with acuteness, and with a comprehensive knowledge of the heathenism of the other Celtic nations.

[2] Mone, Th. ii. p. 457.

leaves; and if the mistletoe was found growing on a tree, a priest, ascending the tree, severed the sacred plant with a golden knife. A festival on the happy occasion was held under its branches, attended with the sacrifice of two white bulls.[1]

With respect to the doctrines and learning of these western Brahmins, what Cæsar ascertained was very similar to that which Alexander had formerly found among those on the Ganges. They taught the immortality of the soul, its transmigration from one body to another, and—founded on this belief—inculcated a contempt of life.[2] They professed a considerable knowledge of the heavenly bodies and their motions; discoursed on the magnitude of the world, and of its countries; the nature of things; and the virtues and power of the immortal gods.[3]

In the druidic order, and in that of the knights or equestrian order, was vested the chief authority of the country. The druids were subordinate to a high-priest chosen by themselves, though arms occasionally decided

[1] Plinii H. N. xvi. c. 95. Max. Tyr. Dissert. xxxviii.
[2] Lucan. lib. i. v. 460. A Triad of the druids—(Davies's Celtic Researches, p. 182), "The three first principles of wisdom are obedience to the Laws of God, care for the welfare of man, and fortitude under the accidents of life"—is found also as the principle of the gymnosophists, in Diogenes Laertius (Prooem. § 5), Σέβειν θεοὺς, καὶ μηδὲν κακὸν δρᾶν, καὶ ἀνδρείαν ἀσκεῖν.
[3] Cæsar, B. G. vi. 14. [Of their gods, the chief was one to whom Cæsar (vi. 17) gives the name of Mercurius: "Deum maxime Mercurium colunt: hujus sunt plurima simulacra." Tacitus (Germ. ix.) says in the same words of the Germans: "Deorum maxime Mercurium colunt;" thereby meaning Wodan, the chief god of the Germanic nations. Hence Wodensdæg (Wednesday) = dies Mercurii. See Grimm's 'Deutsche Mythologie,' p. 76 sq. On other deities of the Britons Cæsar bestows the names of Apollo, Mars, Jupiter, and Minerva.—T.]

the fate of the Celtic pontificate. Through the administration of the judicial functions they became accurately versed in temporal affairs, and thus secured to themselves worldly influence, and to justice the sanction of religious awe. Their human sacrifices,[1] which were usually limited to criminals and captured foes, we regard with horror; yet posterity should not too severely judge them, since, without the plea of religious infatuation, it had for two thousand years deliberately persisted in similar sacrifices, before doubts as to the lawfulness of capital punishments became a subject of national consideration. As the knight was attended by military followers, so was the druid surrounded by studious disciples, to whom twenty years seemed not too long a period for the acquisition of the required knowledge,—astrology and magic, as well as acuteness in judicial decisions,—together with the privilege of directing the sacrifices, and of proclaiming the dreaded excommunication, and the temporal advantage of exemption from taxes and military service.[2] Their precepts, which were in verse, were delivered orally, it being forbidden to commit them to writing; though in recording the common con-

---

[1] From Cæsar, vi. 16, it appears that the human sacrifices of the Britons were not limited to public occasions. "Qui sunt adfecti gravioribus morbis, quique in proeliis periculisque versantur, aut pro victimis homines immolant, aut se immolaturos vovent, administrisque ad ea sacrificia druidibus utuntur." For the larger sacrifices he informs us that they framed immense images of twisted osier, the members of which they filled with living beings, and then set the mass on fire. The victims were generally criminals, but when these could not be supplied, innocent persons were taken: "etiam ad innocentium supplicia descendunt."—T.
[2] Cæsar, B. G. vi. 13–16. Plinii H. N. xxx. cc. 3, 4. Tac. Ann. xiv. 30.

cerns of life they are said to have used the Greek letters.[1]

With the druids the bards (beirdd) were closely connected [2] who wrote in verse on the descent of their princes, and, together with didactic and epic, had also lyric poetry, which was sung to the sound of the *chrotta*.[3] Though none of the productions, nor even the names of the more ancient bards have been transmitted to us, yet all that is related of them allows us to suppose that their works resembled those still extant of the bards of the sixth and following centuries, from which, when treating of later times, we must not withhold our attention. That bards were known to Posidonius and Lucan,[4] is a convincing proof of the antiquity of the Celtic settlement in Britain, for wandering people carry no poems about with them, scarcely even the most meagre traditions. The Anglo-Saxons and Northmen brought no poetic store from their ancient home to their new country. The peace, leisure, and prosperity of a nation, dwelling in its old native abode, are indispensable to the cultivation of national song.[5]

Together with the druids, the ruling order was, as before said, that of the chieftains or knights. In

[1] A hieroglyphic bardic writing is also said to have been in use, consisting of sixteen characters, and formed from the figures of plants. The characters of the runic alphabet are also named chiefly after natural objects, some of them from trees, as oak, birch, and thorn. See Davies, p. 245 sq.

[2] Diod. v. 31. Strabo, iv. Lucani Phars. i. *v.* 447 sq. Athenæus, vi. Ammian. Mar. lib. xv. 24.

[3] "Crotta Britanna." Venant. Fortun. lib. vii. c. 8. [The crowd (rote) of later minstrelsy. See Graff. 'Althochdeutscher Sprachschatz,' ii. col. 487.—T.]

[4] Athen. lib. iv. c. 37. Pharsal. lib. i. *v.* 447 sq.

[5] May not an instance to the contrary possibly exist in the original saga of Beowulf?—T.

Cæsar's time, both these noble orders had reduced to a state of dependence the greater part of the rest of the people of Gaul, who were oppressed by debts, taxes, and the tyranny of the powerful, exercising towards them all the rights of masters over slaves.[1] The Roman conquest itself might also have contributed to the completion of an already existing state of clientship of the indigent class to the opulent, such as is still to be found in the very pure patriarchal customs of the clans in the Scottish highlands and isles.

The land was divided among many tribes and their kings,[2] who, slightly connected through the priesthood, lived independently near each other, cherishing their love of strife, and training up their youth in civic quarrels, without manifesting at a later period, in the days of the destruction of the common liberty, the judgment and energy necessary for a general resistance.[3] The power of these princes was much limited by the before-mentioned castes, and consisted chiefly in military command, although the occasional rule of queens makes it probable that this authority was heritable.

In the southern parts of England, more especially in Kent which had become more civilized through commerce, the cultivation of grain, to which the mildness of the climate was favourable, had been greatly improved by the art of marling.[4] The daily consumption was taken from the unthrashed corn,

[1] Cæsar, B. G. vi. 13.
[2] The royal authority and even military command could also be exercised by a female, as in the instances of Cartismandua and Boadicea.
[3] Diod. lib v. 21. Tac. Agric. c. xii.
[4] Plin. H. N. xvii. 4. Tac. Agric. xii. Diod. v. 21.

preserved in cakes, which they prepared for food, but did not bake as bread.[1] Horticulture was not in use among them, nor the art of making cheese;[2] yet the great number of buildings, of people, and of cattle appeared striking to the Romans. Copper, and bits or rings of iron, served, according to weight, as money.[3] Their custom of painting themselves with blue and green, for the purpose of terrifying their enemies, as well as that of tattooing,[4] was retained till a later period by the Picts of the North. At certain sacrifices, even the women, painted in a similar manner, resembling Ethiopians, went about without clothing.[5] Long locks and mustachios were general. Like the Gauls, they decorated the middle finger with a ring.[6] Their round simple huts of reeds or wood resembled those of that people,[7] and the Gaulish chequered, coloured mantles are still in common use in the Scottish Highlands. Their clothing, more especially that of the Belgic tribes of the South, enveloped the whole body; a girdle encircled the waist, and chains of metal hung about the breast.[8] The hilts of their huge pointless swords were adorned with the teeth of marine animals;[9] their shields were small.[10] The custom of fighting in chariots (called by them esseda, covini),[11] on the axles of which scythes were fastened, and in the

[1] Diod. v. 21.   [2] Strabo, lib. iv.   [3] Cæsar, B. G. v. 12.
[4] Cæsar, B. G. v. 14. "Virides Britanni." Ov. Amor. lib. ii. 16. "Cærulei Britanni." Mart. Epig. liv. Plin. H. N. lib. xxii. 2. Claud. Prim. Cons. Stil. lib. ii. v. 247. Pomp. Mela, iii. 6. Sol. Polyh. c. xxi. 1.
[5] Plin. H. N. xxii. 2.   [6] Plin. H. N. xxxiii. 6.
[7] Strabo, iv. Diod. v. 21.   [8] Dio. ap. Xiph. lxii.
[9] This was rather the custom of the inhabitants of Ireland. Sol. Polyh. c. xxii.—T.
[10] Tac. Agric. xxxvi.   [11] Pomp. Mela, iii. 6.

management of which they showed great skill, was peculiar to this and some other of the Celtic nations, occupying generally level countries, where the horses were not sufficiently powerful to be used for cavalry. The charioteer was the superior person, the servant bore the weapons. They began their attacks with taunting songs and deafening howls.[1] Their fortresses or towns derived a natural defence from the impenetrable forests.[2] In the interior of the country were found only the more rugged characteristics of a people engaged in the rearing of cattle, which, together with the chase, supplied skins for clothing, and milk and flesh for food.[3] The northern part of the country seems in great measure to have been abandoned to the shaft and javelin of the roving hunter, as skilful as he was bold.[4] That every ten or twelve men of near relationship possessed their wives in common, but that the one earliest married was regarded as the father of all the children, is probably a mere Roman fable.[5] Simplicity, integrity, temperance, with a proneness to dissension, are mentioned as the leading characteristics of the nation.[6] The reputation of bravery was more especially ascribed to the northern races.[7]

A much more favourable picture of the social condition of the ancient Britons may be drawn from the

[1] Cæsar, B. G. iv. 33, v. 16. Strabo iv. Tac. Agric. xii. Diod. v. 21. Dion ap. Xiph. lxii. Pomp. Mela, iii. 6.
[2] Cæsar, B. G. v. 21. Strabo, iv.
[3] Cæsar, B. G. v. 14. The abundance of milk and skins is mentioned in Eumenii Panegyr. ad Constan. Aug. c. ix. Cf. eund. ad Constan. Cæs. c. xi.
[4] Dion ap. Xiph. lxxvi. 12.
[5] Cæsar, B. G. v. 14. Diodorus does not mention this custom.
[6] Diod. v. 21, 22. Pomp. Mela, iii. 6. Tac. Agric. xii.
[7] Dion ap. Xiph. lxxvi.

Triads of Dyvnwal Moelmud, who is said to have lived several centuries before the Christian era,[1] if those Triads have even the slightest claim to be considered genuine which have reached us only in a very modern manuscript, and exhibit not only traces of Roman and Saxon influence, but also of numerous interpolations subsequent to the introduction of Christianity.[2]

Of the British tribes, the first to be mentioned are the Cantii, or men of Kent. They were governed by four princes,[3] within whose lands lay the towns of Dorovernum Comtiopolis (Cantesbury), Rhutupiæ (Richborough), and Reculver. Northward of the Thames, as far as the river Stour, in the present counties of Middlesex and Essex, dwelt the Trinobantes, whose capital, London, was already a considerable emporium. To the north of the Stour, in Suffolk, dwelt the Cenimagni, a

[1] ["Before the crown of London and the supremacy of this island were seized by the Saxons, Dyvnwal Moelmud, son of Clydno, was king over this island, who was son to the earl of Cernyw, by a daughter of the king of Lloegyr. And his laws continued in force until the time of Howel the Good, son of Cadell." 'Ancient Laws and Institutes of Wales,' pp. 89 and 630. In a note the learned editor, Mr. A. Owen, adds, "Dyvnwal, according to the Chronicle of the Kings, in the book of Basingwerke (a Welsh version of Geoffrey of Monmouth's compilation), flourished from anno B.C. 694 to 667." Of these Triads Mr. Owen says (Pref. p. vii.), "Their antiquity is very dubious, but in their present form and phraseology, they may be attributed to the sixteenth century." —T.] See also 'The Ancient Laws of Cambria' translated by W. Probert, 1823. Cf. Gervinus in den Heidelberg. Jahrbüchern 1831, Ss. 46-49, and Palgrave's 'Rise and Progress of the English Commonwealth,' vol. i. c. ii.

[2] [For a passage in the original work omitted from this translation by Mr. Thorpe, see "Supplementary Notes," at the end of the second volume.]—B. C. O.

[3] Cæsar, B. G. v. 22. Ptolemy places London in the territory of the Cantii. [See also Anc. Laws and Instit. of Engl., p. 14, fol. ed.—T.]

tribe of the Iceni; in Norfolk, Cambridgeshire, and Huntingdonshire, the rest of the Iceni, whose chief town bore the common Celtic appellation of Venta. The Catuvellani, or Katyeuchlani of Ptolemy, inhabited the present counties of Hertford, Bedford, and Buckingham. Their territories included Stratford and Verulam, spots destined to become sacred in the history of our modern culture.

The Coritavi (Coriniaidd), who, as the Triads relate, had migrated from a Teutonic marshland, possessed the present counties of Northampton, Leicester, Rutland, Lincoln, Nottingham, and Derby. Beyond them, in the eastern part of Yorkshire, dwelt the Parisi.

The most powerful people were the Brigantes, who held the country to the north of the Humber and the Mersey, comprising the counties of York, Durham, Lancaster, and Westmoreland, to the southern boundary of Scotland. The Caer, or city, Luel (Luguvallum, Lugubalia, or Carlisle), in the country of the Cumbri. on this side of the Picts' wall, remained long the seat of its original inhabitants. Cataractonium and Vinnovium may here also be distinguished as having evidently preserved themselves under the names of Catterick and Binchester. To this people belonged also the Jugantes and the Cangi.

The ancestors of the Welsh were the Ordovices, whose territory comprised the counties of Montgomery, Merioneth, Caernarvon, Anglesea, Denbigh, and Flint; the Dimetæ in Caermarthen, Pembroke, and Cardiganshire; and the most powerful tribe of those parts, the Silures, inhabiting the present shires of Hereford, Radnor, Brecknock, Monmouth, and Glamorgan.

Hampshire, Somersetshire, and Wiltshire, from the English to the Bristol Channel, were occupied by the

Belgæ, where a city, Venta, is still to be recognised in the modern Winchester.

The ancient tin country, the Bretland of the Northmen, now Cornwall and Devonshire, was inhabited by the Dumnonii or Damnonii. The Roman incursions not having reached this south-west corner of the province, we consequently possess the fewest accounts of the period relative to that part of the country which was first known to the three ancient divisions of the globe.

Between the Dumnonii and the Belgæ, in the present Dorsetshire, dwelt the Durotriges: in the counties of Gloucester and Oxford, the Dobuni. The Atrebates, whose chief city was Calleva,[1] were settled in Oxfordshire. In the vicinity of these we are to look for the small tribes mentioned by Cæsar, of the Segontiaci, Ancalites, Bibroci (Bibracte in Bray Hundred, on the Thames, below Windsor), and the Cassi.[2]

The Cornabii, or Carnabii, inhabited the present counties of Warwick, Worcester, Stafford, Salop, and Chester, and probably a part of Flint. In the last-mentioned county, or in that of Chester, was seated the monastery of Bangor (Banchor Iscoed), the most celebrated reli-

[1] Anton. Itin.,
[2] For the geography of Britain under the Romans, Camden's 'Britannia' is especially to be consulted. See also the works of Horsley and Stukeley. The appendix to the first book of Henry's 'History of Great Britain' contains a very useful illustration and comparison of the texts of Ptolemy and Antoninus, and of the extracts relative to Britain in the 'Notitia Imperii Occidentalis.' The itineraries of Antoninus and of Richard of Cirencester, with the illustrations by Gale, Horsley, and Stukeley, are given by Whitaker at the end of his 'History of Manchester.' The notions of the ancients regarding the form of Britain and its coasts, as given by Ptolemy, are most ably illustrated by Mannert. [The localities of the several tribes given in this translation are from Petrie's Corpus Historicum.—The itinerary of Rich. of Cirencester is a forgery, and no statement dependent on it can be relied on.]

gious foundation in the island, till its destruction and the slaughter of its inmates by Æthelfrith of Northumbria.[1]

The Scottish and Irish races (for a knowledge of whose names we are chiefly indebted to Ptolemy) form matter exclusively for the separate history of those nations. Here it is only necessary to observe, that to the north of the Brigantes dwelt the Mæatæ, consisting of five tribes, and beyond them the Caledonians.[2]

The Britons had lived hitherto without intercourse with the south of Europe, except, as before mentioned, through the medium of a few travellers, and an inconsiderable commerce, carried on for the most part by intermediate agents, when they learned that the mighty Roman people from the South had already advanced upon, and subdued many of their Gaulish brethren. Valiant, and mindful of their own danger, the Britons endeavoured, though vainly, by sending succours to the Veneti, to support the Gauls against their victorious foe;[3] but this inefficient help served only as a ground for Roman policy, or a pretext to the Roman general for risking an attack on the unsubdued island. Its inhabitants soon received intelligence from foreign traders, that the Roman commander was making preparations for an invasion, and they beheld a Roman captain, C. Volusenus, in a ship of war reconnoitring their coast.[4] Some of the British tribes, either terrified by the fame of the conquerors of more regions than they had ever heard of, or with the view of amusing the enemy by negotiations, sent ambassadors across the sea to the Roman camp, promising hostages and submission.

[1] Beda, ii. 2. Sax. Chron. a. 607. Ric. Corin. lib. i. c. 6, § 27. "Banchorium monasterium totius insulæ celeberrimum, quod in contentione Augustini eversum, non postea resurrexit."—T.
[2] Dion ap. Xiph. lib. lxxvi. 10. [3] Cæsar, B. G. iii. 9. [4] B.C. 55.

They were received in the kindest manner by their ambitious enemy, whom they assured of the early fulfilment of their promises, and were accompanied on their return by a chieftain named Commius, whom the Romans favoured, on account of his valour, his judgment, and his reputation, and had placed as king over the Gaulish Atrebates [Arras], and who now undertook the commission of persuading the Britons to have reliance on the Roman people, and of announcing the early arrival of their general. Scarcely, however, had Commius made known his commission in the public assembly, when—although it was the duty of their princes to protect the sacred character of an ambassador—the enraged people, divining the drift of the deceitful words, seized on the speaker, and loaded him with chains. Whether Commius had intended again to betray his countrymen, or whether he was a traitor to the Romans, is a question that must remain unanswered. The Britons collected their hordes, which they skilfully posted on the eminences along the shore.[1] The Romans, of whom the infantry of two legions had crossed over the country of the Morini,[2] did not at first venture upon landing, but observing the moment of the ebb, they attempted it upon a level tract of shore about seven miles distant.[3] Here were British cavalry and war-chariots arrayed before the foot-soldiers, who for some time skilfully and boldly held the invaders in check: but the eagle-bearer of the tenth legion, after exhorting his comrades, leaped into the sea, and rushed to the onset, when the missiles of the enemy, Roman valour, enthusiasm for their leader, the great Caius Julius Cæsar—under whom it was regarded a greater disgrace to see the glory of

[1] Where Dover now is.—T.   [2] Orosius, vi. 9.
[3] Near the present Deal.—T.

victory even slightly tarnished, than to be beaten under any other general—but above all, superior discipline, effected the hostile landing.[1]

In these encounters, the war-chariots of the Britons called forth the admiration of their invaders. Their manner of fighting from chariots was this:—At first they rode in all directions, casting their darts, and with the dread of their horses and noise of their wheels generally succeeded in disturbing the ranks of the enemy. Having made an opening in the bodies of cavalry, they would leap from the chariots and fight on foot: meanwhile the charioteers gradually withdrawing from the battle, would post the chariots so that, if pressed by numbers, their comrades might find a certain retreat; thus evincing both the rapidity of cavalry and the firmness of infantry. From constant exercise they could drive their horses at full speed down a declivity, or along a precipice, checking and turning them instantaneously; and could run along the pole, sit on the yoke and thence in an instant reseat themselves in their chariots.

The Britons, in their first consternation, imagining the danger greater than it really was, sent ambassadors to Cæsar, accompanied by the prince of the Atrebates, Commius, offering to give hostages, to place themselves under the protection of the Romans, and entreating forgiveness for the outrage committed on his ambassador.

In his glad surprise Cæsar could not do otherwise than lend a willing ear to these proposals; the British warriors were therefore sent back to their fields, and their princes came to Cæsar, for the purpose of commending themselves to his protection. They soon,

[1] Aug. 26. Anno U.C. 699. B.C. 55. Cæsar, B. G. iv. 21-23.

however, remarked that the valour of their enemy had deceived them with regard to his numbers, and moreover learned that the ships, which had been expected with the cavalry and grain, were dispersed in a storm. Hereupon the resolution soon ripened among them of freeing for ever their native land from this daring foe. They withdrew from the Roman camp, gathered their warriors, and attacked the seventh legion that had gone out to forage, but to which Cæsar sent timely help. Some days afterwards, in an attempt upon the Roman camp, they were repulsed with loss, though, for want of cavalry, not pursued. On the same day they sent messengers to sue for peace, from whom Cæsar demanded a number of hostages, the double of that which he had previously required, and the equinox being at hand, hastened to avoid a dangerous contest with the elements by a speedy return to Gaul. The Romans at home were, however, elated at his account of their new acquisition, and in celebration of it decreed a festival of twenty days' continuance.[1] Thus terminating what—save for the gratification of his own vanity—may be considered a bootless adventure.

But this light prelude was soon to be followed by a sterner contest. The following summer Cæsar again trod the British shores with a greater power[2]—five legions, two thousand cavalry, and all their military engines, added to which was an elephant armed with scales of iron, and bearing a tower containing archers and slingers,[3]—and met with no resistance, the inhabitants of the coast, who had at first appeared in

---

[1] Cæsar, B. G. iv. 20–38. Dion Cass. xxxix. 51–53. Luc. ii. v. 572.
[2] B.C. 54. In the Triads the Romans are called "Cesariadid," 'Archæology of Wales,' p. 58.
[3] Polyæn. Strat. viii. 23.

arms on the level shore, terrified at the magnitude of the approaching fleet, having retired to the higher points of land. An internal dissension, fostered by Mandubratius,[1] the son of Imanuentius, the powerful prince of the Trinobantes, who had been slain by Cassivellaunus (Caswallon), devastated the country. Small was the benefit which the barricades, erected in the forests against domestic foes, afforded against the Romans, in comparison with the detriment they suffered, through their want of union, in allowing a foreign enemy to land unassailed, to repair his fleet, and, after victories easily achieved, to march forward to the heart of the country. The Britons at length sacrificing their petty quarrels to the pressing necessity of struggling for independence, intrusted the chief military command to the brave prince of the Cassi, Caswallon, who had hitherto been engaged in constant warfare with the neighbouring states. In their incursions and attacks great valour was displayed by the Britons, yet was lack of discipline the cause of much disorder after a mischance, and a preventive to their engaging in a general battle. The enemy had advanced as far as the Thames, which at a shallow ford they passed, unhindered by the strong piles that had been driven into the bed of the river by order of Caswallon, remains of which existed in the time of Beda,[2] after an interval of seven hundred

[1] Cæsar, B. G. v. 20. Orosius (vi. 9) calls him Androgorius.

[2] "Quarum vestigia sudium ibidem usque hodie visuntur, et videtur inspectantibus quod singulæ earum ad modum humani femoris grossæ, et circumfusæ plumbo immobiliter erant in profundum fluminis infixæ." H. E. i. 2. The exact point at which Cæsar crossed is not known with certainty; Camden supposes it to have been at Coway Stakes, near Lalcham. See Archæol. vol. i. p. 184; ii. 134, 168.—T.

years. The treachery of the Trinobantes and other tribes, who had submitted to the invaders, disheartened the British leader, whose fame has been preserved to us only in the honourable testimony of Cæsar. His well-planned forest-fastness was, with great difficulty, at length taken, and even then he attempted an attack upon the Roman camp on the coast of Kent, with the design, by destroying their fleet, of turning the land they had conquered into a prison. No other resource being left him, Commius negotiated for his submission, by which the Romans obtained what alone they could seek in this to them inhospitable land—the glory of victory; while Caswallon gained that which, even with the disgrace of apparent humiliation, was not too dearly bought—the evacuation of his native country by hostile armies. This time hostages were actually led home by the Romans, grain was delivered to them, and Rome was dazzled [1] by Cæsar's account of the riches of this new portion of the world, and by the sight of a corselet adorned with British pearls which he dedicated to Venus:[2] yet the promised yearly contributions were not paid, and, with the exception of the hostages, the Britons were as free as they had been the year before, ere a passing cloud had for a moment darkened the sunshine of their independence. The steady yet powerful influence of the vivifying rays of the Roman sun could not fail to reach the Britons, and the coins of their prince Cynobellin, the Cymbeline ennobled in

---

[1] Not so the better informed. Cicero, in a letter to Atticus (iv. 16), writes, "Britannici belli exitus exspectatur. Constat enim aditus insulæ esse munitos mirificis molibus. Etiam illud jam cognitum est, neque argenti scripulum esse ullum in illa insula, neque ullam spem prædæ, nisi ex mancipiis." Cæsar, v. 8–23.

[2] Plin. H. N. ix. 57. Sol. Polyh. c. liii.

tradition and by Shakspere's muse, prove that the Roman alphabet was intelligible to the natives, and that Roman art was cultivated in Britain.[1]

[1] See Pegge's 'Essay on the Coins of Cunobeline:' London, 1766. In Whitaker's 'History of Manchester' representations of these coins are given. See also Henry's 'History of Great Britain,' vol. ii.

CHAPTER II.

A.D. 43-120.

Invasion by Claudius—Caractacus—Conquest of Mona—Boadicea—Agricola—Mode of Government—Guilds—Celtic Tongue—Princes—Laws—State of country.

A CENTURY had nearly elapsed, and the Britons had seen on their soil no other Romans than peaceful merchants. The duties levied in Gaul on their trifling exports and imports were moderate.[1] On the rumour of an intended invasion, envoys were sent by them to the emperor Augustus;[2] yet Rome heard of no homage from Britain, except the offerings said to have been made by some petty princes to the Capitol,[3] and in the empty compositions of poets and panegyrists. And it is probable that the Britons would never have yielded to Roman sway—for the strength of the latter was already on its wane, their power near the summit from which it was soon to descend—had not pernicious discord prevailed among the British princely races, and reduced their country under a subjection of four hundred years' duration.

Adminius,[4] the son of Cynobellin, a successor of Caswallon, having been banished by his father, had, with a few followers, placed himself under the power of Caligula, who, as if the whole island had been sur-

[1] Strabo, iv.   [2] Dion Cass. liii. 22.   [3] Strabo, iv.
[4] Orosius (vii. 5) calls him Minocynobellinus.—T.

rendered to him, immediately sent despatches to Rome announcing the glorious intelligence. The forces raised for the German war were hereupon ordered to the coast, and there arrayed, with their military engines in readiness. In suspense as to what was to follow, they beheld the emperor embark on board a trireme, in which he proceeded a short distance from the shore, but soon returning he placed himself on a lofty throne, from whence he gave a signal as if for battle, and to the sound of trumpets ordered them to gather, and fill their helmets and bosoms with shells, which he called "the spoils of the ocean." As a monument of victory, he caused a lofty tower to be built, which at the same time should serve as a beacon; gave considerable rewards to the soldiers, and commanded the shells to be borne in triumph to Rome.[1]

The treachery of Cynobellin, however, proved hurtful only through the example which it soon after afforded to an exile named Beric, at whose instigation the emperor Claudius resolved on sending an army to Britain.[2] The warlike reputation of the natives was so universally acknowledged, that the four legions destined to contend with them, under the command of Aulus Plautius, could scarcely be induced to break up their quarters. Surprised, however, by the landing of the enemy, the Britons were not in a condition to oppose it, and proved their valour only in a warfare of skirmishes. The Gaulish allies of the imperial forces, even if at the

[1] Suet. de Calig. c. xlvi. Dion Cass. lix. 21. A.D. 40.
[2] A.D. 43. Dion Cass. lx. 19. Suet. de Claud. c. xvii. Orosius says (vii. 6), " Expeditionem in Britanniam movit, quæ excitata in tumultum propter non redhibitos transfugas videbatur." The fugitives were probably Beric and his associates, and the disturbance, caused by the emperor's refusal to deliver them up, seems to have served him as a pretext for invading the island.—T.

outset they spared the lives of their kindred, and only slew their chariot-horses, could not fail in the end to cause them injury. The glory of the first important victory in Britain, and the honour of a triumph at home, belong to Cn. Osidius Geta.[1] This country was the palæstra of the Roman emperors. Vespasian, at the head of the second legion, accompanied by Titus, fought here thirty battles, subdued the Isle of Wight, overcame two nations, and took twenty places.[2] The war now assuming a more serious character, Plautius, as he had been previously instructed, resolved on sending for the emperor. Claudius was accompanied by Galba, the administration of the state being conducted by Vitellius during the absence of the emperor. Cynobellin was now dead; of his sons, Togodumnus and Caractacus, or Caradoc, the former had fallen in battle, the latter was driven across the Thames, and Claudius, honoured with the surname of the Britannic, entered their chief city, Camulodunum.[3] From this place, by means of negotiations and arms, he began to mould the south-eastern parts of Britain into a Roman province, the administration of which was committed to Plautius, and afterwards to P. Ostorius Scapula.[4] A prince named Cogidubnus obtained some territories in or about Sussex, which he was proud to govern under the title

[1] Dion Cass. lx. 20.

[2] Dion Cass. lx. 20. Eutrop. lib. vii. c. 19; Suet. de Vespas. c. iv.; de Tito, c. iv.; de Galba, c. vii. Tac. Agric. c. xiv.

[3] Dion Cass. lx. 21. Suet. de Claud. xvii. Camulodunum is usually supposed to be the town of Maldon, but the cogent reasons assigned by Mannert and others induce us rather to identify it with Colchester. See 'Geogr. der Griechen und Römer,' p. 157. [Roy. Milit. Antiq. p. 187. Archæol. iii. p. 165.—T.]

[4] A.D. 50. Tac. Agric. c. xiv. Camden (edit. Gibson, p. 300) supposes the Oyster hills near Hereford to have been one of his camps. Ostorius came in the year 47.

of an imperial legate, and devoted the rest of his life to the establishment of the Roman power in his native country.[1] The majority of the inhabitants who had attached themselves to the conqueror had, however, soon cause to repent that step, on perceiving that while the duty of subjects was exacted from them, they were at the same time deprived of the right of bearing arms. While the west was submitting to the Roman camps on the Avon and the Severn, the Iceni in the east were the first to declare themselves against the new tyranny; and history, when relating their defeat, celebrates at the same time their many and brilliant achievements. Their misfortune disheartened the similarly disposed neighbouring states; but the Cangi and the Silures, under the national hero, Caradoc, continued a war of annihilation and despair. The Brigantes also, in the yet unconquered northern parts, now rose for the protection of the common liberty; but before the league among them had become general, and they could appear prepared for the contest, they were, for the time, reduced by Ostorius, who with his army marching rapidly against them, caused the few who had taken up arms to be slain; the others were pardoned.[2]

[1] Tac. Agric. c. xiv. The hypothesis of several commentators on this passage of Tacitus, which Lingard also adopts, that Togodumnus and Cogidubnus were the same person, appears, on comparison with Dion, untenable. The writers of the 'Universal History' (vol. xlvii. p. 32) make him the son of Cartismandua, and to fall, instead of Togodumnus, in battle against the Romans. At Chichester, in 1723, an inscription was dug up with the words, "Ex auctoritate Tiberii Claudii Cogidubni regis legati Augusti in Britannia." See Gale in Philos. Trans. 1723, Oct. 31. Horsley, Brit. Rom. No. 76, pp. 192, 333; also Henry, 'History of Great Britain,' i. p. 336. The fac-simile, with a somewhat different explanation, is given in Hearne's Preface to Adam de Domerham.
[2] Tac. Ann. xii. 32.

With the design of securing the subjection of the vanquished, and of those who were honoured with the name of allies, as well as of establishing a stronghold in the country for Roman interests and civilization, a colony of hardy veterans was placed at Camulodunum.[1] The Roman eagles were already displayed over the plains of Britain, when the Silures, Ordovices, and other mountaineers, who had flocked around Caradoc, began a new struggle, which for some time seemed ruinous to the enemy; yet were their love of freedom, their reverence for the gods of their country, their craft and valour forced to give way before regular warfare. Caradoc's stronghold (Caer Caradoc[2]) was taken; his wife, daughter, and brothers fell into the hands of the conqueror. He himself sought shelter and help among the Brigantes, whom he had formerly befriended; but their queen, Cartismandua, expecting to obtain less by a noble struggle for the independence of her people than through the favour of the Romans, sought to purchase the latter by the treacherous surrender of her guest to his enemies, whom he had stoutly resisted during a space of nine years.[3] But though compelled to appear with his family as a glorious spectacle to proud, triumphant Rome, who looked on this fruit of treachery as equal to the most brilliant victories of Publius Scipio, and Lucius Paullus, yet were the brave mountaineers whom Caradoc had led still unsubdued. The Silures attacked the Roman legions appointed to erect fortresses among them, and although they often gave way,

[1] Tac. Ann. xii. 32.
[2] A lofty hill on the river Ony, near the junction of the Clun and the Teme, in the south-eastern part of Shropshire, still bears the name of Caer Caradoc, and exhibits traces of ancient fortifications.
[3] A.D. 51.

the enemy could boast of no victory: his forces—which could hope only with the last of the Silures to quell the spirit of British independence — were daily diminishing, while the allies of the Britons daily increased. Ostorius died of grief.[1] His death was justly celebrated as a victory by the Britons, for his successor Aulus Didius Gallus was, by reason of his advanced age, far less formidable. Some years had passed when Venusius, the husband of Cartismandua, from whom he had parted, and who had married Vellocatus, one of his shield-bearers, placed himself at the head of his people, in opposition to the Romans, whose arms, however, under the skilful guidance of Cæsius Nasica, succeeded in producing a momentary tranquillity. Didius was succeeded by Veranius.[2]

The Britons of the present England were now, to all appearance, nearly subjected to the Romans; and the prefect or legate, Suetonius Paullinus, the successor of Veranius, after two years of tranquil administration, resolved on the reduction of the Isle of Mona (Anglesea),[3] the chief seat of druidism, and a receptacle for fugitives. To this end he ordered the construction of shallow vessels for the transport of the foot-soldiers, while the cavalry should either swim or wade across the strait. On arriving at the opposite shore they found a dense band of armed men, between whose ranks women like furies were seen passing, clad in mourning, with dishevelled locks, and bearing torches; while the druidesses with upraised hands poured forth maledictions on the invaders. Appalled and, as it were, petrified at this spectacle, the soldiers stood aghast and exposed to the missiles of the enemy, till, on the

[1] A.D. 55.   [2] Tac. Ann. xii. 40, xiv. 29. Hist. iii. 45.
[3] A.D. 61.

exhortation of their general, not to fear a band of fanatics and women, they rushed to the onset, overthrowing and destroying in their own fire all who had courage to resist. A garrison was then left on the isle, and the groves, stained with the blood of human victims, fell under the axe of the legionaries. But while the general was thus engaged,[1] the Britons were nearly proving successful in extirpating the Romans from the country. These, as well as the other provincials, were bitterly exasperated by the heavy taxes, in the levying of which they were exposed not only to the rapacity of Roman usurers—among whom was Lucius Annæus Seneca,[2] in whom the love of wisdom and of base lucre existed in a rare, though not unparalleled combination—but also by the most intolerable oppression of the procurator Catus, and of other Roman officials.

No tribe endured the incorporation of their country as a province more impatiently than the Iceni. Their king, the wealthy Prasutagus, in the view of securing both his kingdom and family from the officers and farmers of the revenue, and, according to a practice then prevalent, seeking in degradation a safeguard against insult, had made the emperor his joint heir with his two daughters. The atrocities perpetrated by the insolent and profligate officials of the provinces (whom vice instigated more than the desire of possession, and who had been excited by wantonness to a recklessness of all the rights of humanity, as well as of their own well-understood interest), met at length with a well-merited vengeance. Under the conduct of Boudicea, the magnanimous widow of Prasutagus, who had been scourged as a slave, a multitude of a

[1] Tac. Ann. xiv. 29.   [2] Dion ap. Xiph. lxii. 2.

hundred and twenty thousand Britons[1] surprised the Romans, destroyed Camulodunum, the important emporium London,[2] and Verulam, and slaughtered seventy thousand Romans (including the ninth legion under the legate Petilius Cerealis), and their traitorous British allies, with all the fury of vengeance to which the violation of their temples, their honour, and their domestic hearths could impel them.[3] Suetonius Paullinus, in a contest of despair, gained, through his wedge-shaped order of battle, a bloody victory,[4] in which eighty thousand Britons fell, while Boadicea who would not survive them, ended her days by poison.[5] Yet neither the want of regular discipline, nor the reinforcements of the Romans, but only a scarcity of corn in the following winter compelled the Britons again to submit to the dominion of the Cæsars. One point, however, was gained: the necessity of a mild administration became understood at Rome. The procurator Catus was succeeded by Julius Classicianus: the general by Petronius Turpilianus; his followers

[1] Dion ap. Xiph. lxii. 1. sq.
[2] "Londinium, cognomento quidem coloniæ non insigne, sed copia negotiatorum et commeatuum maxime celebre." Tac. Ann. xiv. 33.
[3] Dion ap. Xiph. lxii. The grove of Andraste or Andate, the British goddess of victory, is mentioned as the chief place where these atrocities were perpetrated.—T.   [4] A.D. 62.
[5] Tac. Ann. xiv. 31-37. Boudicca is described by Dion (ap. Xiph.) as of the largest size, most terrible of aspect, most savage of countenance, and harsh of voice; with a profusion of yellow hair which fell down to her hips, and wearing a large golden collar. She had on a party-coloured flowing vest drawn close about her bosom, and over this a thick mantle fastened by a clasp. Such was her usual dress, but at this time she also bore a spear. By the same authority we are informed that she died of disease.—T.

were the contemptible Trebellius Maximus, and the inactive Vettius Bolanus, under whose inefficient command the Roman soldiery became more licentious, the Britons more bold.[1] Among the Brigantes, Venusius had fostered enmity to Rome and her ally Cartismandua; and they might have hoped to overpower the Romans, had not Vespasian, at that time emperor, appointed Petilius Cerealis to the dignity of consular legate, who, after an entire year of contest, succeeded in subduing them: yet these mountaineers rose again and again with renewed strength.[2] The Silures could only be withheld from further strife by his successor Julius Frontinus,[3] who was followed in the administration of the province by Cneius Julius Agricola,[4] a leader whose glorious memory will for ever live in the noble monument raised to his father-in-law by the great historian of the empire.

The first campaign of Agricola, after his arrival, was against the Ordovices, who had attacked and nearly annihilated a body of Roman cavalry stationed on their border. Having destroyed the greater part of this people, he directed his attention to the reconquest of Mona, which had recovered its liberty on the sudden departure of Paullinus to quell the insurrection under Boudicea. Though without vessels for the transport of his soldiers, the energy of Agricola was not to be subdued. He caused such of his auxiliaries as were most expert in swimming, and who were acquainted with the locality, to cross the strait, on whose unlooked-for approach the surprised inhabitants sued for peace, and again yielded to the Romans.

[1] Tac. Ann. xiv. 38. Agric. c. xvi.; Hist. i. 60.
[2] A.D. 70-75.   [3] A.D. 75-78.
[4] Josephus de Bell. Jud. vii. 4. Tac. Agric. c. vii.

But Agricola knowing by experience that tranquillity can be best maintained by removing the causes of discontent, and, acting on this conviction, undertook the work of reform, wisely beginning with his own household. He checked the abuses connected with the levying of the taxes, which were even more intolerable than the taxes themselves. The summer immediately following [1] was employed in improving the state of the army, in the formation of camps, and other measures for the security of the province; and the winter was passed in introducing among the rugged natives the luxuries and refinements of the capital.

To this end neither exhortations nor aid were wanting on the part of Agricola. Temples, baths and other structures, both public and private, were erected; the British youth were instructed in the language and learning of Rome; elegant and costly entertainments became fashionable, and with the toga the vices of the imperial city were adopted. Among the inexperienced this passed under the name of politeness, while it was a part of their servitude.

In the third year of his government Agricola conducted his forces as far as the Tay, where he established strong garrisons. In his fourth year, for the security of his conquests, he caused a line of forts to be erected between the Firths of Forth and Clyde.[2] With a view to the future subjugation of Ireland, to which he had

[1] A.D. 79.
[2] On the subject of the Roman walls in Britain, the reader will find a very able digest in a work entitled 'Eburacum, or York under the Romans, by C. Wellbeloved,' 8vo, 1842: which contains also much valuable matter connected with the latest discoveries in Yorkshire and the North, as well as with the state of Roman Britain in general.—T. [See also J. C. Bruce, on the Roman wall; Tyne to Solway.—E. C. O.]

been excited by the representations of an exiled chief, Agricola, in the year following, extended his conquests to the western shores of Britain, where he stationed numerous forces, to be in readiness for ulterior operations.

In the summer of his sixth year he proceeded with an army to the country beyond the Forth, while a fleet coasting along the eastern shore seconded his designs. At the sight of the ships the Britons were struck with amazement, while the Romans were equally alarmed by accounts of the valour and activity of the Caledonians. These in the night attacked the ninth legion, and, having slain the sentinels, were already engaged in a sanguinary contest within the camp, when Agricola, informed of their movements by his scouts, commanded the fleetest of his horse and foot to follow in their track. The Caledonians having now an enemy to contend against in front and rear, were compelled to seek for safety in the shelter of their marshes and forests.

In the last year of his administration Agricola resolved on another expedition into Caledonia. For this purpose he assembled his sea and land forces, having added to the latter a corps of tried British auxiliaries. With these he advanced to the Grampian hills, where he found the Britons, under their general Calgacus, to the number of thirty thousand, drawn up in battle array, their foot being posted in lines on the declivity, while the chariots and horse occupied the level plain. In the centre of his battle Agricola placed eight thousand auxiliary foot; his legions were posted in front of the camp; three thousand horse were at the wings. As long as they fought with missiles the advantage appears to have been on the side of the natives; but on the attack of three Batavian and two

Tungrian cohorts with their pointed swords, the Britons, whose long, ponderous swords without points and small targets were but ill fitted for close action, were compelled to give way. On the advance of other cohorts their horse were put to flight, and the chariots driven in disorder among the infantry. Those of the Britons who had occupied the summit of the hills now descended, with the design of attacking the rear of the Romans, but were repulsed by a body of cavalry which had been held in reserve by the foresight of Agricola. The following day exhibited to the victors the spectacle of a vast solitude, with the smoke of burning dwellings in the distance, but not a vestige of a living being. The loss of the Britons in this conflict is estimated at ten thousand, that of the Romans at three hundred and sixty. The army then retired into winter quarters, and the fleet having made the circuit of the island, returned to Sandwich (Portus Trutulensis), from whence it had sailed. Triumphal ornaments and the honour of a statue were decreed to Agricola, who shortly after delivered up his province to a successor, returned to Rome, which, according to order, he entered by night, and, after a cold reception by Domitian, sank into obscurity amid the servile crowd.[1]

The quiet of the latter years in the greater part of South Britain, not less than the power of arms in other districts of the country, had now (after the Celtic tribes of the continent, notwithstanding the fruitless endeavours of Cl. Civilis in Belgic Gaul,[2] had also submitted to the Romans) greatly promoted the union of Britain with the Roman empire. The politic and wise administration of Agricola completed the Romanizing of the British Celts, and gave to the larger portion

[1] Tac. Agric. c. vii.-xl.   [2] Tac. Hist. iv. 15.

of Britain the form under which for several centuries it was governed, and at the same time caused the political division of the country into the parts which from later settlers have obtained the names of England and Scotland. The form of government under which the country was acknowledged as a part of Europe, while it destroyed the national unity of the Britons, must in its connection with the whole administration of the empire be here briefly delineated.

The division into Britannia Inferior and Superior [1] is nearly identical with the present one into England and Scotland. The provinces were: Britannia Prima, or the district to the south of the Thames and the Bristol channel; Britannia Secunda, the present principality of Wales; Flavia Cæsariensis, so called from the master of Agricola, which extended from the Thames to the Mersey and the Humber. Beyond the Humber, to the distance of twenty-five miles north of the Picts' wall, was the province of Maxima Cæsariensis, bordering on the fifth province Valentia, which extended to the firths, to the country beyond which the name of Vespasiana had, it is said, been given; but of which, as the memorial of a fruitless occupation, mention is made only in the work of Richard of Cirencester, discovered (if not fabricated [2]) in the middle of the last century.

The supreme civil and military power in Britain was at first vested in a governor, who bore the high title of Legatus, or Consularis.[3] The Procurator or Quæstor administered the concerns of the imperial

[1] Dio. Cass. lv. 23.

[2] [The work *De Situ Britanniæ*, referred to is now known to be a fabrication.—E. C. O.]

[3] The title of Præfectus or Proprætor of Britain occurs only in later writers, and was held, according to their authority, by Agricola to the year 84; Sallust Lucullus (Sueton. Domitian, c. 10); Julius

treasury, levied the land-tax, the poll-tax, and those laid on certain natural productions. Severus divided the government into two portions.[1] When Constantine parted the empire into four governments, Britannia fell to that which was placed under the Præfectus Prætorio Galliarum, who at first resided at Treves and subsequently at Arles. Under a vicar of the prefect, two consulars were appointed to the provinces of Maxima Cæsariensis and Valentia, and three presidents over those of Britannia Prima, Britannia Secunda, and Flavia Cæsariensis.[2] For the revenues of the country, a Rationalis Summarum Britanniarum, a Præpositus Thesaurorum Augustensium in Britanniis, and a Procurator Cynegii in Britannia Biennensis[3] were subordinate to the Comes Largitionum of the West. Under the Comes Largitionum Privatarum there was a special Rationalis Rei Privatæ per Britannias.[4] We can here give only an imperfect outline of the administration; the details, such as the amount of revenue, its increase or diminution, are totally unknown to us. It was not, however, till after the time of Appian[5] that the receipts of the state began to cover the expenses of the government. The military force in Britain under the Magister Militum Præsentalis, which was intrusted to the Comes Militum

---

Severus (Dio apud Xiph.); Cl. Prisc. Licinius (Camden, p. lxvii); Lollius Urbicus, 146; Ulpius Marcellus, 180; Clodius Albinus, 190-197.

[1] Herodian. iii. 24.   [2] Zosim. ii. 33. Not. Imp. Occid. c. lxviii.

[3] Not. Imp. c. xxxiv. For *Biennensis* Pancirol. (p. 68) reads *Dremtensis*, but without adding any explanation. Grævius (Thes. tom. vii.) has *Bentensis*, and *cynegii* instead of the *gynecii* of the earlier editors.

[4] Not. Imp. c. xli.   [5] See his preface.

Britanniarum, consisted of 2200 infantry and 200 cavalry; under the Comes Tractus Maritimi (at a later period, Litoris Saxonici per Britannias) 3000 infantry and 600 horse; and a larger force under the Dux Limitum Britanniarum, of 14,000 infantry and 900 cavalry, forming together an army of 19,200 infantry and 1700 cavalry. The British Count had thirty-seven castella to defend; the Count of the Saxon shore, nine fortresses situated on the coast of South Britain, from the straits of Dover to Brancaster in Norfolk and Pevensey in Sussex.[1] The frontier fortresses were numerous and required strong garrisons.

The number of these officials and—when compared with the others of the empire—the narrow limits of the British province lead us to infer the existence of a sufficient object, both for the activity and cupidity of those employed in the administration and their subalterns; an inference, indeed, which seems incompatible with the current opinion of the want of all civilization in the country. More important, however, for the Britons than those forms in which the ambition of a few Romans found a step to higher objects, or the rapacity of others sought the means of gratification, must have been the economy of the civic constitution; and here we recognise the advantages, which even an enemy always brings to a previously isolated country.

[1] Not. Imp. co. xix., lxxii., and Pancirol. ibid. p. 157. The title of Comes Litoris Saxonici first occurs in the Notitia Imperii Occident. composed in the time of Arcadius and Honorius. The conservation of peace on the British coast on the Atlantic fell much more naturally to the Gaulish coast troops under the command of the Dux Tractus Armoricani (Not. Imp. Occid. i. 86); though the chief command over the marine in those parts may, as in the instance of Carausius, have sometimes been held by one individual.

When the Romans abandoned Britain it contained twenty-eight cities, besides a considerable number of castella, ports, and small communities. Among the first, we know of two municipia, York and Verulam; nine colonies, Camulodunum (Maldon or Colchester), Rhutupiae (Richborough), Londinium Augusta (London), Glevum Claudia (Gloucester), Thermae Aquae Solis (Bath), Isca Silurum (Carleon in Monmouthshire), Comboricum (Chesterford near Cambridge), Lindum (Lincoln), and Deva Colonia (Chester); also ten cities which had obtained the right of Latium: Pterotone (Inverness), Victoria (Perth), Durnomagus (Caistor in Lincolnshire), Lugubalia (Carlisle), Cattaractone (Catterick), Cambodunum (Slack in Longwood), Coccium (Blackrode in Lancashire?), Theodosia (Dumbarton), Corinum (Cirencester), and Sorbiodunum (Old Sarum), the last colony to the south-west in the country of the free Damnonii. Volantium (Ellenborough in Cumberland), so rich in Roman remains, preserves an inscription, from which we learn that it had Decurions who assembled in a public building destined for the purpose.[1] These cities, therefore, possessed a council (Decuriones, Curiales, Municipes), with magistrates of their own choosing (Duumviri and Principales), and the right of contentious, as well as of voluntary jurisdiction. To them was committed the levying of taxes in their districts, and it is known how the joint security of the civic decurions became both a burthen to themselves and brought the greatest obloquy on their order. That these abuses had also found their way into Britain, we learn from an ordinance of Constantine for the remedying of the same in this country.[2] Subsequently

[1] Most of the above statements rest only on the fabrication *de Situ Britanniae*. But cf. Petrie, C. H. p. cxiii. No. 123. Horsl. B. R. 68.   [2] Cod. Theod. xi. tit. 7, 2.

to the time of that emperor, the Defensor elected by the whole city, more especially against the oppressions of the governor, had become of consideration. The establishment of corporations at Rome, into which certain artizans and handicraftsmen were united, was extremely advantageous to them when they were removed into foreign provinces. We find much information concerning these colleges in ancient inscriptions; and it is very probable that, together with the trades of Rome, this form of social unions, as well as the hereditary obligation under which the former were conducted, was propagated in Britain, and was the original germ of those guilds which became so influential in Europe some centuries after the cessation of the Roman dominion.[1]

Great caution is necessary in endeavouring to show what ancient British elements were preserved under the Romans. From the Latin authors we can extract very little upon the subject, and the old British accounts have reached us in a form comparatively modern and demonstrably much corrupted. In the larger eastern portion of the country, it is chiefly in the names of rivers and mountains that the old British denominations have been preserved;[2] those of tribes and of places being either wholly lost, or in their Roman disguise scarcely to be recognised; while in Gaul the old names may easily be traced. As rare exceptions may be mentioned a few places known through commerce prior to the Roman conquests in the north of Europe, viz. Vecta (the Isle of Wight), Dubris (Dover), the

[1] 'Collegium lignatorum,' inscrip. at Middleby in Scotland : 'fabrorum,' inscrip. at Chichester. Horsley, B. R. pp. 337, 342. Petrie, C. H. pp. cxii., cxiii. Cf. also Wilda, 'Das Gildenwesen im Mittelalter.'

[2] For a copious enumeration of these with illustrations, see Chalmers's 'Caledonia,' vol. i. p. 33-36.

county of Kent, and that universal mart on the Thames which, though dignified by the Romans with the name of Augusta, has still preserved its ancient appellation of London.[1]

It was otherwise beyond the mountains, the British Apennines, which separate the country into two portions, where, in the later territory of the Cymry—comprising Cumberland, the south-east of Scotland, Westmoreland and Lancashire; and in Wales, Cornwall, Devonshire, Man and Anglesea—every philological deduction justifies the inference of a purer preservation of the British stock. Of the dialects and literature of Wales we shall have occasion to speak hereafter; it may, however, be here observed, that Cornwall, so late as the twelfth century, was by the Norwegians called Bretland,[2] and until the middle of the sixteenth century only the primitive British or Lloegrian tongue was there spoken; since which time, through the reformation of the church and the spread of English printed books, it rapidly declined, till, about half a century ago,[3] on the death of its last preserver, a very aged woman, it was entirely blotted from the list of living dialects.[4] Still longer has the

[1] "Lundinium vetus oppidum, quod Augustam posteritas adpellavit." Amm. Marcell. xxvii. 8.

[2] See Theodoric the monk of Trondhjem, in Hist. et Antiq. Regum Norwégiœ, apud Langebek, Scriptores Rerum Danicarum, t. v. p. 315.

[3] [The author wrote in 1833.—E. C. O.]

[4] From 1560 to 1602 the Cornish dialect greatly declined, and became limited to the western part of the county, where it was preserved till the beginning of the last century. Lhuyd ('Archæologia Britannica,' p. 225-253) gives a grammar of the Cornish. The printed books in this dialect are few, and only three or four in manuscript. Latterly, however, we are indebted to the late Davies Gilbert, Esq., for 'Mount Calvary,' and 'The Creation of the World,' 8vo. The first is in old Cornish with a slight mixture of

old Celtic tongue been preserved in the Isle of Man, which may perhaps be due to the earlier admixture of Anglo-Saxon words.[1] With the old British territories may perhaps be reckoned the tract of country extending from the Humber to the Firth of Forth, which after the departure of the Romans was formed into two states, the names of which, Deifyr and Bryneich, are undoubtedly British. Here are also several British names of places that have undergone but little corruption.

That British princes of the old reigning native families were acknowledged by the Romans under Trajan after the death of Cogidubnus, is by no means improbable, as, according to their wise policy, it was thought useful, in the other provinces of the empire, to preserve such mediators, as it were, between themselves and nations wholly differing from them in speech, habits, and notions of right. Yet as no mention of their names is to be found even in the accounts of the several insurrections in Britain, nor on coins or other monuments, they must have acted a part little beyond that of rich private individuals, who were

---

Saxon or Norse. The other is in more modern Cornish, written in 1611. To both are added translations made by J. Knigwin in 1682, together with several small Cornish pieces. Cf. Borlase's 'Antiquities of Cornwall.' Oxf. 1758, folio. W. Price, 'Archæologia Cornu Britannica, containing a Cornish Grammar and Vocabulary.' Sherborne, 1790, 4to. Daines Barrington on the expiration of the Cornish language, in Archæol. vol. iii. p. 279, vol. v. p. 81; also the treatises in Grose's 'Antiquarian Repertory,' vol. ii.

[1] See Henry Rowland's 'Mona Antiqua restaurata, with an Appendix containing a comparative table of primitive and derivative words.' Lond. 1722 and 1766, 4to. Also 'A Practical Grammar of the Ancient Gaelic, or language of the Isle of Man, usually called Manks,' by John Kelly, Lond. 1808. Some translations of the Scriptures exist in this dialect.

regarded by their oppressed countrymen with the respect due to their lineage, as well as with lively sympathy, and, sometimes, with secret hope. British tradition speaks of princes of Colchester, of Cornwall, and among the 'Gewissi' in Warwickshire and Worcestershire, during the sway of the Romans, and this may afford ground for a probable hypothesis of the existence of certain princely families, from whom many of the ancient, noble and wealthy races derived their origin.[1] But it would seem safest to assume that such princely families, enjoying independence, could only have held their ground in those parts of western England which were not traversed by Roman roads, and whose coasts were left to the guardianship of the inhabitants.

In no part of England are there fewer Roman remains than among the Damnonii and in Wales. To explain this slight influence of the Romans by the supposition of greater pliancy and weakness in the natives of those parts is not justifiable, when we call to remembrance the noble struggles of the Silures. On the contrary, both from the above circumstance and from the fact that the western coasts of England continued free from attacks from the opposite shore of Ireland, we may conclude that those people who were able to preserve the most striking sign of distinct nationality in their native tongue, continued in reality as respected allies of the Romans. In such a case, the Roman chancery too might find it easy to forget that, to the unity of their power in Britannia Prima and

---

[1] The continuation of such princes in Britain with a subordinate authority is adopted by Whitaker ('History of Manchester,' vol. i. p. 247). By Gibbon (c. xxxi. note 184) the hypothesis is rejected, while Palgrave ('Rise and Progress,' i. p. 324) favours it. What is here stated may perhaps suggest new grounds for the supposition.

Secunda, some districts were wanting, while the treasury might have been alike willing to abstain from demanding the contributions of the coast-lands of the Atlantic.

This view of the limits of the real dominion of Rome, and of the condition of the western tribes, is in many respects important for later history. It explains and supports the British traditions, the accounts of the first introduction of Christianity, the state of the country after the departure of the Romans, and, in a degree, marks the limits of the Anglo-Saxon conquests, which may frequently be traced by those of Roman Britain.

A fact worthy of notice in this place, is the existence down to recent times of the old British law of succession in Wales, Kent, and some parts of Northumberland, called Gavelkind. As far as we are enabled to understand it in its mixture with Anglo-Saxon law, all the sons of the same father inherited, but the youngest possessed the homestead; the eldest, or the next following capable of bearing arms, had the heriot, that is, the arms offensive and defensive of his father, and his horse. Even the son of an outlaw could not be deprived of the entire succession, but of the half only.[1]

Of events in Britain under the Romans there is but little to relate. A province has no individual existence; its dreamlike, vegetative life no history. Most of the occurrences of which it may have been the theatre, even the changes and modifications in the machine of its government, belong to the history of the empire or of its metropolis. The laurels won by

[1] 'Ancient Laws and Institutes of Wales,' p. 266, and on the subject of Gavelkind in Kent. See 'Statutes of the Realm,' vol. i. The greater part of the usages there recorded are purely Germanic.

British legions in distant lands seldom came to the knowledge, and still more seldom touched the hearts, of their countrymen. This last acquisition of a fragile state-colossus was particularly unfortunate: the culture of the Romans, grafted with violence on the wild stock, not being that of a higher intellectual life and exalted moral feeling, but of an age in which talent and mental powers, deaf to the inner voice, under, and in harmony with, which they ought to be cultivated, were subservient only to sensuality, to all the failings of humanity, and to the then prevailing disregard of the social bond. Roman customs, Roman garb, and Roman extravagance found entrance among the barbarians, with the temples, language, and law of the metropolis of the world; and every benign as well as every hurtful influence of victory combined to destroy the nationality of a conquered people amalgamated with its conquerors. Agricola extended the limits of the British province to the interior of Scotland, but his struggles and the later victories of the Caledonians belong rather to Scottish than to English history, although they were not without influence on Britain, which was the road that led direct to the theatre on which northern and Roman valour played their several parts.

CHAPTER III.

A.D. 120-350.

Picts and Scots; their Resistance against the Romans—Conflicts between Roman Commanders—Emperor Severus brings Reinforcements to Britain—Roman Losses—Truce with northern Tribes—Romans build Wall of defence in the North—Tranquillity restored ; but disturbed again by arrival of Saxon Pirates— History of Saxon Tribes—Carausius; his Influence on the Settlement of Saxons along the Frankish and British Shores—Constantius and his wife Helena in Britain—Their Son, Constantine the Great, proclaimed Emperor in Britain—Spread of Christianity in Britain—Agreement of the British with the Eastern or Byzantine Church—Persecutions—Civilizing Influence of Romans — Roads — Churches — Picts and Scots — Princely Families—Tyranny of Roman Officials.

FROM Scotland came the movement which, in the time of the emperor Hadrian, awakened the spirit of British freedom to new life, and to an apparently well-founded hope of totally casting off the imperial yoke.[1] Though the Roman armies maintained themselves in the elder province, the emperor, nevertheless, deemed it advisable to retire from the boundary line drawn and fortified by Agricola in Scotland,[2] and, between the

[1] Æl. Spart. Had. c. v. Britanni teneri sub Romana ditione non poterant.— Fronto de Bello Parthico, § 4. Hadriano imperium obtinente, quantum militum a Britannis cæsum !—Orosius, vii. 17. Severus victor in Britannias defectu pene omnium sociorum trahitur. Ubi magnis gravibusque prœliis sæpe gestis, etc. Cf. also Cassiodorus. [2] Tac. Agric. c. xxiii.

Tyne and Solway Firth, to cast up a rampart with a ditch—the Picts' wall still existing to the height of six feet—which should defend what was more strictly the Roman province.[1] An irruption of the Mæatæ, dwelling in the south of Scotland, was attended with the support and junction of many of the Brigantes, and probably of other Britons, seeing that they were able to penetrate to the Ordovices. They were, however, driven back by the proprætor Lollius Urbicus, who erected the rampart of earth bearing the name of his master, the emperor Antoninus Pius, between Caerriden on the Forth and Alcluid (Dumbarton) on the Clyde.[2] Of a war in Britain during the reign of Marcus Antoninus,[3] we know little more than the name of the Roman general, Calpurnius Agricola.[4] The emperor who, in the tranquillity of his palace, meditated on lessons of recondite wisdom, was satisfied if his name was bestowed on the northernmost monument of Roman sway; and the orator flattered both him and his people with the conceit that, in the delightful enjoyment of science and learning, he directed the helm of the mighty vessel of the state, as well as this remote warfare.[5] Under

---

[1] A.D. 120. Æl. Spart. Had. c. xi.
[2] Jul. Capitol. de M. Anton. c. v. Horsley, B. R. p. 160. Petrie, C. H. p. cvii. sqq. The account given in the text is the one generally followed, and in Graham's dyke traces of the rampart seem to be preserved: the inscriptions there found also refer to Antoninus; still under this supposition the words of Pausanias (viii. 43, § 3) remain to be explained, although his account agrees with the passage cited of Capitolinus, and is compatible with the hypothesis, that the vallum of Antoninus may have been raised near that of Hadrian, which had been destroyed by the Britons.
[3] A.D. 161–180.
[4] J. Capit. de M. Anton. c. viii.
[5] Fronto, cited by Eumenius (Panegyr. Const. Cæs. c. xiv.)

Commodus[1] the boundary wall was broken through by the Britons, to repel whom proved an arduous undertaking to the Roman general, Ulpius Marcellus.[2] He was succeeded by Clodius Albinus, who accepted the title of Cæsar, which had been offered to him by Commodus, from Severus,[3] whose sole motive in conferring that honour seems to have been to lull suspicion in the mind of a vain but potent officer, of whom he was jealous, and on whose destruction he had resolved. On the intelligence that Severus was advancing with a hostile army, Albinus crossed with his forces over to Gaul; the armies met on the plain of Trevoux, near Lyons. For some time victory seemed to incline to the side of Albinus, Severus being unhorsed and having disappeared from the field; but the arrival of fresh troops to his aid changed the face of things. The army of Albinus was routed, and himself seized and beheaded in Lyons, where he had shut himself up from the commencement of the conflict. Having settled the affairs of Britain, Severus, as has already been observed, divided the government into two provinces.[4]

At this time the power of the northern tribes had become so formidable, that the propraetor, Virus Lupus, was compelled not only to purchase with a considerable sum a short respite from the inroads of the Maeatae, but to solicit either an additional force or the presence of the emperor himself. Though advanced in years and afflicted with gout, Severus obeyed the summons with alacrity. Attended by his sons, Antoninus Caracalla and Septimus Geta, he soon arrived in Britain, where

[1] A.D. 190–197. [2] Dion ap. Xiph. lxxii. s. 8.
[3] Herodian, ii. 48, iii. 16–23. Dion ap. Xiph. lxxii:. 14. J. Capit. cc. xiii., xiv. Aur. Vict. c. xx. Oros. vii. 17.
[4] Herodian, iii. 24.

BRITAIN UNDER THE ROMANS, A.D. 120-350. 53

he lost no time in making the most efficient preparations for the subjugation of the barbarians. To his younger son, Geta, he committed the civil administration of the province: Caracalla accompanied his father. On the arrival of the Romans beyond the limits of the province, the natives, though unfitted for regular warfare through the want of discipline and of defensive armour, harassed the Romans, who, nevertheless, continued to advance on their march, felling woods, levelling hills, rendering marshes passable, and constructing bridges. At length, with a loss of fifty thousand men, they nearly reached the extremity of the island, where, having entered into a treaty with the natives, according to which a considerable portion of territory was to be yielded to the Romans, the emperor, who during the whole expedition had been borne in a covered litter, returned to York. On the intelligence of a fresh insurrection, Severus, whom age and sickness compelled to remain inactive, resolved on sending an army under Caracalla to extirpate the barbarians. That prince, however, who was far less intent on prosecuting the war than on corrupting the soldiery, in the view of excluding his brother from all share in the empire, on the death of his father, which shortly after took place at York,[1] entered into a truce with the natives and returned to Rome.[2]

Whether, after his expedition against the northern tribes, Severus enlarged and strengthened by a wall the rampart of Hadrian or that of Antoninus,[3] is to the

[1] A.D. 211.
[2] Dion ap. Xiph. lxxv. 5, lxxvi. 11-16, lxxvii. 1. Herodian, iii. 46-51.
[3] The latter opinion has been started by Mannert; but would Dion (ap. Xiph. lxxvi. 12) have said of the wall of Severus, if it

antiquary a question not devoid of interest; but in either case it is manifest that the south of the present Scotland was always a very insecure possession to the Romans, and in the hands of extremely doubtful allies, and that it was only in the modern England that Rome held any considerable influence.

The tranquillity which Britain enjoyed, with the exception of the northern border districts, began in this century to be disturbed by an event which, new in its kind and consequences in the history of the world, had an incalculable influence on this country. The ocean which had set a salutary limit to the hostile desolating wanderings of the savage, which is, as it were, appointed to be the securest medium and freest path for civilization and varied intercourse, was, in the north of Europe, in a state ill adapted to the purpose either of separation or communication. It was at that time infested with swarms of those daring pirates, to whom for many ages after it served as a home, and who, in their frail barks, exposing themselves to all the perils of the stormy ocean, evinced in every conflict the most desperate valour, with an endurance and skill in warfare, which, if applied to higher purposes, would have renewed in history the dazzling glory of Sparta and of ancient Rome.

In the historical records that have been handed down to us, the name of the Saxons does not occur before the end of the second century, when they are noticed as the

were in Scotland, without thinking of that of Hadrian, that *it divides the island into two parts?* He must also (l. 15) have spoken in other terms of the new hostilities of the Mæatæ and Caledonians, if both people had, by the wall, been placed in a totally different position with regard to the Romans. Cf. also Smith's Beda, App. No. V.

BRITAIN UNDER THE ROMANS, A.D. 120-350. 55

possessors of the islands at the mouth of the Elbe, and probably also of the opposite districts of Holstein and Hadeln.[1] In the following century they became so troublesome to the Roman empire, through their piracies, that, for the purpose of warring against them and for the protection of the northern coasts, a commander was appointed by the emperors Diocletian and Maximian, in the person of Carausius, a Menapian,[2] whose successor bore the title of Count of the Saxon shore, "Comes litoris Saxonici.[3] But of such importance was this appointment, in consequence of the formidable power of the adversary, that Carausius, probably availing himself of the distraction caused by

---

[1] Ptol. Geogr. ii. 2.
[2] A.D. 287-296. 'Pirata.' Claud. Mam. 'Menapiæ civis.' Aur. Vict. de Viris Illust. c. xxxix. 'Bataviæ alumnus.' Eumen. 'Genere infimus.' Oros. vii. 25. 'Vilissime natus.' Eutrop. ix. 21. 'Juvenis in Britannia ex infima gente creatus.' Geof. of Monm. v. 3. Richard of Cirencester, i. viii. 14, in speaking of the two Menapias (the Irish, and the present St. David's), says, "Harum unam, quam nam vero incertum, patriam habebat Carausius." [But see note to Preface.]
[3] This title first occurs in the 'Notitia Dignitatum Imperii,' compiled under Arcadius and Honorius. Earlier writers name him 'comes maritimi tractus;' a circumstance not to be overlooked, on account of the importance of the 'litus Saxonicum' for the history of the Saxons. Of Carausius, Eutropius (ix. 21) says, "Cum apud Bononiam, per tractum Belgicæ et Armoricæ, pacandum mare accepisset, quod Franci et Saxones infestabant, etc." Eumenius also in Constantio (c. xii.) says of the fleet of Carausius, "Quæ olim Gallias tuebatur."

[The leading tribes of these Northmen became of great importance to the rest of Europe, during the middle ages, but above all to Britain, where, under Norman rule, the Anglo-Saxon people became welded into a settled community, whilst it still preserved the spiritual characteristics and civic freedom which have since secured to it a proud eminence among other nations of the earth.]

the Gaulish Bagaudæ, ventured, after entering into a compact and alliance with the Saxon pirates, to withdraw himself from subjection to the Roman sceptre, to fortify Boulogne, and to assume the imperial title in Britain. The emperor Maximian found himself compelled to acknowledge him as a joint ruler, but without seeing an end put to the piracies, by which the coasts of the German ocean, of the Atlantic, and even of the Mediterranean were held in constant dread. Carausius had governed in this country for seven years, even after the loss of Boulogne, victorious against the Caledonians, and powerful in his internal administration, when he fell by the hand of an assassin, his companion Allectus,[1] who occupied his place for three years, when Asclepiodotus, the prefect of the emperor Constantius, having destroyed him and his forces, stormed London, and soon restored their most northern province to the dominion of the Cæsars.[2]

The deeds of Augustus Carausius are of great moment for the later history of the country. Through him Britain first learned that it could maintain itself independent of Roman supremacy, and in security

[1] Orosius, vii. 25. Aur. Vict. c. xxxix. Eutrop. ix. 22. Cf. Genebrier, Geschichte des Carausius aus Münzen (from the French, in the appendices to the 'Allegemeine Welthistorie,' Th. vi.). Stukeley's 'Medallic History of Carausius.' Some coins of Carausius and Allectus are given in Havercamp's 'Orosius,' p. 527. See also 'Eumenii Oratio pro restaurandis Scholis,' cc. xviii., xxi.

[2] Eumenius (Paneg. Const. cc. xv.–xvii.) is the only one of the ancients extant who gives the circumstances of the destruction of Allectus, with whose account Geoffrey of Monmouth agrees so closely, that we must suppose this extraordinary writer to have used ancient Latin works no longer in existence. Even the name given by him of the defender of London, 'Livius Gallus,' is probably, like his other Roman names, genuine.

against its northern enemies; and the slumbering national spirit became, through this consciousness of self-dependence, powerfully excited.[1] He reigned chiefly by the help of Frankish warriors, under Roman forms of government, which, from their connection with his memory, may have been held in a higher degree of veneration in the minds of later races.[2]

But not less has Carausius influenced the later Germanizing of Britain by the Saxons. A German by extraction, and a Menapian by birth, he at least promoted if he did not cause the settling of the Saxons along the Saxon shore, in Gaul as well as in Britain by his alliance with them.[3] The prevailing opinion, that the 'Litus Saxonicum' borrowed its name from the enemy to whose attacks it was exposed, appears as contrary to the principles of sound philology as it is unhistorical.[4] By the probably contemporaneous settlements of the Saxons on the Litus Saxonicum

[1] A few years earlier a prefect of Britain, under the emperor Probus, having raised a rebellion, had by some artifice (περινοίᾳ οὐκ ἄφρονι) been circumvented and put to death by a minister of the emperor sent over for the purpose. Zosimus, i. 66.

[2] That the coins of Carausius, bearing the impress of the wolf and twins, were copied by the Bretwalda Æthelberht of Kent, can hardly be placed to the account of mere caprice. The circular temple, that remarkable and venerable relic which, till destroyed by the hand of modern barbarism, stood on the banks of the Carron, though in later times attributed to Julius Cæsar and to Arthur, was at a remoter period considered to be the work of Carausius. See Stukeley; also Palgrave, vol. i. pp. 376, 377. Nennius, c. xix. Camden, and 'De Mirabilibus Britanniæ' at the end of Hearne's Robert of Gloucester, p. 576.

[3] Eutropius, ix. 21, speaks only of the Belgian and Armorican coasts, Beda (H. E. i. 6) here copies Orosius, who takes his account from Eutropius.

[4] See Palgrave, vol. i. p. 384, who takes the same view.—T.

near Bayeux (to which, perhaps, the circumstance may partly be ascribed, that the manners and language of the French found slower admission into that place than into the other parts of Normandy[1]), the weakness of the Romans, even on the coasts of Gaul and elsewhere across the channel, is authentically shown, as well as the proneness of the Saxons to similar settlements, of which also the 'Litus Saxonicum in Belgica Secunda' (Flanders)[2], not less than the just application of language, affords a further proof. The emperor Probus sent a number of Franks as colonists to Britain, where they became permanent settlers, manifesting at first considerable devotion to the emperor.

During the reign of Constantius Chlorus, the position of Britain in the Roman state must have been very prominent. Swayed both by inclination and probably by matrimonial connections—his wife Helena being, it is said, the daughter, or at least the relative of a British prince[3]—and perhaps by the wish also to

[1] Grannona in litore Saxonico. Not. Imp. Occid. c. lxxxvi. Du Chesne, Hist. tom. i. p. 3. In the capitularies of Charles the Bald this district is called 'Otlingua Saxonica.' Bouquet, vii. p. 616. 'Saxones Bajocassini.' Greg. Turon. v. c. 27, a. 578, x. c. 9. Fortunati Carm. iii. 8, says, at the end of the sixth century, speaking of Felix, bishop of Nantes,

"Aspera gens Saxo, vivens quasi more ferino,
Te mediante, sacer, bellua reddit ovem."

[2] See Warnkönig, 'Flandrische Staats-und Rechtsgeschichte,' vol. i. p. 95.

[3] Panegyr. Vet. pp. 193, 207. Henry of Huntingdon (lib. i., we know not on what authority) and Geoffrey of Monmouth (v. 6, 11) give to this prince the name of Coel (of Colchester). On the other hand, in the 'Gesta Treberorum,' c. xxix., it is said, "Helena Treberorum nobilissima." Huntingdon relates, that the walls of London, existing in his time, were built by Helena. [It seems

preserve this country to Rome, Constantius passed the greater part of his life in Britain. He died at York, where his son Constantine was proclaimed emperor. A German prince supported his nomination, a circumstance from which we may infer the presence of German warriors.[1]

The name of Constantine the Great immediately reminds us of the rapid diffusion of Christianity during his time, and through him.

The Christian faith found at an early period, among both the Celtic and the German races, ready admission into Britain, and, even when persecuted, had, in solitary retirement, borne promising fruits for the future. It is, down to the latest times, so closely interwoven with the social constitution, and, consequently, with the leading events of this country, that a glance at the history of religion is often indispensable for the illustration of political events. The account that, less than thirty years after the death of the Redeemer, a lady of distinction—Pomponia Græcina, the wife of that Plautius whose victories in Britain had gained him the honour of an ovation—adopted Christianity, stands probably on no better foundation than other tales of a similar nature, it being improbable that this lady ever set foot in Britain; yet as early as the close of the following century, Christianity had advanced even into parts of Britain not subject to the Romans,

---

almost superfluous to remark, that Colchester derives its name, not from Coel, but rather from its ancient appellation, Colonia (Camulodunum).—T.]

[1] " Præcipue Eroco, Alamannorum rege, auxilii gratia Constantium comitato, imperium capit." Aur. Vict. Epit. c. xli. May not the name Erocus be a corruption of Ertocus, a Latinization of the Old-Saxon Heritogo (A.-S. Heretoga, Ger. Herzog), *dux*?

by which Cornwall and Wales are particularly to be understood. The agreement of the British with the Eastern churches respecting the celebration of Easter,[1] shows a conformity which is perhaps most satisfactorily to be accounted for by the supposition of an historic basis for the several legends respecting the preaching of the doctrines of Christ by oriental apostles. It is even probable that the first tidings of the new faith did not come from Rome, where it was still under oppression, but rather from one of those congregations of Asia Minor, which the Mediterranean had long held in connection with Gaul, and from whence, by the great public roads, the spirit of conversion easily found its way to Britain.[2]

We cannot, however, attach any very special significance to these traditions. The zealous historic inquirer might wish perhaps to find in the remains of the ancient monastery of Glastonbury corroborative evidence of its traditional foundation by Joseph of Arimathea, since it has been perhaps too hastily assumed that its walls had served to shelter the earliest apostles of the Christian faith in ancient Britain. But although these cloistered walls are not silent, they proclaim no more than that in their architecture they may have followed that of the

[1] It appears that in the beginning of the fourth century the Britons and Romans kept Easter on the same day. Euseb. Pamph. de Vita Constant. iii. 19. κοινῇ πάντων ἤρεσε κρίσει, τὴν ἁγιωτάτην τοῦ Πάσχα ἑορτὴν μιᾷ καὶ τῇ αὐτῇ ἡμέρᾳ συντελεῖσθαι. Cf. also Socrat. Hist. v. 22. Conc. Arelat. (Spelman, pp. 40, 42) and Lingard, H. E. vol. i. p. 45 *note*, edit. 1837.—T.

[2] For the traditions respecting Glastonbury, see Will. Malmesb. 'De Antiquitatibus Glastoniensis Ecclesiæ, apud Gale,' t. i. Also Warner's 'History of the Abbey of Glastonbury,' 1826, 4to, who, by the way, gives credit to the tradition of St. Paul's preaching in Britain. [See also in reference to the history of the building Professor Willis's volume on Glastonbury Abbey.—E. C. O.]

ancient Anglo-Saxon churches of England; while the immediate result of the numerous excavations that have been made on the spot, has been to show that it had served in earlier times as a British fortification, which from the presence of coins of Vespasian and Hadrian's time, and the traces of roads, had probably been known to the Romans.

Less objectionable seems the tradition of the adoption of Christianity by the British Prince Lever Maur (the Great Light), or Lucius, on comparing it with the testimony of Tertullian.[1] Lucius is reported to have sent Fagan and Dervan to Rome, for the sake of receiving from the bishop Eleutherius more accurate instruction in the doctrines of Christianity; whereupon Roman missions passed over to Britain, and there founded three archbishoprics and twenty-eight bishoprics[2]— denominations which are of course to be understood in the sense of the time. The supposition seems by no means unreasonable, that the Anglo-Saxon Romanists, in their disputes with the British followers of the Eastern church, would, in such tales, provide themselves with a weapon of controversy; yet how is it that we find them in a complete form precisely in those authors who have translated the old British authorities?[3]

[1] Adv. Jud. c. vii.
[2] This number is, no doubt, connected with the catalogue of the twenty-eight cities of Britain mentioned in Nennius, c. ii.
[3] Beda (H. E. i. 4) places Lucius (who, according to Geoffrey of Monmouth, died in 156) in the time of Marcus Aurelius, to the beginning of whose reign he assigns the date 156, instead of 161. In lib. v. c. 24, he places Eleutherius in the years 167-182. Nennius gives 167 as the year of the conversion of Lucius. In his 'Chronicon' Beda places this event in 180, which agrees better with the regnal years of pope Eleutherius, 167-182, or, according to 'Anastasii Vitæ Pontificum,' 179-194, where mention is made of

Gaul, in the time of the predecessors of Eleutherius, had very numerous Christian congregations, which have been ennobled by the persecutions they underwent at Lyons and Vienne, in the year 177; fleeing from which, many of their members may have increased the number of believers among the kindred Britons. The controversy between the Jewish and the heathen Converts upon several external matters, and especially the celebration of Easter, had already at that time engaged the minds of men, and, among the new converts who belonged to neither party, but had at once sprung from druidism, occasioned new scruples. Without, therefore, attaching much importance to later embellishments of the account of a mission from a distinguished British chieftain to Eleutherius, we may, perhaps, assume, that the former might have applied to the head of the Western church, with the view of effecting an arrangement of the contradictory opinions prevailing among the Christians under his dominion.

Lucius in the words used by Beda in his history, "Hic accepit epistolam a Lucio, Britanniæ rege, ut Christianus efficeretur per ejus mandatum," of which passage the last three words are wanting in Beda's 'Chronicon.' On the other hand, Anastasius agrees with the 'Chronicon' in mentioning, under Victor, the successor of Eleutherius, the document (libelli) of the latter relative to the celebrating of Easter. If Beda had had the 'Vitæ Pontificum' before him, the account of Lucius must gain considerably in point of historic credibility; at the same time the confusion in the chronology is quite inexplicable. Not less hazardous does it appear to assume that the author of the 'Vitæ Pontificum' had both of Beda's works at hand. A thorough examination of the 'Gesta' or 'Vitæ Pontificum' would probably lead to the discovery of a common source to both authors. With regard to the accounts of Geoffrey of Monmouth, it may not be amiss to notice that he appeals (iv. 20) to a work of Gildas, 'De Victoria Aurelii Ambrosii.' See Pref. to Stevenson's edit. of 'Gildas,' p. xi.

The gradual spread of Christianity in Britain drew upon it the unpropitious notice of the pagan emperors, and the persecution of the Christians under Diocletian has also in this country left behind it a terrific remembrance. The glory of the martyrdom of St. Alban at Verulam, and of Aaron and Julius, the two citizens of Caerleon upon Usk, could not be obscured, even in the succeeding times of relapse into paganism.[1] The Christian faith and the measures adopted for its preservation were, however, not yet entirely suppressed. Under Constantius, the mild successor of Diocletian, Christianity again ventured to show itself, and under Constantine we meet with the names and dioceses of three British bishops, who were present at the first Council of Arles; Eborius of York, Restitutus of London, and Adelfius of Lincoln,[2] and at the same time learn the differences of their tenets from those of the Romish church. This account supports a tradition, which has been too much called in doubt, that, besides the above-mentioned, Wales also (Britannia Secunda) had a bishop at Caerleon, and the most northern province one at St. Andrews (anciently Albin), and that each of these bishoprics was divided into twelve districts.[3] However erroneous this tradition may be in naming five archbishoprics and sixty bishoprics, it may, nevertheless, not be essentially void of foundation.

[1] Gildas, c. viii. Beda, i. 7.
[2] A.D. 314. Spelman, Conc. t. i. p. 42. The see of Adelfius is there called " Colonia Londinensium," for which, with Henry, we prefer reading 'Col. Lindum,' than to render it by ' Richborough.'
[3] Girald. Cambr. (' De Jure et Statu Menev. Eccl.,' ap. Wharton, 'Anglia Sacra,' t. i. p. 542) appeals to "tomum Anacleti papæ, sicut in pontificalibus Romanorum gestis et imperialibus, directum Galliarum episcopis."

The first half of the fourth century is chiefly remarkable as regards Britain, on account of the harmony with which the natives and Romans, as well as other settlers —brought together in no small number by their common faith—united in the arts of peace.[1] The cultivation of grain had been carried to such a height, that Britain became the granary of the northern provinces of the empire, and by yearly exports supplied other countries with food, while it enriched itself.[2] Civic establishments were so flourishing, that builders and other artificers were demanded from Britain for the restoration of the desolated provinces.[3]

The country was crossed by high-roads in various directions, many of which have served the later settlers in their marches, as well as their commercial operations. It is probable that the Romans themselves found some of these great highways already in existence, which were afterwards known by the names of Watling Street, leading from the southern shore of Kent, by Rhutupiæ and London, through St. Alban's and Stony Stratford to Towcester, Weedon, South Lilbourne, Atheriston, Gilbert's Hill (now the Wreken), Wroxeter, Stretton, and Cardigan to Caernarvon (Segontium) and Ikenild, or Rikenild Street, from Tynemouth, through York, Derby, and Birmingham to St. David's. The Irmin (Ermin) Street led from the latter place to Southamp-

[1] "Britannia . . . terra tanto frugum ubere, tanto læta numero pastionum, tot metallorum fluens rivis, tot vectigalibus quæstuosa, tot accincta portubus." Eumen. Paneg. Const. Cæs. c. xi. Cf. ejusdem Paneg. Const. Aug. c. ix.
[2] Amm. Marcell. xviii. 2. Libanii Orat. x. t. ii. p. 281. Zosimus, iii. 5. Julian. Imp. ad S. P. Q. Athen. Epist. Eunapii Legat.
[3] Eumen. Paneg. Const. Cæs. c. xxi.—T.

BRITAIN UNDER THE ROMANS, A.D. 120-350. 65

ton; the Foss from Cornwall through Devonshire and Somersetshire, by Tetbury, Coventry, Leicester and Newark to Lincoln.[1] These roads, which, if not formed, were at least greatly improved by Roman labour, prove by their direction a lively internal traffic, as well as a commercial connection with the countries lying east and west of Britain.[2]

We are accustomed to regard Roman influence and Roman civilization in Britain as considerably less than in the southern provinces of the empire, chiefly because the language of modern England is not immediately based on that of Rome, and but few ancient monuments have been preserved in the country. Of these the number has been greatly diminished by frequent and early devastations, more especially in the richest provinces, and those first occupied by the Romans; yet, even in our days, many have been discovered, which sufficiently prove to us the importance of Roman Britain.[3] Many remains of Roman buildings, on sites long since traversed by the ploughshare, or from which, as from seed, modern towns have sprung up, were visible as late as the twelfth and thirteenth centuries.[4] Besides the two municipal towns, the remote Caerlon (the City of the Legion, Isca Silurum) also had its theatres, temples, and palaces, of which Giraldus speaks in terms of high

[1] H. Hunt. lib. i., followed by Robert of Gloucester, 'Ric. Corinæus de Situ Britanniæ,' lib. i. c. 7, and 'Commentary on the Itinerary,' p. 110 sq. edit. 1809. R. Higden, Polychron. lib. i. cap. 'De Plateis Regalibus.' Whitaker's Hist. of Manchester, vol. i. p. 102 sq.
[2] The course of these roads is very uncertain. Compare Ric. Corin. with Higden.—T.
[3] See Horsley, 'Britannia Romana.'
[4] Will. Malmesb. de Gestis Regum, lib. i. c. 1. Id. de Gestis Pontificum, lib. iii. Prooem.

VOL. I. F

admiration,[1] and for which like Bath (Aquæ Solis), it may have partly been indebted to its hot springs. At a later period we have an account of various subterranean antiquities in the city of Chester (Deva).[2] To the excavated remains of a temple of Neptune and Minerva at Chichester we are indebted for some highly important disclosures relative to the history of Britain under the Romans; but the most complete idea of Roman building is presented to us in a villa discovered at Bignor in Sussex; also in the antiquities at Woodchester in Gloucestershire.[3] Beda likewise mentions the Roman towns, lighthouses, roads, and bridges existing in his time.[4] Many a sacred spot of antiquity offers itself to our knowledge through the holier consecration it has received from Christianity, always ready to apply and hallow every legacy of the past. St. Peter's church and abbey at Westminster, St. Paul's cathedral in London, will appear to us only the more venerable, if we call to mind that at the former, in times remote, the worship of Apollo contributed to the culture of a rugged race, and at the latter, that a temple of Diana had ministered to the faith of so many peoples. Thus the Angles and the Saxons, when they had established themselves in Britain, dwelt within Roman walls, and were surrounded by spacious structures and beautiful works of Roman art. Ought it then to surprise us, if,

[1] Girald. Cambren. Itin. Camb. lib. i. c. 1. ap. Camden, p. 836.
[2] R. Higden, Polychr. ap. Gale, i. 200.
[3] See Sam. Lyson's splendid work on this subject, London. 1797, 1815: also his 'Reliquiæ Britannico-Romanæ,' 3 vols. fol. Lond. For Roman temples and other buildings at Bath, see Lyson's, also Carter's 'Ancient Architecture of England.'
[4] H. E. i. 11. Vita S. Cuth. xxvii. Malmesb. de Gestis Pontif. ap. Savile, p. 258.

BRITAIN UNDER THE ROMANS, A.D. 120–350. 67

when first made sensible, on their conversion to Christianity, of the necessity of new and ample edifices, they strove to restore the architecture of the Romans in their country, and that structures in imitation of these buildings were afterwards erected, which have erroneously been regarded as original productions of Saxon art? Of Roman vestiges, those of ramparts and fortresses are oftenest to be met with, though it is not to be denied that these, through their equivocal character, have but too often given rise to misconceptions and inveterate errors. As undoubted Roman remains may be cited those at Richborough (Rhutupiæ), Lincoln (Lindum), Burgh Castle in Suffolk (Gariannonum), and Chester (Deva). At Dorchester vestiges of an amphitheatre are still visible.

From the great number of Roman towns and garrisons in Britain, it may be inferred that an intimate connection subsisted between the Romans and the natives. Hence the Roman language also had found general admission among the provincials, as is evident from the number of Latin words occurring in the Welsh tongue. In modern English, as in the olden Anglo-Saxon, we find preserved many of the words brought to Britain by Cæsar and his legions. When, moreover, we take into consideration that the conquest of England by the Saxons was but slowly achieved, it becomes obvious that the Roman tongue must have been repressed with equal slowness. Considering, too, the number of Latin books, some of which are well written, that have come down to us from the Anglo-Saxon times, we must assume that owing to the large number of persons who were acquainted with the language of Rome, the later introduction of Norman French must have been comparatively easy. Indeed in the British historical traditions, as they have been preserved by Nennius, Geoffrey of Monmouth, and others, we meet with too many points of resemblance with Roman history and tradition, to allow the supposition of a total abolition of the Roman tongue, with the cessation of Roman sway and the temporary extinction of Christianity.

For their superiority as shipmen it has been thought that the Britons were indebted to the Romans, though we know that the Roman troops stationed in the island were by no means a match by sea even for their usual enemy, the Saxons,[1] and that they were not practised in sea-fights. The inhabitants of the shores of the Mediterranean may, perhaps, have taught the rovers of the North an improved style of ship-building, but confidence on the rocking element, the direct dartlike course over and through the wild towering billows, the placid gaze which spies the wind, ere its approach, on the far distant curling surge, the unquenchable delight in the amphibious life of a seaman—these have been brought to Britain only by Saxons and Northmen; and not only does the English language, but even those of southern Europe declare, who are the people called by nature to be master alike of vessel and of wave.

We must now turn from the subject of Roman civilization in Britain, and cast a glance on the nations which chiefly contributed to its extirpation—the Picts and Scots—who are first mentioned as making their appearance in the present Scotland in the fourth century. Both these tribes were nearly related

[1] The passage of Eumenius (Paneg. Const. c. xii.) which has been cited in proof of the maritime proficiency of the Romans, rather says that Carausius employed many foreigners—"exercitibus nostris in re maritima novis."

to the Caledonians, and Mæatæ, though they appear to have been more barbarous. It is certain that the Scots, and probably the Picts likewise, passed over from Ireland and reduced the earlier inhabitants to subjection. Their name, Picti, is by no means an appellation bestowed on enemies with painted bodies, but is a Roman corruption of Peght.[1] They dwelt in the north-eastern part of Scotland, on both sides of the Grampian hills, from Inverness and Elgin to Dumbarton, or from the Firth of Murray to those of Forth and Clyde, but at, a later period, in the south-west of Scotland, as far as the Picts' wall, where, on the river Nith in Dumfriesshire, we meet with a particular tribe of them, the Nithwaras.[2] In the south of Scotland the rustic still points to many a memorial of the Picts, consisting of old walls and excavations. The Scottish kings in the ninth century included their name among their titles. Pictland was attacked by the Norwegians, and in the famous battle of the Standard, in the year 1138, also in that of Clithero, the Peghts of Galloway[3] fought with their native savage valour. As no remains exist of a particular tongue spoken by this people, nor even any accounts of its existence or decay, British antiquaries have indefatigably contended, some for a Gothic, and others for a Celtic origin of the Pictish language—a dispute certainly about less than words,

[1] Even Wittekind gives them their right name. Eumenius (Paneg. Const. c. vii.) is the first who mentions them, "Caledonum aliorumque Pictorum silvas et paludes." Amm. Mar. xxvii. 11. "Britanni Pictis modo et Hibernis assueti hostibus."
[2] Bedæ Vitæ S. Cuthb. c. xi. Cf. ejd. H. E. i. 1; iii. 4; v. 21, and Chron. a. 452.
[3] See the Rev. R. Garnett's communication to the Philological Society, June 9, 1843, p. 123. —T.

for one or two very ancient names of mountains, which at the present day we are unable to explain by our insufficient knowledge of the old Gaelic, can afford no proof of a distinct Pictish tongue, which probably differed from that of other British and Irish tribes only in being a more barbarous dialect.

Together with the Scots, mention is also made of the Attacotti.[1] A tribe of these, the Dalreudini, in the southern part of Argyleshire and the neighbouring isles preserved the name of their original home in Ulster. Historeth, son of Istorin, was the name of their leader, a name which has probably no more historic truth in it, than that of Reuda assigned to him by other traditions.[2] These were followed by their countrymen from Irin (Ierne, Hibernia) in multitudes, and it is probable, that under the name of Scots, against whom the Romans fought, we must frequently understand their kinsmen also, who left Ireland solely for the purpose of joining them. From West Wales, or the territory of the Dimetæ, as far as which they had endeavoured to extend their conquests, it is related that they were for ever driven by Cunedda Wledig, afterwards Prince of Gwynedd, who with his sons came from Manau Guotodin, before the Romans had yet left the other parts of the island.[3]

The consideration of the old British princely families began to revive when the pressure of the Roman

[1] Amm. Mar. xxvi. 4; xxvii. 8. Hieron. Epist. lxxxii. ad Oceanum. Nennius, c. viii.
[2] Nennius, c. viii. Beda, H. E. i. 1.
[3] Nennius, c. viii. lxvi. Appen. As Cunedda is said to have come to Gwynedd 146 years before the reign of Mailcun, who died A.D. 547, the date 370–380 is here given. Guotodin is supposed to have been on the eastern coast of the south of Scotland.

BRITAIN UNDER THE ROMANS, A.D. 120-350. 71

government was lightened. The princes of Strathclyde and North Wales traced their descent from Cunedda Wledig, or the Glorious (a title answering to that of Cæsar Augustus), and to his ancester Coel, as did the Cornish dynasty to Bran ap Llyr,[1] the ancestor of Arthur, and of these other heroes whose valour enabled them to avert the total subjection of their mountain followers by the Romans, and afterwards by the Saxons and the Danes.[2]

Under Constantius, the son of Constantine, the condition of Britain was rendered particularly deplorable by the tyranny of the notary Paulus, a Spaniard by birth, who had been sent by the emperor for the purpose of prosecuting certain individuals of the army accused of participation in the conspiracy of Magnentius. This man, availing himself of the opportunities afforded him by his station, hesitated not, by means of false accusations, to sacrifice the liberty and life of those individuals whose fortunes offered a temptation to his rapacity. Martinus the pro-prefect, who had long lamented the sufferings of the innocent, finding his intercession vain, threatened to resign his charge. Alarmed hereupon for the permanency of his own power, Paulus took measures to involve him in the common ruin, when, urged by the feelings of the moment, Martinus attacked the notary with his sword, but failing to strike a mortal blow, he plunged the blade into his own side, a victim to his hatred of oppression and cruelty. Paulus now freed from restraint set no bounds to his barbarity; many, loaded with chains, were led to torture, while many were proscribed and

[1] So called in Geoffrey of Monmouth.
[2] See Gunn in 'Historia Britonnum,' p. 119.

driven into exile, or perished by the sword of the executioner. Though he was applauded for his services by Constantius, the succeeding emperor, Julian, condemned Paulus to be burnt alive.[1]

[1] Amm. Mar. xiv. 5, xx. 2.

CHAPTER IV.

A.D. 350-446.

Roman Generals—British Settlements in Armorica—Roman Legions retire — St. Germain — Christianity in Britain — Pelagius— Miserable Condition of the Country.

IN the century after the death of Constantine the Great, during which Britain still continued a part of the Roman empire, we know little more of the country than that it was the theatre of devastations, caused by the Celtic and Germanic tribes. It had indeed long been a school of war by land and sea for the Romans, out of which arose many a conspicuous character as well as many a germ of rebellion. The anti-emperor Bonosus, who vainly strove to wrest from the emperor Probus the island of Britain—which usually fell to those tyrants who had made themselves masters of Gaul—was the son of a rhetorician or pædagogue of British origin named Magnentius.[1] The Pannonian Valentinus, when banished to Britain, found both friends and aid in his rebellion against Valentinian, the suppression of which, even after the capture and death of the chiefs, required all the prudence of the general Theodosius.[2] This success, but yet more his glorious

---

[1] A.D. 280. Vopiscus de Probo, c. xviii. [Domo Hispaniensis fuit, origine Britannus: Galla tamen matre; ut ipse dicebat, rhetoris filius; ut ab aliis comperi, pædagogi litterarii. Id. de Bonoso, c. xiv.—T.]
[2] Amm. Mar. xxviii. 3.

triumph over the Picts and Scots,[1] who had advanced as far as London and slain the general, Fullofaudes, and the count of the marine district, Nectaridus—the re-establishment of the province of Valentia—the restoration of the towns and garrisons—the security of the camps and frontiers—and the amelioration of the civil government, obtained for the British leader that renown and influence which raised him to the rank of magister equitum, and contributed to the elevation to the imperial purple of his yet more fortunate son, by whom that dignity was once more, and for the last time, ennobled. Britain possessed also an upright, though severe governor in Civilis, and in Dulcitius, a general distinguished for his knowledge of the art of war.[2]

But the spirit of independence had already struck too deep a root for the example of Carausius ever to be without imitators. Maximus, of a distinguished British family,[3] had gained the highest reputation in the wars against the Picts and Scots.[4] He was, against his will, proclaimed emperor by the army;[5] and in the treason of the warrior posterity would have seen only the strong national feeling of the noble Briton, had he not left his island-realm, and, seduced by early success, been desirous of founding at Treves a Western Roman empire, which was at first acknowledged by Theodosius. He was taken prisoner at Aquileia and put to death.[6] His young son Victor,

[1] A.D. 368.
[2] Amm. Mar. xxviii. 3; xxvii. 8. Claud. de Consul. Honorii.
[3] See the authorities in Palgrave. vol. i. pp. 381, 383.
[4] Prosp. Tyro, a. 382.
[5] Prosp. Tyro, a. 381. Prosp. Aquitan. a. 384. Sulp. Sev. Vita S. Martini, c. xx. Orosius, vii. 34. and from him, Beda, H. E. i. 9. Paulus Diac. lib. xi. Greg. Turon. i. 38. [6] A.D. 388.

whom he had declared emperor and left behind in Gaul, shared the same fate.¹ Hence, though we must look with great mistrust on the Welsh pedigrees,² which derive the independent princes of Gwent and Powys, as well as the more powerful ones of Cumberland and Strathclyde, from Constantine, who is described as the eldest son of this emperor, yet the impression which was made on the Britons by the deeds of Maximus must be acknowledged to have been extremely deep.

An event connected with the history of this prince may not be passed without notice ; namely, the settlement of a Roman military colony (milites limitanei, læti), consisting of British warriors, in Armorica, which has given name, as well as a distinct character and history, to the province of Bretagne.³ Though that country had from the earliest times, by descent, language, and druidism, been related to Britain, yet the new colonists, who were followed by many others, both male and female,⁴ served unquestionably to bind more closely and to preserve the connection between Bretagne and the Britons of Wales and Cornwall ; and but for this event, the heroic poetry of France and

¹ Prosp. Aquitan. a. 388. Orosius, vii. 35. Paul. Diac. lib. xii. Nennius, c. xxvi.
² See Gunn in Hist. Brit. p. 141.
³ Gildas, c. x. Nennius, c. xxiii. Beda (H. E. i. 12) copies the words of Gildas. It is not apparent why Gibbon (c. xxxviii. note 136), who else frequently follows these authors, here wholly rejects them. See also Palgrave, vol. i. p. 382.
⁴ The tradition of St. Ursula and the eleven thousand virgins who followed the colony of warriors, is recorded by Geoffrey of Monmouth, lib. v., according to whom the arrival of many of them in the Rhenish districts is not unfounded. See also the present author's little work on Heligoland, note 17.

Germany had probably been without the charm cast over it by the traditions of the Sangraal, of Tristan and Isolde, of Arthur and of Merlin. But Britain was thereby deprived of her bravest warriors, and thence the more easily became an early prey to foreign invaders.

Scots, Picts, and Saxons continued to trouble Britain, and even the excellent administration of the vicar Chrysanthus came too late to restore the disturbed condition of the country. Stilicho indeed felt himself at first powerful enough to send a body of Roman troops to the aid of the afflicted province, who both fulfilled the object of their mission, and, as tradition informs us, exhorted the natives to construct a wall across the island from sea to sea, as a barrier against the northern barbarians.[1] But the Roman general himself soon stood in need of all his united forces for the defence of Italy against the hordes of Alaric. The troops, a few years after, returned to Britain, but the country had in the meanwhile suffered new devastations from the Celtic invaders.

The Roman legions were soon afterwards, on the occupation of Gaul by the Alani, the Suevi, and the

[1] [Or rather to restore the one already constructed.—T.] See Gildas, c. xii. This tradition is remarkable for the confusion it has caused: having been adopted by Beda (H. E. i. 12. and Chron. a. 426) it has frequently been copied. Nennius (Rubric to c. xxiv.) mixes the story with the older accounts of the wall of Severus, by the interpolation of a new emperor, Severus II., who built a wall from Boggenes (Bowness) to Tynemouth; consequently, where Hadrian had caused the first wall of earth to be raised. Rich. Corinæus (De Situ Brit. ii. 1. 37) also considers the wall as the work of Stilicho, and appeals to the passage of Claudian (In Prim. Cons. Stilichonis, ii. 247:—

"Me (Britanniam) quoque vicinis pereuntem gentibus, inquit, Munivit Stilichon," etc.

Vandals,[1] withdrawn from the island by the emperor Honorius, who was compelled to leave it to its fate. An emperor of Britain was elected in the person of Marcus,[2] who, being slain, found a successor to his dignity and his fate in Gratian, a burgher of a British municipal town.[3] The memory of Constantine the Great was, after the lapse of a century, so highly revered in his real or adopted country, that the possession of that illustrious name, which at the time was borne by a humble soldier, procured for him the vacant British throne; though the vigour which also gained him the dominion of Gaul and Spain,[4] might well justify the supposition, that a descent from the emperor Constantine and consanguinity to British princes raised him to that eminence.[5] He probably yielded to the hope of rendering his dignity and power hereditary; his son Constans having, it is said, exchanged the cowl for the diadem.[6] Honorius saw himself compelled to acknowledge Constantine as emperor;[7] but the count Gerontius having proceeded to Gaul with an army, shut him up in Arles, took him prisoner and put him to death.[8] Constans his son was also slain at Vienne by count Gerontius.[9] Britain, however,

[1] Oros. vii. 40, and from him Paul. Diac. Beda, i. 11.
[2] A.D. 406.
[3] Oros. i. 1. Olymp. ap. Photium. Zosim. vi. 2. Sozom. ix. 11.
[4] A.D. 409. Oros. vii. 40, who adds, "sine merito virtutis." Olymp. ap. Phot. Zosim. vi. 3. Sozom. ix. 11. Procop. i. 2. Prosp. Aquit. a. 407.
[5] Procop. (i. 2) calls him οὐκ ἀφανῆ ἄνδρα.—T.
[6] Oros. vii. 40. Geof. Mon. vi. 5, who says that he had been a monk at Winchester.
[7] Olymp. ap. Phot. Zosim. v. 43.
[8] A.D. 412.
[9] Oros. vii. 42. Procop. i. 2.

never returned to Roman subjection, but continued under rebellious tyrants or pseudo-emperors.[1]

A new inroad of the Picts and Scots appears to have occasioned a mission from Britain to Rome, which, clad in mourning weeds, had to deprecate the murder of the Roman generals in the last rebellion, and to implore forgiveness and protection.[2] Roman troops came over once more, to defend a province which contained no inconsiderable amount of Roman property and was closely associated with Roman interests. Perhaps also, under the pretext of punishing the rebels, these cohorts were sent to get possession of the remaining treasures of the inhabitants;[3] but having repelled the invaders they were obliged to hasten away to warfare in distant regions, after having repaired the forts along the wall, and the watch-towers on the sea-coasts, and left behind them arms for models, with instructions how to use them.[4]

This gift availed but little—the Britons being not only strangers to the use of arms, but, in a still greater degree, to concord—for the re-establishment of the common good in the forsaken land, in which every town and every petty chieftain aspired to perfect independence. The Roman officials who had been left behind were driven from the island, and the emperor Honorius, conscious of his weakness, renouncing for the present all hopes of replacing them, charged the British states to undertake their own defence: but liberty proved as useless to the Britons as did the

---

[1] Procop. i. 2.   [2] Gildas, c. xii. Nennius, c. xxvii.
[3] "Hac tempestate præ valitudine Romanorum vires funditus attenuatæ Britanniæ." Prosp. Tyro, a. 409. Cf. also Sax. Chron. a. 418. Nennius, c. xxvii.
[4] Gildas, c. xiv. Nennius, c. xxvii.

cunning with which the court of Ravenna appeared to grant what it had not the power to hinder.¹ The enemies from the north of the island soon returned, and the feeble inhabitants were unable either to defend their towns, or to escape from the murderous weapons of their foes. To this state of helplessness were added famine, and the pestilence which at that time raged throughout Europe.²

Of one victory only, which for a short time checked the progress of the piratical Saxons and the Picts, has any tradition been preserved : and this, from the battle cry, bears the name of the Hallelujah victory.³ The Gaulish bishop, St. Germain of Auxerre, during his stay in the island, in the year 429, is said to have led the orthodox Britons on this occasion, strengthening them by the penetrating virtue of his spiritual promises.⁴

Yet once again a supplicating embassy was sent to

¹ Zos. vi. 5, 10, an. 409 and 410. The Saxon Chronicle (which places the landing of Cæsar in the year 60 B.C.) is in agreement with this: it says (a. 409) that "they (the Romans) altogether ruled in Britain 470 years since Caius Julius first sought the land." So likewise Beda, H. E. i. 11, and v. 24, a. 409, " Roma a Gothis fracta ; ex quo tempore Romani in Britannia regnare cessarunt."
² Gildas, cc. 19, 22.
³ " Alleluiam tertio repetitam sacerdotes exclamant." Beda, i. 20.—T.
⁴ Gildas, c. xviii., seems to allude to this victory. Cf. Beda, i. 17; Chron. a. 459. Nennius. Prosp. Aquit. a. 429. Constan. Vita S. Ger. c. l. 28, also Beda, i. 20, where the reading ' Saxones,' sanctioned by the best MSS.; and by the life of Germanus by Constantius, written within forty years of his death, ought not to be questioned. To this expedition of the Saxons the accounts refer which place the first landing of the Saxons in Britain in the year 428 or 429 ; in the Appendix too of Nennius (Petrie, C. H. p, 77), where " Felice et Tauro consulibus " indicates the year 428. Nennius, c. xi., reckons, that till the ourth (twenty-fourth) year of King Mervin, in which he wrote viz. A.D. 858, 429 years had passed since the

the Roman general Ætius, during his third consulship, in the year 446. "The barbarians," said the ambassadors, "drive us to the sea, the sea to the barbarians, if we are not massacred we must be drowned."[1] Ætius

Saxons first landed in Britain; for which event, therefore, the half of 858, or the year 429 is to be assigned. At a later period also this date is given. Osbern, Precentor of Canterbury in the eleventh century, in his 'Life of Dunstan,' speaking (cap. i.) of the year of Dunstan's birth, says, "Regnante Anglorum rege Ethelstano, anno quidem imperii ejus primo, adventus vero Anglorum in Britanniam quadriugentesimo nonagesimo septimo." The editors ('Acta Sanctorum' ed. Papebrock. Maii 19, t. iv. 359. Wharton, 'Anglia Sacra,' ii. 90 and 94) have been desirous of altering this number into 479, and, supposing the year 449 as that of the coming of the Saxons, have placed the birth of Dunstan in the year 928, which is the fourth of the reign of Æthelstan, thereby making Dunstan so young, that Wharton (p. 94) accuses Osbern of falsehood. But Osbern was not thinking of the year 449, but of 428, according to which Dunstan would be born in 925, with which the Saxon Chronicle agrees, which year is also the first of the reign of Æthelstan. In the edition also of Nennius by Mark the Hermit, the landings of the Saxons are confused between the years 429 and 447. In the beginning of his work (p. 46) Mark gives the date of its composition very accurately, viz. "Quintus annus Eadmundi, regis Anglorum," or A.D. 946, according to our reckoning, or 976 according to the reckoning of the Welsh, if we may here accept the testimony of Mark, c. i., and Nennius, cc. xi. xxix., who take the year in which we place the birth of Christ for that of his passion, and thus reckon thirty years more than we do since the birth of Christ. Mark, p. 62, is sufficiently explicit, "Saxones a Guthergirno suscepti sunt anno 447 post passionem Christi. A tempore quo advenerunt primo ad Bryttanniam Saxones [viz. 429] usque ad primum imperii regis Eadmundi 542. ad hunc in quo nos scribimus annos, traditione seniorum 547 didicimus." A chronology dating from the death of Christ rarely occurs (Cf. Ideler, 'Handbuch der Chronologie,' ii. p. 411), and never without adding the usually adopted year of the nativity.

[1] Gildas, c. xvii. Nennius, c. xxvii. Beda, i. 13, and from Beda's Chron. Paulus, Diac. xiv. Ric. Corin. lib. ii. i. 39. Sax. Chron. a. 413.

BRITAIN UNDER THE ROMANS, A.D. 350-446. 81

was unable to help them. The clergy entertained a better hope, and showed greater courage. The state of the church in Britain during this early period is indeed too remarkable not to claim a short notice in this place.

The ordinances of the Christian communities were observed in Britain, though many districts of a country exposed to the rapacity of the Roman officials were unable to satisfy the modest claims of the clergy. Three Britons, therefore, were the only bishops at the Council of Ariminum, in the year 359, who accepted the offer of the emperor Constantinus, to receive their subsistence at the expense of the state.[1] That not only Romans in this country, but others also of British race, were devoted to Christianity, is proved by the existence of British versions of the Bible.[2] Of the state of Christianity in Britain some idea may also be formed from the early opposition there manifested to the doctrines of Arius, and the subsequent strong tendency to that heresy. The holy places of Palestine, which the British Helena and her imperial son had adorned, were soon visited by their countrymen, to whom even to pray at the pillar of Symeon Stylites[3] seemed a sufficient motive for a perilous journey by sea and land, and the best pretension to the reward of everlasting life. The pilgrims returned with intelligence of the cloisters that were forming in the East; and the monastery of Bangor[4] was a foundation—as ancient as it was memorable—of a society of brethren

[1] Sulp. Sev. lib. ii. c. 55.—T.
[2] Chrysost. Opp. P. viii. p. 111. edit. Savile.
[3] Theodoreti Relig. Hist. c. xxxvi.—T.
[4] Bangor, the great circle, is an universal denomination for a congregation or monastery. See Gunn in Hist. Brit. Pref. p. xx

in this country (probably grafted on druidism) devoting themselves to pious contemplation and traditional wisdom, but who, however beneficial to individuals, contributed little to the spread and inculcation of Christianity, and were even unable to hinder its extinction and oblivion.

We are enabled to form some judgment of the acuteness and capacity of the British ecclesiastics by the celebrated heresy of the Briton Morgan, better known under his latinized name of Pelagius,[1] as also of the Scot Cælestius, by which Christendom was long agitated, and which, having been propagated in their native country by the Pelagian Agricola, found such favour, that the orthodox, through the intervention of Palladius, who afterwards became the first Scottish bishop, prevailed on the pope Cælestinus to send hither

[1] Bishop Stillingfleet has the following notices of Pelagius, who appears to have followed the doctrines of the Greek fathers and the Eastern churches, and was approved by the council of Diospolis; and, as the bishop observes, was condemned by men who did not understand his meaning. "St. Augustine," he adds, "saith of Pelagius, 'he had the esteem of a very pious man, and of being a Christian of no mean rank.' And of his learning and eloquence St. Augustine gives sufficient testimony in his epistle to Juliana, to whom Pelagius wrote an epistle highly magnified for the wit and elegance of it. And he saith, 'He lived very long in Rome, and kept the best company there.' Pelagius wrote letters to clear himself, first to Pope Innocentius, and then to Zosimus, who was so well satisfied, that he wrote to the African bishops in his vindication, although he afterwards complied in condemning him :"— "so that Pelagius and Cœlestius, by their own natural wit, had in all probability been too hard for a whole succession of popes, Innocentius, Zosimus, and Xystus, had not the African fathers interposed, and told them what the true doctrine of the Church was." Orig. Brit. p. 114, where also honourable mention is made of the piety, learning and eloquence of two British bishops charged with Pelagianism, Fastidius and Faustus.—T.

Germanus, bishop of Auxerre, and Lupus, bishop of Troyes,[1] to confute their opponents in a public disputation, such as was seen in later ages in the noted scholastic encounters between Luther and his opponents. Their first attempt proved that the majority were not incorrigibly devoted to the new doctrine. Scriptural passages, relics, together with the address with which Germanus came to the assistance of the Britons, in the conflict before mentioned with the Picts and Saxons, all fought together against Pelagius.[2] In a second journey, in the year 446, which probably preceded the above-mentioned mission of the Britons, but certainly stood in close connection with it, Severus, bishop of Treves, accompanied Germanus to Britain, where, in the expulsion of the Pelagians,[3] they performed one of the last acts of Roman power in this country. This measure indicating the weakness of that religious conviction which was so soon to be totally annihilated, allows us to attribute the earliest occupation of a Roman province by the pagans to the same contentious sectarian spirit, through which, a thousand years later, the last fragment of the unwieldy political conglomeration fell, in like manner, a prey to infidels.

The spectacle which Britain now presented is one of the saddest, but, at the same time, most memorable in

[1] Prosp. Aquit. an. 429, 431. Constant. Vita S. Germani. Vita S. Lupi.
[2] For the miracles said to be performed by Germanus, see Usher, Annal. Hector Boetius relates that he caused the Pelagians to be burnt, by the care and order of the magistrates. See Jortin, Six Dissertations: the Second contains an historical account of this controversy, so much connected with the early history of Britain, abridged from Le Clerc, Bibl. Chois. viii. 308.—T.
[3] Beda, i. 21. Vita S. Germani.

the history of the world. It was relieved from the rapacity of the Roman procurator; it was freed from the insolence of the Cæsarian cohorts; but for this liberty the people were not indebted to their courage and higher impulses; for them, therefore, liberty was helplessness, independence, anarchy. However much the historian may strive to show that corruption had long been gaining ground in the country; that the government had become gradually perverted; that of the events and views of later times types are to be found in its earlier history and that many fundamental principles were constantly preserved, while the outer shell alone was changed; it cannot yet be denied, that no country ever so quickly cast aside a polished language, which had for many generations been the mother-tongue, not only of the settlers but of the natives. Equally true is it that the Christian religion had never so rapidly been exchanged for paganism and infidelity, leaving not a trace behind. Indeed such a political and moral degradation as took place in the greater part of Roman Britain, after so many a mournful lesson, appears an inexplicable enigma.

This was the deplorable state of the country whose nationality had been destroyed by Roman lust of conquest, after the annihilation of which it possessed not the power to resist its most barbarous enemies. And yet on this foundation a people was ere long to arise which should prove one of the firmest bulwarks of Christianity, and which while it produced some of the wisest and noblest of rulers, and created a literature such as no other nation in that age can show, was destined to develope a power, which in the course of time should not only exceed that of all other states of the modern world, but far outstrip the might of ancient Rome. May this glorious people never forget the example of its ancestors, nor forfeit the moral support and sympathy of the nations most nearly connected with it by the bonds of a common origin.

PART II.

FROM THE LANDING OF HENGEST AND HORSA TO
THE ACCESSION OF ECGBERHT, A.D. 449-800.

CHAPTER V.

Vortigern — Northern Auxiliaries—Hengest and Horsa — British Traditions—Chronology of Anglo-Saxons—Their Races—Modes of Reckoning.

AFTER the extinction of the Roman power in Britain, the country had for many years been a prey to internal discord and foreign assailants, when, to subdue his northern foes, Vortigern,[1] a powerful prince in Kent and the southern parts of Britain, with the concurrence of his counsellors and in the true spirit of Roman policy, formed the resolve to avail himself of the help of those German warriors who for many years had been known to the country only as formidable enemies. This resolve was executed; but these mercenaries took advantage of the weakness of the land, and, with the

[1] Vortigern was the son of Guorthenou, or Guortheu, the great-grandson of Gloui, who, according to the British tradition, built Cair-Gloui (Gloucester). Such is the account given by Nennius, c. liv. A later tradition ascribes the building of that city to the emperor Claudius, whom it states to have been the father of Gloui by a British girl named Genissa. See Geoff. Mon. iv. 15. Malmesb, de Gestis Pontif. iv. p. 283.

aid of succeeding cognate tribes and kinsmen, subjected it to their dominion; a drama which, in the following century, was in a similar manner enacted in the north of Italy by the Lombards, who had been called in by Narses.

That the employment of the Jutish "heretogas" or leaders, Hengest and Horsa, who, banished[1] from their native home, had been driven to gain for themselves a new country, was no very striking event, and that the number of their followers was not considerable, is evident from the obscurity which shrouds the history of England during the years immediately following their arrival. This is further shown by the small number of their vessels (ceylas[2]), as well as from the fabulous traditions (though unknown to Gildas and Beda) with which these years were filled up by the later Welsh writers, as soon as the growing preponderance of the Saxons in the British islands had contributed rather to excite the imagination than to cherish and freshen the memory.

Hengest, when, according to the British tradition, his band, after Dido's example, had measured with a hide, or, with greater probability, had, according to Roman usage, received as a reward, the fertile isle Ruoihin, by the Saxons called Thanet,[3] which was rendered im-

---

[1] The banishment is mentioned not only by Geoffrey, but also by Nennius, c. xxviii. "Interea venerunt tres chiulæ a Germania in exilio pulsæ, in quibus erant Hors et Hengist, qui et ipsi fratres erant." Beda (i. 15) speaks only of the invitation, but Wittekind gives a circumstantial account of a mission of the Britons to the Saxons, and recites their speech, referring, for further information, to an 'Historia Anglo-Saxonum.'

[2] "Tribus cyulis, nostra lingua, 'longis navibus.'" Gildæ Hist. c. xxiii.

[3] "Felix Thanet sua fecunditate—insula arridens bona rerum

portant by its position commanding the Thames, he sent for new allies from his native country, together with his son Ochta, Abisa [1] the son of Horsa, and for his daughter Rowena, so highly prized for her beauty. The British prince, Vortigern, at a feast given by the Saxons,—who, in the accounts of the time, are represented as addicted to gluttony and drunkenness,—received from Rowena a full golden cup, with the old German salutation, " Wes hal," and learned the answer, " Drinc hal." [2] Vortigern now forgot all regard for the Christianity which he outwardly professed, and, excited by love and wine, declared the fair Jute his consort, whom her father granted to him in return for the cession of Kent, at that time suffering under the maladministration of a certain Gnoirangon.[3] His subjects saw with indignation the partiality for the strangers with which their king was inspired, in consequence of this connection, and placed his son Vortemir on the throne. Hengest, who, according to Geoffrey of Monmouth, had called over three hundred thousand of his

---

copia, regni flos et thalamus, amenitate, gratia, in qua tanquam quodam elysio, etc." Cf. Jocelinum de Vita Milburgæ. eund. de Vita S. Augustini, ap. Leland Collect. t. iii. p. 170, t. iv. p. 8. The British name of this isle, of which we have documentary evidence as late as the year 692 (Thorne, p. 2234), shows, together with other proofs, that the British tongue had not been driven out of Kent by the Latin.

[1] Later traditions relative to these individuals will be noticed, when we come to the founding of the kingdoms of Northumbria.

[2] See von Arx, in ' Monum. Germ. Hist.' t. ii.

[3] Nenn. c. xxxvii. Gorongus Will. Malmesb. lib. i. c. 1. [Some suppose this name to signify a title, as viceroy, governor, but from the words of Nennius it would rather seem to be a proper name : " Gnoirangono rege regnante in Cantia," though some MSS. omit the word ' rege.'—T.]

ANGLO-SAXON SETTLEMENT, A.D. 449-800. 89

countrymen to Britain, under the pretext of defending the Picts' wall against the Scots, with whom he afterwards entered into an alliance, had by the victorious arms of Vortemir been beaten in three battles—on the Darent, at Episford,[1] in which Horsa and Categirn, a son of Vortigern, were slain, and at Folkestone,[2]—and for some years driven out of the country, but had been recalled by his son-in-law, after the latter (whose son had been poisoned by Rowena) had re-ascended the British throne. On the refusal of the Britons to restore to the Saxons their previous possessions, a conference was appointed of three hundred of each nation, during which, on the exclamation of Hengest to his followers, "Nimath eowere seaxas," they, with their long knives, which they had held concealed, fell on their opponents and murdered them.[3] The ransom of Vortigern was three provinces, distinguished by their later denominations of Essex, Sussex, and Middlesex, over which Hengest, and after him his son Ochta, reigned.[4]

In the perusal of this narrative, drawn from the writings of those who have recorded the British traditions, we feel at no loss with regard to the several elements of which it is composed. The Triad of the

[1] Nenn. c. xlvii. *Br.* Saissenaeg haibail, so called, says Camden, because the Saxons were conquered there. The Saxon Chron. a. 455, reads Æglesthrep and Æglesford.

[2] This reading is founded on a conjecture of Somner and Stillingfleet, that for Lapis Tituli (Nenn. c. xlvii.) we should read Lapis Populi; while others suppose that Stonar, in the Isle of Thanet, is the place intended.

[3] Davies (in his 'Mythology and Rites of the British Druids') would perceive in the 'Gododin' of Aneurin, a bard of the sixth century, an allusion to this event. Turner's refutation (b. iii. c. 4) is very satisfactory, though his own interpretation seems no less arbitrary.

[4] Nenn. c. xlix.

druidic religion and of British fiction furnishes the groundwork and the standard, according to which all events, without any chronological data, are shaped. Here British and Roman traditions are mingled and embellished, and the Old-Saxon saga of the craft and valour with which the Saxons landed in Hadeln, gained possession of Thuringia, bought land, and murdered the inhabitants with their knives, is again placed in account against them by the Britons. The principal assertion in this narrative is, moreover, the least true,— that Hengest received the above-mentioned three provinces, which never fell to his share, but to that of other German chieftains, and a part of them in much later years.

The evident worthlessness of these traditions renders the more necessary a strict examination of the accounts of their conquests in Britain given by the immigrants themselves. We find these in Beda,—who, however, records but very few circumstances relative to that event from his own sources, but, for the most part, transcribing Gildas, mingles both traditions,[1]—and in the earliest English chroniclers, among whom Henry of Huntingdon, from his greater detail, is particularly valuable and interesting. As these narratives are accompanied by dates, the first point to be ascertained by the historic inquirer is, the system, according to which these dates were calculated, before the Christian writers, through whom only they are transmitted to us, reduced them to the Julian calendar and the Christian

[1] Beda, i. 15, 16, 22, from Gildas, cc. xxiii. xxiv. xxv., while Henry of Huntingdon copies Beda, adding, however, the accounts which are substantially given in the Saxon Chronicle. The passages copied from Beda should be carefully detached from the rest, in order to form a correct idea of the view here taken.

era. Britain, in the latter half of the fifth century, could no longer have reckoned its years by the Roman consuls and emperors; the epoch of the birth of Christ, first introduced by Dionysius Exiguus in the sixth century, could not in any case have been adopted before its close, and before the conversion of an Anglo-Saxon prince, and probably not before the Christian religion had gained a considerable footing in the country.[1] Of the chronology brought by the Saxons into Britain we know little more than that they reckoned by lunar years, and increased their year (which, like that once in use among the Romans, consisted of ten months only[2]) by the addition of two new months, and of an intercalary month, on the adoption of the Christian Roman calendar.[3] Hence, in assaying, as it were, such chronological data, and whatever is dependent on them, we must have the greater regard to their intrinsic credibility, seeing that, for a period of nearly a hundred and fifty years, we are unable to adduce a single trustworthy authority for the history of the pagan Anglo-Saxons.

The Anglo-Saxon narratives are given to us by the chroniclers in the following words:—

In the year 449, on application made by Vortigern, king of the Britons, to the " æthelings " or chiefs of the Angles, or Saxons,[4] for aid against the Picts and Scots, the leaders Hengest and Horsa, the sons of Wihtgils, a

[1] On the dates of the Anglo-Saxons subsequent to the introduction of Christianity, Kemble's Introduction to the 'Codex Diplomaticus Ævi Saxonici' may be consulted with advantage.—T.

[2] See Idcler's 'Chronologie' and Niebuhr's Roman History.

[3] Beda de Ratione Temp.

[4] Beda, i. 15. Sax. Chron. a. 443, which probably follows some other narrative in assigning the year 443, or the following year, to the invitation of the Angles.

great-grandson of Woden, who, in the sixth generation, descended from God, land with their followers from three ships at Ypwines-fleot[1] (Ebbsfleet) in Kent. The Picts and Scots had already advanced to Stamford in Lincolnshire. While on the one side they fight with darts and spears, on the other with battleaxes and long swords, the Picts, unable to withstand such force, seek for safety in flight.[2] The victorious Saxons triumph over the enemy whithersoever they advance, and gain vast booty. The strangers inform their countrymen in Saxony of the fertility of the island, and the sloth of its inhabitants; whereupon a fleet of sixteen sail immediately brings over a larger body of warriors, which, added to the former band, form an irresistible army. A fixed habitation is assigned them by the Britons, as reward and pay for the further defence of Britain, according to the three races: to the Jutes in Kent, to the Saxons in Wessex and Essex, to the Angles northwards. The story of Rowena is here mentioned merely as a British tradition.[3] Beda further relates, that Horsa fell in a battle against the Britons, and that his monument was yet to be seen in the eastern part of Kent.[4] The Saxons afterwards come in greater numbers, and form an alliance with the Picts.[5] He then gives some words from Gildas on the battles of

[1] Sax. Chron. (which in other particulars of this event merely copies Beda). Ethelwerd, lib. i. It is remarkable that the Goths migrated in three ships; see Jornandes, p. 98: the Winili or Longobards in three divisions; see P. Warnefrid, i. 3: the Waräger under three leaders; see Nestor.
[2] H. Hunt. lib. ii.
[3] H. Hunt. "dicitur a quibusdam." Cf. Nenn. cc. xxxvii. xlix.
[4] At Horsted. Archæol. vol. ii. p. 107; Hasted's Kent, vol. ii. p. 177.—T.
[5] This account of Beda, i. 15, is not to be found either in Gildas

Ambrosius Aurelianus with the Saxons, and immediately, through one of those singular hallucinations under which he occasionally labours, passes on to the battle of Bath, which he places in the year 492, or in the forty-third year after the arrival of the Saxons. On a later occasion he calls the son of Hengest, Oeric (Eric), surnamed Oisc[1] (Æsc), from whom the royal race of Kent derived its patronymic appellation of Oiscings[2] (Æscings). The other traditions which we are about to relate, were therefore unknown to, or regarded by Beda as unworthy of notice.

In a battle where Ambrosius Aurelianus, a chief of Roman lineage, with two sons of Vortigern, Gortimer and Catigern, lead each a separate body, Hengest and Horsa, though with an inferior number, each with his band, march boldly to the encounter.[3] This battle may be identical with that of the Derwent, recorded without particular details by the British traditionists. In the sixth or seventh year after the coming of the Saxons, was fought the battle at Æglesthrep, supposed to be the present Aylesford, where tradition

---

or Nennius, who would hardly have omitted it, had it been founded. It may possibly have arisen from a misunderstanding by Beda of the passage in Gildas, c. xxiii. " testantur se cuncta insulæ rupto fœdere (sc. cum Vortigerno inito) depopulaturos."

[1] It may be well to observe that, in the orthography of personal proper names, Beda uses the Northumbrian dialect, writing oi for æ and e, œ and i for e, a and æ for ea, u for w, c and ch for h, d for th (ð). Examples of all these changes occur in the following, Oidilualch, Coinualch, Cœnred, Alcfrid, Ædwine, Sœberct: for Æthelwealh, Cenwealh, Cenred, Ealhfrið, Eadwine, Sæberht.—T.

[2] Beda, H. E. ii. 5.

[3] H. Hunt. lib. ii. The battle between Aurelianus and Hengest is also mentioned by Gildas, c xxv., though without details.

declares the British structure known by the name of Kits Coty house to be the sepulchral monument of Catigern. At the outset Horsa attacked the band led by Catigern with such impetuosity that, like dust, it was scattered in all directions, and the son of the king was struck by him to the earth. His brother Gortimer, however, a very valiant man, burst from the flank into the array of Horsa, and slew that hero. The remnant of Horsa's band fled to Hengest, who still fought unconquered with the wedge-formed-battle array of Ambrosius. The whole weight of the conflict having now fallen on Hengest, who was also pressed by the brave Gortimer, after a long resistance, and a great loss on the side of the Britons, he who had never fled was now compelled to flee. This battle, though, from its name, regarded as the second mentioned by Nennius, agrees in its consequences more with the third and last recorded by him.[1]

In the eighth year after the coming of the Germans, the Britons led four large bodies under as many valiant chieftains to Crecganford (Crayford) in Kent, against Hengest and his son Æsc. Nevertheless, when they had begun the game of war, they ill withstood the Saxons, who, strengthened by a body of newly-arrived chosen men, with their battle-axes and swords, had fearfully hewed the bodies of the Britons, never ceasing from the conflict until they beheld the slaughter of four thousand of their adversaries, who in dismay fled towards London, and never again ventured to enter Kent with a hostile purpose.[2] Hengest and his son Æsc[3] then assumed kingly power in Kent.

[1] Sax. Chron. H. Hunt. a. 455.
[2] Sax. Chron. Ethelwerd. Flor. of Worc. H. Hunt. a. 457.
[3] Sax. Chron. Flor. Wigorn. a. 455. Huntingdon places the

Eight years later, in 465, Hengest and Æsc assembled an invincible army, against which all Britain went forth in twelve noble warlike hosts. They fought long and bravely, until Hengest slew the twelve British chieftains, took their standards, and put the panic-struck bands to flight; but he there lost, together with other noted leaders and kinsmen, his valiant thane Wipped, after whom the battle-field, which, from the preceding narrative, we ought not to look for in Kent, received the name of Wippedes-fleot. This battle was followed by so many tears and so much sorrow, that neither people for a considerable time ventured beyond their own boundaries.[1]

Again, after a term of eight years, in 473, Hengest and Æsc gained another victory over the Britons. The very name of the field is forgotten; and although they made vast booty, the Britons fled before them as from fire.[2]

In the fortieth year after his arrival,[3] or twice eight years after the last battle, Hengest died, and after him

---

assumption of the kingly power by Hengest and his son in 457, where the mention of Æsc seems a later addition to the text, the verb being left in the singular: " Exinde *regnavit* Hengist et Esc filius suus." Ethelwerd also (rightly I suspect) omits all mention of Æsc, saying merely, that Horsa being slain, Hengest "cepit regnum." Whether Hengest's assumption of the royal dignity was a consequence of Horsa's death or of the complete expulsion of the Britons from Kent, is doubtful, though the latter seems the more probable cause.—T.

[1] Sax. Chron. Ethelw. Flor. of Worc. H. Hunt. a. 465.
[2] Sax. Chron. a. 473.
[3] H. Hunt. a. 488. " Mortuus est Hengist xl. anno post adventum suum in Britanniam." The Sax. Chron. Ethelw. and Flor. of Worc. make no mention of the fortieth year, which is, moreover, un-doubtedly incorrect, and added apparently through prepossession for the number eight and its multiples.—T.

Eric, surnamed Æsc, the patriarch of the dynasty of the Æscings, reigned twenty-four years, increasing his territory at the expense of the Britons, until the end of the eighth cycle of eight years after the coming of the Germans into England. From this time for the following eighty years, the history of the kingdom of Kent affords no chronological data, and records little beyond the names of the first Æscings, which forcibly remind us of those of the heroes of Asciburgum of the Lower Rhine and the Asgaard of the Northmen, namely, Octa or Ocha, the son of Eric or Æsc, and Eormenric, the son or brother of Octa. Under the year 568 Æthelberht is named, who reigned forty-eight years, and whose successor Eadbald was followed by Earconberht, each of whom reigned twenty-four years.

The great importance in the history of England of the conquests of Hengest must justify us in occupying some space in an attempt more accurately to determine the value of the foregoing narratives. The first point for consideration is the year of the landing, which, according to the later Anglo-Saxon chronicles, is 449. The more ancient Beda, in three different places,[1] merely says, that the first landing of the Saxons took place during the seven years' reign of Marcianus and Valentinianus, the beginning of which in his History he places in the year 449, but in his Chronicon in 459: the right year is known to be 450. The English accounts being thus evidently incorrect, the hitherto apparently neglected statement of the older and nearly contemporaneous Prosper Tyro becomes important, namely, that Britain, as early as in the year 441, fell

---

[1] Beda, H. E. i. 15, v. 24, "quorum tempore Angli a Britonnibus accersiti Britanniam adierunt." Chron. a. 459.

under the dominion of the Saxons.[1] With this year the mission of the Britons to Ætius, at that time resident in Gaul, might possibly be brought into connection : yet Beda himself, in other parts of his work, where he gives the dates with greater exactitude, fixes 446, that of the third consulship of Ætius,[2] for the year of the landing of the Angles and Saxons. It would seem that Beda, whose glaring deficiency in historic criticism has never been duly attended to, followed in the one account the Kentish narratives, in the other, the North-Anglian authorities, both of whom may be correct for their respective localities. On the first-mentioned account of Beda later chroniclers have founded the beginning of their Saxon era.

The oldest Anglo-Saxon chronologists reckoning their years from the arrival of the Saxons, we have, in the adoption sometimes of the year 445 and sometimes 449, an explanation why the dates of the earliest annals so frequently differ from each other by exactly four years.[3] The year 428, to be found in writers of no

[1] "Britanniæ usque ad hoc tempus variis cladibus eventibusque latæ (laceratæ) in ditionem Saxonum rediguntur." Pr. Tyro, a. 441, ap. Canisium, and Petrie, C. H. p. lxxxii. 2.

[2] Beda, H. E. v. 23, "anno adventus Anglorum in Britanniam, circiter ducentesimo octogesimo quinto, Dominicæ autem incarnationis anno septingentesimo tricesimo primo." Id. i. 23, "anno decimo quarto ejusdem principis (Mauricii, hoc est anno 696) adventus vero Anglorum in Britanniam circiter centesimo quinquagesimo." The 'Northumbrian Chronology' (Wanley, p. 288; Petrie, C. H. p. 290) places the arrival of the Angles 292 years before 737, consequently in 445. See also Petrie, p. 120, note ª. Nennius (c. xxviii.) assigns a period of forty years from the extinction of the Roman power in Britain till the landing of the Germans, where it is evident that, as well as in other parts of his history, he mixes up Anglo-Saxon with British traditions.

[3] See also the 'Annales Juvavienses Majores,' where the death

very late times, as that of the landing of the Saxons in England, having been already considered, need be merely mentioned in this place.

We have endeavoured in the above details to draw attention to a circumstance hitherto overlooked,—that the events in the saga of the Æscings, or founders of the kingdom of Kent, take place in an eight times repeated cycle of eight years. If so many traces of fiction did not betray a poetic source from which these meagre chroniclers derived their narrative, those numbers would yet awaken the suspicion, that in regard to this people, who have preserved no ancient chronological notices, and whose genealogies, ascending in the tenth or twelfth generation to the first Creator of the world, betray a very short historic memory, we have here only a fragment, arbitrarily taken by the Scalds, of a myth founded on some historic sagas.

Though so little of the Old-Saxon traditions has been transmitted to us through the literature of the Christian Anglo-Saxons, we possess, however, two poetic pieces in which Hengest appears as a conspicuous character: the one a fragment only, " The Battle of Finnesburh,"[1] the other an episode in Beowulf,[2] the

---

of Æthelberht of Kent is mentioned under the year 620, but which is usually assigned to 616, while, according to a contrary calculation, the year of the death of Finnan bishop of Lindisfarne is placed in 658, instead of 662. A similar confusion occurs in the year of the death of Penda of Mercia, which is usually given in 654, but in the Northumbrian chronology, already cited, in 658.

[1] See Hickes, Thes. t. i. p. 192; Conybeare's 'Illustrations,' p. 173, and Beowulf by J. M. Kemble, vol. i. p. 238.

[2] [First published by Thorkelin at Copenhagen in 1815, 4to, whose text abounds in the grossest errors, but from which his

oldest national epic extant of Germanic Europe. We should therefore not be startled at the supposition of poems, founded on his most memorable deed, sung by heathen Anglo-Saxons in the first century after it took place;[1] nor if, in the history of the later founded Anglo-Saxon kingdoms, we detect many traces of poetic conception in the fragments preserved by the chroniclers. Whether the number eight was merely the division given by the probably historic numbers forty and sixty-four, or whether it had an astronomic allusion, or was founded on some myth, we are unable to discover. That the Saxons were not strangers to astronomic traditions, appears probable from their primitive saga, in which 354, the number of the ships with which their forefathers migrated from the land of sunrise,[2] corresponds with that of the days of the lunar year. We find the number eight in the division of the twenty-four hours, from one morning to another, usual among the Anglo-Saxons and Icelanders. A similar division exists in the eight watches among mariners. As at Rome the period of eight days was superseded only by

---

original transcript, now at Copenhagen, is, singularly enough, in great measure exempt. His "versio Latina" is worthy of the text. An edition of a different character appeared in 1833, and again, with considerable improvements, in 1835, by J. M. Kemble, M.A., which was in 1837 followed by a prose translation of the poem, a valuable glossary and body of notes by the same able hand.—T.] The name of Hengest [as well as that of Huæf], though occurring several times in the poem, has at each time been misunderstood by Thorkelin!

[1] This is perhaps not exactly the place to remark, that in Büsching's 'Volkslieder' there is a child's song in which allusion is made to the Saxon invasion of Britain. The mention therein of the Old-Saxon weapon, the long knife (seax), is remarkable.

[2] See i. a. Sachsenspiegel, lib. iii. c. 44.

the Jewish-Christian week of seven days, so both German and Scandinavian colloquial terms point to a similar division of time in the heathen North. This number reminds us, moreover, of the ὀκταετηρίς of the Greeks, so frequently occurring in their games and other institutions.

If, in considering the cyclic chronology of the dominion of the Æscings, we recollect how many centuries of history are a later work of men, we shall be unable wholly to suppress our doubts regarding the existence in Kent of the first founder of that race. Among the reasons against the historic truth of the traditions of Hengest and Horsa, the first that presents itself is the extraordinary, and, except in poetical tradition, almost unheard of circumstance, of two leaders, at the same time, at the head of a band of followers. Beda gives the story of the two brothers as a tradition only.[1] Their synonymous names are yet more striking, which have been considered as bearing allusion to the horse held sacred by the Germans,[2] to their military banner,[3] and to the white horse, the arms of the county of Kent. The poems of the founding of the kingdom of Kent are unfortunately, through the early decay of that power, irretrievably lost, and there is as little hope of illustrating the traditions from historic narratives as from the heroic compositions of the bard or gleeman.[4]

[1] H. E. 1. 15. [The circumstance of two brothers being joint kings or leaders, and bearing alliterative names, is far from unheard of in the annals of the North: as instances may be cited the sons of Ragnar, Ingvar and Ubba, of whom hereafter ; also two kings in Rumedal (Snorre. t. i. p. 81), Herlaug and Hrollaug. See also the early Danish chronicles.—T.]

[2] Tac. Ger. c. x.   [3] Ibid. c. vii.   Ejd. Hist. iv. 22

[4] According to a tradition of Ocka Scharlensis, a Frisian historian of the tenth century (printed at Amsterdam in 1507), Hengist and

The inquiry into the chronology of the Anglo-Saxons naturally leads to the question, what were the means employed by them to aid the memory, and preserve to posterity the remembrance of past generations? That the art of writing was not very general among them we must conclude from their numerous symbolical legal usages; nevertheless the Anglo-Saxon, and in part English expressions for writing and alphabetic signs, viz. writan, *to write*, and stæf, *letter*, and the many Anglo-Saxon derivatives from these roots, as stæfcræft,

---

Horsa were the sons of Udolph Haro, the seventh and last duke of the Frisians, and of Svana, a daughter of the noble Witgistus (Wihtgils?), dwelling near Hamburg, and sister of two earlier individuals deceased, named also Hengist and Horsa. I am acquainted with this story (which is justly rejected by Verstegan and later English writers) only through the work of Suffridus Petri, 'De Frisionum Antiquitate et Origine,' Colon. Agrip. 1590.

Having, since the foregoing was written, received the original work of Ocka, revised and enlarged by John Vlitarp and Andreas Cornelisz (Leeuwaarden, 1597, fol.), I find that, in speaking of Hengist, born in 361, and Horsus, who had already served in the army of Valentinian, and landed in Britain in 385, the author generally follows Geoffrey of Monmouth. According to the Frisian historian this Hengist was hanged in the year 389 by Eldol (Cf. Galfr. Monum. vi. 6), and the conquest of Britain was achieved by the followers of the sons of the second Frisian king Odibalt, who were born in 441, and likewise called Hengist and Horsa, and had been taught the art of war under the Northern kings, but were at last slain by Gormund and his Irishmen. In Ocka's work no mention is made of Svana nor of her father 'Wæthgist' (Wihtgisl, Wihtgils). [From the tale of the scop or gleemen in Beowulf, Hengest certainly appears as (what he has always till of late been considered) a Jutish leader. The whole episode will be found at the end of the volume, accompanied by what I believe to be a literal translation, with a few conjectural readings of the text, which do not, however, affect the parts relating to the country of Hengest.—T.]

art of letters, grammar; stæfen-row, *alphabet;* stæf-gewrit, stæflic, stæf-plega [*school*], etc., justify the conclusion, that if the Anglo-Saxons had appropriate names for writing and objects connected with it, the art itself could not have been unknown to them. Of runes, the use of which among the Germans seems to have been known to Tacitus,[1] many traces still exist in England, where the word *rune*, however, rather signified a mystery, than, as among the Scandinavian nations, an alphabetic character. That the Germans brought alphabetic writing with them to Britain appears partly from the circumstance that they were acquainted only with the old runic alphabet of sixteen letters, and that their characters closely resembled those of the northern Germans,[2] but particularly from the adoption of some of the Saxon characters into the Roman alphabet introduced by the Christian priests, which was found inadequate to express all the Anglo-Saxon sounds. These are the runes, Þ, afterwards expressed by V or W, and Þ or þ (for which the later Ð, ð was also used), now expressed by Th. During the early culture of the Anglo-Saxons by the missionaries, the other runic characters the sooner fell into disuse

[1] Ger. c. iii. "Aram Ulixi consecratam, monumentaque et tumulos quosdam Græcis literis inscriptos in confinio Germaniæ Rætiæque adhuc extare." Ib. c. x. "Virgam frugiferæ arbori decisam in surculos amputant, eosque notis quibusdam discretos super candidam vestem . . . spargunt." Were these twigs, used for casting lots, marked with runes? [See a passage connected with this subject in 'The legend of St. Andrew,' edited by J. M. Kemble for the Ælfric Society, or in Archæol. vol. xxviii. p. 332.—T.]

[2] Cf. W. C. Grimm, 'Ueber Deutsche Runen,' Göttingen 1821, and his supplement to that work in the 'Wiener Jahrbücher,' 1828, Bd. 43. Geijer, 'Svea Rikes Häfder,' t. i. 131-185, with whom I agree in the result, though not in particular points.

from being unknown to the Britons, who at a later period exercised considerable influence on the mission schools. Although we have to regret the loss of all the alphabetic writings of the Anglo-Saxons from the time of paganism, which recorded on perishable wood the genealogies of their kings, legal documents and poems, more durable though somewhat later monuments inscribed with them are yet not wanting, from which we may conclude that here, as in the North, they were in use as the writing of the people for some centuries; and hence we meet with them on boundary stones, fonts, and similar public monuments.

The Anglo-Saxon and Scottish missionaries carried the knowledge of these runes into Germany, while the use of runes as a peculiar kind of writing may be traced in England till the fourteenth century;[1] if we err not they continued in use both there and in Germany for inscriptions and seals to even a later period, in consequence of the superior facility which their right-lined forms afforded to the engraver over those of the usual round monkish characters. That we have failed in discovering their numerals is much to be regretted, since an acquaintance with these figures might have made many an enigmatic myth of the North susceptible of an historic interpretation. From the undoubted connection of the runic characters with the Phœnician and, consequently, with the ancient Greek alphabet, we may perhaps conclude that the runic numerals were those characters in

[1] See Cod. Sangallens. 270 and 878; it. Cod. Isidor. Paris. in Grimm. tab. ii., and ibid. tab. iii.; from later A.-S. manuscripts in Hickes, t. i. pp. 135, 136, and t. iii. tab. 6; Duncan und Repp's account of the monument in Ruthwell Garden, Edinb. 1833 [and J. M. Kemble on Anglo-Saxon Runes, in Archæologia, vol. xxviii.—T.].

their ancient order, which we know from some manuscripts; a supposition which as far as the number 19 finds confirmation in the notation used on the old runic calendar, in reference to the cycle of nineteen years.[1] If we further consider how long these characters continued in use among the common people and perhaps in commerce, the question, however repugnant to received opinion, may be asked, whether, notwithstanding the influence of the Arabian or Indian numeral system on our own, the present so-called Arabian first eight numerals are not eight runes, to which, as they appear in ancient manuscripts, they bear a closer resemblance than to the real Arabian ciphers?—thus, for instance, in the sixth Anglo-Saxon rune called *cen*, we have, with its closed under half, our cipher 6. That this supposed similarity is less striking in the Northern than in the later wide-spread Anglo-Saxon runes, seems in favour of the hypothesis. Planudes indeed says, that the numerals used by him are of Indian origin;[2] but how different from our ciphers are the figures which we find in his time and, some centuries earlier, in the writings of Roger Bacon, as well as in other manuscripts! It would be rash to pretend to decide on a point regarding which our materials for judging are so scanty and so uncertain; yet the doubt may be forgiven on calling to remembrance that science and art have often been found nearer to their home than shortsighted learning imagined.

Of greater inportance for historical investigation would be the knowledge of the numeral system in use

[1] Hickes, t. i. p. 34.
[2] See Montucla, 'Histoire des Mathématiques,' i. p. 375 sq. The second rune Ur resembles in all the alphabets the cipher for two as it appears in manuscripts of the fourteenth century.

among the Saxons. I am inclined to the belief that the octonary, on account of its facility of division, was the one followed, and that herein may be found a further reason for the frequent use of the number eight in the Anglo-Saxon narratives. From this system it appears also probable that the name of the eighth rune, "hûn," is nearly connected with *hundred;* also, that both Scandinavians and Germans had a small and a great hundred and thousand, by the latter of which the numbers 120 and 1200 were denoted,[1] and hence perhaps the frequent occurrence of the number 12 (3 × 4). The greatest weight usual in the North, which emphatically bore the name of 'vætt,' contained eighty pounds, and was increased to a hundred[2] in later times only. The Anglo-Saxons placed the words "hund" before the numbers 70 to 120, a practice evidently derived from a time when that syllable had not acquired its later signification of number, but indicated only a certain multiplication; which notation might perhaps have connection with the number of the sixteen ancient runes, the eleventh of which might denote 20, and so on, the fifteenth 60, and the last 100; in like manner, at a later period, after six new runes had been added, the twenty-first might have been employed for the great hundred, and the last rune for its multiple, the great thousand. As an idiom now lost in the English tongue, but as showing the close relationship subsisting between the Anglo-Saxon method of reckoning and that of the

---

[1] Rask, Anvisning til Isländskan, p. 130. Mone, Gesch. des Heidenthums, ii. 79, p. 89. For traces of a reckoning by a great hundred see Diss. on Domesday Book, p. xlvii. Ellis, Introd. to Domesday, vol. i. p. 148.

[2] Grágás II. in Gloss., though Björn Haldorsen, voc. Vætt, explains it by 'octoginta pondo, nonnunquam *olim* centum pondo.'

Scandinavian and other Germanic people, may be cited the use of the word "healf," half, which they subtract from the following whole number, while in other tongues the half is added to the preceding number (as half-four instead of three and a half). This idiom receives illustration from the custom adopted, in writing the numerals during the middle ages, of drawing a stroke through the whole number, thereby signifying that a half is to be subtracted from it.

CHAPTER VI.

MIDDLE OF FIFTH CENTURY.

English Language — Saxons — Angles — Jutes — Frisians -- The various Tribes in Britain—Resistance of the Lloegrians or Britons—Success of Saxons.

BEFORE we resume the subject of the settlement of the Germans in Britain, the manifest deficiency of the historic picture,—which in this instance has very little claim to be regarded as a faithful mirror,—renders it necessary to give a more detailed account of the descent of these people. This is the more important, as with greater rapidity and more lasting results than any other invaders they converted their newly acquired land, in language, laws and customs, into a native country for their posterity.

It is a remarkable circumstance attending the invasion of Britain by the Germanic races, that people whose language was sufficiently formed to supplant both the old mother-tongue, and the language of business, and culture, and of the church,—while in every other province of the Roman empire, with the exception of border districts, the language of the barbarians expired,—should have preserved only meagre genealogic memorials, but no ancestral tradition, historic records, or even any distinct allusions to the country which they had previously occupied. But this want of native history will appear the less singular, when we call to mind that the immigration did not take place in great bodies, but gradually and frequently by very small settlements, which spread themselves over the greater part of England and the south of Scotland, during the course of one or two centuries. In the English language, particularly in the rural districts, where the Norman French has exercised less influence, we still possess living evidence of the identity of the invaders with the inhabitants of the banks of the Lower Elbe and of the neighbouring countries, to the north and south, from the mouths of the Rhine to Jutland. The existing monuments of the old Lower Saxon dialect, especially the 'Harmony of the Four Gospels,' of the ninth century, known by the name of the Heliand,[1] agree much more closely with the Anglo-Saxon in the formation of words, in inflexion and the whole vocabulary, than the Upper German writings of the same period. Widely as the modern English tongue deviates from the present German, there, nevertheless, yet lives in the various dialects of England, and particularly of Scotland, a rich store of Old-Saxon, and the speech and the song of the Scottish ploughman not unfrequently receive their best illustration by a comparison with the expressions of the Holsteiner, Hadeler, or Frisic husbandman or mariner.

An insight into the very close, immediate connection between the Anglo-Saxon and Low German dialects is not without important results for many centuries of English history, affording as it does a firm footing for the elucidation of the civil institutes in both these neighbouring countries. The Scandinavian dialects are far more remote from the Anglo-Saxon, and we are

[1] Heliand. Poema Saxonicum seculi noni, edidit J. A. Schmeller. Monachii, Stutgartiæ et Tubingæ. 1830, 4to. Also, Glossarium Saxonicum e Poemate Heliand, ib. 1840.—T.

fully justified in regarding the traces yet to be found in English of the old Norse tongue as the echo of the invasion of the Jutes, and yet more of the later ones by the Danes or Northmen, and are enabled to fix with confidence the period of the introduction of certain Northern elements, which, as legal antiquities, sometimes present themselves as still extant in the present day.

To the proofs derived from language regarding the native land of the Saxons who passed over to Britain, belongs the resemblance both of the personal names of the Anglo-Saxons, and of local names in the eastern parts of England to those of Lower Saxony. Though with respect to the former, the comparison is rendered very difficult by the want of old Lower Saxon documents, few of which reach beyond, or even so far as the twelfth century, besides being exposed to much uncertainty, through the early spread of originally national proper names by wanderings and intermarriages. But the resemblance of local names, exclusive even of those that preserve historical and mythological recollections, is too striking not to have been long ago called into notice;[1] yet the lists may be greatly increased, and gain in value by the aid of more ancient records. The most important names to us must be those which, occurring in Old-Saxony only, lead to the inference of similar political institutions. Thus it is worthy of notice that the name of the Anglo-Saxon noble, "æthel," is to be found in Ethelingstede,[2] and that the

---

[1] See Ch. U. Grupens, Abh. ' De Lingua Hengisti ' in Observat. Rer. et Antiquit. Germanic. et Romanar.; and, with particular reference to districts on the Elbe, Wedekinds noten zu deutschen Geschichtschreibern, Bd. i.
[2] Now Tellingstädt in the Dithmarsh.

local termination in *Wick, wich*, so frequent in England with its compounds *Wykgraf, wykvogt, Wykscheffel* (wispel), are not common to all Germany, but exist only in Old-Saxony and Friesland.

Of greater and more immediate interest for the history of England is the agreement between the public and private legal institutions of the Germans and those of the English Saxons, which abundantly manifests itself as well in their general characteristics as in incidental notices and detached fragments, the further consideration of which we defer for the present, as an opportunity will hereafter be given for the discussion of them in connection with the history of the Anglo-Saxon constitution.

But if, on every close comparative consideration of the copious language, numerous settlements, and civil institutes of both nations, new proofs of identity shall be found, a more favourable and more faithful picture will present itself of the state of civilization of the continental and of the insular Saxons than the meagre narratives of the older historians have been able to supply. Even though it were the petulant, rugged youth who first forsook their home, and took possession of a foreign land, yet these emigrants, unconsciously to themselves, had their share in the transmission to England of the most valuable possession of their country, in language and customs, which succeeding multitudes of their older and more peaceful kinsmen afterwards fully effected. But let the modern world not forget, that the existing notions of property, and of inheritance, and the institutions founded thereon, are the slow and artificial production of many centuries, and that states of society sometimes present themselves to the geographer and the historian exhibiting no inconsiderable degree of mental culture, yet with no consciousness of the necessity of those fundamental principles of present social order. The system of an annual changing, or at least changeable possession of land, and the custom necessarily attending it, of migrating, prejudicial as they were to the solid interests of nations, nevertheless required activity and strength of mind: the individual too, whose home afforded him no permanent settlement, would not respect that of a stranger; while piracy, ennobled by stratagem and valour, is indebted only to an established system of social order for the odium in which it is held and for its liability to punishment. Even in later times the prince of the Hebrides bore without scruple the title of "archpirate." The Barbary States also afford examples of odious but not wholly savage communities, professing piracy as a trade; and the letters of marque of the Europeans prove how easy, even to ourselves at the present day, is the suspension of the fundamental principles of our whole legal system, and the return to lawful private robbery.

The ancestral traditions of the Saxons scarcely belong to the province of history. The tradition that they sprang from the Danes and Northmen, though questioned by Wittekind, was probably founded on the transient dominion of the Danes over the northern Saxons,[1] and receives some countenance in the intermediate position of these people between Germany and the North. As neighbours of the Danes, on the confines of the Cimbric Chersonesus, the Saxons were known to Ptolemy. We find them soon afterwards in the South, extending

[1] "Confinalis Daniæ est patria quæ nominatur Saxonia, quæ antiquitus et ipsa ex Dania pertinere dicebatur." Geog. Raven. iv. c. 17.

themselves along the sea-shore towards the Rhine.[1] With both these traditions, a third, to which the monks of Corvey gave full credit, is not incompatible, viz. that the Saxons having come to their neighbourhood in ships, and first landing, in Hadeln, drove the Thuringians thence by craft and violence. If this event took place, it cannot have been later than at the time stated, that of the emperor Vespasian, as we soon afterwards find the Saxons in league with the Franks. Wittekind does not inform us whence these Saxons came who landed in Hadeln, and there is no ground for controverting it, but, in accordance with other narratives and with the ordinary march of nations from north to south, we may assume that they were from the north shore of the Elbe, or Nordalbingian Saxons, who took possession of the southern shore of that river, and soon spread themselves over those tracts, as far as the Weser and the Rhine,[2] until, in the time of Charles the Great, they

---

[1] "Saxones, gentem oceani in litoribus et paludibus inviis sitam." Orosius, vii. 32, whose words here as elsewhere are copied by Paulus Diac. de Gest. Roman. lib. xi. In geographical notices the unaltered confirmations of a copyist are sometimes of value. The 'Insulæ Saxonum' of Ptolemy are probably to be sought for in the present North Friesland: Eiderstedt, Nordstrand, Wicking-Harde and Böking-Harde. See Falck, Schleswig-Holsteinsches Privatrecht, Th. ii. p. 10.

[2] This is the country which Beda, Ælfred and other English writers call Old-Saxony in contradistinction to the newer Saxon realm in England. Herewith also agrees the account of Adam of Bremen, i. 3, that the Saxons first had their habitation on the Rhine, and thence passed over to Britain. To seek for Old-Saxony in Holstein, with Camden and others after him, is not admissible, as in the oldest accounts we always find the latter country written Holsatia. Adam. Brem. ii. 8. "Holsati dicti a sylvis quas accolunt." And from him, Annalista Saxo a. 983. "Holcetæ dicti a sylvis quas incolunt." Cf. also Albert. Stad. a. 917. The Sachsenspiegel (b. iii. art. 64, § 3) has 'Holtseten.'

ANGLO-SAXON SETTLEMENT, A.D. 446–800. 113

were in possession of the territory forming the eight bishoprics founded by him, or of the "gaus," or districts, of the later Upper and Lower Saxony and Westphalia. In the account which makes the Saxons to have passed from Britain to Hadeln,[1] a later inversion of the tradition is to be recognised, originating, perhaps, in the return of some bodies of Saxons from England.[2]

That a considerable portion of the German invaders of Britain were strictly Saxons[3] is the more probable, as the names of the territories occupied by them, Essex, Sussex, Middlesex and Wessex, prove their Saxon origin. Even at the present day, after all the immigrations of other races, their Celtic neighbours, the Highland-Scots, the Welsh, the Irish, and the Bretons, speak of the English only under the denomination of Saxons, though other hordes either accompanied or followed them. Among these the Angles are chiefly conspicuous, whose origin is, nevertheless, involved in very considerable obscurity—though they were undoubtedly more numerous than even the Saxons, and sufficiently powerful to impart their name, as a national denomination, to the whole new Germanic land, to the exclusion of that of the Saxons,[4] until, for

[1] Meginhard, Transl. S. Alexandri, and Adam. Brem. i. 4, from Einhard.

[2] Gildas, Hist. c. xxv. Beda, i. 16. Geof. of Monm. vi. 13.

[3] The oldest continental writers for the most part mention only the Saxons as immigrants. Prosp. Aquit. a. 441. "Britanniæ . . . . . . in ditionem Saxonum rediguntur." Geog. Raven. v. § 31. "In oceano occidentale est insula quæ dicitur Britannia, ubi olim gens Saxonum, veniens ab antiqua Saxonia, cum principe suo, nomine Anschis, modo habitare videtur;" also Wittekind, lib. i. [The territories occupied by the Saxons were small in comparison with those of the Angles.

[4] Already in a letter of Gregory I., a. 596, the inhabitants of 'Saxonia transmarina,' as they are denominated in the superscrip-

VOL. I. I

the sake of convenience, historians introduced that of ANGLO-SAXONS. Both Beda and Ælfred distinctly mention the district of Angeln as the original seat of this people,[1] a name now confined to the country between the Slie, or Schley, and Flensburg, but which anciently must have comprised a much larger territory.[2] The former predominance of the people of Angeln seems to derive confirmation from the ancient Danish Saga, which represents Angul and Dan as the founders of their nation. The testimony of Beda, who lived in one of the states founded by the Angles, and scarcely a century from the time of its foundation, is here valuable. The old British tradition makes Hengest and his companions embark for Britain from the Isle of Angul,[3] although they are otherwise spoken of as Saxons, while the peopling of the kingdom of Kent, founded by them, is ascribed to Jutes.[4]

---

tion, are in the text called 'gens Anglorum.' Hardt. iii. p. 509. Du Chesne, t. i. p. 897. So also in all the letters of the same pope in Smith's Beda, Appendix vi., and in Bedæ Opera Historica Minora, Appendix, ed. Stevenson.

[1] Beda, i. 15. "Porro de Anglis, hoc est, de illa patria quæ Angulus dicitur, et ab eo tempore usque hodie manere desertus inter provincias Jutarum et Saxonum perhibetur, Orientales Angli, Mediterranei Angli, Merci, tota Nordanhymbrorum progenies, id est, illarum gentium quæ ad boream Humbri fluminis inhabitant, ceterique Anglorum populi sunt orti." Ælfred's Account, § 3. Ohther's Voyage, § 10. Dahlmann's Forschungen. Th. i. p. 418 sq. Nestor also, the Russian chronicler, makes mention of the Angles.

[2] See Ethelwerd, lib. i., who mentions Sleswick, by the Danes called Haithaby, as the capital of that country.

[3] Nennius, c. xxxvii. "Hengistus . . . cum suis senioribus, qui secum venerant de insula Angul." [Some MSS. read Oghgul.—T.] Gerv. Tilb. ed. Maderus, p. 41. "Ab illis Saxonibus ab Engla insula venientibus seminarium ortum est Anglorum."

[4] Beda, i. 15. Procopius, lib. iv., says, Βριττίαν δὲ τὴν νῆσον ἔθνη

The Angles[1] possessed in Britain those parts which afterwards formed the kingdoms of East Anglia, Mercia, and Northumbria (in the ancient and literal acceptation of that name, comprising the country to the north of the Humber, viz. the county of York and the present Northumberland, the latter, if it were already included under that appellation, forming but a small, and the most remote portion of it), or, in other words, the country to the north of the counties of Hertford, Northampton, and Warwick. This northern portion of England is distinguished from the south by two denominations, which can be ascribed only to the Angles. Thus while the parts inhabited by the Saxons were divided into hundreds, the like division in the Anglian territories bore the name of *wapentake*,[2] which is still retained in the county of York, and partially in those of Derby and Lincoln. It will hardly be objected that this appellation was introduced at a later period by the Danes, since, of all the Anglian states, East Anglia, which first fell under a regular Danish govern-

---

τρία πολυανθρωπότατα ἔχουσι ... 'Αγγίλοι τε καὶ Φρίσσονες καὶ οἱ τῇ νήσῳ ὁμώνυμοι Βρίττωνες, without mentioning the Saxons.

[1] Of the Old Angles we possess a remarkable monument in the laws of the Angles of Haithaby, generally known under the title of 'Leges Angliorum et Werinorum,' for which Dahlmann acutely proposes to read 'Angliorum Etverinorum,' or 'Hetverinorum.' See Kraut on the Lex Angl. et Werin. in Falk's Eranien, iii. [The reading 'Werinorum' is, however, as old as Cnut's Forest Laws.—T.]

[2] Leges Edw. Conf. xxx. "Everwichescire, Nicholescire, Notingehamscire, Leicestrescire, Norhamtunescire, et usque ad Watlingestrete, et VII. milliaria ultra Watlingestrete, sub lege Anglorum. Et quod alii ('Angli,' some MSS.) vocant hundredum, supradicti comitatus vocant wapentagium." 'Ancient Laws and Institutes of England,' folio edit. p. 196.

ment, is the only one where it does not occur. In the present counties of Northumberland and Durham, which had early and long been Danish, as well as in Cumberland and Westmoreland, the division called *a ward* is met with, which may, however, date only from the Norman times. Another national denomination of the Angles accords precisely with the preceding, viz. that of the civic establishment, the "by." Frequently as local names with this termination occur to the north of Warwick, we shall vainly seek for them southwards of that town.[1] To the distinction between Angles and Saxons it may, perhaps, also be ascribed, that beyond the Watling Street, many of the local names end or begin with "kirk" (church), while to the south we find "minster" (monastery). These remarks on isolated differences of expression between Angles and Saxons, here confined to local instances, may be extended to the important and well-ascertained variations in dialect prevailing between the inhabitants of Mercia and those of Wessex.

The testimony of manuscripts of the same work in the dialects of Wessex and Mercia,[2] and of a period when the Danes, having scarcely obtained their first peaceful settlement in England, could exercise no in-

[1] The correctness of this observation, with reference to the earliest times, cannot indeed be proved, in consequence of the want of documents. Derby, in which I have first met with this termination, owed its name of Deoraby to the Danes, having been originally called Northweorthig. Ethelwerd, iv. 2.

[2] In that of Mercia is the Cambridge MS. of the Chronicle (C. C. S. 11, Wanley, p. 130), and a MS. of Ælfred's Boethius used by Rawlinson in his edition. [I believe the genuine Anglian dialect to be that which is usually denominated the Northumbrian. For the near resemblance between the Northumbrian and East-Anglian dialects, see Lufa's Testament in 'Analecta Anglo-Saxonica,' p. 119.—T.]

fluence over the language and culture of their territory, seems to place the age of both dialects, and, consequently, the difference of both races, beyond a doubt; and will, when the investigation is rendered more easy, probably remove all uncertainty regarding the descent of the Angles.

Another hypothesis must not, however, be entirely overlooked, according to which the Angles were either the Anglii of Tacitus, or the Angrivarii, the inhabitants of the later duchy of Engern. Ptolemy relates that a nation, bearing the name of Angles, dwelt to the south of the Elbe, in a territory which, perhaps, may be sought for in the old North Thuringia.[1] No account of, not even the slighest allusion to, any connection between these southern Angles and those of Sleswig is extant; yet, if the supposition be not groundless, that the Saxons moved southwards from the northern bank of the Elbe, it is not improbable that hordes also of their Anglican neighbours in the north might have accompanied them.

Nor may we seek for the Anglian settlers in the middle of the German continent, seeing that the grounds alleged in favour of that opinion rest on a manifest misunderstanding.[2] At an early period the servility of

[1] Von Wersebe, Beschreibung der Gauen zwischen Elbe und Werra, p. 69. Von Ledebur, Land und Volk der Bructerer, p. 274. This writer, in what he says about the Old-Saxons, is far from satisfactory ; and, in what he states concerning the Angli and Warni, he misunderstands the passage of Procopius, lib. iv., who does not consider the Angli and Warni as allies in England, but speaks of the Angli who from Britain overcame the Warni encamped on the opposite coast of Belgium.

[2] In Adam. Brem. i. 4, where he speaks of the Saxons who had gone over to Britain, the words " et vocati sunt Angli," after " Saxones circa Rhenum sedes habebant," are wanting in the Vienna MS.

genealogists had declared Hengest and Horsa to be sons of the duke of Engern, with the view of bestowing on those individuals an origin that should be welcome both to the Saxons and English.[1] But we ought to be extremely distrustful of an argument, however specious, founded merely on blazonry. The duchy of Engern bore, it is said, a white horse in its banner, whence that charge came into the shield of the dukes of Lüneburg and the present Guelphs.[2] The same is also borne by the county of Kent, where, according to tradition, Hengest and Horsa, whose very names may have been merely allegorical, first landed and ruled. But here all dates are wanting, and Kent, as we have already seen, was not occupied by a race of Angles.

Of the laws of the Angles there is no collection extant; the loss of them, more especially those of Offa, is matter of deep regret, as they would, no doubt, have afforded us some important data whereby to judge of the identity of the British Angles with one of the continental races. We know, however, from detached

[1] Gobelini Personæ Cosmodrom. ætate vi. "Duces exercitus illius, qui de Saxonia in Britanniam profectus est, filii ducis Angariæ sive de Engere fuerunt, . . . et inde forte est quod arma ducis Saxoniæ sunt equus albus." See also Verstegan, p. 131.

[2] Not the device of the Saxons, who, according to Wittekind, bore an eagle hovering over a lion and a dragon. The golden dragon was the royal standard of Wessex. H. Hunt., lib. iv. "Edelhun præcedens Westsexenses, regis insigne, draconem scilicet aureum gerens," etc. The horse in the arms of Brunswick-Lüneburg was not added till the year 1362. See Müller in Neue vaterländische Archiv, 1832, p. 176; Scheidt vom deutschen Adel, p. 228. The horse borne in the arms of the electoral bishopric of Cologne, has been referred to Frederick Barbarossa's conquests in Westphalia and Engern, but it is shown by a bull of Pope Alexander III. that it had long before been borne in the Cologne arms. See Privileg. Eccles. Metropol. Coloniens.; and Hugo, 'Rights of the Brunswick-Lüneburg House,' p. 293.

sources, that the laws of the southern and northern English, or of the Saxons and Angles, even in their later form, differed in many points from each other.¹ The law of Mercia is usually cited as agreeing with that of East Anglia;² hence an accordance of the law of Mercia with that of the continental Anglians ought not to be overlooked. In the latter of these, among all the written German laws, the denomination "adaling" (ætheling) is alone to be found, while both codes fix the wergild of the free at two hundred shillings.³ The disproportion in the wergild of the noble among the Anglians may perhaps be accounted for by the circumstance, that a new nobility, the "sixhyndesmen," formed out of the military retainers that had passed into Britain, had stepped into the place of the old nobles, while the wergild of the old nobility by birth was doubled, and their rank raised in proportion. We possess, however, a very remarkable testimony of the origin of the wergild of the free from the law of the Anglians, and of its validity in England, in the Forest Laws of Cnut, which seems to place even the later application of that law in England beyond a doubt.⁴

But the accordance of the laws of the Anglians with those of the Anglo-Saxons is in general, and even in

---

¹ See Laws of Æthelred, vii. 9, 13, and the title 'Wergilds,' in the 'Ancient Laws and Institutes of England.'

² Cnut's Sec. Laws, lxxii.

³ See tit. 'Mercian Law,' in Anc. Laws and Instt. Lex Angl. et Wer. tit. i.

⁴ Const. de Foresta, xxxiii. . . . "emendet secundum pretium hominis mediocris, quod secundum legem Werinorum, i. Thuringorum, est ducentorum solidorum," [The reading ' Churingorum,' for 'Thuringorum,' given in Spelman's Glossarium, is apparently a mere clerical or typographical error: Canciani has, "hoc est Thuringorum."—T.]

many individual points, very remarkable. Particularly important in the former is the precept regarding the succession to inheritances in the male line[1] (*lancea*, the *spear-side* of the Anglo-Saxons[2]); the Saxons also acknowledging only heirs male, to which, as far as the fifth generation, they give the preference over descendants in the female line. Alike important is the title 'De Postestate Testandi,' or, Of freedom in testamentary bequests.[3] The higher fine imposed for injury done to the hand of the harper, the goldsmith, and the embroideress,[4] of which no mention occurs in the other German laws, calls to mind the harp of the North, of Denmark and of England, at the same time that the several female ornaments[5] imply the existence of cities, such as from the foregoing we may suppose Haithaby to have been. A striking characteristic of the Anglians was the sanctity of domestic security, which manifests itself in the heavy penalty affixed to its violation, implying both civilization and notions of property, the later advancement of which appears in the great respect shown by the laws for the house of the English burgher.[6]

[1] Lex Angl. et Wer. tit. vi. Leges Henrici I. lxx. § 20, where, though the passage is copied from the Leges Ripuariorum, c. lvi., yet it in principle agrees with the Anglian law, and can have been adopted only in consequence of its conformity with the Anglo-Saxon.

[2] See Testamentum Ælfredi Regis. Hence is also the proverb to be explained, " Bicge spere of side oδer bere: lanceam eme de latere, aut fer eam," which in Leges Edw. Conf. xii. is thus cited in the law of 'Manbote,' "Emendationem faciat parentibus, aut guerram paciatur."

[3] Lex Angl. et Wer. tit. xiii. That the Anglo-Saxons were acquainted with this appears from Cnut's Sec. Laws, lxxi. LL. Hen. I. lxxv. § 11. See also Anc. Laws and Instt. p. 185.

[4] Lex Angl. tit. v. 20.   [5] Lex Angl. tit. vii. 3.

[6] See title ' Hamsocn,' in Anc. Laws and Instt. of England.—T.

In the laws of the Anglians and of the Anglo-Saxons is found also the common principle, that those who first forcibly enter another's property shall pay a heavier fine than those who follow.[1] According to both laws a thief might be slain, if his crime was affirmed by oath.[2] Whether the enactments of the Anglians regarding duels, which were allowed in all cases of two shillings and upwards, show any connection between their laws and those of the Anglo-Saxons, will be doubted by those who deny the existence of that mode of judicial proof among the latter, on the ground that the word for single combat, "eornest,"—though certainly Germanic,—is not of Anglo-Saxon[3] origin; yet William the Conqueror speaks of the judicial combat as a known English custom. It is evident, however, from the language of their law, which says, "let the field (campus) decide,"[4] that the Anglians themselves lacked an appropriate term. The omission of all mention in the Anglo-Saxon laws of this undeniably existing custom may, perhaps, justify the inference, that the laws of East Anglia contained circumstantial provisions regarding judicial combats. The existence, however, in England of another means of proof in judicial proceedings, similar in form and application to what is enacted in that old Germanic law, is undoubted—the fire, or iron test, for accused females, which consisted in walking over nine red-hot ploughshares.[5]

[1] Lex Angl. tit. x. o. 9. Laws of Æthelberht, xvii.
[2] Lex Angl. tit. vii. 4. Laws of Ine, xvi. xxxv. Laws of Wihtræd, xxv.
[3] Palgrave, vol. i. p. 223.
[4] "Campus judicat;" hence, Kampe, *champion, campio;* Kamp, Low Saxon for *field.*
[5] Lex Angl. tit. xiv. Annal. Winton. ap. Du Cange, voce

Thus it may be confidently asserted, that the laws of the Anglians agree, not only in general characteristics common to all Germanic laws, with those of the Anglo-Saxons, and may be regarded as a chief source of them, but also, that no other Germanic laws coincide with them so closely in single points. Hence if all other historic grounds were wanting, we must, nevertheless, place the laws of the Anglians in the nearest relationship to those of the Anglo-Saxons.

The third race which increased the new population of Britain was that of the Jutes, apparently less numerous than either of the before-mentioned, as they possessed only Kent, the Isle of Wight, and a part of Wessex, where for some centuries the Jutish race was distinguished from the Saxon.[1] Kent has certain customs of its own, among which the law of inheritance called Gavelkind is well known, and also a peculiar dialect.[2] Even on a slight glance over the history of England, we must be repeatedly reminded of the distinguishing nationality of the men of Kent. More accurate inquiries, however, into the history of nations than have hitherto been carried on, and especially into the history of England, will alone enable us to ascer-

---

'Vomeres'; Wharton, Anglia Sacra, t. i. Cf. Theodor. Monach. Hist. Reg. Norv. c. xxxiv. ap. Langebek, t. v. p. 340. Capit. ad Leg. Salic. c. ix. Capit. l. iv. App. ii. c. 3. LL. Longob. l. i. c. 10, § 3, and even LL. Hen. I. lxxxix. § 1. Other laws enjoin twelve ploughshares.

[1] Beda, i. 15, iv. 16. Sax. Chron. a. 449. Juti Vectiani, and Cantiani Juti, about the year 900 are mentioned by Wallingford, ap. Gale, i. p. 538.

[2] A remarkable and valuable specimen of the Kentish dialect exists in the 'Ayenbyte of Inwyt' (MS. Arundel. 57), which, though written in 1340, may still be regarded as Anglo-Saxon. See Cædmon, Pref. p. xii.

tain whether the oldest Jutish law resembles the custumal of Kent, and whether the Jutish forefather may yet be traced in the Kentish man of the present day. One circumstance is, however, too striking not to have drawn to it the attention of others—while the other English shires are parted into hundreds or wapentakes, the county of Kent alone is divided into six *lathes*[1] of regular form, and of nearly equal magnitude. These divisions, which have in later times become mere districts for judicial purposes, served at an earlier period for the quartering and muster of the military and of the general levy. But in the Jutish law[2] a military expedition is still called a "lething" (in modern Danish, "leding"); whence the district summoned together for such expedition may have borne that name. In like manner the word "fyrd," the military levy of the Anglo-Saxons,—the old signification of which does not appear to have been preserved in any other monuments of the German tongue,—is still used in Holstein, where it signifies the assembly of the States, originally for military purposes, at Bornhöved. The earliest record known to us of any of the customary laws of Kent[3] refers chiefly to circumstances arising out of the feudal system, while the Jutish Law of King Valdemar the Second, in the thirteenth century, has adopted many Saxon and other foreign principles; both, however, contain the enactment, that the son, in reference to the property of the deceased husband, shall be considered of age in his fifteenth year;[4] a principle

---

[1] LL. Edw. Conf. xxxi. var. lect. 13.
[2] Lib. iii. c. 2, 12.
[3] Statutes of the Realm, vol. i. p. 223-225. Many of the usages there mentioned will, however, be recognised as common Anglo-Saxon law. [4] Jüt. Lov. lib. i. c. 7.

which, though on the one side in accordance with the Danish laws, and, on the other, valid among the socmen[1] in other parts of England, is probably not derived from the Saxon laws, but rather to be referred to the immigration of the Jutes.

It is hardly probable that, in those days of national migrations and military services, so splendid an enterprise as the conquest of Britain should not have allured many bands from the kindred tribes of Germany; these, however, were not, it seems, sufficiently numerous to claim notice in the most authentic narratives. Frisians, on account of their proximity, their skill in seamanship, their language so nearly resembling the Anglo-Saxon, and the traditions already mentioned, we might expect to meet with before all others[2]; but from affinity of language, however, no inference is to be drawn, as it would tend to the exclusion of the

[1] Glanvile, lib. vii. c. 9, § 2.
[2] Fin filius Folcwald, who was a Frisian chief, appears as an ancestor of Hengest in the genealogies as given by Nennius and those following him; but the Saxon authorities, viz. the Chronicle, Asser, Ethelwerd, the Textus Roffensis, also Florence and Snorre, concur in naming Godwulf as the father of this Fin; while in 'Beowulf,' 'The Scôp's Tale' (Traveller's Song), and 'The Battle of Finnesburh,' Fin son of Folcwalda appears, not as an ancestor, but as an adversary of Hengest, by whom he is attacked and slain in his dwelling, Finnesburh or Finnesham, in Friesland. I find it therefore much more reasonable to prefer in this case the Saxon authorities, and to suppose that there were two Fins, living at very distant times, than to seek to reconcile them with an apparent error of Nennius, by the aid of hypotheses hardly in accordance with our notions of a more than semi-barbarous people. In these meagre traditions exist, I firmly believe, faint traces of persons that once had being, and actions that once took place; but that they generally require a mythic interpretation is to me more than questionable. See additional note, and extracts at the end of work.—T.

remoter German races; nor should too much importance be attached to such words as "seax," the long knife of the Saxons, from which they are supposed to have derived their name, and which was common also to the Frisians,[1] and is still to be met with in that country; as on the same ground the Icelanders must also be considered as Saxons.[2] Even the striking similitude between the old Frisic and the Anglo-Saxon public and private law, although affording the most decisive testimony as to the relationship of the two nations, does not allow us to make any further inference with regard to Britain; more especially as our oldest accounts of the Frisians are too defective to enable us to ascertain what influence the connection with the Anglo-Saxons, and the migration of the latter may have had on the tribes of Friesland. The assertion of Procopius,[3] that Angles and Frisians dwelt on the isle of " Brittia," notwithstanding the fables in the rest of the narrative, appears credible on account of its antiquity and other circumstances to be discussed hereafter. Later testimonies show with greater certainty the existence of the descendants of Frisic forefathers in England, but do not prove the establishment of any state or considerable settlement of that people in the country.[4]

[1] Asega-Buch, tit. iii. § 13, tit. v. § 17. [J. Grimm considers the derivation from *sax* (sahs, *a stone or stone weapon, saxum*) as undeniable. D. M. p. 204, and Massmann's 'Abschwörungsformeln,' p. 18. At all events, the coincidence of the words, seax, franca und angul, signifying weapons, with the names of three warlike nations, is, if accidental, not a little remarkable.—T.]

[2] Sax, *machæra*. B. Haldorsen.—T.

[3] De Bello Goth. lib. iv. c. 20.

[4] Vita S. Swiberti: "Egbertus sitiens salutem Frisonum et Saxonum, eo quod Angli ab eis propagati sunt." The Sax. Chron.. a. 897, mentions, that the ships constructed by Æl'red were shaped neither like the Frisian nor the Danish; and also gives us the

Of the participation of the Franks there exist some, though not sufficiently specific accounts: the same may be observed with respect to the Longobards. Little doubt can, however, be entertained regarding either the one or the other, as we elsewhere, in similar undertakings, find Saxons united with Franks and Longobards; the latter especially, when the complete occupation of the British southern or eastern coasts made a new field for conquests desirable.[1]

But little attention has hitherto been paid to the national diversity of the Germanic races which established themselves in Britain, and the collective appellation of Angles, which became common at an early period, as well as the subsequent political unity, have caused us to overlook the variety of elements of which the population of Great Britain is composed; although, at the present day, after a lapse of nearly fifteen centuries, even in the instance of the Celtic tribes, striking

---

names of three Frisians of distinction slain in a sea-fight with the Danes, together with sixty-two men, Frisians and English. The circumstance, however, that they are mentioned separately leads us to regard these Frisians rather as allies than inhabitants. In Vita S. Liudgeri, c. xi., Frisian merchants are spoken of as strangers. Beda also (iv. 22) has a story of a slave bought by a Frisian in London.

[1] See Paul. Diacon. De Gestis Longob. lib. ii. c. 6, and lib. iii. c. 6. Of the connection between the Anglo-Saxons and Longobards we shall again have occasion to speak; but will here observe, that Sceaf, one of the ancestors of Woden in the genealogy of the West Saxon kings, is called a king of the Longobards, and that the old Longobardic kings, Agelmund, Lethus, Auboin, and his son Alboin, are celebrated in Anglo-Saxon song. See "The Song of the Traveller" in Conybeare's Illustrations, p. 9. [Also Cod. Exon. p. 318 ; Beowulf, edit. Kemble ; and Ettmüller's 'Scôpes Vidsidh,' accompanied by a valuable commentary, illustrative of the persons mentioned in the poem and its ethnography.—T.]

varieties in laws and dialect, as well as peculiarities of figure, hair, and eyes, are still discernible, and prove their indelible natural affinity with those of the ancient country. Must not these characteristics have displayed themselves in early times much more manifestly than at present? The answer is obvious; and to this cause, no doubt, may be ascribed the great weakness of the Anglo-Saxon power, when, fleeing before the invading Northmen, the sons yielded the dominion of the land which their valiant forefathers had conquered. The slow introduction of Christianity, the disputes of the clergy in the north and south of England by which it was followed, the disunion which prevailed during the invasion of foreign foes, the treaties with them,—in short, the most important events of the Anglo-Saxon sovereignty, find their true and natural illustration in an attentive consideration of the diversities of race.

These original, though not strongly marked differences among the invaders, lead us to the obvious, though neglected remark, that a considerable part of what we are accustomed to regard as the religion, law, customs, and language of the Anglo-Saxons, arose only in the course of some centuries, from the blending of the several elements. As any attempt at detail of what the immigrants brought with them from their home is not admissible in this place, we shall defer till a future opportunity the discussion of that which may be more strictly regarded as Anglo-Saxon, occasionally adverting to what appears originally to belong to the Saxons, to the Angles, or to the Jutes.

Such were the races which, in the course of a century and a half, succeeded in gaining possession of the eastern or greater portion of Britain. The more Roman the several districts had been, the sooner did the forsaken cities and towns become the prey of the barbarians. Of the resistance made by the Lloegrians, or Britons of the present England, at the outset of the struggle, few accounts are preserved. The discord among the British princes, by which the progress of the enemy was greatly facilitated, seems to have caused in the British traditionists themselves an indifference towards the fallen or lost states. Ambrosius Aurelianus, a chieftain of Roman descent, perhaps one of the British provincial emperors, contemporary, though apparently not in alliance with Vortigern, and though involved in a war with the British prince Guitolin, or Wetheling, withstood the advances of the Saxons with Roman tactics; and it is probable that there were yet both Roman and Romanized warriors in detached fastnesses, who, however, would seem only to have increased the general disorder.[1] A defeat sustained by the Saxons, which compelled them to return home for the purpose of seeking reinforcements, was wisely turned to account by Ambrosius, in exciting the Lloegrians, and strengthening them against a further advance of the enemy. In many successive battles and skirmishes, the Lloegrians were alternately conquerors and conquered. The last considerable defeat sustained by the Saxons was at the siege of Bath; but other though inconsiderable contests took place, which are known to us only through the accounts of the establishing of the several Anglo-Saxon kingdoms.[2]

The contemporary who records the victory at Bath, gained by his countrymen in the first year of his life,

[1] Gildas, c. xxv., and from him Beda, i. 16. Nenn. c. xxviii. "Dum ipse (Gorthigernus) regnabat, urgebatur . . . et a Romanico impetu, necnon et a timore Ambrosii." id. c. i., and Gale, ibid.
[2] Gildas, c. xxvi. Annal. Camb. a. 516.

and who bears witness of its consequences after a lapse of forty-four years,[1] Gildas, surnamed the Wise, considers it superfluous to mention the name of the far-famed victor; but his wide-spread work, and the yet more wide-spread extracts from it in Beda, have reached no region in which the fame of king Arthur had not preceded them. This noble champion who defended the liberty, usages and language of the ancient country from destruction by savage enemies—who protected the cross against the pagans—and who gained security to the churches most distinguished for their antiquity, and for the culture to which a considerable portion of Europe owes both its Christianity and some of its most celebrated monasteries, needed not a historian to secure him through all ages a more brilliant place than any claimed for the heroes of the chronicles, and among these he is counted from the time of Geoffrey of Monmouth. Not to mention the works which, about the year 720, Eremita Britannus is said to have composed on the Holy Graal, and on the deeds of king Arthur,[2] the rapid spread of Geoffrey's work over the greater part of Europe proves that the belief in the hero of it was deeply rooted. In the twelfth century a Greek poem, recently restored to light, was composed, in celebration of Arthur and the heroes of the round table.[3] Still more manifestly, however, do the numerous

[1] Beda, i. 16, has misunderstood this passage, and placed the battle in the forty-fourth year after the coming of the Saxons, i.e. in 492. The 'Annales Cambriæ' give 516 for the year. Matt. Westmon. 520.

[2] See Warton, H. E. P. vol. i. p. x. note ᵇ, edit. 1840.—T.

[3] This fragment of 306 verses was first published by Von der Hagen in his 'Denkmale des Mittelalters,' Berlin, 1824, 8vo. Godfrey of Viterbo also proves how rapidly the story had been spread over

local memorials which, throughout the whole of the then Christian part of Europe, from the Scottish hills to Mount Etna,[1] bear allusion to the name of Arthur; while, on the other hand, the more measured veneration of the Welsh poets for that prince, who esteem his general, Geraint, more highly than the king himself; and even relate that the latter, far from being always victorious, surrendered Hampshire and Somersetshire to the Saxons, may be adduced as no worthless testimony for the historic existence of king Arthur.[2] Even those traditions concerning him, which, at the first glance, seem composed in determined defiance of all historic truth, and which recount the expedition against the Romans, on their demand of subjection from him, appear not totally void of foundation, when we call to mind that a similar expedition actually took place in Gaul. We are, moreover, informed, on the most unquestionable authority, of another undertaken in the year 468, on the demand of Anthemius, by the British general Riothamus,—who led twelve thousand Britons across the ocean against the Visigoths in Gaul, —and of his battles on the Loire.[3] This very valuable

---

Europe through Geoffrey of Monmouth. Part xviii. of his Chronicle contains some stories, in hexameters and pentameters, of Voltiger, Orsus, Engist, Corinna (Rowena), Uterpendragon, Merlin, Hierna (Hidernia), etc.

[1] Gervas. Tilbur. ap. Leibnitz, i. p. 921.

[2] Turner, Hist. of the A.-S. vol. iii. c. 3. He regards Llywarch Hên and other poets as contemporary with Arthur. Similar accounts are also to be found in the 'Historia Angliæ ad primordia Regis Stephani,' ascribed by Bale and Pits to Richard of Devizes (see Stevenson's Preface to Chron. Ric. Div. p. vii.), and in Chron. Radulfi Nigri, composed about 1161, both existing only in manuscript.

[3] Jornandes de Rebus Geticis, c. 45. Sidonius Apollin. iii. ep. 9.

ANGLO-SAXON SETTLEMENT, A.D. 446-800. 131

narrative gives us some insight into the connections and resources of those parts of Britain which had not yet been afflicted with the Saxon pirates.

Arthur fell in a conflict on the river Camlan in Cornwall, against his nephew Medrawd :[1] his death was, however, long kept secret, and his countrymen waited many years for his return and his protection against the Saxons. The discovery of his long-concealed grave in the abbey of Glastonbury is mentioned by credible contemporaries,[2] and excited at the time no suspicion of any religious or political deception. Poem and tradition bear witness to the spirit, and his ashes and their gravestone to the life and name of Arthur. Faith in the existence of this Christian Celtic Hector cannot be shaken by short-sighted doubt, though much must yet be done for British story, to transfer the sense latent in the poems of inspired bards—which have in many cases reached us only in spiritless paraphrases—into the sober language of historic criticism.

[1] So Annal. Cambr. a. 537. According to Geoffery, lib. xi. c. 2, Arthur in the year 542 resigned his crown.

[2] Girald. Cambrens. de Inst. Principis. [Bromton, coll. 1152, places the exhumation in the time of Henry II., Wendover in that of Richard I. His words are, "Eodem anno (1191) inventa sunt apud Glasconiam ossa famosissimi regis Britanniæ Arthuri, in quodam vetustissimo recondita sarcophago, circa quod duæ antiquissimæ pyramides stabant erectæ, in quibus literæ erant exaratæ, sed ob nimiam barbariem et deformitatem legi minime potuerunt . . . cui (sarcophago) crux plumbea superposita fuerat, in qua exaratum erat, 'Hic jacet inclytus Britonum rex Arthurus, in insula Avalonis sepultus.'" Roger de Wendover Chronica, t. iii. p. 48. The veracity of the story seems extremely questionable. Malmesbury (lib. iii.) says, "Arturis sepulchrum nusquam visitur, unde antiquitas næniarum adhuc eum venturum fabulatur."—T.

K 2

CHAPTER VII.

A.D. 477-570.

Arrival of fresh Hordes of Northmen—Resistance of Britons—Ælle —Various Sections of Saxons—Cerdic—Angles—Their History —Northumbria—Britons—Their Territorial Divisions — Germanizing Influences.

WHILE the British nation was more obstinately than successfully defending itself against the power of the Saxons,[1] as it had done of old against the Romans, the greater part of the island was becoming the prey and the home of strangers. The British narratives of this period are extremely deficient, and the Anglo-Saxon accounts, particularly their chronology, seem deeply tinged with the fabulous.

Hengest was yet living when, in the year 477, Ælle (Ælli)[2] and his three sons, Cymen, Wlencing, and Cissa, landed from three ships at the place afterwards called Cymenes-ora,[3] on the coast of Sussex. On the

[1] Many of the natives fled to the ancient seats of the Veneti and Coriosolytani, where it is said that their successors, both in manners and language, still evince their affinity to the Welsh. Einh. Annal. a. 786.

[2] Beda (ii. 5) merely mentions his name as the first Bretwalda. The remaining account is from Henry of Huntingdon, the accuracy of whose excerpts from sources with which we are acquainted is a voucher for the same quality in those from lost or unknown authorities. See also Sax. Chron. Of the two forms (Ælle, Ælli) that in 'i' is the more ancient.

[3] Keynor on Selsea. The locality of Cymenes-ora appears from a charter a. 673 in Monast. Angl. t. vi. p. 1103.

landing of the Saxons the Britons raised a loud cry, numerous bodies of them hastened from the neighbouring country, and war instantly commenced. The Saxons, who excelled in stature and bodily strength, received their enemies with undaunted valour, while the latter imprudently hurrying forwards, were, as they approached in disorderly and separate bodies, slaughtered by the compact phalanx of Saxons, each successive band arriving only to witness and share the fate of its predecessor. The Britons were driven into the neighbouring forest of Andredes-leah, while the Saxons established themselves on the coast, and gradually extended their settlements, until, in the eighth year after their landing in Sussex, the princes and chieftains of the Britons, having united their forces, engaged with them in a great battle at Mearcredesburne, the issue of which is doubtful. The armies much injured and weakened, each execrating its conflict with the other, returned to their habitations: but Ælle sent to his German countrymen to demand reinforcements, which, arriving six years after, proceeded with that chieftain to the siege of the strong old Roman city of Andredes-ceaster, or Anderida. The Britons now gathered like swarms of bees, and warred on the besiegers by day with stratagems, by night with attacks. No day nor night passed in which new tidings of disaster did not embitter the minds of the Saxons, who with redoubled ardour continued their assaults on the city; but the Britons were constantly at hand, with their arrows and other missiles, in the rear of the assailants; and when the Saxons, turning from the walls, directed their steps and arms against them, the Britons, who excelled in speed, hastened to the forests, issuing from whence, on the return of the

Saxons to the works, they were again ready to assail them from behind. The Saxons being thus wearied, many too having fallen, divided their army into two bodies, of which while one attacked the city, the other might be armed against the assaults of the British. The citizens, now worn out by hunger, and no longer in a condition to withstand the ardour of the besiegers, found, with their wives and children, their death by the sword. Not one escaped, and Anderida was razed to the ground by the exasperated victors. Henry of Huntingdon knew merely the site of the once noble city; in our days even this is become an object of fruitless research. Ælle, who had assumed the royal dignity in Sussex, was now regarded as the supreme head of all England, as the first Bretwalda of the Anglo-Saxons; so at least we are informed by Beda.[1]

Ælle's death is said to have taken place between the years 514 and 519: it appears, therefore, that to him, as to Hengest, was assigned a term of forty years in England. He was succeeded by his son Cissa,[2] after whom we have a period of a hundred and thirty years, during which neither chronicler nor poet has transmitted to us one line concerning the kingdom of Sussex, which, enclosed between two of the new Germanic states, could not extend its limits by conquests in the British territories. Even the name which it bore before the rise of other Saxon states gave occasion to the distinctive appellation of South Saxons, has not been preserved. We are, however, informed

---

[1] It is remarkable that the genealogy of Ælle, the first Bretwalda, is the only one not given among those of the founders of the several kingdoms of the Octarchy.

[2] His memory is preserved in the name of Cissan-ceaster, now Chichester.

that its thick forest and barriers of rock preserved Sussex, the last hold of paganism, against the arms of the other states; also that Cissa's posterity maintained the royal dignity in Sussex, although their influence, through the rising greatness of the other Germanic kingdoms, was necessarily much diminished.[1] To its first German population belongs apparently the singular division of Sussex into six 'rapes,'[2] each of which is again divided into hundreds. These districts were probably intended for military purposes.

The establishment of the third German kingdom in the south of Britain is, through the supremacy afterwards acquired by Wessex, a subject of paramount interest. Cerdic, a descendant in the ninth generation from Woden, who in conflicts at home had already proved the energy of his soul, in the view of adding to his military renown, landed nine years after the death of Hengest,[3] attended by his enterprising and emulous son Cynric, from five ships at a spot afterwards called Cerdices-ora,[4] the locality of which is no longer known. He posted his Saxons in close order of battle before his ships, where they obstinately maintained their ground against the repeated bold attacks of the islanders, until the approach of night. Cerdic and his son proved their

---

[1] H. Hunt. lib. ii. "Regnavit post eum Cissa, filius ejus, progeniesque eorum post eos : at in processu temporum valde minorati sunt." Æddii Vita S. Wilfridi, c. xl. (South sex) "provincia gentilis, quæ præ rupium multitudine et silvarum densitate aliis provinciis inexpugnabilis extitit." Ædde was contemporary with Beda. The assertion of Matthew of Westminster, that, after Cissa's death, Sussex became a province of Wessex, is of little weight against the foregoing.

[2] The Old Norse 'hreppr' denotes a nearly similar territorial division.

[3] A.D. 495. [4] Sax. Chron. Flor. of Worc. a. 495.

valour also in another battle with the Britons, and extended themselves along the sea-shore. The progress of the Saxons, however, was not great until six years later, when Port with his two sons, Bieda and Mægla, landed from two large ships.[1] The error committed on the earlier landings of the Germans, as well as on Cæsar's, and at a later period on that of William the Norman, was here repeated. The disembarkation was not prevented; the country was called together with great clamour; uncombined attacks, boldly commenced by great numbers, were repulsed by the firmness of the enemy; the imprudent Britons fled in their excitement, and Port remained victor on the spot, which from him, as it is said, derives the name of Portsmouth. Mention is made of the death of a noble young Briton in one of these conflicts, probably Geraint ab Erbin, prince of Dyvnaint, whose fall in the battle of Llongborth is lamented in the elegies of his friend Llywarch Hên.[2] With extraordinary pomp of diction [3] the war is announced of the greatest king of the Britons, Nazaleod or Natanleod, but who is described elsewhere only as a general of the British king Uther. All Britain united against the foreign intruders; Cerdic on his side formed an alliance with Æsc king of Kent, with Ælle the great king of the South Saxons, also with Port and his sons. Cerdic and Cynric led the two orders of battle. Of these Natanleod attacked the most powerful, the right wing commanded by Cerdic;

[1] A.D. 501.

[2] So Turner, who does not, however, notice an inconsistency in the chronology of 29 years. Palgrave t. o, vol. ii. p. ccxxxiv., says that Geraint was slain in the year 501, and at p. cclxiii. in 530.

[3] H. Hunt. "Bellum scripturus sum quod Nazaleod, rex maximus Britannorum," etc. Cf. Sax. Chron. a. 508, and ibidem Gibson. Flor. of Worc.

the Saxon banners were beaten down, their ranks broken; Cerdic fled, and vast slaughter was instantly made among his forces. His son, however, at the head of the left wing, pressed on the rear of the pursuers; a new and bloody fight began; Natanleod fell, and with him five thousand Britons, while the rest found safety in their speed.

A few years only had passed in the tranquillity of secure possession, when new auxiliaries arrived for new exploits. In the year 514 Stuf and Wihtgar, nephews of Cerdic, came with three ships and landed at Cerdicesora. On the following morning the British leaders arrayed their forces according to the rules of war. As one division advanced over the hills, and another was proceeding cautiously through the valley, the beams of the rising sun, which just shone out, gleamed on their golden shields; the hills around were illumined with their brilliancy, and the air seemed brighter. The Saxons, seized with great dread, advanced in terror to the encounter; but when these two great armies met in conflict, the energy of the Britons was extinguished. Stuf and Wihtgar conquered many districts, and Cerdic's power through them became formidable: he now marched through the land confident in his strength. After twice eight years, Stuf and Wihtgar with their uncle gained a great victory in the Isle of Wight, at a place which afterwards bore the name of Wihtgares-burh (Carisbrook). This victory put Cerdic in possession of that isle, which he bestowed on his two nephews.[1]

Cerdic also fought a great battle against the Britons at a place afterwards named Cerdices-ford (Charford in Hampshire), in which the latter displayed great valour,

[1] A.D. 530.

until, on the approach of evening, the Saxons gained the victory. Though the loss sustained on this occasion by the inhabitants of Albion was great, it would have been yet greater had not the setting sun put an end to the conflict.[1]

Having now passed thrice eight years in Britain, in the midst of battles, Cerdic and Cynric assumed the kingly title. The original kingdom of the Gewissas,[2] or West Saxons, was, as is evident from the site of the last-mentioned battle, hardly more extensive than the other Germanic states in Britain, and barely reached beyond the borders of Hampshire and the territory of the Sumersætas. These provinces are stated to have been surrendered to the Saxons by King Arthur, after he had given a check to their further advances near Bath;[3] the possession of them, however, implies also that of a portion of the land of the Dorsætas and the Wilsætas. Eight years afterwards the Gewissas gained another great battle over the Britons at Cerdices-leah.[4] Cerdic's

[1] A.D. 1519. H. Hunt. lib. ii.

[2] Beda, iii. 7, and Smith's note. "Occidentales Saxones, qui antiquitus Gevissæ vocabantur." — So called either from their western locality, analogously with Visigothi, or from Gewis, the great-grandfather of Cerdic. Asser, Vita Ælfr. *init.*, says, "Gewis, a quo Britones totam illam gentem Gegwis nominant." The British historians also, who never distinguish the other tribes, know the Giuoys. See Annal. Camb. a. 900. Geoffrey of Monm. iv. 15, v. 8, viii. 10, xii. 14, [who speaks of Gewissi in Warwickshire and Worcestershire during the time of the Romans. The denomination as applied to a British tribe, was probably derived by the traditionists of that nation from Gevissa, the mother of Glovi, from whom, according to them, the city of Gloucester was named.—T.]

[3] Gildas, c. xxvi., where see Stevenson's pref. p. viii. Radulphus in R. Higdeni Polychron. p. 224. Ric. Divisiensis MS. ap. Langhorne, Chron. Regum Angliæ, p. 70.

[4] A.D. 527.

death is recorded in the sixteenth year of his reign, over the West Saxons, and like that of Hengest and Ælle, in the fortieth after his arrival in Britain,[1] a number, it would appear, used merely to denote a long reign, the precise duration of which is not known. A similar custom of using this number for any undetermined large number prevailed also among the Persians, even when the real number was known to be larger. Cynric succeeded his father in Wessex: the Isle of Wight was given, as a kingdom dependent on Wessex, to his cousins, of whom Wihtgar, it is said, was a son of Cerdic's sister.[2] The Isle of Wight was peopled by Jutes; hence it is probable that Cerdic's sister was married to a powerful Jute, whose sons led their victorious followers from Jutland, if not from Kent, which had been long inhabited by that people.

Cynric gradually extended the boundaries of his kingdom, the capital of which was Winchester (Wintanceaster), the old Venta Belgarum. A vast army of Britons being assembled to attack him, he, in conjunction with the forces of his friends, hastened to encounter them, and near Searobyrig (Old Sarum[3]) totally defeated and put their numerous host to flight. Less favourable to Cynric and his son Ceawlin was a great battle fought some years later against the united forces

---

[1] So W. Malm. According to the Sax. Chron., which places his death in 534, he died in the thirty-ninth year after his arrival, according to the calculation of the lunar year before noticed with regard to Hengest. [According to five MSS., Malmesbury assigns a reign of only fifteen years to Cerdic; only two MSS. have sixteen.—T.]

[2] Asseri Vita Ælfredi, init. W. Malm. lib. i. c. 2. According to H. Hunt. lib. ii. this donation took place in 534, shortly before the death of Cerdic.   [3] A.D. 552.

of the Britons, in which the latter were indebted to their order of battle, according to the rules of Roman tactics,[1] for their preservation from the defeat with which they were threatened by the strength and valour of the Saxons. The chronicles assign to Cynric a reign of twenty-six years, yet state his death to have taken place in the sixty-fifth year after his landing in Britain; but an account seems to have existed, according to which he, like the son of Hengest, died in the sixty-fourth year after his arrival, and consequently in the twenty-fourth year after the death of Cerdic.[2] Contradictions between historic traditions and the verses of the poet were from the first difficult to reconcile, and they are much more so now. All that is incumbent on us is to point out the great uncertainty of the several accounts, though the facts which are recorded may in their general outlines be acknowledged as authentic.

Although it may excite no surprise that, in a time of universal dissolution, the occupation of isolated tracts of coast by an enemy attracted at first but little notice, and that at a later period the reward of historic glory was bestowed only on the new and powerful lords of

---

[1] A.D. 556. H. Hunt. lib. ii. "Novem acies ... tribus scilicet in fronte locatis, et tribus in medio, et tribus in fine, ducibusque in ipsis aciebus convenienter institutis, virisque sagittariis et telorum jaculatoribus equitibusque jure Romanorum dispositis." A similar passage occurs shortly after, "Cum autem Britones more Romanorum acies distincte admoverent."

[2] Sax. Chron. Fl. of Worc. a. 560. H. Hunt. "Regnum Westsexe incipit anno adventus Anglorum lxxi., anno ab incarnatione Domini 519." "Cerdic regnavit xvii. annis in Westsexe." According to this account Cynric succeeded his father in 536, or twenty-four years before his death; though the same chronicler says, "Kinric cum regnasset xxvi. annis mortuus est."

the soil, it might, nevertheless, have been expected that circumstantial and trustworthy accounts would have informed us of the events connected with the city of London, a place of prominent interest in every age, through its commerce and the arts inseparable therefrom. But the pen of the genius of trade is, like the net of the fisher, devoted only to the contemplated gain. No territory ever passed so obscurely into the possession of an enemy as the north bank of the Thames, where the kingdom of the East Saxons comprised the counties of Essex and Middlesex, of which the latter continued probably for some time in a state of independence. The year 527 is mentioned as that of the first landing of the Saxons there; and Æscwine, or Ercenwine,[1] as its first prince, a son of Offa, a descendant of Seaxneat (Saxnôt), the abjuration of whose worship, together with that of Thor (Thunaer) and Woden, was, after a lapse of ages, exacted from the Saxon converts of the continent.[2] Æscwine is said to have reigned during a patriarchal period of sixty years: his name reminds us of Æsc, the prince of the Jutes, on the southern shore of the Thames, and of the race of the Æscings, though that of his father would indicate a relationship to the Offings, the royal race of Mercia; while his descent from the Saxon gods, as well as the name of his kingdom, speak for his pure Saxon lineage. The geographical position of this state may, however, be rather in favour of the supposition of a mixture of several races, to which the account of a more critical chronicler, who gives Sleda, in the year 587, as the first king of Essex, seems no

[1] H. Hunt. Geneal. in Fl. of Worc.
[2] See Grimm, D. M. p. 203. Massmann's 'Abschwörungsformeln,' pp. 14, 67   Pertz, Monum. Hist. Germ. t. iii. p. 19.—T.

contradiction;[1] though it is far from improbable that the earliest settlements of the Germans on this coast reach up to a much more remote period, and have connection with the appellation of 'Litus Saxonicum.'

Northward of the East Saxons was established the kingdom of the East Angles, in which a northern and a southern part (Northfolc and Suthfolc) were distinguished. It is probable that, during the last period of the Roman sway, Germans were settled in this part of Britain; a supposition that gains in probability from several old Saxon sagas, which have reference to East Anglia at a period anterior to the coming of Hengest and Horsa. The land of the Gyrwas, containing twelve hundred hides, which was also accurately divided into a southern and a northern portion, comprised the neighbouring marsh districts of Ely and Huntingdonshire, almost as far as Lincoln. Of the East Angles Wehha or Wewa,[2] or more commonly his son, Uffa or Wuffa, from whom his race derived their patronymic of Uffings or Wuffings, is recorded as the first king.[3]

The neighbouring states of Mercia originated in the marsh-districts of the Lindisware, or inhabitants of Lindsey (Lindesig), the northern part of Lincolnshire. With these were united the Middle Angles.[4] This kingdom, divided by the Trent into a southern and a northern portion, gradually extended itself to the borders of Wales. Among the states which it comprised

[1] W. Malm. lib. i. c. 6. He makes no mention of his father, but says merely that he was the tenth in descent from Wodon, which involves no inconsistency with the other accounts.

[2] Fl. of Worc. Geneal. ap. Petrie. Nennii App.

[3] Beda, ii. 15. H. Hunt. a. 571.

[4] Beda, i. 15, iii. 21. Malmesb. de Antiq. Glaston. Eccles. ap. Gale, i. p. 295.

was the little kingdom of the Hwiccas, conterminous with the later diocese of Worcester, or the counties of Gloucester, Worcester, and a part of Warwick. This state, together with that of the Hecanas, comprising the ancient bishopric of Hereford, bore the common Germanic appellation of the land of the Magesætas.[1]

Henry of Huntingdon, though a writer abounding in traditions, and, at the same time, a native or inhabitant of those parts, gives us no legends relative to the establishment of the two last-mentioned states. After the victory at Cerdices-ford, and probably at an earlier period, many chieftains passed over from Germany to those territories, and, in emulation of each other, possessed themselves of several tracts. Their number has caused their names to be forgotten; but their territories towards the end of the century were united with the two last-mentioned kingdoms.[2] Creoda, or Cridda, the son of Cynewald, and tenth in descent from Woden,[3] appears as the first king of Mercia.

In addition to the doubts attending the descent, and even the name of the Angles, the genealogies of their kings demand and merit discussion. In that of the kings of Mercia we find three names in succession, which accord with a similar unbroken series in the Danish traditions, viz. the descendants of Woden,

[1] Fl. of Worc. Appen.
[2] H. Hunt. p. 313. "Ea tempestate venerunt multi et sæpe de Germania, et occupaverunt East-angle et Merce." Matt. Westmon. a. 527. Radulphus ap. Higden Polychron. lib. v. p. 224, has the year 492. Florence says of Mercia merely, "Post initium regni Cantuariorum, principium extitit regni Merciorum." But of East Anglia, "Regno *posterius* Cantuariorum, et *prius* regno Occidentalium Saxonum exortum est;" consequently before the year 495.
[3] Sax. Chron. a. 626.

Wihtlæg, Wærmund, and Uffa[1], who stand in the Danish chronicles as Wiglet, Wermund and Uffo, descendants of Odin, and ancestors of the conquerors of Britain.[2] Even the resemblance of the names of Offa's posterity, Angeltheow and Eomer to the Danish Ingeld and Iaomer is very remarkable; and after what has already been stated, it seems the more worthy of notice that the progenitors of Woden, both in the Anglo-Saxon and Scandinavian genealogies, have many names in common, and that among these Sceaf is regarded in the latter as a king of Sleswick, or the country of Angeln. An inquiry into the value of these resemblances in an historic point of view would here, perhaps, be out of place; but attention should be directed to the evidence furnished by this accordance of the traditions, in favour of deriving the origin of the Angles and Mercians from the country north of the Eider.

The history of the Angles receives some light from a Byzantine historian. Procopius, who died in 562, before Uffa reigned in East Anglia, mentions a king of the Angles in Brittia or Britain, in the years 534–547, whose sister was betrothed to Radiger, king of the Warni, but who, on the death of his father, in violation of his engagement, married his stepmother, a sister of the Frankish king Theudebert. To revenge the slight, the Anglian lady, after a fruitless expostulation by embassy, sailed, with an army, and attended

[1] Sax. Chron. In Nennius, Guithleg, Guerdmund, and Offa.
[2] See Erici Chron. Sax. Grammat. Sv. Aggonis Hist. Reg. Dan. c. i. has only the two last. The Icelandic Langfedgatal also omits the first, and calls Uffo, Olaf. It seems pretty evident that this genealogy, though given as Danish in the Danish Chronicles, is that of the Anglian kings of Sleswick, the ancestors of the kings of Mercia.

by one of her brothers, to an outlet of the Rhine. In a battle which followed their landing, the Warni were defeated, and their prince, being captured in his flight, was brought bound into the presence of the Angle, who, to his glad surprise, after reproaching him for his want of faith, and on his promise to atone for it by renouncing his stepmother and fulfilling his prior engagement, restored him to liberty and treated him honourably. Their marriage followed as a matter of course.[1] However fabulous other accounts communicated by that writer may be, concerning some Angles sent to the emperor Justinian at Constantinople, the fact is, nevertheless, worthy of notice, that Angles and Frisians are mentioned by him as inhabitants of the island, as also a king of the Angles, which proves (as in the before-mentioned laws) a connection between the Angles and the Warni. The same author also states, that the powerful king of the Franks, Theudebert, took advantage of the emigration of some Angles to his country, and of the distracted condition of Britain, to arrogate to himself the appearance of a supremacy over it, which was in conformity with the pretensions of the Frankish monarchs to the dignity of Emperor of the West, and also finds additional grounds in the ancient provincial administration, under which Britain was considered a diocese subordinate to Gaul. Political relations between the Anglo-Saxons and the court of Byzantium of a tendency hostile to the Franks, were in the following century apprehended by the latter,[2]—a suspicion which at least implies other close connections between them. It may be with reference to such relations that the Welsh bard, Lawarch Hên, who lived in

[1] De Bello Gothico, iv. 20. [2] Beda, iv. 1.

this century, speaks of the warriors of Wessex as Franks. Pope Gregory the Great also, in a letter to the Frankish kings, Theuderic and Theudebert, relative to his design of converting the Angles, appears to speak of them as subjects of those princes; from which, however, nothing is perhaps to be inferred beyond pretensions, which he deemed it advisable to treat with delicacy and favour in his intercourse with his royal Christian allies.[1] We think, moreover, that in the account given by the Byzantine writer of this war, and its relations to the Frankish kings, we have grounds for assuming that the ancient Roman province of Britain was already known to the rulers and writers among other nations under the name of England,—a name destined more than once to assert its supremacy in both hemispheres. Yet in this—the sixth century—we find that the Pope, Gregory the Great, still knows and speaks of the inhabitants of Southern Britain only under the name of Angles, whilst the name of the more powerful Saxons prevailed still longer in the land, and never wholly disappeared from the nomenclature of their Celtic neighbours.

The history and the poetry of those remote and unlettered ages have long lain reconciled in the same grave, and we cannot awaken the ashes of the one without—and often unconsciously—bringing the other back to light. As connected with this remark, we must not omit to mention that East Anglia contains a

---

[1] Gregorii Epist. lib. vi. c. 58. Bedæ Opera Minora ed. Stevenson, p. 234 . . . "magnam de vobis materiam præsumendi concepimus, quod subjectos vestros ad eam converti fidem per omnia cupiatis, in qua eorum nempe reges estis et domini. Atque ideo pervenit ad nos Anglorum gentem ad fidem Christianam, Deo miserante, desideranter velle converti."

little known and still less investigated rich store of old traditions: among others the saga of King Atla of Northfolk, the founder of Attlebury; of Roud, king of Thetford;[1] also the yet more wide-spread one of Havelok, or Cuharan (Cwiran), king of Northfolk, and son of Ethelbert the Dane, who dwelt in that country before the time of Hengest and Horsa,[2]—traditions which seem to confirm that which history, from the days of Carausius, renders far from improbable.

The country to the north of the Humber had suffered the most severely from the inroads of the Picts and Scots. It had been at an early period separated into two British states, the names of which were retained for some centuries, viz. Deifyr (Deora rice), afterwards Latinized into Deira, extending from the Humber to the Tyne, and Berneich (Beorna rice), afterwards

[1] This poem, consisting of about 12,000 verses, was originally either in Anglo-Saxon or Semi-Saxon, and was translated into French verse at the desire of a certain countess, *when the original could not be understood* (i. e. by the Anglo-Norman nobility), probably in the thirteenth century; which version was translated into Latin by John Brame or Brome, who informs us that the French differed considerably from the English original. The original name of the king appears to have been Waldeus, not Atla. The Latin elaboration of the poem is in the library of C.C.C. Camb. A manuscript of the French Romance of King Atla, once Mr. Heber's, is now in the possession of Sir T. Phillipps, Bart. See Sir F. Madden's note in Warton, H. E. P. vol. i. p. 41, edit. 1840.—T.

[2] A limited edition of 'The Ancient English Romance of Havelok the Dane,' 4to, accompanied by the French text and a valuable glossary, was published in 1828 by Sir F. Madden. The tale of Havelok is also given in 'L'Estorie des Engles, solum la Translation Maistre Geffrei Gaimar,' ap. Petrie, C. H. p. 764. Later English chroniclers likewise (as Knyghton, lib. i. c. 5, make mention of the story. [In 1868 'Havelok the Dane' was re-edited by the Rev. W. W. Skeat, M.A.—E. C. O.]

Bernicia, from the Tyne to the Clyde. Here also the settlements of the German races appear anterior to the date given in the common accounts of the first Anglian kings of those territories, in the middle of the sixth century. The traditions respecting Hengest relate that he founded for his son Octa, and for Ebusa the son of Horsa,[1] Germanic states in the north of Northumbria, or, according to the older traditions, beyond the Firth of Forth, whither they sailed with forty ships, but which seemed inconsistent with the account, that Hengest himself, when driving before him the Picts and Scots, did not advance further than Lincolnshire. According to a much neglected account, Deira had already been separated from Bernicia by Soemil the son of Zegulf (Sæfugl), whose grandson Guilglis (Wihtgils) was the father of Hengest, and grandfather of Yffe (Yffi), of whom we are about to speak;[2] and we know also, from other accounts, that both Hengest and Yffe descended from the same son of Woden, Wecta or Wægdæg.[3] This tradition is important from the information it contains that the Saxon settlements in the North of Britain were older than those in the

[1] Nennius, c. xxxviii. W. Malm. lib. i., who calls Octa the brother of Hengest and Ebusa the son. A confirmation of these accounts may be found in Geoffrey of Monm. lib. i. c. i., where Modrawd promises to Childeric the country between the Humber and Scotland, and that which in Vortigern's time Horsa and Hengest possessed in Kent. According to Geoffrey, who is here very prolix, Octa son of Hengest received York, and his cousin Eosa, Alcluyd with the remaining country bordering on Scotland. See lib. viii. c. 6, 8, 18, 21, 23. Abisa, Ebusa, Eowis, Eosa denote the same individual.

[2] Nenn. App. Soemil and his son Swearta (Swerthing) are wanting in the genealogy given in the Sax. Chron. Swerthing, a prince of the Saxons, was the slayer of Frothi IV. See Saxo. pp. 273, 282, edit. Müller.

[3] Sax. Chron. a. 560, etc.

South. Attention must also here again be drawn to the circumstance already noticed, that while the South-English chronicles fix the landing of Hengest and Horsa in, or rather after, the year 449, the oldest North-English authorities place the arrival of the Angles in 445 or 446, not to mention the earlier invasion of these people. Nennius fixes 447 for the year of Hengest's landing, from which it would seem that the Saxon chieftains of the North threw off the supremacy of the Kentish kings after a lapse of a full century, instead of founding, according to the received tradition, a new kingdom in the year 547. Fifty years later, or about the year 500, the city of Eboracum is said to have been taken by the Saxons, and the archbishop to have fled to Armorica, where he founded the bishopric of Dol. Nor perhaps is the story to be totally rejected that Colgrim and his brother Baldwulph conquered these countries, but were beaten by Arthur in the year 516, on the river Duglas.[1]

Ida, the son of Eoppa, a descendant of Woden (to whom in this genealogy five forefathers are assigned), is, according to the Anglo-Saxon traditions, regarded as the founder of the Anglian kingdom of Bernicia, in the year 547; or rather as the first who freed the land, hitherto governed by nine subordinate rulers, from the supremacy of the kings of Kent.[2] He arrived with forty or sixty ships of the Angles,[3] and, after having reigned twelve years, is said to have fallen in a battle against Urien of Cumberland and Reged, leaving

[1] Nenn. c. lxiv. Geof. of Monmouth, lib. ix. c. 1, and from the latter, Matt. Westm. a. 516.
[2] Scala Chron. Cf. Gale ad Nennium, c. lxv. W. Malm. lib. i.
[3] Chronol. ap. Wanley and Petrie. Flor. of Worc. Sim. Dunelm Wallingford.

twelve sons. Bebbanburh, now Bamborough, perpetuates the name of his consort Bebbe.[1] His immediate successor seems to have been Glappa, who was followed by Adda, Æthelric, and Theodric, sons of Ida. About the same time Ælle son of Yffe (Yffi), of descent equally illustrious, conquered the greater part of the kingdom of Deira.[2]

So trivial, and yet more uncertain, are the accounts left us of the conquest of a great kingdom by the barbarous dwellers on the shores of the German Ocean, and of the spoliation perpetrated among structures and other property, the fruits of Roman civilization, on a people accustomed to servitude, who knew but little how to use them and still less to defend them.

The Britons were soon restricted to the western parts of the island, where they maintained themselves in several small states, of which those lying to the east yielded more and more to Germanic influence; the others, protected by their mountains, preserved for a considerable time a gradually decreasing independence. As opportunities for touching on the history of these small British states will hereafter be but

[1] Sax. Chron. a. 547. According to Nenn. App. Bebbe was the consort of Æthelfrith, the grandson of Ida. "Eadfered Flesaurs regnavit xii. annis in Berneich, et alios xii. in Deur, . . . et dedit uxori suæ Dinguo Aroy, quæ vocatur Bebbab, et de nomine suæ uxoris suscepit nomen, id est, Bebbanburch." The passage in Beda (iii. 6) does not decide who was the husband of Bebbe.

[2] Sax. Chron. a. 560. In stating the perplexed genealogy of the kings of Bernicia to the year 592, the authority has been followed of the chronicle in Wanley and Petrie, and of Simeon, who in matters connected with Northumbria is particularly trustworthy. These two authorities, though slightly differing in the regnal years, agree in the order of succession, while the lists in Florence and Nennius are irreconcilable both with the above authorities and with each other.—T.

rarely afforded, a short notice of them is the more desirable; though some separate states occasionally occur as united into one, while others may have arisen from comparatively later partitions.

In the south-west we meet with the powerful territory of Damnonia, the kingdom of Arthur, which bore also the name of West Wales. Damnonia, at a later period, was limited to Dyvnaint, or Devonshire, by the separation of Cernau, or Cornwall. The districts called by the Saxons those of the Sumorsætas, of the Dornsætas (Dorsetshire), and the Wilsætas were lost to the kings of Dyvnaint at an early period; though for centuries afterwards a large British population maintained itself in those parts among the Saxon settlers, as well as among the Defnsætas, long after the Saxon conquest of Dyvnaint, who for a considerable time preserved to the natives of that shire the appellation of the ' Welsh kind.'

Cambria (Cymru), the country which at the present day we call Wales, was divided into several states, the chief of which were—Venedotia (Gwynedd), consisting of the greater part of North Wales. The king of Gwynedd was supreme over the other states; his residence was at Aberfraw;[1]—Dimetia (Dyved), or West Wales,[2] comprising the district bounded by the

---

[1] Now a village on the west coast of Anglesea. Its name *aber Fraw, the efflux of the Fraw*) is derived from being situated where the brook Fraw flows into the sea. Glossary to Anc. LL. and Inst. of Wales.—T.

[2] Or South Wales; but as Cornwall is sometimes called South Wales, in like manner the name of West Wales is applied to Dimetia. Much valuable information respecting the old geography and inhabitants of Wales is to be found in the 'Itinerarium,' 'Cambriæ Descriptio,' and ' De Illaudabilibus Walliæ' of Giraldus. [See also Ancient Laws and Institutes of Wales, from which, and

Tywi on the south-east, and the Tewi on the north-west, or, in a wider sense, the country over which the ecclesiastical supremacy of the see of Mynyw or Menevia (St. David's) extended. The residence of the Dimetian princes was at Dinevwr.[1] To the east of Gwynedd and the mountains, of which Snowdon forms the highest point, was Powys, the princes of which resided at Mathraval.[2] In Deheubarth, or South Wales, were several small states, the southernmost of which, Gwent (Monmouthshire), or South-east Wales, the country of the Silures, forming the present diocese of Llandaff (Landav), the royal seat of which was at Caerleon upon Usk, while Morganwg (Glamorganshire) lay on the northern bank of the Severn. Near, if not comprised within this state, between the rivers Usk and Taff, was the small principality of Gleguising. Along the Irish Channel lay Ceredigion and Brecheiniog, whose names are easily recognised in those of the present counties, and which appear to have been under separate rulers.

The chief tribes of the Britons, or, as they call themselves, Cymry, are distinguished by the various dialects of their common mother-tongue, among which the Venedotian, the Dimetian, and that of Glamorgan, are the principal. The Cymrian tongue was polished by illustrious poets,—Aneurin and Taliesin in the sixth,

---

from Mr. Owen's notes, the account of the ancient territorial division of Wales given in this translation has been chiefly compiled.—T.]

[1] Near Llandilo vawr, in the Vale of Tywi. Some remains of the castle are visible.—T.

[2] Situated in the upper part of the Vale of Meivod, near the junction of the two streams which form the river Evyrnwy. Gloss. ut sup.—T.

and Llywarch Hên and others in the next following centuries, whose works in a state of tolerable purity have been preserved to the present time.[1]

The usages and laws of the Cambrians were in all these states essentially the same. An invaluable and venerable monument of them, although of an age in which the Welsh had long been subject to the Anglo-Saxons, and had adopted many of their institutions and customs, are the laws of the king Howel Dda,[2] who reigned in the early part of the tenth century, which, with some local modifications, were acknowledged as valid in the other states of Wales.

The partition of Cambria into several small states is not, as it has often been supposed, the consequence of a division made by king Rodri Mawr, or Roderic the Great, among his sons; but which, supposing it to have taken place, could have reference only to the sovereignty over territories which many centuries before occur as separate states. Of Dyfed, during the first centuries after the coming of the Saxons, we know very little; but with regard to Gwynedd, which was in constant warfare with Northumbria and Mercia, our information is less scanty: of Gwent also, as the bulwark of Dimetia, frequent mention occurs. On the whole we are less in want of a mass of information respecting the Welsh, than of accuracy and precision in that which we possess. While the Welsh, in their historic narratives,—as remarkable for singularity of

[1] See Turner's Vindication of the genuineness of the ancient British poems, at the end of the last volume of the third and following editions of his 'History of the Anglo-Saxons.'
[2] In the Venedotian and Dimetian Codes, Howel styles himself 'king' or 'prince of all Cymru;' in the Gwentian Code, 'king of Cymru, when the bounds of Cymru were in his possession.'—T.

expression as for their poetic garb, give either no dates whatever, or dates on which no reliance can be placed, the several states and their rulers are seldom spoken of in the Anglo-Saxon chronicles otherwise than under the universal appellation of the Britons, and their kings : hence a comparison of their respective accounts is frequently impracticable, each nation usually speaking only of its victories, very rarely of its reverses.

An obscurity still more dense than that over Wales involves the district lying to the north of that country, comprised under the name of Cumbria. This territory, sometimes united under a supreme chief, or Pendragon, called also Tyern (Tyrannus), who, like the other British princes, considered themselves not only as the successors, but also as the descendants of Constantine, or of Maximus, consisted of three principal parts. The southern, or Cumberland, properly so called, comprised, besides the present county of that name, also Lancashire and Westmoreland, which latter appears likewise as a petty kingdom—Westmere. It extended into the later kingdom of Northumbria; and as the little state of Elmet seems also to have belonged to it, the town of Leeds must have been on its border. The old Roman Lugubalia, or Carleol, was its largest city, in which Arthur, Rhyddrich Hael, or the Liberal, and other princes celebrated in ancient song, are said to have held their Round Table or court.[1] The two northernmost kingdoms of the Britons, Reged and Strathcluyd, belong to the history of Scotland ; yet as England extended as far as Edinburgh, they must not be passed without mention. Reged, a territory in the south of Scotland, in or near Annandale, is rendered worthy of notice on account of the protection offered to the bard

[1] A.D. 561.

Taliesin by its prince Urien, celebrated by Llywarch Hên, who was himself a prince of Argoed in Cumberland. The kingdom of Strathcluyd, comprising Clydesdale or Dumbartonshire—where its chief city, Alcluyd, was situated—the counties of Renfrew and Dumfries, and probably those of Peebles, Selkirk, and Lanark, in the east, continued to a much later period; and, although in constant warfare with the Anglo-Saxons, as well as with the Picts and Scots, its chiefs extended their power over all Cumberland, from which they were not expelled till the early part of the tenth century, when Cumberland, under Anglo-Saxon suzerainty, became a principality held by the heir of Scotland.

With respect to the first institutions adopted by the German chieftains in the conquered country, how the relations of service and tribute were fixed; how the Germans gradually united themselves into considerable kingdoms; how far the remains of Roman civilization, when they afforded no apparent or palpable advantage, were respected,—with regard to all this we have little beyond supposition; though the result, the Saxonizing of Britain by the Germanic heretogas, or ealdormen, and their followers, is as manifest as the Romanizing of Spanish America by Columbus and Pizarro. Of the history of these kingdoms from their foundation till their gradual conversion to Christianity, there exist scarcely any written accounts besides the series of their kings, which, in detached traditions, form but a very insignificant component of the national history.

While Anglo-Saxon sources are wanting, the British ones also either fail us, or must undergo a stricter critical ordeal than they have hitherto passed through, before any reliance can be placed on them. Even the earliest Anglo-Saxon laws are too recent, and too exclusively restricted to the Germanic scale of penalties and atonements, to aid us in drawing a picture of the condition of the country immediately after the Saxon conquest. Their silence on many points leads us, perhaps, on comparing them with the laws of other Germanic conquerors, to divine more than their scanty diction expresses.

(157)

CHAPTER VIII.

FROM THE MIDDLE OF THE FIFTH TO CLOSE OF SIXTH CENTURY.

Condition of Britain—The Dignity of Bretwalda—Kingship among Germans and Northmen—Ceawlin of Wessex—Marriage of Æthelberht with Berhta—Conversion of Men of Kent—British Churches—Gregory—Augustine—Interview between King and Augustine—Baptism of King—Conference between Augustine and British Bishops—Arrogance and want of Conciliation on both sides.

PUBLIC affairs in Britain had, in consequence of the departure of the Romans and the inroads of enemies, fallen into the utmost disorder. The property both public and private that had formerly belonged to the Romans became, either by purchase or usurpation, a new unsettled possession in the hands of a people who had long forgotten how to govern. The inhabitants of the island were at that time, as their language sufficiently shows, scarcely to be called Romanized : on the contrary, the posterity of the Romans among them had rather assimilated themselves to the original Britons. In this state of dissolution it must have been an easier task to the conquerors of Britain than their warlike brethren found it in the better organized states of Europe, to obtain possession of the objects of their ambition without causing the rights of the stronger to be felt in the most oppressive manner. The former Roman property, which in the south, and especially on the coasts, must have been considerable, would satisfy the small number of strangers. That a certain portion of landed property, of rents, or of produce, was regularly set apart for the conquerors, as was the custom in other Germanic states, is not probable, as in the accounts of the later conquests of the Anglo-Saxons in Britain, we meet with nothing leading to such a conclusion. Indeed the very gradual progress made in the occupation of many parts of Britain by detached hordes, independent of each other, and of various races, almost induces us to regard it less as a conquest than as a progressive usurpation of the British territory. From the circumstance that the Anglo-Saxons had to pass over in ships to the country destined for their future home, it follows that they brought with them but few women and children; and as Vortigern had no repugnance to an union with the daughter of Hengest, it is probable that the German warriors, with the exception, perhaps, of a few of noble race, would not disdain to unite themselves with the British women. If thereby the natives soon became intermingled with the strangers, still the latter, in virtue of the almost exclusive advantage of the male line with respect to inheritances, would not find such marriages prejudicial to their political independence. Many Britons fled before the pagan Germans, but the facility of flight weakened the power of resistance, and accelerated the advances of the enemy. Those Britons who, not being prisoners of war, peaceably remained, appear to have preserved their previous rights; since we find no considerable difference between the Britons and the Saxons,[1] with regard to the wergild, the capability of bearing witness, and other rights.

[1] Laws of Ine, xxiii., xxiv., xxxii.

A most important subject for consideration, as we early observe, was the dignity of Bretwalda, which was only borne by one of the most influential of the Anglo-Saxon princes during the period of his life, and which is said to have been recognized as supreme over all the inhabitants of Britain. The desire to trace the continuance of Roman institutions has also led some enquirers to see in this dignity an imitation of that of the Roman emperors of the West, acknowledged at the same time both by Saxons and Britons.[1] The acknowledgment of the Britons, who were still united under a sovereignty of their own, may be most confidently denied, but that a passion for imitation in the Saxon warriors could prompt them to favour one of their fellows, who aspired to the authority of their most formidable and hated enemy, may be very strongly doubted. The pretensions of the most powerful Anglo-Saxon king scarcely extended over the Germanic provinces of the southern part of Britain: to other portions of the Roman dominion they never reached. Imitation, both in the uncivilized and the weak, begins with the tinsel of unsubstantial show, with the assumption of an empty name, of neither of which any trace appears among the Anglo-Saxons till after the lapse of some centuries. With the inquiry into the origin of the office of Bretwalda, which in its later form exhibited perhaps some traces of Roman imperial influence, may, in the absence of more satisfactory accounts respecting the duties and rights ascribed to that dignity, be joined the questions, what notions the Germans brought from their native country, and what occasion they found in Britain for the appointment of that relative supremacy?

[1] Palgrave, vol. i. p. 563.

To the North-Germanic and Danish nations kings ruling over the whole race were unknown, each people being divided under several chieftains;[1] and we know that among these, although the consideration of birth prevailed, their leaders in war were chosen from the most valiant. To them nothing could be more foreign than to found the dominion of a whole race on a common language or on kinship.

Of the Jutes and Danes especially, we know that they for several centuries lived under a great number of kings, but that they acknowledged the supremacy of the kings of Leire—in like manner as the Swedish kings were subordinate to those of Upsala—and that monarchy (einvalld) was a later institution among them.[2] The Frisian chiefs also acknowledged a superior. In Britain a connection between the southern and northern Saxons was, as we have already seen, established as early as the first conquests of Hengest. The necessity of a common chief over all the Germanic provinces arose in Britain partly from the great number of independent kings, ealdormen and other potentates, whose states only in the course of time lapsed into the kingdoms of the 'Heptarchy;' and partly from the necessity of opposing a united resistance to the Britons, combined against the divided power of the foreign intruders, as well as to the Picts and Scots. For this purpose the Germans in Britain must have soon found an alliance among their tribes indispensable, and of no other form of union is a trace to be discovered, nor even conceivable. A common warfare of several states without a dictator was not to be conceived; and the call to that post was on the most powerful, or on

[1] Cf. Dahlmann's 'Forschungen,' Bd. i. p. 431 sq.
[2] Snorre, Ynglinga Saga, c. xlv.

him whose territory was most exposed to hostile inroads. The latter case we find the most frequent. Sussex is said to have first enjoyed that supremacy when it had to defend Kent. Kent laid claim to it while it yet possessed rights of suzerainty in the north, and subsequently obtained it; possibly as an indemnity for its renunciation of such rights.

Wessex next formed the bulwark; but this state having strengthened itself, and the struggle being carried on more northwards, the chief military command passed to East Anglia, and lastly to Northumbria; neither of whose Anglian states acknowledged the authority of the Bretwalda[1] until the condition of affairs had become changed. That those states used the transient power for the aggrandizement of their territory was in the nature of things, and, at the same time, not inconsistent with the object of the institution. The elective emperor of the Germans, whose dignity was not attached to hereditary states, nor to descent, but to the importance of the individual, represents what the Bretwalda might have been, if the general interest could have been conceived by the barbarian conquerors from a higher point of view. It is probable that not only the choice of the other kings, but also of the collective nobility and ealdormen, determined the nomination of the Bretwalda; for as, according to the words of an old writer, he possessed sovereign power

---

[1] Beda, i. 25. "Rex Ædilberctus in Cantia potentissimus, qui ad confinium usque Humbræ fluminis maximi, quo meridiani et septentrionales Anglorum populi dirimuntur, fines imperii tetenderat." Lib. ii. 5. "Ædilberct . . . tertius quidem in regibus gentis Anglorum, cunctis australibus eorum provinciis quæ Humbræ fluvio et contiguis ei terminis sequestrantur a borealibus, imperavit." See also lib. ii. 3.

over all these,[1] it is to be inferred that, in the spirit of Germanic forms of government, the appointment was the result of a preceding free election.[2]

[1] "Omnia jura regni Anglorum, reges scilicet et proceres et tribunos in ditione sua tenebat." H. Hunt. lib. ii.

[2] The sole source, whence all our information regarding these paramount kings is derived, is Beda (H. E. lib. ii. 5), who supplies us with a list of seven. The Saxon Chronicle, after copying Beda (a. 827), adds Ecgberht as an eighth. The first of them is Ælle, who landed in Sussex from three ships; and, five or six years after, having received considerable reinforcements from Germany, crushed the Britons and destroyed their stronghold Anderida; in consequence of which success he appears to have obtained a preponderance that either prompted him to assume, or his followers, or the contemporary chieftains, to confer on him, the title of Brytenwalda, or Bretwalda (lord over the Britons). Ceawlin, king of Wessex, the second in the list, obtained the title, according to all probability, in like manner, by his successes against the Britons. How Æthelberht, king of Kent, the third on the list, acquired it, history omits to inform us; though Beda tells us that he held sway over all the country as far as the Humber, and might, therefore, well be "walda," or ruler, over a considerable British population; as the Germanic state of Mercia was then in its early infancy. Equally unknown to us is the way in which Rædwald, king of East Anglia, obtained the title. He possibly assumed it on the defeat of Æthelfrith of Northumbria, and, if an evidently corrupt passage in Beda (lib. ii. 5) may be so interpreted ("qui etiam, vivente Ædilbereto, eidem (eundem?) suæ genti ducatum præbebat") during the lifetime of Rædwald. The three Northumbrian kings, Eadwine, Oswald, and Oswiu, either assumed, or had the title of Brytenwalda conferred on them by their people, as one denoting supremacy, without regard to its primitive signification, as is the case at the present day among ourselves. For who now in an usher (huissier, from old Fr. huis, *door*), whether of the black or the birchen rod, sees a door-keeper? or in a marshal (Olg. maruh, *horse*, and scalh, schalk, *servant*), whether city- or field-, a horseboy?* And does not the protestant sovereign of England

---

* The French, in the word *maréchal* (a farrier), have retained something of the primitive signification.

Notwithstanding the high estimation in which this dignity was held from a very early period, Beda is yet unable to inform us who was invested with it after Ælle, until Ceawlin, the grandson of Cerdic, became its possessor. A noble Æscing, the young Æthelberht of Kent, disputed it with him, and invaded with his arms the territory of Wessex. A defeat at Wibbandun (Wimbledon in Surrey)[1] humbled the

---

still retain the title of defender of the (Roman Catholic) faith, conferred by the pope on Henry VIII., for having written against the protestant faith? and until recently that of king of France? and are there not still kings of Cyprus and Jerusalem? From the foregoing it will be seen that I do not place implicit confidence in the words of Beda, whose information regarding the southern states of the "Heptarchy" was far from perfect, but rather incline to the supposition, that the title in question was either assumed by its bearer, or conferred on him by his army or people without regard to its primitive import. Whether he bore the name of Brytenwalda, or Bretwalda, seems doubtful.

Mr. J. M. Kemble ('Saxons in England,' ii. p. 20), would render Brytenwalda by "an extensive, powerful king," deriving its first component from the verb breótan, *to distribute, divide*; but this interpretation I think hardly applicable to the case, although I admit that it seems countenanced by Ethelweard, who, translating the Saxon Chronicle, renders the word by *pollens potestate*. But is bryten, in the sense of *extensive*, &c., ever found in prose? I believe not. Against this rendering is also Mr. Kemble's own citation from the Codex Diplomaticus (V. pp. 217, 218), viz., "Ego Æthelstanus, Angul-Saxonum necnon et totius *Britanniæ rex*," which is afterwards expressed in Saxon by "Ic Æthelstân, Ongol-Saxna cyning and *brytænwalda* eallæs ðyses iglandæs;" ib. p. 22 he says: "I am not prepared to admit the probability of a territorial title, at a time when kings were kings of the people, not of the land." But what is "totius Britanniæ rex"? not to notice numerous similar instances in the Codex Diplomaticus. The word Bretwalda occurs but once (Sax. Chron. a. 827), and Brytenwalda only in the charter of Æthelstân just quoted.

[1] Sax. Chron. a. 568. W. Malm. lib. i. H. Hunt. lib. ii.

bold aspiring youth, whose disgrace was not effaced till twenty years afterwards, when he attained the object of his ambition. To his brother Cuthwulf, whom he unfortunately lost in the same year, Ceawlin was indebted for a most important victory over the Britons, which brought the towns of Lenbury, Aylesbury, Bensington and Eynsham under his dominion.[1] Not less fortunate was Ceawlin some time afterwards, when, with the aid of his brother Cutha, or Cuthwine, after a battle at Derham in Gloucestershire, in which three British kings were slain—Conmail, Farinmail (probably of Gwent), and Condidan or Cyndillom (of Pengwern or Shrewsbury)—he won three cities, Bath, Gloucester, and Cirencester.[2] The last-mentioned places did not, however, continue under his dominion; probably because he did not fight with his West Saxons only, but with the Angles also, in his character of Bretwalda, since we find the territory of the Hwiccas, in which those cities lie, subsequently attached to Mercia. The Britons were now confined to their mountains and forests. A great victory at Fethanleah (Frithern) on the Severn, which gained him many towns, much treasure, and vast booty, was yet granted to Ceawlin, though purchased with the life of his valiant brother Cutha, and probably also with that of his own son, of whom the former fell in the beginning of the contest;[3] of the other no further mention occurs in the chronicles. With those friends Ceawlin lost much; the star of his prosperity was set. Great guilt must have accumulated on the head of him,[4] against whom,

[1] Sax. Chron. a. 571. [2] Sax. Chron. a. 577.
[3] Sax. Chron. an. 568, 597. Flor. of Worc. W. Malm.
[4] Malmesbury says of him, " Diebus ultimis regno extorris, miserandum sui spectaculum hostibus exhibuit. Quin enim in

after thirty years of prosperous sway and successful warfare, his kindred, even though instigated by the ambition of Æthelberht of Kent, could be induced to enter into a disgraceful league with the Britons and Scots.¹ He was defeated in a great battle fought in his own territory at Wodnesbeorh in Berkshire, not far from the frontier of Mercia, and compelled to abdicate the throne, which Ceolric, the son of his brother Cutha, ascended,² and Æthelberht was now acknowledged as Bretwalda. Ceawlin, who for centuries ranked as the mightiest monarch of the Anglo-Saxons, died two years afterwards in all the misery of exile.³ His successor, Ceolric, survived him only five years.⁴

The strife and discord which tore and threatened destruction to the Anglo-Saxons was, however, soon to be met by the kindliest palliative. The grandsons of the Saxon conquerors had been so far civilized by peaceable possession and gradual acquaintance with the arts of peace, that they could lend their ear to the preaching of Christianity. Of all the people of unmixed Germanic race the first converted to the faith of Christ, the Anglo-Saxons were called to impart its sanctity, and all the highest moral feeling attached to it, to the rest of Germanic and Northern Europe. The Roman civilization which they found in England had expanded the narrow boundary of their habits, their

---

odium sui quasi classicum utrobique cecinerat, conspirantibus tam Anglis quam Britonibus apud Wodnesdic, cæso exercitu, anno xxxi. regno nudatus in exilium concessit, et continuo decessit.

¹ Forduni Scotichron. lib. iii. Cf. also Langhorne ut sup.
² Sax. Chron. Flor. of Worc. a. 591.
³ Sax. Chron. Flor. of Worc. a. 593. W. Malm. lib. i.
⁴ Sax. Chron. Flor. of Worc. a. 591.

energies, and perhaps of their activity, without, at the same time, destroying the nationality of their institutions, their laws, or their language. Their mental cultivation, which must have been much promoted in their intercourse with the Britons, had no doubt greatly refined even their pagan notions. Hence we see that Christianity was received by the Anglo-Saxon states in the order according to which they had been favoured over others, by greater extent of settlements and length of peaceable possession.

An important event, through which the Anglo-Saxons first approached the pale of the Christian commonwealth of Europe, was the marriage of king Æthelberht with Berhta, daughter of Charibert, king of the Franks. Such a connection between these princes admits the supposition of an intercourse between their subjects, which, at a somewhat later period, does in fact appear to have subsisted as at the great commercial fair of St. Denis, which was visited by Anglo-Saxons.[1]

The ordinances of the Christian church, simple and humble as they were, could not maintain themselves in the new pagan Anglo-Saxon kingdoms, where royalty and the sacerdotal office were in close connection. We find them longest in the North, where the Angles established themselves but slowly as independent states. Samson, about the year 500, was nominated bishop of York, in which well-fortified city a Christian Roman school may probably have continued till the occupation of the place by the Angles. The Anglo-Saxons could not be otherwise than ill-disposed to the

[1] Charter of Dagobert of the year 629, ap. Bouquet, t. iv. p. 629, and more correct in Marini, 'Papiri Diplomatici,' p. 97, in which those Saxons only who came from beyond sea to Rouen and Quentavic to fetch honey and wood are to be held as Anglo-Saxons.

worship of Rome and of their enemies in Britain, as well as to other Roman institutions, which might threaten to be prejudicial to their independence: the teachers of Christianity, therefore, found among their most barbarous Celtic neighbours earlier admission than among the German invaders. The pupil of Germanus, who is said to have accompanied him on his visit to Britain, St Patric, the son of a deacon on the southern shore of the Clyde, who died in 493, continued in Ireland, as Palladius (since the year 430) among the Scots, successfully to spread the faith of Christ during the time when the Saxons were establishing themselves in Britain. Among the southern Picts, Christianity is said to have maintained itself from the period of their conversion by the Briton Nynias in the year 394, and Christian Anglo-Saxons, in later times, celebrated their worship in the stone church of St. Martin, founded by him at Hwitern (Candida Casa) in Galloway, when that territory had been annexed to the kingdom of Bernicia.[1] In the year 563 St. Columba passed over from Ireland to the northern Picts, with whom, employed in the propagation of his faith, he continued thirty-two years,[2] and formed excellent disciples, through whom a pleasing image of pious zeal, deep learning, and varied acquirement attaches itself to the memory of the Scottish monks. St. Columba received from the Pictish prince the island of Hii, now Iona or I-Colm-Kill (the isle of the church, or cell of Columba), which his name has consecrated, and which, in honour of him, continued for ages to be the real or fabled

[1] Beda, iii, 4.
[2] Adamni Vita S. Columbæ ap. Canisii Lectt. Antiquæ. His biographer was one of his successors in the abbey at Iona, and is known also by his work, 'De Locis Sanctis.'

burial-place of many Northern princes, as of those of Scotland, Ireland, Norway, and even Northumbria.[1]

In the Cambrian or Welsh states, as also in Cumbria, no apostasy from the Christian faith had taken place, though no conformity with the church of Rome existed; and the later accounts, which ascribe to Rome the sending of the before-mentioned missionaries, appear for the most part very unworthy of credit.[2] Contrast, and their contests with the pagans, must have strengthened a faith among them which reserves its noblest crown for the martyr. Many churches in Wales trace their foundation back to those British saints, who, in the time of Cerdic and his immediate successors, sought protection for their faith and tranquillity for self-contemplation behind the rocks and in the sylvan solitudes of that country.[3] The connection into which the church had already entered with the state, as well as that very peculiar one, which almost identified the form of the Western empire with the existence of the clergy, became known also in this country, and preserved its ecclesiastical institutions. Of these we may mention the distribution into seven bishoprics, also the monasteries of Bangor, and Avallon or Glastonbury. We find bishops at the election of kings. Thus Dubritius, first bishop of Llandaff, subsequently of Caerleon, where there were two ecclesiastical seminaries, crowned king Arthur in the year 516.[4]

---

[1] According to Simeon (De Eccles. Dunelm., cix.), Ecgfrith king of Northumberland was buried at Iona.

[2] As regards Patricius, cf. Neander's ' Geschichte der christlichen Religion,' Bd. ii. 259.

[3] See the genealogies of the Saints in ' Archæologia Britannica,' by Edward Lloyd.

[4] This report, as far as the bishop's name is concerned, seems

St. David, who transferred the see from Caerleon to the ancient Menevia, exerted himself at a British synod, held in 519, to eradicate the traces of the Pelagian heresy.[1] Mention also occurs of three provincial synods of the bishopric of Llandaff,[2] which, although they testify to a knowledge of existing vices and to a desire to remedy them, at the same time justify the mournful picture which the monk of Bangor has with black lineaments and chastening zeal drawn of his contemporaries in the British church. Gildas may unquestionably be numbered among the most distinguished men of his age, as of all writings of a similar description, it has transmitted his alone to posterity and to the present time. Though his style be bombastic, his conception bordering on the absurd, his historic delineations undefined, without chronology, he is, nevertheless, a very instructive voucher at a period, the other relics of which would, without his labours, be much more obscure and questionable than they are at present. We believe we err not, if in him we recognise the speaking representative of the more serious and pious Britons of the time, and a model of

---

doubtful, as he may have been mistaken for Dibric, who died in 612. See Annal. Camb. and Monast. Angl. t. vi. p. 1220.

[1] This synod is not to be placed, as it is generally, in the year 519. The Annales Cambriæ record it, with the death of bishop David, under 601, and (according to a later MS.) the synod of Victoria, perhaps too early, in 569. The historians who place David, Daniel of Bangor (ob. 584, see Annal. Camb.), and Dubritius, in the beginning of the sixth century, have not considered that Giraldus, their chief authority, here only follows Geoffrey of Monmouth.

[2] Spelm. Concilia, t. i. p. 62 sq. Wilkins, Conc. t. i. p. 17. Usser. Primord. Eccles. Angl.

Christian British Roman culture. What pious, modest, apt sentiments, what rare learning, what pure aims prevailed in the British church, we know from the favourable testimony of an opponent, the Venerable Beda, who praises and exalts no catholic Anglo-Saxon ecclesiastics so highly as he does those of the Britons and Scots, held out to them as patterns. The struggle between both churches in Britain is not less interesting from the sympathy which we cannot refuse to the fathers of the national church, than from the incalculable political importance of its suppression.

The points of difference between the catholic and the British churches had reference to the time of celebrating Easter, the form of the tonsure, the administration of baptism, the ecclesiastical benediction of matrimony, the marriage of priests, the manner of the ordination through presbyters of the British bishops (of which almost every church possessed one), and other trifling differences; but, above all things, to the refusal to acknowledge the supremacy of the pope and the councils. Of these points, however, those only regarding the computation of Easter and the administration of baptism were insisted on by Augustine, with the condition that the British priests should unite with the missionaries in preaching to the Angles.

The British church, established probably on the oldest direct traditions from Judea, in closest connection with conversions of the highest importance in the history of mankind, appeared no less by its geographical position than by its exalted spiritual endowments, fitted to become the foundation of a Northern patriarchate. Its counterpoise to Rome and the rest of the South, its guardianship over a Celtic and Germanic population, and its adhesion to the doctrine of Christ, might have made it the instrument to impart to those within its pale the freedom for which both meditative and ambitious men, in the middle ages, sometimes ventured to strive, but which, in comparatively modern times, Martin Luther first endeavoured to extort for Romanized Europe.[1]

The struggles between the Britons and the Anglo-Saxons were carried on for centuries with so much rancour, that it ought to excite no astonishment, and still less call for blame, that the former did not attempt the conversion of their barbarous enemies and oppressors. Most worthy therefore of admiration appears pope Gregory the Great, who first conceived the idea of gaining the Anglo-Saxon states for Christendom and the Catholic church, and applied to the holy work with a perseverance and caution worthy of the happy result by which it was followed. The obstacles, amid which the introduction of Christianity among the Anglo-Saxons was effected, were, indeed, very great, and it

---

[1] On the old British church see bishop Münter's treatise in Ullmann's u. A. 'Theologischen Studien und Kritiken,' 1833. Döllinger ('Kirchengeschichte,' t. i. sect. 2), proceeding on catholic principles, explains several points by much research, but is too zealous in endeavouring to obliterate all traces of views and discipline, in which the ancient British church differed from that of Rome, ascribing to the former an acknowledgment of the Roman supremacy. The passage he quotes from the Epistle of Gildas does not prove that the British procured for themselves at Rome dignities in the church of their own country, but merely that some of them had surreptitiously obtained ordination in transmarine parts, perhaps Ireland or Bretagne. The mention made of the bishop of Caerleon, in the letter of the abbot of Bangor to Augustine, in which the supremacy of the Roman pontiff is not recognised, will no longer, after what has been before said of bishop David, raise critical doubts, but may be reckoned among the tests of its authenticity.—T.

required almost a century for the completion of the task. The language of the Roman missionaries proved the first check to the convincing powers of their eloquence. Even though a prince, by family connection, by means of preaching and papal briefs, which flattered his vanity, as well as by presents—such as are given in modern times and for a similar purpose to the savages of remote regions—might have felt favourably disposed to the new faith, and acknowledged himself a Christian, yet his court and the rest of his people might still remain unconverted. On the death of such a convert, as the history of all the large Anglo-Saxon states testifies, his successor would probably raise again the banner of paganism. Nor, in attempting the spiritual conquest of any of the small states, was there a prospect of any great result, since, from their slender connection with each other, and the inconsiderable influence of the Bretwalda—which, in this case especially, proved wholly ineffectual—the conversion of a kingdom was for the neighbouring ones the occasion of a more vigilant opposition. At the same time, however, it must be noticed, as a favourable circumstance, that, notwithstanding repeated relapses into paganism, Christianity in one or other of the states always preserved an altar and a sanctuary.

The wish and the plan to draw the Anglo-Saxons within the pale of the Roman Catholic church must have been long entertained at Rome. Yet the external impulse, necessary to the production of the greatest events, had been wanting, which at the first glance is wont to appear so incredible, that it might be pronounced as too wonderful for accident, yet the following is accepted as the true version of the manner in which the Anglo-Saxons first received Christianity.

Some young Angles were standing in the Forum at Rome, there to be sold as slaves. By whom they had been conveyed thither is wholly unknown; they possibly formed a portion of the booty taken in the wars of the Bretwalda with the Northumbrians, and had been brought from the public market at London. These foreign boys, distinguished by their beautiful countenance, fair skin, and—that which was the sign of good descent—their comely locks, attracted the notice of Gregory, who some years afterwards was elected pope, and was so famed for his attention to the education of youth, that for more than a thousand years after his death they were accustomed to celebrate the day dedicated to his name. On learning that they were from Britain and heathens, he loudly lamented that they with such bright countenances must become the prey of the prince of darkness; and that such grace of aspect was not accompanied with the grace of inward light. On being told that they were called Angles (Angli), he exclaimed, "And rightly so, for they have an angelic mien, and should be the co-heirs of angels in heaven." On inquiring the name of the province from whence they came, he was answered, that the people to which they belonged were called Deiri. "It is well," said he, "de ira eruti," snatched from wrath and called to the mercy of Christ. On being informed that their king was named Ælle, "Alleluiah," said he, in allusion to the name, "the praise of God the Creator ought to be sung in that country." Whereupon he hastened to the pope, for the purpose of beseeching him to send some ministers of the Word to Britain, who might convert the inhabitants to Christ, offering to accompany them himself. But though the pope was willing to grant his request, the people would not admit of his absence from the city for so long a period; yet Gregory, immediately after his elevation to the papacy, executed his serious purpose by sending missionaries to the land of the slaves who had been the objects of his commiseration.[1] These, under the guidance of Augustine, had performed but an inconsiderable part of their journey, when they were so terrified at the description given them of the barbarity of the savage pagans, of whose speech even they were entirely ignorant, that, on their arrival in Provence, they sent home Augustine,[2]—who was destined to be bishop of the Angles, and who on all occasions appears rather as a faithful instrument subservient to general opinion and higher command, than as an inspired preacher of the Word which brings life, —for the purpose of supplicating the pope to release them from so dangerous, laborious, and doubtful a mission. But Gregory exhorted them to continue their journey, recommended them to the protection of the Frankish kings, Theuderic and Theudebert, and to their powerful grandmother, Brunhild, also to the several bishops, and caused Frankish interpreters to accompany them. On the isle of Thanet, the earliest Anglo-Saxon acquisition, Augustine likewise made his landing, with a number of monks, which Anglo-Saxon tradition fixes at about forty. To the king of Kent, Augustine announced his coming from Rome, with a message that promised to the obedient eternal joy in heaven, and a kingdom without end with the true and living God. Though Æthelberht might not have paid attention to the faith professed by the great number of his subjects forming the oppressed British population, he must, nevertheless, have had some knowledge of the religion

[1] Beda, ii. 1.   [2] Id. i. 23.

of his consort Berhta, who, by the terms of her marriage contract, enjoyed the free exercise of her worship, the duties attending which were fulfilled by Liudhard,—a Frankish bishop, who had accompanied her to England,—in the church of St. Martin near Canterbury, which had been preserved from the time of the Christian Romans.

The king, soon after their landing, proceeded to the isle for the purpose of meeting the strangers, where, apprehending the influence of their sorcery under a roof, he received them seated and in the open air. The missionaries approached, bearing, in place of a banner, a silver cross, also a representation of the Saviour painted on a board, and singing litanies, supplicating for the eternal salvation of themselves and of those for whom and to whom they were come. The words and promises of the sermon preached before the king seemed to him beautiful, yet being new and uncertain, he would not renounce the faith of the whole nation: at the same time he gave the foreigners an hospitable reception in his chief city, Canterbury, and allowed them, by their preaching and example, to propagate their faith among his people, to baptize, and to solemnize their worship in the church of his queen. The conversion and baptism of Æthelberht himself,[1] which soon followed, was attended with the restoration of the old British church of the Holy Saviour in the royal city, and with the acknowledgment of the archiepiscopal authority of Augustine, who had made a journey to Arles, where, by command of Gregory, he had received consecration at the hands of the archbishop Virgilius,[2] and who on his

[1] Beda, i. 26. A.D. 597, on the feast of Pentecost, or June 2. See Smith's note, also Stevenson's.—T.
[2] A.D. 597. Beda, i. 24 (where see Smith's note) and id. i. 27.

return sent Laurentius and Petrus, two of his companions to announce to Gregory the progress of his mission. These brought back with them several coadjutors, among whom were Mellitus, Justus, Paulinus and Rufinianus, together with gifts for the new church, consisting of holy vessels and vestments, books and relics, also letters from the pope to Augustine, granting him the use of the pall. Gregory now saw the general conversion of the nation assume a definite form,[1] and the active head of the church, in the leisure which his great mind was able to command for the purpose of recording the fruits of his profound and learned contemplations, could thank the Almighty, that the inhabitants of Britain, whose language had erst been employed only for heathenish and barbarous purposes, now chanted forth the Hebrew Hallelujah to the praise of God.[2] Who does not here call to mind his early wish? Well might he rejoice in the progress of the great work of which he had laid the foundation!

It would be a proof, alike of ingratitude and ignorance, to deny that the greatest event that could befall a people, the noblest benefit that could be conferred upon it, was the introduction of the Christian faith, which taught all men to recognise one common origin and one common aim in the attainment of eternal life,

[1] Beda, i. 27. 29. We learn from a letter of Gregory to Eulogius, bishop of Alexandria, that before the following Christmas more than ten thousand of the English had been baptized by Augustine and his followers. By Thorne it is stated that Æthelberht resigned Canterbury and the surrounding country to Augustine, and retired to Reculver: " Ipse Ædilberctus Regulbium demigravit, ibique novum sibi palatium condidit." See Smith's and Stevenson's notes.—T.

[2] Expositio Jobi ap. Bedæ II. E. ii. 1.

and to acknowledge that all were equally dependent for help on the hand of the Almighty, and all bound together by one common hope of redemption. It is true that doctrines which could only be presented to rude demoralized races under the mask of emblems and images, could not instantaneously turn earthly strife into heavenly peace; but seldom has the influence of the Christian religion left so permanent an impression on the entire social culture, and the political unity and stability of a people as in the case of the Anglo-Saxons before the ocean again fell under the dominion of the pagan Northmen, and gave the Christianized British island a prey into their hands.

The failure of an important step contemplated by Augustine proved a check to the more rapid spread of Christianity. In Wales the Christian faith as well as a great degree of Roman civilization had been preserved, especially through the schools of Bangor and Llancarvan; and Augustine was not slow to perceive how desirable for the propagation of Christianity an union would be between the Roman and the British clergy. Through the influence of Æthelberht a meeting between the missionaries and the heads of the British church was effected, at a spot afterwards known by the name of Augustine's Oak,[1] on the confines of Wessex and the territory of the Hwiccas. Here, after a long and fruitless discussion of the points on which the two churches were at variance, the chief of which, it appears, was the time of celebrating Easter—Augustine, as we are told by Beda, having, in proof of his

[1] The conference was, without doubt, literally held in the open air, under the spreading branches of an oak. On this interesting subject see Palgrave, vol. i. p. 238 sq.—T.

authority, miraculously restored a blind man to sight,[1] —the meeting was adjourned to a future day.

Previous to the second conference, which was attended by seven British bishops, by the abbot Dinoot, or Dunawd, and several learned divines from Bangor, the Britons consulted a certain hermit, who was held by them in high veneration, as to whether, in compliance with the preaching of Augustine, they should renounce their own traditions? He answered, "If the man is of God, follow him." To their inquiry, "How are we to prove this?" he replied, "The Lord says, Take my yoke upon you, and learn of me, for I am meek and humble of heart. If, therefore, Augustine is meek and humble of heart, it is to be believed that he himself bears the yoke of Christ, and offers it to be borne by you; but if he is arrogant and proud, it is manifest that he is not of God, and that we need not heed his words." To their further question, "But how shall we ascertain this?" "Order it so," said he, "that he and his followers be the first at the conference, and if he rise up to meet you, do you, knowing him to be the servant of Christ, hear him obediently; but if he contemn you, and will not rise up to you, you being in number the greater, be he contemned of you."

On their arrival at the place of conference, finding Augustine seated, they, according to the instructions of the hermit, as well perhaps as from predisposition, met all his proposals with a refusal. Whereupon he said,

[1] From an extract of a letter from Gregory to Augustine, it appears that the great work of the latter was promoted by the intervention of other miracles besides the one here recorded. In this letter the pontiff exhorts the missionary not to be presumptuous on account of such miracles. See Beda, i. 31; and, for the remainder of the letter, ejd. Opera Minora, ed. Stevenson, p. 218.—T.

"Though in many points you act contrary to us and to the universal church, yet, if you will agree with me in these three,—to celebrate Easter at the proper season; to perform baptism, whereby we are born again to God, after the manner of the holy Roman and apostolic church; and, together with us, to preach the word of God to the Anglian nation,—we will kindly bear with you." They answered, that they would do none of those things, nor acknowledge him for their archbishop. In reply, Augustine, in a threatening tone, is said to have predicted to them, that, if they would not accept peace with their brothers, they should have war with their enemies: and if they would not preach the way of life to the Angles, they should suffer vengeance at their hands. The fulfilling of the prophecy, or what was regarded as its fulfilment, will be seen hereafter.[1]

From the above it will, perhaps, appear obvious to the unprejudiced reader, that the arrogance of the foreign missionary on the one side, and, on the other, the stubbornness of the British ecclesiastics, called into activity by that arrogance, were the chief causes why a conference, held for so holy a purpose, ended in evoking feelings the reverse of those of peace and goodwill to men.

With more satisfaction we, at the present day, regard the wisdom and liberality with which Gregory answers the questions of Augustine, as to the course he was to follow with regard to the diversity prevailing in the customs of the Roman and Gallican churches. "It is my wish," writes Gregory, "that you sedulously select what you may think most acceptable to Almighty God, be it in the Roman, or in the Gallican, or in any other church; and introduce into the church of the Angles

[1] This important narrative is wholly taken from Beda, ii. 2.—T.

that which you shall have so collected; for things are not to be loved for the sake of places, but places for the sake of good things. Choose, therefore, from the several churches whatever is pious, and religious, and right, and these, gathered as it were into one whole, instil, as observances, into the minds of the Angles."[1]

[1] Beda, i. 27.

(181)

CHAPTER IX.

SEVENTH CENTURY.

Conversion of Essex—Rædwald of East Anglia a Convert—Æthelfrith of Northumbria's Opposition to Christianity—Eadwine's Marriage—His Influence on the Destinies of the People—Conversion of Eadwine and his Ealdormen—Paulinus becomes Archbishop of York—Peace and Prosperity of Northumbria—Eadwine resigns his Crown—Calamities of Northumbria—Penda of Mercia—Death of Eadwine—Murder of his Son Eadfrith—Oswald acknowledged as Bretwalda—His Valour and Piety—His Warfare with the British—His Conflicts with Penda—Conversion of Wessex—Ceolwulf of Wessex—He falls in Battle.

A CONNECTION similar to that which had caused the introduction of Christianity into Kent facilitated its entrance into Essex. Ricole, a sister of Æthelberht, was the mother of Sæberht (Sæbriht), king of that small state, which was however rendered important on account of the cities it contained.[1] The king soon attached himself to the new faith of his uncle and Bretwalda, and his people, following the example of their prince, yielded to the preaching of Mellitus, to whom, through the influence of Æthelberht, a church in London, dedicated to St. Paul, was assigned as an episcopal see, where had formerly stood a temple of Diana; while Justus was by Augustine consecrated to the see of Rochester, in which city a church, dedicated

[1] Beda, ii. 3. Sax. Chron. i. 601.

to St. Andrew the apostle, was founded by Æthelberht, and, as at Canterbury, endowed with lands and other possessions.[1]

It was the happy lot of Augustine to pass to the higher reward of his deeds with no cause of anxiety for his great acquisition for the church, which gathered strength under the powerful sceptre of Æthelberht. He had made a very praiseworthy choice of a successor in his associate Laurentius, who, in conjunction with Justus, renewed the attempt to unite the Britons with his church, and even took similar steps among the Scots of Ireland.[2]

Mellitus was in the meanwhile gone to Rome on business of the church: it happened, therefore, that Boniface IV. counted in the Synod then sitting[3] one Anglo-Saxon bishop. In Kent the wholesome influence of the Roman ecclesiastics was manifested also in the circumstance, that Æthelberht caused to be recorded, in the language of his country, the first written collection among the Anglo-Saxons—perhaps among all the Germanic nations—of the ancient laws of his people, comprising those newly introduced by the Christian priests. But the welfare of the church was not to rest on the written letter. On the death of Æthelberht,[4] which was soon followed by that of Sæberht, the faith had been established among the Anglo-Saxons about twenty-one years, when it was suddenly brought near its suppression. Eadbald, the son of Æthelberht, having not only refused to listen to its doctrines, but, yielding to the frenzy of the most passionate excitement,

[1] A.D. 604. Beda, ii. 3.
[2] A.D. 605. Beda, ii. 3, 4, where see the letter of Laurentius to the Scottish bishops and abbots.—T.
[3] A.D. 610, Feb. 27.   [4] Sax. Chron. a. 616.

had not hesitated to espouse his father's widow. The sons of Sæberht, who had also refused to receive baptism, had granted to their subjects permission to return to the worship of idols, and driven Mellitus from the kingdom for having refused to desecrate the bread of the eucharist by administering it to them at a feast. Mellitus and Justus fled to Gaul, whither Laurentius was preparing to follow them, when a sudden change in the mind of Eadbald, occasioned by the last representations of the archbishop, was followed by the suppression of idolatry in his dominions, the dismissal of his step-mother, and the restoration of Christianity.[1]

Not so soon did the East Saxons become sensible of their error, though the three sons of Sæberht had fallen in a battle. Mellitus succeeded Laurentius, in the archiepiscopal dignity, but his former diocese still persisted in their idolatry.[2] It was a new generation only that followed king Sigeberht the Good, and the

[1] The device by which these desirable events were brought to pass, though unfit to be recorded on the pages of history at the present day, affords, nevertheless, too striking an example of the means, it is to be feared, but too frequently employed in propagating the new faith among our simple forefathers, to be wholly unnoticed. We are told by Beda (ii. 6), that Laurentius, on the eve of his departure, had directed that his bed should be placed in the church of St. Peter and St. Paul. In the dead of the night St. Peter appeared to him, and scourging him asked, why he abandoned the flock entrusted to his care? In the morning he presented himself before the king, and showed him his body lacerated with the scourging, and, on his inquiry who had dared to inflict such stripes on a man like him, received for answer, that he had been so wounded and tormented by the apostle of Christ, for the sake of his (Eadbald's) salvation. Thereupon, the prince abjuring his old idolatry, dismissed his stepmother, adopted the Christian faith, and received baptism. See also Sax. Chron. a. 616.—T.

[2] Beda, ii. 6.

majority of the Anglo-Saxons, who now generally professed the doctrines of Christianity. Yet even then the appearance of an unusually destructive pestilence, called the yellow plague, prompted the East Saxons to look for aid in the restoration of the heathen temples, while Sigehere (Sigeheri), one of their two kings, relapsed into paganism; but the example given by the pious king Sebbe (Sebbi), together with the spiritual exertions of bishop Jaruman, led to the final destruction of the old national idolatry with its temples, and to the permanent establishment of the new faith.[1]

While on a visit to Æthelberht of Kent, Rædwald, king of the East Angles, had also declared himself a convert to Christianity, a step the more important, as, after the death of Æthelberht, the dignity of Bretwalda had passed over to the Uffings. Induced, however, by the importunity of his wife and friends, Rædwald soon rejected the newly acquired faith, but, in the view of satisfying both parties, caused to be erected in the same temple an altar to Christ by the side of that devoted to the rites of paganism.[2]

His neighbour beyond the Humber, Æthelfrith (Æthelferth), the son of Æthelric and grandson of Ida, who had forcibly united Deira, the kingdom of Ælle his deceased father-in-law, with his own paternal state, Bernicia, was a foe to Christianity. He had acquired a reputation for great valour in the glorious victory, purchased with the loss of his brother Theodbald, at

---

[1] Beda, iii. 22, 30. Fl. of Worc. a. 653. From the date given in the margin of the latter of these chapters of Beda, it might seem that the reign of Sighere and Sebbe commenced in 665; but in Wulfhere's charter of endowment to Peterborough abbey, dated 664, their names as kings appear among the signatures. See Sax. Chron. a. 657.   [2] Beda, ii. 15.

Dægsanstan, or Degsastan,[1] over Aidan, the son of Gabran, king of the Dalreods or Albanians, the remembrance of which long deterred the latter from further contests with the Angles of Northumbria. His wars had hitherto been chiefly with the Britons, vast numbers of whom he had exterminated, or rendered tributary to his sceptre; and the fear which those conquests spread among his neighbours occasioned an alliance, till then unheard of, between Anglo-Saxon and British princes. Eadwine (Eadwini), the son of Ælle, a child of three years, had it appears, on the seizure of his inheritance by Æthelfrith, been committed for safety to the care of Cadvan, king of Gwynedd,[2] and there educated under the British clergy till he had attained the age of manhood. Cadvan, for the sake of his ward, having formed an alliance with Brocmail, king of Powis, the patron of the poet Taliesin, hazarded a war with the persecutor of Eadwine, which ended in a battle fought near Chester (Caerlegion, Lægacester) and the destruction of the celebrated monastery of Bangor, the seat of Celtic Christian learning.[3] Previous to the battle Æthelfrith espied an

[1] Beda, i. 34. Sax. Chron. a. 603. Dalston near Carlisle, according to Gibson, whose supposition is favoured by the various reading, Deglastan. Dawstane in Liddlesdale has also been conjectured as the spot. Tigernach makes no mention of this battle, unless he alludes to it a. 600, "Prælium Saxonum contra Ædanum, ubi cecidit Eanfrnc (Eanfrith) frater Etalfraich, occisus a Maeluma, filio Baodani, in quo victor erat." Annal. Ulton. a. 599, "Bellum Saxonum, in quo victus est Aeda.'

[2] Vaughan, Diss. on Brit. Chronol. Laghorne, Chron. Angl., though in other respects confuting Geoffrey of Monmouth considers this tradition as probable.

[3] In 607 according to the Sax. Chron. Fl. of Worc. a. 603, says "longo post tempore (Æthelfrido) collecto exercitu," etc. Annal. Camb. and Tigern. 613. Beda, ii. 2, does not give the year of this

unarmed body, standing apart in a place of apparent security. On being informed that they belonged for the most part to the monastery of Bangor, and had with others assembled on that spot to pray, under the protection of Brocmail, he exclaimed, "If they cry to their God against us, and load us with imprecations, though unarmed, they fight against us:" whereupon he ordered them to be attacked and put to the sword. Eadwine fled before his brother-in-law and persecutor to Mercia, whence, finding no security there, he took refuge with Rædwald of East Anglia; and thus, a homeless wanderer, established, through the protection which he there sought and obtained, a connection which was followed by a result far more important than that attending his previous alliance with the Britons.

To the first and second application of Æthelfrith, for the death or delivery of the fugitive, though accompanied by tempting pecuniary offers, the Bretwalda gave no ear; but on the third solicitation, and the proffer of a larger sum, and threatening war in case of refusal, the faith of Rædwald gave way, and he promised compliance with the wishes of the Northumbrian. It was night, and Eadwine was preparing for rest, when a faithful friend, calling him from his chamber, informed him of Rædwald's promise, and engaged to convey him to an asylum, where neither the one nor the other should be able to discover him. "Thanks for your good will," said Eadwine, "but I cannot yield to your proposal, and be the first to break my compact with a king who has done me no injury,

---

event. The British kings, Scysil son of Conan, Jacobus son of Beli, and Cetul are named among the slain.

nor shown any ill-will towards me. If I am to die, let him rather than a less noble hand deliver me to death. Whither can I flee, who, in striving to escape from the snares of my enemies, have so long been a wanderer through all the provinces of Britain?" His friend, departed, and Eadwine was left alone sitting on a stone before the palace, sad and at a loss what to do, or whither to bend his steps.

While thus sitting, wrapt in agonizing thoughts, he was startled by the approach of a stranger, who, after greeting him, asked why, when others were at rest, he was there so lonely? "Yet think not," continued he, "that the cause of your affliction and your vigil is unknown to me: I know who you are, and why you are depressed, and the impending evils which you dread. But say, what reward would you give to any one, if such there be, who should free you from these cares, and prevail on Rædwald neither to do you aught of harm himself, nor to deliver you to your enemies?" On his answering, that for such a benefit he would be grateful to the utmost of his power—" But what, if he should promise that you shall destroy your adversaries, and be a king more powerful not only than any of your forefathers, but than any who has ever reigned over the Angles?" On Eadwine repeating his assurances of gratitude, the stranger, a third time, asked, "If he, who shall have truly promised such great benefits, should impart to you doctrines of life and salvation, better and more efficacious than any one of your relatives has ever heard, would you obey him, and listen to his admonitions?" On receiving the promise of Eadwine, the stranger laid his right hand on the prince's head, saying, "When this sign shall be repeated, remember this hour and this discourse, and delay not to fulfil that which you now promise." Having uttered these words, it is said, he suddenly disappeared, that he might be known to be no man but a spirit.

The royal youth remained. His mind, though gladdened by the consolation he had received, was yet not free from anxiety, when his before-mentioned friend returned to him with a joyful countenance, and informed him that he might safely retire to rest, and that Rædwald had resolved to keep his faith; for that on communicating to the queen the promise he had made to Æthelfrith, she had made manifest to him how ill it became so great a king to sell his best friend in his distress for gold, and to break his faith, more precious than all ornaments, through love of money.[1]

The Bretwalda having thus resolved on the juster course, marched with a powerful well-appointed army against the Northumbrian, who met him with inferior forces in a battle fought on the eastern bank of the river Idle in Nottinghamshire, on the border of Mercia. Rædwald remained master of the field, which was covered with bodies of the slain, among whom was Æthelfrith himself, who, in an impetuous onset, having destroyed one of the three divisions into which the adverse army was divided, together with its valiant leader Ræginhere (Ræginheri), the son of Rædwald, and being overpowered by numbers, was found far from his

[1] Beda, ii. 12. Regarding this legend of the child of Ælle as too beautiful and graphic, as well as too intimately connected with the account of his conversion, to be omitted or even abridged, I have, at the risk of censure, not hesitated to give it entire and almost literally from the work of the 'Venerable' father of English history, who, for his love of the legendary and fascinating descriptive powers, may be not inaptly called the Walter Scott of the eighth century.—T.

followers amid the slain heaps of the enemy.[1] After this victory, which was attended with most important results for Britain, Eadwine took possession of his paternal kingdom as well as of the vacant throne of Bernicia. One of his earliest deeds seems to have been the conquest of the little British territory of Elmet,[2] which had existed as an independent state under its king Cerdic—a name susceptible both of a British and Saxon interpretation—whom he expelled, for having, under the guise of hospitality, received and afterwards poisoned Hereric, the nephew of Eadwine, who, like his uncle, had been persecuted by Æthelfrith.[3]

The states of kindred origin now attached themselves to the North Angles, and the first Bretwaldaship over all the Anglo-Saxons, with the exception of Kent, devolved on their mighty and widely allied king. The British states and even the Isle of Man, were subject to him; also the Island of Mona, which, though from the colonists brought thither it had re-

[1] Beda, ii. 12. Sax. Chron. a. 617. Fl. of Worc. H. Hunt. a. 616.
[2] A district in Yorkshire about Leeds. Camden conjectures that the ruins visible at Barwick in Elmet indicate the site of the palace of the Northumbrian kings.
[3] Nennii App. "Eaguin, filius Alli, . . . occupavit Elmet et expulit Certic, regem illius regionis." Beda, iv. 23. " Cum Hereric exularet sub rege Brittonum Cerdice, ubi et veneno periit." The above passage will, it is hoped, justify the view I have taken of this event, which receives confirmation from the respect shown by Eadwine to Hild, the daughter of Hereric, with whom, it appears, she received the rites of baptism: " Cum quo (Æduino)," says Beda, ibid., "ad prædicationem beatæ memoriæ Paulini, primi Nordan-hymbrorum episcopi, fidem et sacramenta Christi suscepit." Hereric, the son of the elder deceased son of Ælle, was therefore dead before the death of Æthelfrith : whereby it appears how Eadwine, Ælle's second son, succeeded Æthelfrith without opposition. Cf. also Annal. Camb. a. 616, and Fl. of Worc. Geneal.

ceived the name of Anglesea,[1] afterwards resumed its Celtic character. Eadwine, after the death of his consort Cwenburh, a daughter of the Mercian king Ceorl, obtained the hand of a Christian princess of the family of the Æscings, the former suzerains of his country, Æthelburh or Tate, a daughter of Æthelberht of Kent. This marriage had been permitted under conditions and expectations similar to those attending that of the Frankish princess Berhta with Æthelberht himself. The bishop Paulinus accompanied the young queen, to preserve her in the Christian faith and attend to the duties of divine worship. Shortly after letters, accompanied by precious gifts, arrived from pope Boniface[2] " to Eadwine, king of the Angles, and Æthelburh, his consort," for the purpose of effecting the conversion of the former. Precious jewels for both the royal consorts accompanied the letters, being offered by the pontiff in the hope that by securing a favourable hearing for his messengers, his gifts might bring back a hundred-fold of treasure to the papal chair. Eadwine was probably neither unprepared nor unwilling to receive baptism, to which he must have often been invited in his earlier years: he, nevertheless, weighed the difficulties and the danger of such a step with regard to his subjects. Two events, which occurred almost at the same moment, appear to have accelerated his conversion. Cwichelm, king of the West Saxons, anxious to free himself from the supremacy of Northumbria, had recourse to the arm of an assassin. His

[1] Beda, ii. 5, 9.
[2] As Boniface V. died Oct. 22, a. 625, his letters must have been written in that year, though probably not received till the spring following; a supposition which may account for their being placed by Beda after events of 626.

emissary, Eomer, reached the royal residence on the first day of Easter, and, while delivering a feigned message from Cwichelm, suddenly started up, and drawing from under his garment an envenomed two-edged dagger, rushed on the king, when an affectionate Thane named Lilla threw himself between them, and at the price of his own life saved that of his master. So violent was the stroke that Eadwine was wounded through the body of his follower, nor did the assassin fall beneath the swords of those present until he had slain Forthhere (Forthheri), another Thane of Eadwine's. On the same night Æthelburh was delivered of a daughter, named Eanflæd; when Eadwine, in the presence of Paulinus, returning thanks to his gods for the gift, the bishop rendered thanks to Christ, assuring the king that it was to his prayers that the queen owed her safe and happy delivery. Moved by these words, Eadwine promised to renounce his idols and serve Christ, if he would grant him the victory over that king who had employed an assassin to destroy him, and, in pledge of his promise, intrusted his daughter to Paulinus, by whom she was baptized with eleven others of his household. Being cured of his wound, he collected an army and marched against the West Saxons, who were defeated with great loss, five kings being mentioned among the slain.[1]

On his return, though he abstained from the worship of his gods, he was yet unwilling, without due reflection, to partake of the sacraments of the Christian faith. But, listening to the discourses of Paulinus on the one hand, and of his priests on the other, he meditated in private on their respective arguments, when a means of hastening his resolve presented itself to Paulinus, such

[1] Sax. Chron. a. 626. Beda, ii. 9.

as spiritual superiority has seldom scrupled to apply for the attainment of an adequate object.

The predictions of the vision were now realized, but the sign had not been repeated, when Paulinus, as Beda conjectures, already apprised in spirit of what had taken place,[1] approaching the solitary king, while wrapt in deep meditation, laid his right hand on his head, and asked him whether he acknowledged that sign? Eadwine, trembling, was about to cast himself at the feet of Paulinus, but the latter, raising him up, addressed him thus: "By the grace of God you have escaped from the hands of your enemies; by his bounty, you have obtained the kingdom which you desired: be mindful not to delay the promise you made, to receive his faith and keep his commandments, and, by promoting his will, as announced by me, to free yourself from everlasting punishment, and become a partaker of the heavenly kingdom."[2]

The king promised to receive the faith, and, with the view of effecting the universal adoption of Christianity, called a meeting of his friends and witan. On Eadwine's inquiring of each one separately his opinion of the new doctrines, Cæfi, the high priest,[3] immediately answered, "Judge you, O king, of that which is now announced to us; but I must truly confess to you, that the religion which we have hitherto followed has neither power nor utility. For not one of your subjects has more diligently attended to the worship of the gods than I; and, nevertheless, there are many who have received from you greater benefits and

[1] Beda, ii. 12. [2] A.D. 626. Beda, ii. 12.
[3] "Primus pontificum" (regis). Beda, ii. 13, who in his Anglian or Northumbrian dialect, writes the name 'Coifi': one MS. of Ælfred's version reads 'Cœfi,' and 'Cefi,' another has 'Cyfi.'

greater honours, and prosper more in all their undertakings : whereas, if the gods were worth anything, they would rather favour me, who have so zealously served them. If therefore, on examination, the new doctrine shall appear to you better and more efficacious, let us, without further delay, hasten to adopt it."

One of the ealdormen approving these words, added, "Such seems to me, O king, the present life of man, in comparison of the time which is hidden from us, as when you are sitting with your thanes and attendants, in your hall at your repast—in the winter season, with a fire lighted in the middle, and the apartment warm, but the chilling storms of rain and snow raging without—a sparrow rapidly flies through, entering at one door, and instantly escaping by another. While it is within it is not touched by the winter's storm, but, after having passed through a very short space of serenity, it goes forthwith from storm to storm, and vanishes from your sight. So also seems the short life of man: what follows or what precedes we know not: if, therefore, this new doctrine brings us something more certain, it is also my opinion that it should be adopted." In accordance with this were the sentiments of the other ealdormen and witan. Cæfi now expressed his wish to hear Paulinus discourse concerning God: his conversion was the result, and Eadwine also convinced by the preaching of the bishop, and renouncing idolatry, professed himself a believer in the doctrines of Christianity.[1] To the inquiry of Paulinus: Who would be the first to profane the altars and temples of the idols, with their enclosures?[2] Cæfi answered,

---

[1] Beda, ii. 14. Sax. Chron. a. 627.
[2] The " septum " around a temple was the " frithgeard," or asylum.

"I; for who is fitter than I am to destroy, through the wisdom given me by God, and as an example to all, that which I have worshipped in my folly?" Whereupon he prayed of the king that arms and a horse might be given to him—it being forbidden to the sacrificing priests both to bear arms and to ride except on a mare—and, girded with a sword, and with lance in hand, having mounted the horse, he proceeded to execute his design. The people thought him mad, but he, hastening to the temple, instantly profaned it by casting his lance against it, and in his exultation commanded his associates to set it on fire with all its enclosures. This event took place at Godmundingaham, now Godmundham, in the East Riding of Yorkshire. Eadwine was baptized at York on the following Easter-day, in a church built of wood, and dedicated to St. Peter the Apostle, which he had there caused to be erected, but which was shortly after replaced by a larger one of stone on the same spot. York was assigned as an archiepiscopal see to Paulinus, who received the pall from pope Honorius.[1]

Paulinus preached also on the other side of the Humber, and converted the inhabitants of Lindisse, a territory the name of which is preserved in that of Lindsey. Its chief, Blecca, a descendant of Woden, and his household, were his first converts.[2]

The peace and tranquillity which the power of the Bretwalda procured for his kingdom must have been very favourable to the spread of the new doctrine, such

---

See Law of the Northumbrian Priests, liv. in Anc. LL. and Instt., and Gloss. *v.* Friðgeard.—T.
[1] A.D. 627. Beda, ii. 13, 14.
[2] Beda, ii. 16. Sax. Chron. a. 627. Geneal. ap. Florentium.

security being said to have prevailed that, according to the Anglo-Saxon proverb, a woman with her new-born babe might have travelled from sea to sea without sustaining injury. By the conduits which he had caused to be constructed on the high roads, he directed brazen cups to be suspended, which no hand touched save that of the parched wanderer. Eadwine loved the display of authority: not only were ensigns borne before him in battle, but even in the public ways he was constantly preceded by the Roman *tufa*, or tûf as it was called by the Anglo-Saxons.[1]

Eadwine zealously exerted himself for the propagation of the new faith, and though it appears that he raised no altar in Bernicia,[2] he succeeded in the thorough conversion of Eorpwald, the son of Rædwald, king of the East Angles; and though the murder of Eorpwald by a pagan,[3] plunged East Anglia into darkness and strife, yet Eadwine lived to see the return and establishment of Christianity in that country after a lapse of three years. Sigeberht, who had received the doctrines of Christianity while in Gaul, whither he had fled from the hostility of his step-father Rædwald, now conjointly with his brother Ecgric took possession of the throne, chiefly, it would seem, for the sake of propagating his newly adopted faith. In the work of conversion he was aided by Felix, a Burgundian bishop sent to him from Kent by Honorius, archbishop of Canterbury, under whose wise guidance it prospered

[1] Beda, ii. 16.
[2] This is manifest from Beda, iii. 2, a. 635, where, speaking of Oswald's cross, he says, "Nullum, ut comperimus, fidei Christianæ signum, nulla ecclesia, nullum altare in tota Berniciorum gente erectum est, priusquam hoc sacræ crucis vexillum," etc.
[3] A.D. 627. Beda, ii. 15.

admirably. Desirous of improving the minds of his people, Sigeberht founded a Latin school on the plan of those he had seen in Gaul, in which laudable undertaking he availed himself of the counsel of Felix, who supplied fitting persons as teachers, according to the Kentish practice.[1] On the foundation of the see of Domuc (Dunwich), Felix was appointed its first bishop.[2]

Scarcely had these events taken place when we find the King of the East Angles—following the old Frankish example—resigning his crown, and, giving the earliest instance of an Anglo-Saxon royal monk. The sceptre now devolved on Ecgric, who was already a sharer in the government of this small state. So deeply rooted was the conviction which led the East Anglian to a renunciation of earthly sway, that not even the danger of his native land, at that time suffering under the cruel ravages of Penda, king of Mercia, could induce him to forsake the quiet of his cloister. When forcibly brought forth by his subjects, in the hope that the sight of a leader, once honoured for his valour, might cheer and stimulate his warriors, he stood still amid the raging battle, with a staff in his hand, until he was slain together with his kinsman Ecgric. Christianity was not, however, again driven from East Anglia, Anna, the successor of the slain prince, being not only devoted to its doctrines, but, becoming, at the instance of Fursæus,

[1] Beda, iii. 18. "Juxta morem Cantuariorum." Malmes. de Gestis Pont. lib. ii. "Scholas opportunis locis instituens, barbariem gentis sensim comitate Latina informabat." The above passage of Beda has been adduced in the dispute between Oxford and Cambridge, to prove the higher antiquity of the latter. See Smith, Append. xiv. ad Bedam. The proof is, however, wanting that Cambridge, formerly Grantabrycge, belonged to East Anglia, and not, as is generally understood, to Mercia. [2] Beda, ii. 15.

—a pious man of Scottish race, from Ireland—the founder of several monasteries.[1]

But a season of calamity was now at hand for Northumbria. Penda, the son of Wibba, and successor of Ceorl, had rendered Southumbria, or Mercia, independent of Eadwine,[2] and, in alliance with the powerful British prince Cædwalla of Gwynedd, the son of Cadvan, made war on. Eadwine, who, together with his son Osfrith, was slain in a great battle fought at Hæthfeld.[3] Another of his sons, Eadfrith, who had fled to his relation Penda as a suppliant, was by him treacherously murdered. Eadwine's queen, Æthelburh, and the archbishop Paulinus fled to Kent, where they met with an honourable reception from her brother Eadbald and the archbishop Honorius, who appointed Paulinus to the see of Rochester. Wuscfrea, another son of Eadwine, and Yffe (Yffi), son of Osfrith, were subsequently, from fear of her own brother Eadbald of Kent, and Oswald of Northumbria, sent by the queen to the Frankish king Dagobert, through the mediation of the archbishop Paulinus. The early death of these children, the heirs of the founder of Edinburgh (Eadwines burh), prevented probably an early example of

[1] A.D. 635. Beda, iii. 18, 19, Vita Ethelredæ. According to the Chronicle and Florence, Eorpwald's conversion took place in 632, the preaching of Felix in 636. In the above, Beda has been followed.

[2] According to the Chronicle, Penda had been king of Mercia from 626; but Beda, ii. 22, says expressly, that he was of royal race (de regio genere Merciorum), and reigned twenty-two years. Therefore, as the accounts concur in placing his death in 655, he must have been king from 633 only, the year of his victory over Eadwine.

[3] Beda, ii. 20. Sax. Chron. Oct. 14, a. 633. Flor. of Worc. Oct. 12. Annal. Ult. and Tigernach, a. 631. Camden suppos·s Hatfield, in the West Riding of Yorkshire, to have been the spot.—T.

the Frankish influence so often exercised in after-ages on the fate of North Britain; but a sepulchre within the church long bore witness both to the antiquity of this connection, and to the asylum afforded by the monarch.[1]

The respect paid to the royal races of the Anglo-Saxons is strikingly proved by the circumstance, that neither Penda, who retained only his paternal kingdom of Mercia, nor the king of Gwynedd took possession of the conquered state, the northern part of which, Bernicia, the land of Æthelfrith, devolved on his son Eanfrith, who, after the death of his father, had with several friends wandered to the Scots or Picts, and adopted Christianity, according to the doctrines followed among those people. The southern portion, Deira, was held by Osric, the nearest kinsman of Eadwine, who had been baptized by Paulinus. Both relapsed into the errors of paganism, which was perhaps not surprising in the case of Eanfrith who belonged to a country in which the Odinic faith was still observed. Osric was slain at York, in an attempt to surprise Cædwalla, who had shut himself up in that city; Eanfrith fell by the same hand, being treacherously murdered by him when, accompanied by twelve followers only, he came to sue for peace. Their countries were ravaged by the Britons in the most cruel manner. The names of these apostate princes were erased from the catalogue of Christian kings, and the unhappy year of their reign assigned to Oswald, their pious successor.[2]

[1] Beda, ii. 14, 20.
[2] Beda, iii. 1. Sax. Chron. Flor. of Worc. a. 634. Eanfrith is the Anfraith, whose decapitation is mentioned by Tigernach a. 632.

But the apostasy of these princes and the sufferings of the Northumbrians may be said to have constituted the turning point, as it were, not only of the immediate fortunes of the North Angles, but of the successful struggle of Christianity against paganism. Oswald, a younger son of Æthelfrith, bred like his elder brother among the Scots, placed himself at the head of a small force, and at Hefenfeld, not far from the Roman wall, near Denisburn, in the neighbourhood of Hexham, having erected a cross, the first sign of Christian devotion in Bernicia, assembled his followers before it, commanded them to kneel, and having sent forth a fervent prayer to the God of armies, attacked the numerous warriors of Cædwalla, who lost their leader, and—what in those days was the usual consequence of such a loss—betook themselves to flight.[1] With Cædwalla expired the last renowned hero of the old British race: in fourteen pitched battles and sixty encounters he had revived and confirmed the military fame of his country, and acquired dominion over a considerable part of Lloegria (Lloegyr). No wonder then if his life and death, though claiming a far higher degree of historic credibility than Arthur's, were soon surrounded by the glittering imagery of tradition,[2] and that we are now unable to ascertain the truth, either in the apotheosis of his adoring countrymen, or in the vindictive narrative of the Anglo-Saxons.

History informs us that Oswald's cross decided the

[1] A.D. 635. Beda, iii. 2. Flor. of Worc. a. 634. Nennius (Appen. calls the battle, bellum Catscall., Annal. Camb. a. 631, b. Cantscaul. (Cædwealla).

[2] Geof. of Monm. lib. xii. Llywarch Hên, Elegies. Cf. Turner, vol. i. p. 366.

fate of Britain for ever. Oswald obtained the sovereignty of Bernicia, and also of Deira, being entitled to the latter country by his maternal descent, his mother "Acha," the sister of Eadwine, being descended from Ælle.[1] He was acknowledged as Bretwalda, the sixth who held that dignity, and is said to have reigned over the four tongues of Britain,—of the Angles, the Britons, the Picts, and the Scots. Oswald combined great vigour with much mildness and religious enthusiasm. By him Christianity was introduced anew into his kingdom, but it was that of his teachers, the Scots, by whom Aidan was sent to him from the isle of St. Columba (Hii or Icolmkill), and to whom he granted, as an episcopal seat, the isle of Lindisfarne, now Holy Island, the hallowed abode of many heroes of the Christian faith.[2] Severity towards himself and the powerful, humility and benevolence towards the poor and lowly; activity in the cause of religion, zeal for learning, were the admirable qualities that were praised in Aidan, and shed the purest lustre on the old Scottish church to which he belonged. And few will feel disposed to doubt that the general impression which the lives of such men made on the minds of people disgusted with paganism, together with the internal truth of the Christian doctrines, has always more powerfully contributed to their first conversion than even the most convincing and solid arguments. How else could the so-often vainly attempted conversion of the Northumbrians have been effected by Aidan, who, sprung from a hostile race, and sent from a hostile school, strove to propagate the doctrines of the defeated Scots and Picts, the former oppressors of the Britons, in a tongue

[1] Beda, iii. 6.
[2] See Beda's prose and metrical Life of S. Cuthberht.

for which Oswald himself was compelled to act as the interpreter?

Of Aidan's fitness for the pious work committed to him, a judgment may be formed from the following anecdote, related by Beda.[1] At the solicitation of Oswald, a priest had been sent by the Scots to preach the word to the pagans of Northumbria, who proving unqualified for the task, and unwelcome to the people, through the austerity of his character, returned to his country, where, in an assembly of his brethren, he declared his inability to effect any good among a people so ungovernable and barbarous. On hearing this declaration, Aidan, who was present at the meeting, said to him, "Brother, it seems to me that you have been harsher than was fitting towards such uninstructed hearers, and have not, in conformity with apostolic usage, first offered the milk of milder instruction, until, gradually nourished by the divine word, they might become capable both of receiving the more perfect, and of executing the higher precepts of God." A discussion, to which these words gave rise, terminated in the unanimous declaration, that Aidan was worthy of the episcopal dignity, and that he ought to be sent to teach the ignorant unbelievers.

In such, and in every other manner possible, Oswald promoted the religion of the cross planted by him, not in his own kingdom only, but in the states encircling his British empire.[2] In this he followed the impressions of his youth and the conviction which had steeled his arm for victory. He might also have cherished the hope, that in a British Christian church the surest

[1] A.D. 634. H. E., iii. 5.
[2] "Oswald totius Britanniæ imperator." Cummini Vita Columbæ, c. 26.

spiritual support would be found to consist in the union of all the tongues of Britain. Yet it must not be overlooked that he protected Christianity even when it was identified with the dogmas of the Western church.

Since the days of the Bretwalda Ceawlin the kingdom of Wessex had been engaged in constant warfare with its British and Saxon neighbours. Though the result may not always have been unfavourable, yet the state, split into many parts, bore the semblance of a great camp. In the year 626 we find mention of at least seven kings of the Gewissas.[1] Ceolwulf had succeeded his brother Ceolric,[2] and fighting against all, had proved against all the valour of the bravest,[3] though of his deeds we know but little. Beda, in general a poor source for the history of Wessex, does not even mention his name. The record of an obstinate battle with the then still apparently independent people of Sussex, in which he had the advantage, has alone been preserved in the annals of his country;[4] though a memorial equally favourable to the warrior has been transmitted to us in the records of his enemies, the Britons. Tewdric or Theodric, the valiant king of Morganwg, had at the beginning of the century renounced the world, having left his crown to his son Mouric, and amid the sylvan scenes of Dindyrn (Tintern), on the pleasant winding shores of the Wye, resigned himself to the enjoyment of solitary reflection, purified from all earthly contamination. Ceolwulf, taking advantage of the reign of the son, marched across the Severn, as far as the Wye.

[1] Beda, ii. 9. Sax. Chron. a. 626.
[2] Sax. Chron. a. 597, where and by Florence he is called Ceol.
[3] H. Hunt. W. Malm. lib. i., "quippe qui nulli unquam ignaviæ locum dederit."
[4] Sax. Chron. Flor. of Worc. H. Hunt. a. 607.

The cry of his faithful people drew the aged hero from his ten years' solitude, and his forces under their old leader were again victorious against the pagan Saxons. The dragon of Wessex was banished to the southern bank of the Severn; but Tewdric received a fatal wound which clove his skull, and was buried at the confluence of the Wye and the Severn.[1] Over his grave an oratory was raised, and at a later period a church, in honour of the royal martyr, on the spot afterwards called Mathern,[2] where for many ages his memory was celebrated by the race of his enemies on the anniversary of his martyrdom. His remains in a stone coffin, exhibiting the cloven skull, discovered in the sixteenth century, bore witness to the valiant heart once dwelling in the breast of the noble Tewdric of Morganwg, and even now the memory of this royal martyr gives an additional charm to the ruined remains of Tintern Abbey—one of the most beautiful monuments of mediæval architecture.

Cynegils, a son of Ceolric, and his son or brother, Cwichelm, succeeded Ceolwulf on the throne of Wessex.[3] It was in the reign of these princes that bishop Birinus landed in England. By the advice of pope Honorius, this missionary had undertaken to penetrate to the innermost parts of the country, for the purpose of propagating the Christian faith; but finding himself on reaching Wessex surrounded by the darkest paganism, he deemed it more useful to remain

[1] Calendar 3rd Jan. For the other particulars see Cod. MS. Eccl. Cath. Landav. in Monast. Angl. t. vi. p. 1222. The year of the battle, being in the time of bishop Oudoceus, the second successor of Dubritius (ob. 612), to whom the oratory was dedicated, must be subsequent to 610. See also Godwinus de Præsul. Angl. edit. 1616, p. 619. Usher, de Primord. c. 292. Langhorne, p. 148.

[2] From Merthyr Tewdric. He was accounted a martyr, having lost his life in fighting against pagans. [3] A.D. 611.

in those parts than to prosecute his original design. Cynegils, convinced by his preaching, was baptized at Dorchester,[1] being received from the font by Oswald of Northumbria, who had visited him for the purpose of marrying his daughter. In the following year Cwichelm also, a short time before his death, professed himself a convert to the new doctrine. To Birinus, who had also baptized Cuthred,[2] the son of Cwichelm, Dorchester was assigned as an episcopal see; and though Cenwealh, the son of Cynegils, after his father's death not only refused baptism, but strove to effect in Wessex a relapse into paganism, similar to that which had taken place in other states, yet his expulsion and conversion, which followed soon after, through converse with Anna, the pious king of the East Angles, and his steady adherence to the Christian faith after his restoration, prove that his conviction was sincerely shared by his people.[3]

To Oswald, not less distinguished for his energy and activity than for his fervent Christian beneficence, but a short duration of life was decreed. The restless foe of his country, Penda of Mercia, involved him in a war, in which he fell at a place called Maserfeld.[4] His last words when, surrounded by arms and enemies,

[1] A.D. 635.
[2] A.D. 639.
[3] Beda, iii. 7. Sax. Chron. a. 643.
[4] Sax. Chron. a. 642. Beda, iii. 9, " in loco, qui lingua Anglorum nuncupatur Maserfelth." There is a place called Maserfield near Winwich in Lancashire, but the site of the battle seems with more probability to have been Oswestry in Shropshire. See Monast. Angl. and Camden Brit. By the Britons this battle is called "bellum Cocboy" (or Chochui). See Nennius and Annal. Camb. a. 644, where it is said that Eoba (Eowa), the brother of Penda, also fell. Tigernach places the battle in which Oswald fell in 639: and another battle, unknown to our chronicles, of Oswiu against the Britons, in 642. See Annal. Ulton. aa. 638, 641.

death appeared inevitable, were a prayer for the souls of his people.

The scornful treatment to which the corpse of Oswald was exposed, bears witness alike to the ferocity of the pagan conquerors and to the fear in which they had stood of the Christian Bretwalda. Penda ordered the head and arms to be severed from their trunk and fixed on poles: these were removed by Oswiu in the year following, who caused the head to be buried at Lindisfarne, and the arms and hands at Bamborough, the royal residence. The body of Oswald was some time afterwards, by the care of his niece Osthryth, queen of Mercia, buried at Bardeney, where his banner of purple and gold was placed over his sepulchre.

His amiable character had obtained for Oswald, even among his hereditary foes, the Britons, the surname of "Lamngwin," *the fair or free of hand.* His Christian merits and his martyrdom made him a hero of the Christian world. He had attained only the age of thirty-eight, and reigned eight years, exclusive of the unhappy year assigned by an innocent fiction to his reign, though belonging to that of his predecessors.

Penda withdrew from Northumbria and the coast to his inland kingdom, after having glutted his vengeance and thirst for destruction, but certainly from other motives than those assigned by the credulous monks of those times. He had penetrated to Bamborough, which, defended by its position on a rock and by the waters of the ocean, defied his efforts to capture it either by assault or siege. He, therefore, resolved on its destruction by fire, to effect which he ordered a heap to be raised against the city, formed of timbers, thatch and other combustibles, brought from the ruins of the neighbouring hamlets, which he had commanded to be demolished for the purpose. This, when the wind was blowing towards the city, he caused to be set on fire; but at that instant the wind suddenly, as we are told, at the prayer of Aidan, changed to the opposite direction, driving the flames on the Mercians, of whom some were injured and all terrified.[1]

It is possible that here, as elsewhere in their history, we have evidence that the state constitution of the Anglo-Saxons, though without authority to prevent one kingdom from warring against another, did not permit the arbitrary aggrandizement or incorporation of the greater states, unless based on hereditary right; as in Germany, while under the emperors, we find the principle valid, that two dukedoms might not be united in one hand.

[1] Beda, iii. 16.

(207)

CHAPTER X.
MIDDLE OF SEVENTH CENTURY.

Successors of Oswald—Oswiu—Overthrow of Penda—Progress of Christianity—Oswiu's Efforts to reconcile the British Church with the Papal See—Synod of Whitby—Archbishop Theodore—His influence in asserting the Supremacy of the Romish Church—Bishop Wilfrith—His Character and Conduct—Introduces the Roman Ritual and Rule of St. Benedict.

ON the death of Oswald, his dominions were again separated into their chief constituent parts. His brother Oswiu succeeded to Bernicia and the Bretwaldaship; and two years later, Oswine (Oswini), son of Osric, to Deira. Oswine was distinguished by the comeliness of his person and the amiable qualities of his mind; he was munificent, pious and humble: attracted by his liberality, the noblest men from the provinces dedicated themselves to his service: but the virtues of Oswine availed him little as a shield against aggression on the part of Oswiu. On the eve of a conflict between these princes, Oswine, perceiving that the forces of his adversary were greatly superior to his own, and despairing of success, dismissed his army and withdrew for concealment, accompanied by one faithful follower named Tondhere, to the house of the caldorman Hunwald, near Gilling, by whom he was betrayed to Oswiu, and, together with his attendant, murdered at that king's command by his officer Æthelwine.[1]

[1] A.D. 651. Beda, iii. 14.

Twelve days after his death the venerable Aidan followed his royal friend to the grave. In atonement for his crime Oswiu founded a monastery at Ongetlingum, now Gilling, the spot where it had been perpetrated, near Richmond in Yorkshire.

Oswine was succeeded in a part of Deira by Æthelwald, a son of Oswald, who had just reached the age of majority.[1]

The chief deed of Oswiu, which as a warrior covered him with glory, and had the greatest influence on the history of the Anglo-Saxons, is the overthrow of Penda. This prince, whose name is rendered memorable by many successful enterprises against the other Germanic states in Britain, and on whom the surname of Strenuous [2] has justly been bestowed, presents a striking and almost inexplicable phenomenon. He was ruler of a territory surrounded more than any of the other states by a numerous hostile British population; and which —whatever sense may be given to a few obscure and doubtful traditions—was of all the youngest. This state, protected by marshes, rivers and mountains, had been formed in the middle of the country, by immigrants, who found the maritime parts already occupied. As ruler of this state, the first of the race of Woden among the Teutonic warriors dwelling in this territory; succeeding to power at the age of fifty,[3] yet displaying the

[1] St. Adelbert, a pupil of St. Willibrord, who preached at Kennemaren, and was buried at Hollum, afterwards called Egmond (Annal. Xanten. aa. 690, 694), is said to have been a son of Oswald, king of Deira.

[2] I do not hesitate restoring to Penda this surname, which has been overlooked by modern historians. By Hen. Hunt. he is repeatedly called 'Penda strenuus;' also Beda (ii. 20), in speaking of him, says, "auxilium præbente Penda viro strenuissimo."

[3] Sax. Chron. a. 626. W. Malm. lib. i. Beda, ii. 20 (who pro-

energy of youth; the last unshaken and powerful adherent of paganism among the Anglo-Saxons,—this prince, in alliance with, if not in the pay of, a British Christian king, had, during his reign of thirty years, first assailed the Bretwalda of Northumbria, and afterwards repeatedly the other states of his countrymen, with great success and still greater cruelty, yet, notwithstanding the destruction of five kings, without securing to himself any lasting result. Cynegils of Wessex had alone met him with any powerful resistance in the battle at Cirencester, where both armies, having fought obstinately till separated by the darkness, were, when about to renew the contest on the following morning, so disheartened by the mutual havoc, that terms of reconciliation were easily agreed to.[1] After the above-mentioned wars, with the cause of which we are unacquainted, we find Penda engaged in an expedition against Cenwealh, the son of Cynegils, for the purpose of avenging his sister, whom Cenwealh had married but afterwards repudiated.[2] With his usual success, he defeated Cenwealh and drove him from his kingdom. The fugitive found an asylum and protection with Anna, king of the East Angles, and, after an exile of three years, was, with the aid of his nephew Cuthred, reinstated in his dominions.

The protection afforded to Cenwealh was probably the pretext—if Penda needed a pretext—of a war

---

nounces him "de genere regio Merciorum"), begins his reign in 633, after the death of Eadwine. It may, therefore, not be purely accidental that the Chronicle in aa. 628 and 633 does not dignify him with the title of king.

[1] Sax. Chron. Flor. of Worc. H. Hunt. a. 628.
[2] Sax. Chron. a. 645. Beda, iii. 7.

between the Mercian and the king of East Anglia, in which the latter fell,[1] being the third Uffing who had lost his life in contest with Penda. Æthelhere (Æthelheri), the brother of Anna, succeeded to the throne, whom the conqueror compelled to accompany him in a campaign against the Bretwalda Oswiu. The latter had striven to live on peaceable and even friendly terms with the formidable Penda, the slayer of his brother Oswald. His son Ealhfrith was married to Cyneburh, a daughter of Penda; his daughter, Ealhflæd, to Peada son of Penda, ealdorman of the Middle Angles, who before this union had, with all his thanes and followers, been baptized by Finan of the isle of Hii, bishop of Lindisfarne, the successor of Aidan. Oswiu had delivered to Penda Ecgfrith (Ecgferth), one of his sons, as a hostage, and, in the hope of checking the repeated and intolerable inroads of the Mercians, had promised to their king innumerable royal ornaments and other gifts: notwithstanding which Penda, with his allies, Æthelhere of East Anglia, Æthelwald the son of Oswald, and Catgabail king of Gwynedd, marched against him with the avowed purpose of exterminating the entire nation. His thirty well-appointed legions under experienced leaders were arrayed against the little band of Oswiu, who felt strengthened by their faith in Christ. "If the heathen," cried Oswiu, "will not accept our gifts, let us offer them to him who will, to the Lord our God." He vowed to give twelve estates in land for the erection of cloisters, also to dedicate his daughter Ælflæd, a child of twelve months, to perpetual virginity and a monastic life, if he proved victorious. On the banks of the Winwæd Oswiu and his son Ealhfrith, with their enthusiastic band, began the

[1] Sax. Chron. a. 654.

conflict. On their side fought the God of battles, and the remembrance of five slaughtered kings and of countless victims of foul treachery; but treachery which had hitherto been favourable to Penda, now turned against him. Æthelwald ventured not to fight against his uncle and his country, but withdrawing to a place of security before the beginning of the conflict, awaited its result. Penda fell; and his death was preceded by that of Æthelhere and nearly all the thirty auxiliary chieftains. Catgabail fled under the veil of night, many perished by the sword, but many more in their flight were drowned in the Are, which, in consequence of the heavy rains, had overflowed its banks.[1] Oswiu fulfilled his vows; his victory over the pagans gave to the church six monasteries in Deira and six in Bernicia, but her greatest gain was in the undisturbed diffusion of Christianity. In Mercia the new faith was now firmly established; for, having budded under a pagan king who, at least in his latter years, did not persecute, but was content with despising the Christians, it soon surmounted the dangers of a violent political change. Peada, to whom Oswiu had ceded South Mercia, was in the Easter following murdered, it is said through the treachery of his wife. Two years later Oswiu, who at the time ruled over the whole of Mercia and the southern provinces, was expelled from Mercia by the revolt of three ealdormen, Immin, Eafha, and Eadberht, when Wulfhere (Wulfheri), a younger son of Penda, who had fled on the death of his father, and been long kept in concealment, ascended the throne of his an-

[1] Nennius, c. 66, who names the battle in which Penda fell, 'campus Gai.' The Annal. Camb. place it in 656, and Penda's death in the year following; the Annal. Ulton. in 649; Tigernach places both events in 650.

cestors,[1] which thenceforth derived its support from its adhesion to the Christian faith.

Diuma, a Scot, consecrated by Finan, was the first bishop of the Middle Angles and Mercians; the paucity of ecclesiastics rendering it necessary to place the two people under the spiritual government of one individual.[2] Essex also, whose king Sigeberht had, with the advice of his counsellors, yielded to the earnest remonstrances of his friend Oswiu, whom he frequently visited, abjured idolatry and returned to the faith which had been suppressed in the country since the expulsion of Mellitus. Cedd, an Englishman, consecrated also by Finan, was appointed by Oswiu bishop of the East Saxons.[3] Not long before, Ithamar, on the death of Paulinus, had been nominated to the see of Rochester,[4] being the first Anglo-Saxon raised to the episcopal dignity; and shortly after, Thomas, of the province of the Gyrwas, received the bishopric of the East Angles: even the only archiepiscopal dignity was possessed by an Anglo-Saxon, Deusdedit of Wessex. Already under Honorius, the predecessor of Deusdedit, the pope had remitted to the archbishops of Canterbury and York the journey to Rome for the purpose of obtaining the pall, and transferred to the survivor of either the consecration of the newly chosen archbishop; thereby acknowledging the great independence of the Anglo-Saxon church; but as the archbishopric of York, since the flight of Paulinus, had not been repossessed, Deusdedit received his consecration at the hands of his

[1] Beda, iii. 24.   [2] Beda, iii. 21.
[3] Beda, iii. 21, 22.
[4] Sax. Chron. Flor. of Worc. a. 644. Beda, iii. 14. "Honorius archiepiscopus ordinavit Ithamar, oriundum quidem de gente Cantuariorum sed vita et eruditione antecessoribus suis æquandum."

countryman, the Kentish bishop Ithamar,[1] who was himself succeeded by Damianus, a South Saxon.[2]

The need of a bishop familiar with the language of the country was most openly declared in Wessex. Cenwealh had, after his restoration, elevated Agilbert, a Frank, educated in Ireland, to the bishopric of the West Saxons; but becoming at length weary of a foreign tongue, he established a new bishop at Winchester, in the person of Wine (Wini), an Anglo-Saxon,[3] greatly to the displeasure of Agilbert, who returned to France, where he was raised to the see of Paris. A few years after the departure of Agilbert, the king expelled Wine from his see, so that the West Saxons were for a considerable time without a bishop. Wine betook himself to Wulfhere of Mercia, of whom he bought the bishopric of London, in which he continued till his death.[4] In Mercia also, two Scots (the before-mentioned Diuma, and Ceollach, who soon returned to the quiet of his cloister at Hii) were succeeded by Trumhere (Trumheri), an Anglo-Saxon and relation of king Oswiu, but educated among the Scots.[5] Though a lack of foreign ecclesiastics may be assigned as the cause of these appointments, it was certainly owing to the frequent elevation of natives to the highest spiritual dignities that the English church so early became a national one, that liturgy, ritual, prayers, and sermons so soon resounded in the Germanic dialect of the people and penetrated to their hearts. The retention of German proper names, the peculiarity of the Anglo-

[1] Flor. of Worc. a. 653.   [2] A.D. 664. Beda, iii. 20.
[3] Beda, iii. 7. "Rex, qui Saxonum tantum linguam noverat, pertæsus barbaræ loquelæ, subintroduxit in provinciam alium suæ linguæ episcopum, vocabulo Uini, et ipse in Gallia ordinatum."
[4] Beda, iii. 7.   [5] Beda, iii. 21. Flor. of Worc. a. 659.

Saxon calendar and festivals, the slight influence of the Roman ecclesiastical law, the cultivation of the native tongue by the ecclesiastics, the weakened influence of Rome on the princes,—all these were the beneficial fruits accruing to the church, which thus in reality became enriched by its early wants.

An important measure, both for the benefit of the church and the closer union of the Anglo-Saxons, was reserved for king Oswiu. The Anglo-Saxons, according as they had been converted by Augustine and his followers, or by those of Columba, were attached to the Roman Catholic, or to the British church. The majority of the ecclesiastics, at least of the more distinguished, belonged to the latter; hence arose a difference in religious views and worship not only in the several kingdoms, but in the several provinces, which threatened to become extremely dangerous to the new faith. We see this religious disunion introduced through marriage even among the royal families, and that Oswiu himself celebrated the Easter festival, according to the Scottish practice, on a different day from that observed by his queen Eanflæd, a daughter of the king of Kent.[1] Ealhfrith also, the son and co-regent with Oswiu, was, through the persuasion of his friend Cenwealh, favourable to the Roman church.[2]

[1] The Easter festival was regulated by the commencement of the equinoctial lunation, which, according to the Roman calculation, might begin as early as the fifth, while by the Alexandrian it could not begin before the eighth of March. Another point of controversy was the tonsure. The Romans in defence of their usage, pleaded the example of St. Peter, charging their adversaries with bearing the mark of Simon Magus, against which dire accusation their opponents could shield themselves only under the virtues of those whose example they followed. See Beda, ii. 4, iii. 3, 25, v. 21, and Smith's App. ix.—T.

[2] Eddii Vita S. Wilfridi, c. vii.

Differences of this kind, though affecting externals only, greatly endangered the Christian faith among a people scarcely weaned from the worship of their forefathers, and acquainted with Christianity only in the closest connection with the new external observances. Colman, a Scot, the third bishop of Lindisfarne after the death of Finan, zealously strove to establish the principles of his sect. A synod was called at Streones-' healh (Whitby),[1] in which, under the presidency of Oswiu, the most distinguished ecclesiastics of each church defended their respective doctrines. Among the partisans of Rome were Agilbert, bishop of Wessex, and Wilfrith (Wilferth), the future celebrated bishop of York. The disputation was maintained on both sides with learning and acuteness, and the Scottish clergy might have succeeded in getting for ever a strong barrier against the catholic pretensions of the Roman church, if the king, wavering under the weight of so many conflicting arguments, had not remarked, that the Scots appealed to St. Columba, but the catholics to the apostle Peter; for Wilfrith had not forgotten to adduce, in support of the Roman tenets, that Peter was the rock on which the Lord had founded his church, and that to him were committed the keys of heaven. "Has Columba also received such power?" demanded the king. Colman could not anwer in the affirmative. "Do you both agree that to Peter the Lord has given the keys of heaven?" Both affirmed it. "Then," said the king, "I will not oppose the heavenly porter, but, to my utmost ability, will follow all his commands and precepts, lest when I come to the gates of heaven, there be no one to open to me, should he, who is shown to have the key in his custody, turn his back upon me."

[1] Beda, iii. 25. Flor. of Worc. a. 664.

Those sitting in the council as well as those standing around, noble and vulgar,[1] alike anxious for their eternal salvation, approved of this determination, and were thus, in the usual spirit of large assemblies, and without further investigation of the arguments adduced, impelled to a decision by the excited feelings of the moment. The Scots either returned to their friends or yielded to the opinions of the majority,[2] and thus, by the learning of their school, became useful to the Anglo-Saxons; but, together with these apparently trivial externals, the great latent influence was sacrificed, which their church would probably have acquired in opposition to the then less firmly established one of Rome.

Oswiu himself appears to have been impressed with the necessity of the unity of the Anglo-Saxon church, and his character of Bretwalda—for we occasionally find him influencing, in a manner otherwise inexplicable, the concerns of the church[3]—justified him in, and prompted him to, the execution of this important design. When the archiepiscopal see of Canterbury became vacant by the death of the sixth archbishop, Deusdedit,[4] Oswiu consulted with Ecgberht, king of Kent, who had in the same year succeeded his father,

---

[1] Beda, iii. 25. "Hæc dicente rege, faverunt adsidentes quique sive adstantes, majores una cum mediocribus; et abdicata minus perfecta institutione, ad ea quæ meliora cognoverant sese transferre festinabant." This synod is also mentioned by Liutprand, Chron. a. 664.

[2] Beda, iii. 26.

[3] Beda, iii. 7. Thus, conjointly with Cynegils, Oswald appears as founder of the see of Dorchester. "Donaverunt ambo reges eidem episcopo civitatem quæ vocatur Dorcic, ad faciendum inibi sedem episcopalem." Wulfhere also sold, as we have just seen, the bishopric of London to Wine.   [4] Sax. Chron. a. 664.

Earconberht, concerning the interests of the national church, and concurred with him in recommending the presbyter Wigheard as primate to pope Vitalian, to the end that he might consecrate catholic prelates throughout the whole country.[1] The answers of Vitalian and the presents sent to Oswiu and his queen bear sufficient testimony to the gratitude of the Roman bishop.[2] The death of Wigheard, who fell a victim to the pestilence then raging,[3] soon after his arrival at Rome, was taken advantage of by the pope to set over the Anglo-Saxon bishops a primate devoted to his views, venerable by his age and experience, and distinguished by his rare knowledge and learning. The dignity was, therefore, offered to an African named Hadrian, a monk of Niridano, near Monte Cassino in the kingdom of Naples, who, declining the honour for himself, recommended as worthier of it the monk Theodore, born at Tarsus in Cilicia, a man eminently qualified by his attainments. The recommendation was accepted by the pontiff, on condition that Hadrian should accompany the new primate to Britain. From Rome the travellers proceeded to Marseilles by sea, and from thence by way of Arles to Paris, where they were kindly received by.

[1] Beda, iii. 29. Sax. Chron. a. 667.
[2] Beda, iii. 29, iv. 1.
[3] A.D. 664. This year there was a total eclipse of the sun, which was followed by the yellow plague, which, from time to time, desolated Britain, particularly Northumbria, during a period of twenty years. Among its victims were Catgualet, king of Gwynedd, Earconberht of Kent; Æthelwealh of Sussex; Deusdedit, archbishop of Canterbury; the bishops Wine of London and Tuda of Lindisfarne; Boisil, abbot of Mailros, and Æthelburh, abbess of Barking. In Ireland, it is said that two thirds of the inhabitants perished. The pestilence of which Wigheard died at Rome was probably the same disease. Beda, iii. 27, iv. i. Usher, Antiq. pp. 948, 1164.—T.

Agilbert, with whom having stayed some time, they prosecuted their journey, and landed safely in Kent. Immediately after his arrival, Theodore, accompanied by Hadrian, visited all the Anglo-Saxon states, where, by inculcating the apparently indifferent doctrine regarding the time of celebrating Easter, he effected an universal acknowledgment of the Roman Catholic church, and strove to obliterate all further and even every existing trace of the earlier influence of the Scottish clergy on the choice and consecration of bishops in his province. It was in his time that the Roman or Gregorian chant, which, with the exception of the Northumbrian churches, had been used only in Kent,[1] became general throughout the kingdom; and while he thus united and strengthened the Anglo-Saxon church,[2] and connected it with that of the continent, he exerted himself, by the communication of his own higher acquirements, to place the clergy of this country on a level with that of the rest of the Christian world. We learn also from Beda that to Theodore and Hadrian

[1] Beda, iv. 2. ["Sed et sonos cantandi in ecclesia, quos eatenus in Cantia tantum noverant, ab hoc tempore per omnes Anglorum ecclesias discere cœperunt; primusque, excepto Jacobo, de quo supra diximus, cantandi magister Nordanhymbrorum ecclesiis (Cf. H. E. ii. 20) Æddi cognomento Stephanus fuit, invitatus de Cantia a reverentissimo viro Uilfrido, qui primus inter episcopos, qui de Anglorum gente essent, catholicum vivendi morem ecclesiis Anglorum tradere didicit." To this Æddi we owe the valuable Vita Wilfridi, printed in Gale's collection, t. i., from whom; from Beda; from a metrical life by Fridegod; from Eadmer (ap. Mabillon, Sæc. iii. p. 1), and from W. Malm. (De Gest. Pont. lib. iii.), Smith (App. ad Bed. xix.) has compiled a very useful chronological view of the life of Wilfrith.] [For an account of the introduction of the Gregorian chant into England, see Smith's Appendix, No. xii.—T.]

[2] Beda, iv. 2. "Isque primus erat in archiepiscopis, cui omnis Anglorum ecclesia manus dare consentiret."

the country was indebted for the knowledge of prosody, astronomy, ecclesiastical arithmetic, and also for the training of men who were as familiar with Greek and Latin as with their mother-tongue.[1]

Theodore found a most ardent and able adherent in that devoted champion of the Roman church, Wilfrith, bishop of York, a man eminently distinguished for Christian zeal, rare knowledge and vigorous powers of mind, whose eventful life attracts our attention even for its own sake, and imperatively demands it through its connection with important events in the history of the country, at that time so closely interwoven with that of the church.

Wilfrith, though not of noble birth,[2] was endowed with all those natural advantages, the influence of which over rugged uncivilized people appears almost fabulous. In his thirteenth year, the period at which an Anglo-Saxon youth was considered of age, he resolved to leave his parents and renounce the world. Equipped suitably to his station, he was sent to the court of Oswiu, and, through the influence of the queen Eanflæd, was received into the monastery of Lindisfarne by the chamberlain Cudda, who had exchanged earthly joys and sorrows for the retirement and observances of a cloister. Here he was as remarkable for humility as for mental endowments. Besides other books he had read the entire psalter, according to the emendation of St. Jerome, as in use among the Scots. His anxious desire to behold and pray in the church of the apostle Peter must have been the more grateful to the queen

[1] H. E. iv. 2.
[2] Mulmesb. de Gestis Pont. lib. iii. "Non infimis parentibus apud Northanimbros natus, si quid natalibus defuit gratiæ, generositate morum explevit."—T.

and her Roman Catholic friends from the novelty and singularity of such a wish among his countrymen. In furtherance of his object she sent him to her brother Earconberht, king of Kent, where he made himself familiar with the doctrines of the Roman church, including the psalms according to the fifth edition. He was attached, as travelling companion, to Benedict, surnamed Biscop,[1] a distinguished man, who at a later period exerted himself so beneficially in the cause of the church, and in the civilization and instruction of the Northumbrians. Benedict died abbot of the monastery founded by him at Wearmouth, an establishment not less famed for arts and scientific treasures, than ennobled through its celebrated priest, the Venerable Beda.[2] On Wilfrith's arrival at Lyons,

[1] Eddius (c. iii.) calls him Biscop Baducing, no doubt from the name of his father.

[2] It will be allowed in the history of the Anglo-Saxons, where allusions so often occur indicative of a higher degree of culture among them than has generally been supposed to exist, to call attention to the account, hitherto unnoticed in our histories of art, of the pictures which Benedict, in the year 678, brought from Rome to Wearmouth, which is, moreover, specially interesting as showing not only how much must have been executed, or at least collected at Rome, but that the subjects chosen for representation were the same as those on which artists have been chiefly engaged from that time almost to the present. [The entire passages are so curious that I cannot resist the temptation to give them at length. " Picturas imaginum sanctarum, quas ad ornandum ecclesiam beati Petri Apostoli, quam construxerat, detulit; imaginem, videlicet, beatæ Dei genetricis semperque virginis Mariæ, simul et duodecim apostolorum, quibus mediam ejusdem ecclesiæ testudinem, ducto a pariete ad parietem tabulato, præcingeret; imagines evangelicæ historiæ, quibus australem ecclesiæ parietem decoraret; imagines visionum Apocalypsis beati Johannis, quibus septentrionalem æque parietem ornaret, quatenus intrantes ecclesiam omnes, etiam literarum ignari, quaquaversum intenderent, vel semper amabilem Christi sanctorumque ejus, quamvis in imagine, contemplarentur aspectum; vel

ANGLO-SAXON SETTLEMENT, A.D. 446-800. 221

Dalfinus, the archbishop, was so struck by his judicious discourse, comely countenance, and mature understanding, that he retained him long with him, offered to adopt him for his son, to give him the hand of his brother's daughter, and to procure for him the government of a part of Gaul.

But Wilfrith hastened to Rome, acquired there a thorough knowledge of the four gospels, also the Roman computation of Easter, which, as we have already seen, he afterwards so triumphantly employed; and at the same time made himself familiar with many rules of ecclesiastical discipline, and whatever else was proper for a minister of the Roman church. On his return he passed three years at Lyons with his friend Dalfinus, and extended his knowledge by attending the most learned teachers. He now declared himself wholly devoted to the church of Rome, and received from Dalfinus the tonsure of St. Peter, consisting of a circle of hair in imitation of the crown of thorns, while the Scots shaved the entire front, leaving the hair only on the hinder part of the head. Here he nearly shared

Dominicæ incarnationis gratiam vigilantiore mente recolerent; vel extremi discrimen examinis, quasi coram oculis habentes, districtius se ipsi examinare meminissent .... Dominicæ historiæ picturas, quibus totam beatæ Dei genetricis, quam in monasterio majore fecerat, ecclesiam in gyro coronaret, adtulit; imagines quoque ad ornandum monasterium ecclesiamque beati Pauli Apostoli, de concordia Veteris et Novi Testamenti, summa ratione compositas, exhibuit: verbi gratia, Isaac ligna, quibus immolaretur, portantem; et Dominum crucem, in qua pateretur, æque portantem, proxima super invicem regione, pictura conjunxit. Item serpenti in eremo a Moyse exaltato, Filium hominis in cruce exaltatum comparavit."— T.] One of these pictures, though not specially mentioned, yet perhaps comprised among the 'imagines evangelicæ historiæ,' Beda seems to have had in his eye when describing the three holy kings. Cf. Bedæ Vita S. Bened.

the fate of his unfortunate friend, the archbishop, in the persecution raised against him by the queen Baldhild, the widow of Clovis the second,[1] and the mayor of the palace, Ebruin; but the comely young stranger, through the extraordinary compassion of his persecutors, was saved from the death of a martyr. He now hastened back to his country, where he was honourably received by king Ealhfrith, consecrated abbot of the monastery of Ripon, and regarded as a prophet by high and low. After the disputation with bishop Colman at Whitby, Oswiu and his son with their witan chose the abbot Wilfrith for bishop of York, who passed over to Paris to be consecrated by Agilbert. On his return to Northumbria he was driven by a storm on the coast among the pagan South Saxons, who proceeded vigorously to exercise the right of wreck on the strangers. The chief priest of the idolaters stood on an eminence, for the purpose of depriving them of power by his maledictions and magic, when one of their number, with David's courage and luck, hurled a stone at him from a sling which struck him to the brain. At the fall of their priest the fury of the people was excited against the little band, who succeeded, however, after a conflict four times renewed, in re-embarking with the return of the tide, and reached Sandwich in safety.

So arbitrary at that time was the spirit in which affairs of the highest moment were conducted, so wavering the mind of Oswiu, of so little worth the royal word, that the king, during Wilfrith's absence, influenced by the Scottish party, had consented to the

[1] Baldhild is said to have been an Anglo-Saxon slave. Act. Sanc. Mabill. Sæc. ii. p. 777 sq. Script. Rer. Fr. t. ii. p. 449.

election of the presbyter Ceadda to the see of York. Wilfrith retired submissively to his cloister at Ripon, where he introduced the Roman ritual and the rule of St. Benedict, occasionally performing episcopal duties, at the desire of the kings Wulfhere of Mercia and Ecgberht of Kent. Archbishop Theodore, however, during his visitation of Bernicia and Deira, effected his restoration to his see, while that of Lichfield was by Wulfhere, at the instance of Wilfrith, bestowed on Ceadda.

CHAPTER XI.

LATTER HALF OF SEVENTH CENTURY.

The Arts in England—Mercia—The Mercian King—Wulfhere's Efforts to spread Christianity — Northumbria — Increasing Power of Clergy—Anglo-Saxon Missions Abroad—Scottish Foundations—Ceadwalla — His successive Conquests — Abdication —Wilfrith's Influence in converting the Anglo-Saxon States to Roman Catholic Christianity — Ecclesiastical Institutions —Bishoprics—Disputes with the Scottish and Welsh Clergy of the British Church—Anglo-Saxon Churches and Monasteries.

WITH other arts and knowledge architecture also came to Britain through the Roman church. The Scottish clergy, from the preference perhaps of the northern nations for that material, had built their churches of wood, thatching them with reeds, an example of which existed in the new cathedral at Lindisfarne. It was at a later period only that reeds were exchanged for sheets of lead, with which the walls also were sometimes covered. Wilfrith sent for masons from Kent, and the abbot Benedict for workmen from Gaul. The stone basilica erected by Paulinus at York, which had fallen into a disgraceful state of dilapidation, was restored by Wilfrith, the roof covered with lead, and the windows filled with glass, till then unknown among his countrymen.[1] At Ripon he caused a new basilica

[1] Eddius, cc. xvi., xvii., Beda, Vita Benedicti. "Benedictus . . . Gallias petens cœmentarios, qui lapideam sibi ecclesiam juxta Romanorum morem facerent, postulavit, accepit, attulit. Misit legatarios Galliam, qui vitri factores, artifices vidclicet Britanniis

of polished stone to be erected, supported by pillars, with a portico. The consecration—at which the kings Ecgfrith and Ælfwine were present—was concluded by a festival reminding us of pagan times, which lasted during three days and nights.[1] The four gospels written with golden letters on purple vellum, adorned with paintings, in a case, *bibliotheca*, of pure gold set with precious stones, enables us to judge both of the wealth and munificence of the patrons of Wilfrith. An edifice still more remarkable was erected by the bishop at Hexham, which, it is said, had not its like on this side of the Alps.[2] Benedict's structure too at Wearmouth was the work of masters from Gaul, after the Roman model. Thus we perceive, in the instance of the most memorable buildings of which mention is found in the history of the Anglo-Saxons, how their architecture sprang from that of ancient Rome, however it may have been modified in England to suit a difference of circumstances and climate.

Oswiu had greatly enlarged his dominions by victories over the Picts, and held his state in obedience and tranquillity till his death.[3] His eldest son Ealhfrith had died before him, and his kingdom,

---

eatenus incognitos, ad cancellandas ecclesiæ porticuumque et cœnaculorum ejus fenestras adducerent." [For much curious information on this subject, see Dissertation 'On the Introduction of Learning into England,' in Warton's H. E. P. vol. i.—T.]

[1] Eddius, c. xvii.
[2] Eddius, c. xxii. "Domus, cujus profunditatem in terra cum domibus mirifice politis lapidibus fundatam, et super terram multiplicem domum, columnis variis et porticibus multis suffultam, mirabilique longitudine et altitudine murorum ornatam, et variis linearum anfractibus viarum, aliquando sursum, aliquando deorsum, per cochleas circumductam."
[3] Beda, iv. 5. Sax. Chron. a. 670.

VOL. I.   Q

composed of so many discordant parts, fell to his younger sons Ecgfrith and Ælfwine. Despising their youth, the Picts lost no time in attempting to regain their independence, but the Northumbrian princes, under the direction of the valiant Bernhæth, were enabled for a considerable time to hold them in subjection. A more dangerous enemy threatened them in Mercia, whose king, Wulfhere, seems to have been regarded as Bretwalda. This prince strove to form an alliance with the southern states against Northumbria and to render that kingdom tributary: so unsuccessful, however, was the plan, that Wulfhere, being himself overcome by the Northumbrians, saw his state divided and made tributary, and the territory of Lindisfarne annexed to Northumbria.[1] Wulfhere did not long survive this reverse. He was the first prince who, after some struggles with Wessex, preserved Mercia in a long state of tranquillity and reputation among the Anglo-Saxon kingdoms. His exertions for the spread of Christianity, to which he had converted Æthelwealh,[2] king of Sussex; his endeavour, in conjunction with Wilfrith, by the ministry of the priest Eoppa, to convert the inhabitants of the Isle of Wight;[3] and his friendship for Wilfrith and other

---

[1] Palgrave, vol. ii. p. cccxi, places this event about the year 678, apparently because Beda, iv. 12, says, "quam 'provinciam *nuperrime* rex Ecgfrid . . . superato in bello et fugato Vulfhere, obtinuerat." But Wulfhere died in 675 (see Sax. Chron.), and his successor Æthelred ravaged Kent in 676. Beda, iv. 12. Edde also (c. xx. sq.) places the victory "in primis Ecgfridi regis," before Wulfhere's and several years before Eugobert's death (678). The Chronol. in Wanley and Petrie gives the date 674.

[2] The Sax. Chron. a. 661 erroneously calls this prince Æthelwald.

[3] Sax. Chron. a. 661. [Where it is at the same time st ited that he had previously laid it waste.—T.]

Christian teachers, show that he was susceptible of higher instruction and understood the true policy of his time. Of his last act, which reminds us strongly of his father Penda, we cannot judge with confidence, our knowledge of it being derived solely from Northumbrian sources.

With the increasing power of Northumbria the authority of the bishop of York was in a like degree extended. Clerical influence became exceedingly powerful over the Anglo-Saxons, and among the newly converted people we soon discover the same erroneous notions as those which in that age were so prevalent on the continent. Æthelthryth, the daughter of Anna king of the East Angles, had been first affianced to Tunberht, prince or ealdorman of the South Gyrwas, after whose premature death she was demanded by Oswiu for his son Ecgfrith, then a youth of fourteen years only. This princess, desirous of imitating what in those times was regarded as the acme of female perfection, had made and kept a vow of perpetual virginity.[1] In the view of turning her from her resolve, Ecgfrith demanded the mediation of Wilfrith, promising him lands and money in the event of his success. That Wilfrith's influence was unavailing, or exerted in a way contrary to the king's expectation, may be concluded from the circumstance that, after being for twelve years the wife of Ecgfrith, Æthelthryth became a nun in the monastery of Coldingham. From this event the ill-will of Ecgfrith towards Wilfrith is said to have taken its origin.

After his separation from Æthelthryth, Ecgfrith

[1] Beda, iv. 19, ejd. Chron. a. 688. W. Malm. lib. iv. and her Life by Thomas of Ely, ap. Mabillon, Sæc. ii. [Æthelthryth died abbess of Ely.—T.]

espoused Eormenbirh, sister of the wife of Centwine, king of Wessex,[1] a princess whose violence of disposition seems to have widened the breach between her consort and the prelate, and hastened the outbreak of the dissensions among the higher clergy, and the incipient jealousy of the secular towards the ecclesiastical power. Though Wilfrith had not recovered for his see the old archiepiscopal title, yet the primate of Canterbury could hardly expect that the northern prelate would not seek to regain the ancient rights of his vast province; he consequently delayed not to represent to the kings Ecgfrith and Ælfwine the danger to which the riches and authority of the bishop of York might expose him. The kings and the archbishop agreed therefore to divide the northern bishopric into two dioceses; one at York for Deira, and one at Hexham or Lindisfarne for Bernicia. Though the violence of this proceeding may not meet with approval, the partition of the bishopric seems justified by the example afforded by Wilfrith himself, with whose co-operation the kingdom of Mercia, containing one bishopric of equal extent with itself, was shortly after separated between two, and afterwards among three prelates.[3] East Anglia was also in the time of Theodore divided into two bishoprics.

The personal consideration enjoyed by Wilfrith was powerless in effecting any change in this decision. On the contrary, his opponents were so exasperated, that, on his leaving England,[4] attended by a company of

[1] Eddius, c. xxxix.   [2] Beda, iv. 12.
[3] Malmesb. de Gestis Pontif. lib. iv. p. 288.
[4] Wilfrith's flight must, as by Flor. of Wor., be placed in 677, as in the following spring he had an interview with Dagobert who was murdered in 678. The date 678 given in Beda, iv. 12, and in the

ecclesiastics, the king of Neustria and his powerful mayor of the palace, Ebruin, were prevailed on to cause him to be waylaid on his journey towards Rome. This request implies a closer connection between the two courts than the obscurity in which those times are shrouded enables us otherwise to recognise; though the readiness of the Neustrians to persecute the exile may have been a consequence of the circumstance, that Wilfrith, at the solicitation of the friends of the Austrasian king, Dagobert (Dægberht) the Second,— who, after a long exile, had discovered that prince in Ireland,—had, supported by the arms of his partisans, effected his return to his realm, and presented him with costly gifts. A storm, which drove his vessel to the coast of Friesland, saved Wilfrith; but a delusive similarity of name threw the bishop of Lichfield, Wulfrith, also an exile, into the hands of the waylayers. The landing of Wilfrith in Friesland was productive of the most important consequences, both for the inhabitants of that country, and afterwards for a great part of the north of Europe. Wilfrith found an hospitable reception with the king Aldgisl, as well as protection against the machinations of Ebruin, who even there ceased not to persecute him. Called on by the credulous people, who ascribed to his presence the abundant fishing season and the rich harvest of that year, he preached to them the doctrine of Christ in the intelligible dialect of the Anglo-Saxons, and baptized nearly all the princes, with many thousands of the people.[1]

Chronicle, may have reference to the consecration of his successors. [Some MSS. read septimo for octavo. See Stevenson's note, p. 275 of his edit.—T.]

[1] Eddius, c. xxvi.-xxviii.

It was thus decreed to Wilfrith to be the first of the numerous Anglo-Saxon missionaries and ecclesiastics to whom the countries on the Baltic and German Ocean, also many provinces to the south, are indebted for their conversion to Christianity and the elements of civilization intimately connected therewith. His immediate followers were his pupil Willebrord, afterwards, under the name of Clement, first bishop of the Frisians; Winfrith or Boniface, the apostle of the Thuringians, and archbishop of Mentz; Leofwine, the successful converter of the Saxons; Willehad of Northumbria, the friend of Alcwine (Ealhwine) and first bishop of Bremen; Willebald, first bishop of Eichstädt, and his brother Wunibald. We also find in Germany many devout and zealous Anglo-Saxon ladies, as Leobgyth, who had learned the art of poetry from the abbess Eadburh; Thecla, abbess of the cloister at Kitzingen, and others. In consequence of the connection between Denmark and England, a considerable number of distinguished men followed in the same course, whose influence on the civilization of the North has been generally disregarded, and certainly never sufficiently appreciated. Those remaining behind were cheered and confirmed in the faith by the example and teaching of Aldhelm, first abbot of Malmesbury (Mœldulfsburh), and afterwards bishop of Sherborne, who first among the Anglo-Saxons made the whole heritage of Roman learning his own, and gained the still greater glory of being one of the earliest and best poets in his own Germanic mother-tongue.[1]

[1] Of Aldhelm we have the following testimony: "Aldhelmus nativæ linguæ non negligebat carmina, adeo ut, teste libro Elfredi (manuali libro sive handbuc) nulla ætate par ei fuerit quisquam poesim Anglicam posse facere." W. Malm. lib. v. ap. Savile and

Let us not, however, exalt the merits of the Anglo-Saxons without acknowledging those of their teachers, the Scots, especially as both worked sometimes in common in the same field, and the former are often comprised under the name of the latter. As applicable to both, may be remarked that their emigrations had not always the work of conversion for their immediate object. In consequence of the lack, during several centuries, of regular monastic orders, those desirous of devoting themselves to a severe and contemplative course of life, either alone or with a few kindred spirits, were often induced to leave their home and betake themselves to some lonely cell, or hallowed spot,[1]—a practice long retained among the Scots. At a time when the Anglo-Saxons had scarcely begun to spread a new paganism in Britain, Fridolin, a native of Ireland, had already founded a convent at Seckingen, an island in the Rhine,[2] and dedicated a church to St. Hilarius, the possessions of which have given name to the canton of Glarus.[3] At the beginning of the seventh century, Columbanus, the friend of St. Columba, with his pupil Gallus, travelled to those parts, where the name of the latter is preserved in that of the canton of St. Gall, and where his monastery may be regarded as the choicest storehouse of the learning and poetry of the middle ages. From Columbanus the cloister of Luxeuil, in the Vosges, also that of Bobbio and others derive their

---

Gale; and Wharton, Angl. Sac. t. ii. p. 1. Aldhelm died May 25, a. 709. An edition of Cædmon's Scriptural Paraphrase with an English version, by the translator of the present work, was published in 1832, at the expense of the Society of Antiquaries. Cædmon died in 680.—T.

[1] Osberni Vita S. Dunstani, lib. i. c. i.   [2] A.D. 490.
[3] J. v. Müller's Geschichte der Schweizer, Bd. i. c. 9.

origin. At a later period[1] Kilian, a Scot, with his companions Coloman and Tottman, founded a monastery at Würzburg, the library of which preserves the proof of its descent in precious monuments in the Irish language. Virgilius, a Scot, contemporary with Boniface, was bishop of Salzburg. The convent at Peronne seems also to be among the oldest foundations of the Scots.[2] Gertrude, abbess of Nivelles, a daughter of Pepin, as also a daughter of the mayor of the palace, Grimwald, caused many learned Scots to settle in France. Ultanus was the founder of the abbey of St. Quentin.[3] The convent of St. Martin at Cologne,[4] of St. James at Ratisbon, of St. Mary at Vienna, are only some among the many Scottish foundations to which Germany, as well as other countries, is indebted for the establishment and spread of Christian doctrines, the preservation of learning, and the beneficent applications of worldly goods.[5] The possession of rich benefices often excited the national jealousy against the Scots, who, however, were always able to recover their lost rights.[6] Of the ancient connection between the Scottish

[1] A.D. 680.
[2] Annales Mettenses, a. 690. Beda, iii. 19, and Smith's note; also Gall. Christ. t. ix. 1035, and Mabill. Annal. Ord. S. Bened. xiv. 1, 2.
[3] See charter in SS. Rer. Francic. t. ix. p. 735.
[4] In the Monum. Hist. Germ. t. ii. p. 215, Pertz has, for the first time, printed a chronicle of this monastery, from a. 756 to 1021.
[5] Cf. Murray, Comment. 'De Britannia et Hibernia, sec. vi.-x.' 'Literarum Domicilio,' in Nov. Comment. Soc. Göttingens. t. ii. For Scots in Iceland and other parts of the North, cf. Dicuilus de Mensura Orbis, ap. Langebek, SS. Rer. Dan. t. ii. p. 31, and Adam. Bremen.
[6] As early as the year 846 the French bishops recommended to Charles the Bald that the Hospitalia Scotorum should be kept

cloisters and the mother country, which was never broken, and had often proved of mutual benefit, both in secular and ecclesiastical respects,[1] traces exist even at the present day.

As Germany was especially indebted to British ecclesiastics, whether of kindred or of Celtic race, both for its Christianity and its early mental formation, it may reasonably be inferred that many historic traditions passed over from the old country to the new acquisition of the Saxons. We will here merely allude to the before-mentioned saga of the landing of the Saxons in Hadeln; though the old Danish history is undoubtedly interwoven with traditions of England. With the writings of the Anglo-Saxons, the oldest written chronicles also passed over to Germany, and in the earliest annals of German cloisters are to be found some chronological notices of which all traces are lost in England. To these strangers may also be ascribed the circumstance, that in the oldest small chronicles, in which almost every word must shed some welcome light on dark antiquity, instead of German names and narratives, unintelligible names of British ecclesiastics are often met with; still to these individuals is owing the introduction of Beda's chronology into Germany at that early stage of learning.

In the following year Wilfrith continued his journey towards Rome, after having declined the bishopric of Strasburg, offered to him by his royal friend Dagobert.

according to the intentions of their pious founders. Pertz, t. iii. p. 390. It is in later times only that we find them stigmatized and prosecuted as pseudo-bishops and vagabonds. Hludovici Imper. Capit. Addit. iii. 37.

[1] See hereafter, a. 929.

Bertari, king of the Longobards,[1] a friend and relative of the Anglo-Saxon rulers, received the exile with respect, rejecting with disdain the demand of his enemies to detain him. The protection of the pope had not yet been claimed by Anglo-Saxon churchmen; we may, therefore, considering the connection still subsisting with the old British clergy, as well as the short time that Northumbria had belonged to the catholic church, regard it only as a very bold experiment, when pope Agatho, with the synod assembled at Rome commanded, under threats of spiritual punishments, the restoration of Wilfrith to his former Saxon bishopric.[2] But the thunders of the Vatican proved as powerless as had been for many centuries the decrees of the Capitol. Ecgfrith not only held in contempt the command of the pope, but caused its object on his return to linger nine months in prison, from which he was released only by bold artifice and the representations of Œbba, the sister of king Oswiu and abbess of Collingham. He was, however, compelled to leave the dominions of Ecgfrith,

[1] The passage of Eddius (c. xxviii.), "pervenerunt ad Berchterum regem Campaniæ," has been often misunderstood. The words which he attributes to that prince about his flight to the king of the Huns agree fully with what Paul Warnefrid relates concerning Bertari, who had himself been desirous of seeking aid in England, and whose son Cunibert was married to an Anglo-Saxon lady named Hermelind. See hereafter under Ceadwealla of Wessex, and Paul Diac. v. 32, 37.

[2] Beda, v. 19. Fl. of Wor. a. 679. In his petition to the pope, Wilfrith styles himself 'episcopus Saxoniæ.' See Eddius, c. xxix. In like manner Hwætberht, in his letter to Gregory,—"Hwætberhtus abbas cœnobii beatissimi apostolorum principis Petri in Saxonia." Beda, Vita Hwætberchti. How readily Rome received this appeal, from which a faint dawn of future authority over all the British islands seemed to arise, appears from the acts of this synod. Cf. Alberici Chron. a. 680.

who, moreover, effected his expulsion from Mercia,—
whose king, Æthelred, had married Osthryth, a sister
of the Northumbrian,—as also from Wessex, where a
sister of queen Eormenburh was, as we have seen, the
consort of the king Centwine. As an asylum beyond
the influence of Ecgfrith, the remote territory of the
South Saxons alone presented itself to the fearless
energetic man, who had formerly been driven under
such inauspicious circumstances to their shores, where
the people, notwithstanding the earlier attempt to
convert them, had either persisted in, or fallen back
to, paganism.

The king of Sussex, Æthelwealh, as well as his
queen, Eabe,[1] of the family of the petty kings of the
Hwiccas, had been baptized, and thus to the homeless
exile, whom the secular power would not, and the
highest spiritual power could not protect, the work was
committed, of bringing within the pale of Christendom
the last heathen people of his native land. Here too were
the efforts of Wilfrith successful, as the early establishment of a bishopric in Sussex sufficiently proves, Selsea, which was subsequently transferred to Chichester,
being assigned to him as an episcopal see, together
with sufficient lands and revenues.

Even here the most important events of Britain are
gathered round the person of Wilfrith. Ceadwealla,
son of Cenbyrht,[2] of the race of Ceawlin of Wessex, had
lived an exile in the wilds of Chiltern and Andredes-
weald: he visited the bishop, who received the noble

[1] Eabe had already been baptized in her own country: "Eaba,
in sua, id est, Huicciorum provincia, fuerit baptizata; erat autem
filia Eanfridi, fratris Eanheri, qui ambo cum suo populo Christiani
fuere." Beda, iv. 13.—T.
[2] Ob. a. 661.

youth with kindness; and though yet unconverted, treated him as his son, and was greatly helpful to him in the acquisition of his kingdom.[1] Previously to this event, Ceadwealla (under what pretext, or how Wilfrith's conduct on the occasion is to be explained, we are ignorant) had conquered Sussex,—in defence of which Æthelwealh had fallen,—but had again lost it. Wilfrith now received the bishopric of Wessex from Ceadwealla, who, though still unbaptized, was zealous for the advancement of Christian institutions. Having reconquered Sussex and the Isle of Wight,—the conversion of which was also the work of Wilfrith,—he finally subdued Kent, where his brother Mollo was murdered by the embittered men of Kent, who having surprised him in a hut, set fire to the building, in which he was burnt to death. This event probably accelerated the execution of his design, at all events Ceadwealla resolved not only to adopt the faith professed by the majority of his subjects, but to give an example hardly occurring a second time in the whole course of history,—that of a youthful vigorous prince renouncing his sceptre, to sever himself from paganism by baptism at the hands of the sovereign pontiff, in the church of St. Peter, and in monastic solitude to await in serious meditation the day of admission to a better life.

Wilfrith had in the meanwhile become reconciled with the repentant archbishop Theodore, not long before the death of the latter in 690, and, through his mediation, also with Æthelred of Mercia, who bestowed on him the see of Lichfield,[2]—the fourth that had fallen to him—in his kingdom, and, after the

[1] Eddius, c. xli. II. Hunt. a. 686.
[2] Malmesb. de Gest. Pontif. lib. iii.

death of Ecgfrith, effected his reconciliation with Aldfrith,[1] his successor. Ecgfrith, after an unjust and cruel war on Ireland, the conduct of which he had committed to Beorh,[2] and after the conquest of Cumber-

[1] Aldfrith, who, according to Sim. Dunelm., in the year 685, May 20, succeeded Ecgfrith, has by most English historians (with the exception of Carte, Lingard and Palgrave) been regarded as the same son of Oswiu who ruled jointly, and thirty years previously commanded with his father in the decisive battle against Penda on the Winwæd; but it is to be remarked that Beda, whenever he mentions the eldest son, calls him Alchfrid (in Alfred's version, Ealhfrith), without the slightest allusion to illegitimacy. See H. E. iii. 14, 21, 24, etc. Vita S. Benedicti, p. 293. The later king he always calls Aldfrid (in Alfred's version, Ealdfrith), H. E. iv. 26, v. 19, 21, 24. Vita S. Ceolfridi, Vita S. Cuthb. Ep. ad Ecgb. p. 309, ed. Smith, ed. Stev. p. 219. Sax. Chron. aa. 685 and 705. Alcuinus, do Poutif. Eccles. Ebor. a. 843. Adamnani Vita S. Columbæ, ii. 46. Even in the incorrect printed text of Ædde we find the distinction of the names, c. viii. 56. But we nowhere find that the peaceful Irish student, the inexorable opponent of Wilfrith, of whom he had been the early friend and scholar, and the valiant conqueror of Penda, the rebellious son of Oswiu, were one and the same individual. Malmesbury indeed informs us that Aldfrith was the elder brother ("Is quia nothus erat, factione optimatum, quamvis senior, regno indignus æstimatus, in Hiberniam, seu vi seu indignatione, secesserat; ibi et odio germani tutus, et magno otio literis imbutus, omni philosophia composuerat animum," lib. i.), a fact which, if well founded, proves nothing against Beda's testimony. Alchfrid was in 653 married to a daughter of Penda. Beda, iii. 21. Aldfrid in 705 left a successor eight years of age. The similitude of names need excite no doubt. Aldfrid (Ealdfrith) is well associated with Alchfrid (Ealhfrith) and Ecfrid (Ecgfrith) to suit the Anglo-Saxon usage. Thus Penda's son was named Peada; two brothers, Cedd and Ceadda. Oswiu's daughter married in 653 to Peada, was named Alchfled (Ealhflæd), and one born the year following, Ælflæd. Beda. iii. 21, 24. Tigernach, a. 704, calls him Altfrith mac Ossu. O'Connor (MSS. Stowens. t. i) refers to a poem by him.

[2] Beda, iv. 26. Tigernach, a. 685. "Saxones campum (Bregrae) vastant, et ecclesias plurimas in mense Junii."

land, where he had bestowed Carlisle and the land of Cartmel on the church of Lindisfarne, was slain in an invasion of the Pictish territory, at Nechtansmere (Drumnechtan). Aldfrith was an illegitimate son of Oswiu, who having passed some time in Ireland,[1] devoted to study, and being very eminent at the time for his attainments, had by his brother been destined to hold a bishopric.

But for Wilfrith there was no tranquillity. Though he had declined the succession to the archiepiscopal see of Canterbury offered to him by Theodore, and had even aided Berhtwald in obtaining that dignity, the latter nevertheless, five years afterwards, during which time Wilfrith had recovered possession of the see of York and his other benefices, placed himself, with king Aldfrith, at the head of a synod. At this meeting most of the British bishops were present, who in that spirit of independence of the papal chair which had been maintained for the last twenty-two years, demanded of Wilfrith, in the first place, an acknowledgment of the statutes and ordinances of archbishop Theodore, and, on his refusal, resolved to deprive him of his benefices, excepting only the monastery of Ripon which he had founded.[2]

Wilfrith, far from tamely submitting to his disgrace and to the diminution of the papal authority, again undertook, though in his seventieth year, the perilous journey to Rome, where, however, the agents of the

[1] Beda, Vita S. Cuthb. c. xxiv. "In insulis Scottorum ob studium literarum exulabat—in regionibus Scottorum lectioni operam dabat, ipse ob amorem sapientiæ spontaneum passus exsilium." Also, Vita Cuthb. Anon. § 28. "Qui (Alfridus) tune erat in insula quam Hy nominant."—T.
[2] Eddius, c. xlv.

ANGLO-SAXON SETTLEMENT, A.D. 446–800. 239

archbishop in the character of accusers, strove to anticipate him. Though their efforts against Wilfrith were fruitless, yet the honourable exculpatory decision and mediation of the pope, John the Sixth, availed him little on his return to his native country. The archbishop received him with apparent kindness, but Aldfrith, on whom even Wilfrith's friend and biographer bestows the surname of "the Wisest," was too deeply imbued with the tenets of the old British church to allow the decrees made by his predecessors and himself, with the concurrence of the witan and clergy, to be annulled by a sheet of parchment from the chair at Rome.[1] The death of Aldfrith, and the declaration of his sister, the abbess Ælflaed and other adherents of Wilfrith, that the king in his last hours had desired the restoration of peace, but more effectually, perhaps, the death of Bosa, bishop of York, accomplished at length an accommodation, in the synod on the Nith,[2] which, as far as Wilfrith's pretensions were concerned, can be looked on only as a disregard of the papal authority. He did not even recover the bishopric of York, which was given to John, bishop of Hexham, a man highly venerated for his many virtues; while the vacant see of Hexham, together with the monastery of Ripon, was assigned to Wilfrith. After a few years passed in almsgiving and the improvement of church discipline, Wilfrith died in his seventy-sixth year, at Cundle in Northamptonshire, leaving the memory of a man whose fortunes and activity in the European relations of England, were long without a parallel.[3]

Wilfrith by his own power accomplished what

[1] Eddius, c. lvi.   [2] A.D. 705.
[3] Eddius, c. lxii. Beda, v. 19. Sax. Chron. a. 709.

Augustine, animated by the spirit of Gregory the Great, had begun. The Anglo-Saxon states were converted not only to Christianity, but to catholicism—for secular learning they were chiefly indebted to the Scots and Britons, for their accession to the European system of faith to these two men. The diffusion of the new faith had indeed been the slow work of an entire country, in which the gradually accumulating numbers of converts had more influence than individual cases of conversion amongst even the highest of the land. We meet with no evidence that the new faith was advanced by force, or repressed by persecution on the part of the followers of the old faith when the latter was in the ascendant. Baptisms were performed in large numbers —even by thousands—at the command of a king, priest or noble; and in the church history of the Anglo-Saxons, we derive much useful information in regard to similar occurrences among other Germanic peoples, which have often been falsely interpreted. But however successful Augustine may appear in his first spiritual acquisitions for the church of Rome, the course of Anglo-Saxon history, nevertheless, shows that, although the Roman ecclesiastical system was acknowledged, the influence of Rome was exceedingly weak, and that the Anglo-Saxons, even after they were no longer anti-catholic, continued always anti-papistical. Wilfrith's history itself proves indeed how little even this zealous partisan of the popes could effect; hence it is the more desirable to take a view of the internal relations of religion in England.

We notice, in the first place, in every kingdom a bishop, who, travelling about with his coadjutors, propagated both doctrine and discipline. This kind of church regimen was well calculated to succeed that of the pagan priesthood. The bishops, when chosen by the clergy, always required the confirmation of the prince, but, in most instances, they were nominated by him. In later times it is observable that the royal chaplains always obtained the episcopal dignities. Over these bishops, he who resided at Canterbury, the capital of the Bretwalda Æthelberht, was set as archbishop, in like manner as the bishop of Rome had originally assumed the supremacy over the Roman provinces. The archbishopric of York, established by Gregory the Great, which might act as a check to a primacy of the Kentish archbishop dangerous to the papal authority, ceased to exist after the flight of Paulinus, and was not re-established till a century afterwards, when Ecgberht the brother of king Eadberht, after many representations to the papal chair, received the pall.[1] A third archiepiscopal see was established for the country between the Thames and the Humber by the powerful Offa of Mercia,—who held the dignity necessary for the honour of his kingdom—with the consent of pope Hadrian, to whom this augmentation of his slight influence over the Anglo-Saxon clergy might have been welcome.[2] The old state of things was, however, shortly after restored.

Almost contemporaneously with the bishoprics, some monasteries were founded by the bounty of the kings and their relatives, which served as residences for numerous monks. Many of these cloisters in the north of England were destroyed by the Danes, and their very

[1] Sax. Chron. a. 735. Appendix ad Bedæ H. E. Beda, Epist. ad Ecgberht. Malmesb. de Gestis Pont. lib. iii. Wilfrith never bore the archiepiscopal title. Neither Beda nor Ædde allege anything to justify the supposition, but the contrary.
[2] Sax. Chron. Flor. of Worc. a. 785. W. Malm.

sites are not even now known with certainty. The superintendence over clergy and laity in the larger states soon required more than the single bishop of the territory, whose influence might, moreover, as we have seen in the case of Wilfrith, excite the jealousy of the king. In the choice of episcopal sees and monasteries, especial regard was had to the security of the new establishment; hence the fortified residence of the king, or a spot particularly defended by nature, like the isle of Lindisfarne, was selected. So completely had Christianity perished in Germanic Britain after the departure of the Romans, or so little was it acknowledged by the Saxons, that no religious foundation of Roman times was preserved or could be restored, and only some old Roman buildings and walls were used as churches. A small, probably old British, church was discovered in a wild thorny spot, which gave rise to the foundation of the abbey of Evesham.[1] If the abbey of Glastonbury or Ynisvitrain, which appealed to charters of donation from the ancient kings of Damnonia, seems to form an exception to the above statement, the circumstance must not be overlooked, that this cloister, in the isle of Avallon, where the corpse of Arthur rested, remained long in the hands of the Britons.[2]

[1] Malmesb. de Gestis Pontif. lib. iv. ["constat eum (Ecgwinum) locum illum, quo nunc coenobium visitur, peculiariter amasse, incultum antea et spinetis horridum, sed ecclesiolam ab antiquo habentem, ex opere forsitan Brittannorum." The spurious charters of Coenraed and Ecgwine relating to this foundation are given in Kemble's Codex Dipl. t. i. p. 68 sqq.—T.]

[2] Malmesb. de Antiq. Eccl. Glaston. ap. Gale, t. i. p. 308. The Damnonian charter is, however, dated as late as 601, consequently after the arrival of Augustine, and his conference with the British bishops. [See also the charter of Henry II. printed by Hearne

A glance at the Anglo-Saxon bishoprics, together with a brief notice of the most eminent monasteries, will render the geographical idea of the several kingdoms more familiar. This knowledge is, moreover, indispensable with reference even to the political history of a country in which bishops and prelates shared the privileges and duties of secular nobles.

The little kingdom of Kent contained, besides the archiepiscopal see, the bishopric of Rochester, founded by Augustine. In Essex the only bishopric was that of London, whose diocese comprised the present counties of Essex and Middlesex with the half of Hertfordshire.[1]

In East Anglia dwelt the bishop of Domuc (Dunwich),[2] though, as early as the time of archbishop Theodore, advantage was taken of the death of bishop Bisi to erect a separate see for the North-folc at Elmham, which, in the time of William the Conqueror, was transferred to Thetford, and under William Rufus, to Norwich.[3]

In Wessex the first episcopal see was at Dorcic (Dorchester), from which, as has been already mentioned, a bishopric at Winchester was afterwards detached. The former retained Hampshire and Surrey. A third at Sherborne—famed for its first possessor, Aldhelm, as also for a later one, Asser, the friend of Ælfred,—was, under the Conqueror, in conformity to the canonical

---

from the chartulary of Glastonbury, and Hemingi Cartularium, app. 603.] This is one of the few cloisters of which the charters granted by the early Anglo-Saxon kings have not entirely perished. See Cod. Diplom. t. i.

[1] A.D. 604. Beda, ii. 3. Flor. of Worc. Malmesb. de Gestis Pontif. lib. iii. R. Higden, Polychron. ap. Gale, t. i. p. 204 sq.
[2] A.D. 631. Beda, ii. 15. [3] Malmesb. de Gestis, ii.

prescript for the transfer of episcopal sees from small places to large towns, removed to old Sarum, and afterwards to Salisbury, though not till the following bishoprics had been taken from it, viz. Wells, afterwards Bath; Ramesbury, subsequently reunited to Sarum; Crediton, afterwards transferred to Exeter, with which that of St. Petroc or St. Germain's (Cornwall) was subsequently united. To Sussex belonged the bishopric of Selsea, afterwards transferred to Chichester.

In Mercia, from the original diocese of Lichfield (which comprised also the territory of the Lindisfaras) were detached by Theodore the sees of Worcester, Leicester, Lindesey (at Sidnacester) and Hereford. At the same time the see of Dorchester appears to have belonged to the state of Mercia.[1]

The diocese of York comprised originally the whole of Northumbria, including the south of Scotland. Under Oswald, the see of Lindisfarne or Holy Island—the Iona of the Anglo-Saxons—was founded, containing within its jurisdiction the kingdom of Bernicia, until the establishment by Theodore of another see at Hexham.[2] On the ruin of Lindisfarne by the Danes, the see was transferred to Chester-le-Street, and finally to Durham. That portion of the diocese which was in the present Scotland, fell in the reign of Malcolm Canmore to the see of St. Andrews.

The conquests of the Northumbrian princes were followed by an extension of the diocese of York. Hwitern (Candida Casa), now Whitherne in Galloway, where Nynias had formerly erected a church of bright white stone for the southern Picts, had, in Beda's time,

[1] Malmesb. de Gestis. Higden, Polychron. p. 206.
[2] Beda, iv. 12.

its first Anglo-Saxon bishop, Pecthelm, supposing that the authority of Trumwine—who was sent from Northumbria to the Picts in the year 681, but expelled after the defeat of Ecgfrith—was limited to the northern portion of the Pictish territory.[1] It appears that this bishopric was for some time dissolved, and that its inhabitants were under the charge of the bishop of Sodor and Man;[2] though, on the restoration of the see of Hwitern, the archbishops of York made good their authority over it. At a later period this district, as well as the whole of Strathclyde, belonged to the diocese of Glasgow.

The clergy of Wales refused subjection to Augustine; and although isolated instances may be cited to show the subjection of a Welsh bishop to the see of Canterbury, it is nevertheless certain that no acknowledgment of the English primate on the part of the Welsh took place, previously to the conquest of the country by the English under the Norman dynasty. Of the four dioceses, St. David's (Menevia), Llandaff, Bangor and St. Asaph (Llan Elwy), the first possessed the archiepiscopal title, which at a former period had been held by the church of Caerleon.[3]

Cumberland, as an independent state, had without doubt its own bishop at an early period, though he probably did not reside at Carlisle, which city king Ecgfrith bestowed on St. Cuthberht as an endowment of the see of Lindisfarne. The foundation

[1] Beda, iv. 12, v. 23.
[2] This see, which for a time had been transferred to Iona, was, during the sway of the Northmen, under the archbishop of Trondhjem. See documents in Thorkelin, 'Diplomata Arna-Magnæana.'
[3] Giraldi Camb. Itiner. lib. i. c. 4, lib. ii. c. 1, ejd. Descriptio Cambriæ, c. iv. Particularly his 'Distinctiones VII. de Jure et Statu Menevensis Ecclesiæ.'

of the bishopric of Carlisle is the work of Henry the First.

The dioceses of the present England are, with the exception of a few changes made at the time of the Reformation under Henry the Eighth—when Gloucester, Bristol, Oxford and Peterborough were erected into bishoprics—identical with those of the Anglo-Saxons, as above described. The voice of the bishops in the Upper House is derived from the rights of their predecessors in the Witena-gemôt. The vast differences in their revenues may be immediately traced to the disproportion of the states founded by the Jutes, Angles, and Saxons. Even the Bretwaldaship of Æthelberht, with the functions of which our acquaintance is so imperfect, is to be recognised in the several dioceses comprised in the province of the Metropolitan and Primate of all England. The province of the Primate of England, although containing two dioceses only, preserves in its extensive domains memory of the conquests of Eadwine and Oswiu, as well as that of the firmness and vigour of Wilfrith.

A cloister with a church was the first requisite of the newly introduced faith; a place of meeting and shelter for the missionaries, teachers and disciples, as well as others devoted to piety. The number of these increased rapidly in the larger states; and in their rich endowments, as well as in the numerous ecclesiastics of the noblest and even of royal families, we have a sufficient explanation of the great influence soon possessed by abbots and abbesses. Sigeberht of Essex has been already mentioned, as well as the holy queen Æthelthryth, whose sister Sexburh was her successor at Ely. Æbbe, a sister of Oswiu, was abbess of Coldingham (Coludesburh) on the coast of Berwickshire. Hild, a grandniece of Eadwine, enjoyed a similar dignity at

Hartlepool (Heorutu) in Durham, and subsequently at Whitby (Streoneshealh) in Yorkshire; in the latter she was succeeded by her niece Ælfled, a daughter of Oswiu. A queen of Wessex, consort of king Ine, at one time presided over the abbey of Barking, on the Thames, which had been founded by Æthelburgh, sister of Eorconwald, bishop of London. Previously to the foundation of these monasteries, the need of them among the Anglo-Saxons was so great, that they frequently sent their children to Frankish cloisters for education and consecration to a religious life. In the large number of convents as well as in the names of female saints amongst the Anglo-Saxons, we may recognise the same spirit which attracted the notice of the Romans among the ancient Germans, and was manifested in their esteem and honour of women generally, and in the special influence exercised by their priestess. While the old Germanic character and habits of this people are brought most prominently into view by comparing their language and laws with the earliest remains, and oldest written monuments belonging to their kindred in Germany, we are struck by the fact that in regard to women this difference is to be observed, that south of the Elbe there were very few, and north of it no convents before the thirteenth century, by which time we may assume that these old national characteristics had almost died out. Small cloisters arose from the pious exertions of individuals, as in Northumbria, from an oratory which Wilgis, the father of Willebrord the apostle of Friesland, had founded and dedicated to St. Andrew, and subsequently enlarged, in the cells of which Alcwine, the celebrated biographer of Willebrord, passed his youth.[1]

[1] Alcuini Vita Willebrordi, lib. i. c. 1.

But abuses of almost every kind were not wanting. Wine, one of the first bishops of London, bought his see, as we have seen, of Wulfhere, king of Mercia. Many ecclesiastics were so ignorant of the language of the church, that Beda translated for their use the Creed and Paternoster from the Latin into their mother-tongue. A vice peculiar to the time consisted in the facility with which laymen of rank, ealdormen, and other officials of the king, were permitted to found monasteries for themselves and wives. The land, free from all secular service, was, under this pretext, obtained by money from the kings, and secured to the purchasers and their heirs by royal charter, confirmed by the bishops, abbots, and other dignitaries. In these foundations, the layman, assuming the abbot's staff, devoted to worldly indulgences, free from all burthens, and surrounded by profligate monks,—whose vices had caused their expulsion from other monasteries, or by his own former followers shaven in the guise of monks,—lived without rule or discipline, to the detriment and scandal of the country.[1]

The small number of parish churches was very favourable to the erection of numerous monasteries. A knowledge of their foundations and of the parochial divisions, when attainable, enables us to form some idea of the population and circumstances of the commonalty, and of its increase in times when other sources of information are looked for in vain. But even in England records of the origin of the earliest parish churches are wanting. They seem to have been first erected in the south under archbishop Theodore, and about half a century later, that is, before and during the time of Ecgberht, archbishop of York, in the

[1] Bedæ Epist. ad Ecgb. p. 310 sq., edit. Smith.

northern parts of England. St. Cuthbert, abbot of Melrose,[1] wandered from place to place, to confirm and animate believers by his preaching; yet, when Beda subjoins to this narrative that such was the custom of the clergy at that time,[2] it would follow that in his own days the case was otherwise in those northern countries; at the same time it cannot be doubted that the dioceses or districts there, as in other countries, were, at the beginning, too extensive. We find however in Holstein, very shortly after its conversion by the Anglo-Saxon Willehad, the foundation of four churches for baptism, from the districts of which the later parochial division was established.[3] Similar churches those also appear to have been which, before the time of Theodore, were founded by Cedd, bishop of Essex, at Ythancester and Tilaburg (Tilbury).[4] In the later Anglo-Saxon laws, provisions are not wanting for the regulation of the parochial system.[5] That the laity were soon aware of their rights in the administration of church property, may be inferred both from a similar state of things in the Christian North, and from the community of all Anglo-Saxon property. If proof from the earliest times be wanting for England, we may perhaps assume that the clergy at a later period did not concede ampler rights to the laity than those which they had formerly possessed.[6]

The Anglo-Saxon clergy were, however, by no means so free and influential as their brethren in most of the

[1] Ob. a. 687. [2] Beda, iv. 27. Epist. ad Ecgb. p. 306.
[3] Remberti Vita S. Anscharii, c. xix.
[4] Beda, iii. 22. "Cedd . . . fecit per loca ecclesias, presbyteros et diaconos ordinavit, qui se in verbo fidei et ministerio baptizandi adjuvarent (circa a. 655)."
[5] Laws of Edgar I. i. 2. Eccles. Laws of Cnut, iii.
[6] For a later period see 'Conc. Exancest.' a. 1287.

continental states; for though ecclesiastics sometimes gained power over individual kings, such cases were of rare occurrence and without lasting consequences. That close connection between the Anglo-Saxon states and Rome did not exist, whereby the latter could extend powerful aid to its servants. The archbishop of Mentz, Boniface, himself an Anglo-Saxon, declares, in his letter to Cuthberht, archbishop of Canterbury,[1] that no cloisters were in such a state of slavery as those of the Anglo-Saxons—a declaration confirmed by the language of their charters of donations, whereby they were bound to pay not only the ' trinoda necessitas,' the ' brycg-bôt,' ' burh-bôt,' and ' fyrd,' or contribution for keeping in repair the bridges and fortresses, and for the maintenance of the military levy, but were sometimes also taxable like the rest of the community, and bound to harbour and entertain in their monasteries the king's huntsmen and followers.[2]

Hence the more remarkable will appear a celebrated donation made by Æthelwulf, king of Wessex, to the clergy of his states, after his return from Rome, which some of the older English historians, as William of Malmesbury and other monks, together with Selden, have been inclined to regard as the origin of tithes; an untenable interpretation, partly refuted by the very uncertain tenor of apparently fictitious charters,[3] and partly by the much earlier introduction of tithes, by

[1] Wilkins, Conc. t. i. p. 93.
[2] See Palgrave, vol. i. p. 156, and the documents there referred to. The last-mentioned burthen was often imposed on the cloisters of the continent, though they were relieved from it by the Carlovingian legislation.
[3] A.D. 854, 855. Wilkins, Conc. t. i. Cod. Diplom. t. ii. pp. 50 sq. W. Malm. lib. ii.

the assignment to the church of older imposts belonging to the king and other lords of the soil.[1]

According to a recent interpretation, Æthelwulf bestowed one-tenth part of the land in his kingdom of Wessex and its dependencies, Kent and Sussex, upon the servants of the altar, or for the sustenance of the indigent, exonerated from every territorial tax and duty.[2] But here two donations are blended together; by the one, sometimes called the Testament of Æthelwulf, the obligation is imposed on every ten farmers or farms in his hereditary states[3] to provide one poor person with meat, drink and clothing, and is remarkable as the beginning of secular provision for the poor. The other document, with which we are here more particularly concerned, directs (according to the oldest copies of the Latin text, made probably from an Anglo-Saxon original, as well as according to the interpretation of the oldest and nearly contemporaneous author), that king Æthelwulf, with the advice of his bishops and ealdormen, resolved to exonerate, for monks, nuns and laymen possessing hereditary land, every tenth mansus of their property, or, of smaller possessions, the tenth part, from the before-mentioned three obligations, usually considered as irredeemable, and from all other

---

[1] Excerptiones Ecgberti, iv., v., xxiv. See also Phillips, Angelsächsische Rechtsgeschichte, § 70; with whom, however, we cannot agree in ascribing, on the weak authority of Bromton, either the introduction of tithes to Offa of Mercia, or the confirmation of them to Æthelwulf.

[2] So Palgrave, vol. i. p. 158.

[3] Asser, a. 855, and ejd. Annales: "Per omnem hæreditariam terram suam . . . . in decem manentibus." W. Malm. lib. ii.: "in omni suæ hæreditatis decima hida pauperem vestiri et cibari præcepit." Sim. Dunelm. a. 855: "in decem mansis." Matt. Westm. a. 857: "in decem hydis vel mansionibus."

burthens; for which grace certain masses and prayers were to be said for the souls of the king and of the consenting prelates and ealdormen.[1]

[1] Asser, the friend of Æthelwulf's son Ælfred, is the oldest testimony we have relative to this grant: "Eodem anno (855) Æthelwulfus decimam totius regni sui partem ab omni regali servitio et tributo liberavit." So Asseri Annal., Flor. of Worc., W. Malm.; though the last-mentioned has falsely interpreted it, he nevertheless gives the words so that no doubt can arise as to their essential meaning. "Affirmavi ut aliquam portionem terrarum hæreditariam antea possidentibus omnibus gradibus, sive famulis et famulabus Dei, Deo servientibus, sive laicis semper decimam mansionem; ubi minimum sit, tamen partem decimam in libertatem perpetuam perdonari dijudicavi, ut sit tuta atque munita ab omnibus secularibus servitutibus, necnon regalibus tributis, etc. . . . quo eorum servitutem in aliqua parte levigamus." The last words seem fully to confirm my interpretation. Spelman, Conc. p. 348 (Wilk. t. i. p. 183) has the same text as Malmesbury. Turner is undecided, and misunderstands the word 'minimum,' which does not here signify *the least* or *the smallest*, but *very little, but a little, less than ten mansi*. The widely different text of the document in Matthew of Westminster might be passed without notice, had it not been the cause of errors committed by writers of history. Instead of " portionem . . . servitutibus," he gives "portionem terræ meæ Deo, et B. Mariæ, et omnibus sanctis, jure perpetuo possidendam concedam, decimam scilicet partem terræ meæ, ut sit tuta muneribus, et libera ab omnibus servitiis," etc.

CHAPTER XII.

EIGHTH CENTURY.

Anglo-Saxon Clergy—Canon Law—Church Discipline—Use of Mother-tongue—Pilgrimages—Tithes—Saxon School in Rome—Superstitions—Venerable Beda—Decline of Northumbria—Its Kings and Chieftains - Disturbed Condition of the Kingdom—Pestilence and Wars—First Landing of Northmen on Lindisfarne—Their Ravages—Burning of Wearmouth Monastery—Defeat of Northmen—Continued Convulsions in Northumbria—King Eadwulf seeks help from Charles the Great—Is succeeded by his Son Eanred, who reigns 33 years amid great Dissensions.

THE Roman ecclesiastical canons took root but slowly, and never so deeply among the Germanic nations as among the Romanized people of the continent; the former not being, like the latter, familiar with the Roman law, the fountain of the canon law. We must not suffer ourselves to be misled by the letters of Gregory to Augustine, dictated, as it were, by a conqueror in the flush of victory, who expected to organize the whole country on the capture of the first fortress. Let it be remembered how Kent itself wavered in its new faith, how unfavourable to the papal authority the circumstances were under which the Christian religion was gradually propagated. A few priests only passed over from Rome to England; the majority were Anglo-Saxons, acquainted only with their mother-tongue and the law of their country. Even if not wanting in zeal for the interest of the church, still they were less attached than their continental brethren to the bishop of Rome, who soon became sensible that, at a great distance, even spiritual weapons lose their force. To bishop Wilfrith, neither his profound knowledge of the canon law,[1] nor the sentence of the pope in his favour, proved of any use with the English synod. To the slight regard paid to the papal canon, the great number of Anglo-Saxon ecclesiastical laws, often issued by the king, seem to owe their existence: hence the church law of Anglo-Saxons was, more than that of any other Christian state, a national law. It was only for matters of a purely spiritual nature that the synod was composed wholly of ecclesiastics.[2] The consent of the king appears to have preceded the appointing and summoning of a synod; and it was by his approbation, and by admission among his laws, that its decrees became binding on the laity. Whatever at the same time concerned the right of the laity was treated in the general witena-gemôt with the participation of the clergy. Their own jurisdiction was conceded to the clergy in cases only affecting themselves; every extension of it was strictly guarded against. Mention has already been made of the tonsure and other points, in which the Anglo-Saxons did not follow the Roman practice until at a later period. The long narrow habit was first assumed by the Anglo-Saxons in Rome, when pope John the Seventh seized the occasion to introduce the use both of that and the mitre among the clergy in England, according to the custom of the Roman church.[3] The celibacy of the clergy was not readily established

[1] Eddius, c. xlii. "In omni sapientia et in judiciis Romanorum eruditissimum." [2] Cf. Palgrave, vol. i. p. 176.
[3] See the pope's letter in Baluzii Miscell. t. v. p. 478.

among the Anglo-Saxons,[1] and only the prohibition of a second marriage, and severe penalties for acts of immorality, were observed among them. The Germanic descent of the clergy manifested itself also in the prohibitions occasioned by their propensity to drunkenness.[2] To confine the marriages of the laity within the degrees prescribed by the church of Rome, among a people so impatient of restraint, was impossible; and the pope soon found it necessary to modify for the people of England the restrictions regarding marriage.[3]

In considering the canon law of the Anglo-Saxon church, its relation to the old Scottish law demands our special attention; and here we are led to ask if the English ecclesiastics, and more particularly those of the northern states, who almost all received their training in Ireland, or in Iona or at some other Scottish monastery, may not have brought back to their homes the rules of their respective seminaries, with the dogmas and codes of their venerated masters. May not opinions thus supported by canonical authority have been widely disseminated in an age when the letter was often more closely followed than the spirit? If this be so, it can scarcely surprise us, nay, it rather affords a new and instructive insight into the relations between the different races of the British islands, and the bearing of those national relations on their respective churches, when we discover that the Poeniten-

[1] Even a son of St. Wilfrith is mentioned. Edd. c. lvii. "Sanctus pontifex noster de exilio cum filio suo proprio veniens."
[2] Theod. Pœnitent. xxvi. 2, 4, 3, 13. Ecgb. Penitent. iv. 33, 34, 35. Edg. Can. lvii., lviii. in Ancient Laws and Institutes. Cf. also the systematic view of Anglo-Saxon ecclesiastical law in Phillips.
[3] See Boniface's letter to Æthelbald in W. Malm. lib. i., and excerpt from Gregorii Epist. ad Augustinum in Decret. p. ii. causa 35, qu. 2, c. 20.

tiale of the archbishop of York, Ecgberht, which was drawn up after the closer union of the Anglo-Saxon church with Rome, was for the most part the older work of the anti-Roman, Saint Columba. Supported by evidence of this nature, we can scarcely repress the conviction, that much beyond mere ecclesiastic enactments must have been preserved from the teaching of the old church for the benefit of the people, not indeed through the then limited agency of written works, but by means of the general intercommunication of the several races and of the different grades of society.

The knowledge of Roman law possessed by individual Anglo-Saxons is to be ascribed to the necessity they were under of learning the canon law, which is modified and defined by the Roman. Frequent appeals to the papal court stimulated also many ecclesiastics to a profounder study of the same in Rome itself, as England then possessed no schools appropriated to that object. What such men as Theodore of Tarsus and other foreign or Kentish ecclesiastics may have accomplished in this respect we are without the means of ascertaining, though among the various branches of knowledge possessed by Beda himself, no trace is discernible of his acquaintance with the Roman law; the more remarkable, therefore, appears the knowledge of it manifested by Aldhelm, not only in occasional expressions, but also in a special composition.[1] But exceptional cases such as his wholly disappear as the Anglo-Saxon Church system becomes firmly established.

[1] This fragment was to have been printed under the direction of C. P. Cooper, Esq., among the publications of the late Record Commission. Respecting Aldhelm see also Beda, v. 18, W. Malm. Gesta Reg. Angl. lib. 1., and De Gestis Pont. Angl. lib. v. ap. Gale: his letters are printed in Wharton, Anglia Sacra, and his Latin poetry in Canisii Lectt. Antiq.

ANGLO-SAXON SETTLEMENT, A.D. 446–800. 257

To the distance from Rome, and their slender dependence on the papal chair, the people of England are apparently indebted for the advantage of having retained their mother-tongue as the language of the church, which was never entirely banished by the priests from their most sacred services. Their careless sensual course of life, and perhaps the prejudice which prevented them from learning even so much Latin as was requisite to enable them to repeat the Paternoster and Creed in that language,[1] have proved more conducive to the highest interests of the country than the dark subtilty of the learned Romanized monk, pondering over authorities. Even the mass itself was not read entirely in the Latin tongue. The wedding form was, no doubt, in Anglo-Saxon; and its hearty sound and simple sterling substance are preserved in the English ritual to the present day.[2] The numerous versions[3] and paraphrases of the Old and New Testaments made those books known to the laity, and more familiar to the clergy. That these were not in general circulation in Beda's time, may perhaps be inferred from his omission of all mention of them, though the learned and celebrated Anglo-Saxon poet, Aldhelm, had already translated the psalms, and Ecgberht, bishop of Lindisfarne, the four gospels. Beda is also said to have translated both the Old and the New Testament into his mother-tongue,[4] an assertion which, like a similar one regarding

[1] Conc. Clovesh. a. 742, art. x. ap. Wilkins, t. i. p. 96.
[2] Palgrave, vol. ii. p. cxxxvi.
[3] The Anglo-Saxon Gospels were first printed under the auspices of archbp. Parker in 1571. The second edition is that of Marshall in 1665. The third (probably Ælfric's version) is by the translator of the present volume, in small 8vo, 1842.—T.
[4] Aldred's Northumbrian gloss to the four gospels in the St. Cuthberht's book (MS. Cott. Nero D. IV.) seems not to be earlier

VOL. I.   S

king Ælfred, must be limited in his case to the Gospel of St. John,¹ and, in that of Ælfred, to some fragments of the psalms.² An abridged version of the Pentateuch, and of some other books of the Old Testament by Ælfric in the end of the tenth century, is still extant. The vast collection of Anglo-Saxon homilies, which are still preserved to us, once enlarged and ennobled the language and the feelings of Christianity:³ and the ear which continued deaf to the mother-tongue, in the Anglo-Saxon Church was from an early period yet more sensibly addressed, through the use of musical instruments. Large organs are described and spoken of as donations to the church in the beginning of the eighth century.⁴ The mention of this instrument at

---

than the middle of the tenth century. See Mr. Stevenson's paper, in the 'Graphic Illustrator,' p. 355, and Sir F. Madden's letter to Sir H. Ellis in 'Letters of Eminent Literary Men,' printed for the Camden Society.—T.

¹ W. Malm. lib. i. c. 3. ² Ib. lib. ii. c. 4.
³ These venerable monuments of our early church are published by the Ælfric Society, with a modern English version by the translator of the present work. A MS. discovered at Vercelli by Professor Blume contains not only homilies, but the valuable metrical pieces, printed for the late Record Commission by the present translator, but not published, though now given to the world, with a translation by J. M. Kemble, Esq., for the Ælfric Society. The homilies contained in the Vercelli MS. are all to be found in the various public libraries of England. An Anglo-Saxon version of the Psalms, possibly Aldhelm's, transcribed by the present translator from a MS. in the Royal Library at Paris, has been published at the expense of the University of Oxford.—T.
⁴ Aldhelmus de Laude Virgin. ap. Canisium, t. i. p. 715.

"Maxima millenis auscultare organa flabris
Mulceat auditum ventosis follibus iste,
Quamlibet auratis fulgescant caetera capsis."—

W. Malm. De Gestis Pont. Angl. lib. v. ap. Gale : "Organa, ubi per aereas fistulas musicis mensuris elaboratas, dudum conceptas

Malmesbury affords ground for the conjecture, that it might have been introduced by the musical Welsh. Church music was first brought into Kent by the Roman clergy, and from thence into the northern parts, where it underwent improvement. This was an object of such interest, that the arrival of a Roman singing-master[1] is mentioned by contemporary authors as a matter of almost equal importance with a new victory gained by the Catholic faith over the pagans or the Scots.[2]

A glance at the religious feelings of the people will suffice to show us a striking propensity among them to go on pilgrimages, especially to Rome;[3] and we may discern under the pilgrim's gown not only a longing after the beams of a warmer sun, but also the hereditary craving for restless wandering. The testimonies relative to such wanderers, more especially to the numerous females, are highly unfavourable.[4] The Anglo-Saxon

---

follis vomit anxius auras." Of Dunstan also it is said that he played the organ ("modificans organa"). See Osbern, Vita S. Dunstani, ap. Wharton, Angl. Sac. t. ii. p. 93.

[1] Beda, H. E. ii. 20, iv. 2. Vita S. Bened. a. 678.

[2] With the exception of the Te Deum the Scots had none of the usual Ambrosian and Gregorian hymns, as appears from the antiphoner of Bangor composed in the seventh century, now in the Ambrosian library, but formerly belonging to the monastery of Bobbio. See Muratori Anect. t. iv. These Latin hymns of the fifth and sixth centuries have long lain unheard, and were forgotten, until again brought to light by the praiseworthy researches of modern literati. It is remarkable that some of the hymns of the Scot Sedulius have, in a German version, been preserved in the Protestant church. Cf. Rambach, Christl. Anthol. i. 85, 110.

[3] Beda, v. 7: "Peregrinari .... quod his temporibus plures de gente Anglorum, nobiles, ignobiles, laici, clerici, viri ac feminæ, certatim facere consuerunt."

[4] See Boniface's letter to Æthelbald. To bishop Cuthberht he writes: "Paucæ sunt civitates in Longobardia vel in Francia aut in Gallia, in qua non sit adultera vel meretrix generis Anglorum."

kings established in many places hospitals for the entertainment of pilgrims, the most celebrated of which was that at Rome, known under the name 'Schola Saxonum,' and called at a later period, 'Hospitale di S. Spirito in Vico di Sassia.' A writer of no great authority ascribes the founding of this establishment to Ine, king of Wessex,[1] who, after his abdication, ended his days at Rome.[2] The object of this foundation, which comprised a church dedicated to St. Mary, and a cemetery for the English, was not only to provide for needy West Saxons and other English at Rome, but for the instruction of young Anglo-Saxons in the catholic faith, who were exposed to the danger of many heresies in their native country. For its support Ine is said to have laid, under the name of Rom-feoh or Rome-scot, a tax of a penny on every house in his kingdom, the amount of which was sent to the pope for that purpose. At a later period the St. Peter's penny was a subject of repeated complaints, after its original intention had been lost sight of. William of Malmesbury knew nothing certain relative to the foundation of this institution at Rome, and merely mentions, without any allusion to Rom-feoh, that tradition ascribed it to Offa, king of Mercia. A life of Offa, the fidelity of which has perhaps been too greatly underrated, reconciles both these accounts, by stating that Offa, about

[1] Matt. Westminst. a. 727. His account is rendered rather incredible by his ascribing to the same prince (Ine abdicated in 726) the imposition of Rom-feoh or St. Peter's pence. Spelman (Conc. t. i. p. 290) endeavours, from a manuscript at Chichester, to prove that the Schola Saxonum was founded as early as 714, while the passage refers to Offa of Mercia, from the date of whose death, DCCXCIV., the last o seems to have been omitted. Cf. also J. Ross Antiquarii Warw. Hist. Reg. Angl. p. 72.
[2] Sax. Chron. a. 728. The year of Ine's death is unknown.

the year 790, richly endowed the Saxon school already existing at Rome, and for that purpose introduced the perpetual burthen of Peter's pence.[1] According to a probably contemporaneous account, it appears that in the year 816 the school of the Angles at Rome was burnt.[2] Mention is made of its inmates at the commencement of that century as forming part of the procession which met pope Leo the Third on his return from his visit to Charles the Great.[3] It was again destroyed by fire in the beginning of the reign of Leo the Fourth,[4] when it lay for some years in ruins, till king Æthelwulf, during his stay at Rome,[5] caused it to be rebuilt. The rebuilding of this structure has led some writers to ascribe to that king the introduction of Rome-scot, or rather the transfer of the same to the

[1] This life is ascribed to Matt. Paris, and is to be found, with the Vitæ xxiii. S. Albani Abbatum, in Watts's edit. p. 29: "Rex .... scholam Anglorum, quæ tunc Romæ floruit, ingressus, dedit ibi ex regali munificentia, ad sustentationem gentis regni sui illuc venientis, singulos argenteos de familiis singulis, omnibus in posterum diebus, singulis annis. Et tunc tali largitate obtinuit, ut de regno Angliæ nullus publice pœnitens, pro executione sibi injunctæ pœnitentiæ, subiret exilium .... p. 31, annuum reditum contulit ad sustentationem scholæ memoratæ, propter Anglorum rudium et illuc peregrinantium eruditionem." This passage is extracted in Matt. Westminst. a. 794. Vitæ Abbat. S. Albani, c. i. "Offa .... Romæ scholam peregrinorum pie constituit, ut ibidem peregrini, qui ad Romanam ecclesiam et curiam confluxerant, ex diversis mundi partibus barbari, vel votivæ orationis gratia vel expediendorum negotiorum necessitate, linguas, quas non noverant, addiscerent: quæ schola, propter peregrinorum confluxum ibidem solatia suscipientium, versa est in xenodochium, quod Sancti Spiritus dicitur."
[2] Sax. Chron. a. 816.
[3] "Pastorem .... simul etiam cunctæ scholæ peregrinorum, videlicet Francorum, Frisonum, Saxonum, atque Longobardorum .... susceperunt." Anastasius, ap. Muratori Script. iii. p. 198.
[4] So Anastasius, lib. i. p. 233: "B. Pontificii sui exordio Saxonum vicum validus ignis invasit," etc. [5] Sax. Chron. a. 855.

papal chair.[1] Pope Marinus relieved the school of the Angles from all taxes and burthens, at the request of king Ælfred,[2] who showed his gratitude to that pontiff. Of this privilege king Cnut, during his stay at Rome, obtained a new confirmation from pope John,[3] and in return caused Rome-scot for the pope to be collected with greater strictness.[4]

However interesting the Saxon school may appear to us, especially with regard to the St. Peter's penny, we must nevertheless be careful not to ascribe to it an immediate influence in respect to the legal instruction of the Anglo-Saxon clergy. In its early age it could not have had such a predominant object, although it might occasionally have contributed to it; in later times it was transformed into the hospital nominally still in existence: yet how important would its old archives be, for the social and ecclesiastical history of England, should some fortunate explorer one day discover them![5]

Among the chief objects of attraction to the Anglo-Saxons, both at home and in their pilgrimages, were relics. In finding this superstition so extremely prevalent among them, we are almost led to the supposi-

[1] W. Malm. lib. ii: "Æthelwulfus Romam abiit, ibique tributum, quod Anglia hodieque pensitat, sancto Petro obtulit . . . . scholam Anglorum, quæ, ut fertur, ab Offa, rege Merciorum, primitus instituta, proximo anno conflagraverat, reparavit egregie."

[2] Sax. Chron. aa. 885 and 890. Matt. of Westminst. a. 889. Sim. Dunelm. a. 884, ap. Twysden, pp. 130, 148 and 355.

[3] Rad. Dicet. Abbrev. a. 1031.

[4] Eccl. Laws of Cnut, ix. Law of North. Priests, lvii. Also Laws of Æthelred passim.

[5] The conversion of the school into an hospital is ascribed to Innocent III. See also Spelmanni Vita Ælfredi, p. 7, note. Fea, 'Description de Rome,' t. iii. Some documents relating to probends, claimed by the hospital of S. Spiritus in Saxia de Urbe, from 1284 to 1291, are to be found in Rymer, t. i. pp. 648, 740, 752.

tion that it did not originate in the catholic faith, but was rather, if not entirely produced, at least greatly promoted, by the belief of the Germanic nations, who solemnly buried the bones of the dead in barrows, threw up vast mounds over them, raised monuments of rude workmanship,[1] and thought to conquer in battle with the aid of the corpses of their dead chieftains. The judicial superstition, brought to Britain by the Saxons, that the lifeless body of a murdered person would begin to bleed on the approach of the murderer, also supposes the presence of supernatural powers in the corpse.[2]

No Germanic people preserved so many memorials of paganism as the Anglo-Saxons. Their days of the week have to the present time retained their heathen names; even that of Woden (Wednesday) is still unconsciously so called in both worlds, and by more tongues than when he was the chief object of religious veneration. In the north of England and some parts of Scotland the name of the Yule feast (geohol, geol) has never been supplanted by that of Christmas. That these denominations, throughout ages, were not a senseless echo of superannuated customs, is evident from the Anglo-Saxon laws of later times, which strictly forbid the worship of heathen gods, of the sun, the moon, fire, rivers, water-wells, stones, or forest-trees.[3] It is, however, probable that some of this heathenism may have been awakened by contact with the pagan Northmen. A part of the old theology lost its pernicious power when, reduced to history, it became subservient to the

[1] As did the Jutes for Horsa. Beda, i. 15.
[2] Edg. Can. lxv. Ælfr. Can. xxxv. For Germany see the author's tract, 'Ueber ältere Geschichte und Rechte des Landes Hadeln,' p. 59.
[3] See Laws of Cnut, v.

purposes of epic poetry, as instances of which may be cited the genealogies of the Anglo-Saxon kings and the poem of Beowulf. Of many superstitions, which long maintained their ground, relative to the power of magic, amulets, and magical medicaments, as well as to the innocent belief—so intimately connected with poetry—in elves and swarms of benevolent, or at least harmless unearthly, though sublunary spirits, it is often difficult to point out the historic elements from which they have sprung, since it was precisely in the northern parts of England, where they were longest preserved, that the intermixture of the Britons with the Germans was the most intimate.

The adoption of Christianity does not appear to have been attended with any sudden and important consequences with regard to the political relations of the Anglo-Saxons, and is chiefly indebted to this circumstance for its final settlement. It very soon promoted the general and literary instruction of the nation and brought it into connection with Roman Europe, —operating thereby with increased power on the prospects of the country,—and, by strengthening the state by principles and spiritual means, prevented the threatened dismemberment of the land among military chieftains, striving for independence. These causes soon contributed to augment the power of the larger kingdoms; and the history of the Anglo-Saxons, during a long period, is to be sought chiefly in that of Northumbria, of Mercia, and of Wessex, which subsequently comprised that of all England. These three states were those which, inured to arms, had in earlier times maintained themselves, and extended their dominions by many victories over the Welsh—the kingdoms of Strathclyde and Cumbria, and those of the Picts and Scots.

On Ecgfrith's death, and after the battle of Nechtansmere against the Picts, the boundaries of Northumbria became much contracted. His successor, Aldfrith, acquired the epithet of 'The wisest,' or 'The most learned.' He had been well instructed in the theology and dialectics of the Irish school, which was one day to send forth a Johannes Scotus, or Erigena, the founder of the scholastic philosophy. But other intellectual pursuits were not less welcome to Aldfrith as is proved by the friendly reception given by him to the Gallic bishop Arculf, who had been driven by a storm on the western coast of Britain, on his return from his travels in the East, to which we cannot allude without at the same time mentioning the account of his journey recorded by Adamnan, abbot of Iona, from the mouth of Arculf himself, as well as an extract from it by Beda, which became the foundation of the numerous guides to the land of promise, so characteristic of the knowledge and sentiments of the middle ages.

But no one imparts to the age of the 'Wisest king' greater brilliancy than the man just named, whom the epithet of 'The Venerable' adorns, and whose knowledge was profound and almost universal. Born in the neighbourhood of Wearmouth, he enjoyed in that abbey the instructions of Benedict, its first abbot, of whom we have already had occasion to make honourable mention, as well as those of his successor, Ceolfrith, equally distinguished for his zeal in the promotion of learning. In the neighbouring cloister of Jarrow Beda passed his life in exercises of piety and in varied study, and gave life and form to almost all the knowledge which the age could offer him. If, on a consideration of his works, it must appear manifest that

that age possessed more means of knowledge, both in manuscripts and learned ecclesiastics, than we are wont to ascribe to it; and even if we must recognise in Beda the high culture of the Roman church, rather than Anglo-Saxon nationality, yet the acknowledgment which his merits found in Rome during his life, and, shortly after his death, wherever learning could penetrate, proves that in him we justly venerate a wonder of his age. His numerous theological writings, his illustrations of the books of the Old and New Testaments have throughout many ages, until the total revolution in that branch of learning, found readers and transcribers in every cloister of Europe. His knowledge of Greek, of medicine, of astronomy, of prosody, he made subservient to the instruction of his contemporaries; his work 'De sex hujus seculi ætatibus,' though less used than it deserves to be, is the basis of most of the universal chronicles of the middle age. But his greatest merit, which will preserve his name through all future generations, consists in his historic works, as far as they concern his own native land. If a second man like himself had arisen in his days, who with the same clear, circumspect glance, the same honest and pious purpose, had recorded the secular transactions of his forefathers, as Beda has transmitted to us those chiefly of the church, the history of England would have been to posterity almost like a revelation for Germanic antiquity.

Among the learned contemporaries and countrymen of king Aldfrith, the monk Ecgberht claims especial notice. Like him instructed during a long abode in Ireland, he employed the facility and knowledge there acquired in the conversion of the monks of Iona: but he is more particularly interesting to the Germans through his early wish to undertake personally their

ANGLO-SAXON SETTLEMENT, A.D. 446–800. 267

conversion, and, on renouncing his design for himself, for having sent Willebrord and his companions to the Frisians, thereby stimulating the two Ewalds, the White and the Black, so distinguished from the colour of their hair, to a like attempt among the Old-Saxons, which was however frustrated by their murder.¹

With the death of Aldfrith² the star of Northumbria began to set. Eadwulf, regarding whose pretensions we are not informed, although the general acknowledgment, and the readiness of Wilfrith to receive him amicably, allow us to suppose their existence, assumed the sovereignty, which he was unable to maintain longer than two months.³ Through the influence of Berhtfrith, the most powerful ealdorman of the country, Osred, the son of Aldfrith, a child of eight years, was raised to the throne, and by him protected against disturbers within, and, by a brilliant victory, against the Picts and Scots from without.⁴ While the will of the royal infant was apparently obeyed, and all legitimate forms were observed, the greatest licentiousness burst out among the nobles, to which the clergy would have shown no indulgence, but for the part taken in it by themselves.⁵ The government, during the long minority of Osred, was conducted by his mother Cuthburh,⁶

¹ Beda, v. 10. At Merseburg their memory is celebrated on Oct. 2 (Zeitschrift für Archivkunde, i. 123). According to Beda and the Calendar the day of their martyrdom is, "quinto nonarum Octobrium" (Oct. 3), a. 695.
² Sax. Chron. a 705. ³ Eddius, c. 57.
⁴ This victory was gained between Hæfe and Cære (Caraw, Tindale hundred in Northumberland). Tigernach, a. 711, also mentions it: "Strages Pictorum in campo Manand a Saxonis, ubi Fingaine mac Deleroith immatura morte jacuit."
⁵ Bedæ Epist. ad Ecgbertum.
⁶ I assume this guardianship (although it seems at variance with

sister of Ine king of Wessex, whose failings were forgotten in the subsequent foundation of the abbey of Winburne. Osred followed not in the footsteps of his father, but, sunk in debaucheries, which spared not even the sanctity of the cloister, he was slain in his nineteenth year, in an ambush laid for him by his kinsmen on the southern border by the sea.[1]

The successors of Osred were—1. Cenred, descended from Occa, an illegitimate son of Ida; 2. Osric the son of Ealhfrith; and 3. Ceolwulf, the brother of Cenred. The two years' reign of the first mentioned prince, as well as that of the second of eleven years, are of no importance. The tranquillity of the country during the first years of Ceolwulf was disturbed by violent internal dissensions. The king himself was seized by his enemies, confined in a cloister, and had already

---

the Chronicle which (a. 718) says, that Cuthburh was separated from Aldferth during his life) from the fragment No. 71 among the letters of Boniface, where, speaking of a vision, it is said, " Aspexit .... in poenalibus puteis Cuthbergam simulque Wialan quondam reginali potestate fruentes, demersas usque ad ascellas, i. e. Cuthbergam capite tenus humeroque praeclaram, caeteris membris maculis conspersam; alteriusque, i. e. Wialan, supra caput flammam extendere, totamque animam simul cremari intuebatur." Queen Wiala is unknown to me. This purgatory must have been devised after the death of Boniface, not earlier, as it makes mention of " Æthilbealdus, quondam regalis tyrannus."

[1] Beda, v. 22. W. Malm. lib. i. Matt. Westminst., a. 717, says of him, " belli infortunio interemptus est." Boniface, in his letter to Æthelbald of Mercia (epist. xix.), of which Malmesbury gives only an extract, says, " Osredum spiritus luxuriae fornicantem, et per monasteria nonnarum sacratas virgines stuprantem et furentem agitavit, usque quo ipse gloriosum regnum et inutilem vitam contemptibili et despecta morte perdidit." [R. Wendover, t. i. p. 211. E dem anno (717) " Osredus .... juxta mare pugnans, belli infortunio interemptus est."—T.]

received the tonsure, when his friends replaced him on the throne.[1] Though able to preserve peace on the frontiers of his kingdom, he could not stifle discord within; but of his love for piety and learning, we have the honourable testimony of the Venerable Beda, who dedicated to him his ecclesiastical history of the Angles. During the reign of Ceolwulf, the archiepiscopal dignity was restored to York, his kinsman Ecgberht being the first who received the pall formerly bestowed on Paulinus.[1] He had reigned eight years when he renounced the corroding cares attending the imaginary happiness of rule, and withdrew to the monastery of Lindisfarne, where, apart from worldly anxieties, he lived nearly thirty years.[2]

Ceolwulf on his abdication was succeeded by his cousin and heir, Eadberht, a brother of archbishop Ecgberht and son of Eata,[3] a very able man, fully qualified for the duties of government. Eadberht raised his kingdom to its former estimation, chastised Æthelbald, king of Mercia, who had attacked Northumbria, while he was engaged in warfare with Talorgan mac Fergusa, king of the Picts, and took Cyil in Ayrshire, and the neighbouring lands from Dunnagual, king of Strathclyde, or his father Teudubr, son of Beli mac Elpin (ob. 722). Six years later, in alliance

[1] Beda, v. 23, 24, ejd. App. aa. 731, 737. Sim. Dunelm. a. 731. Tigernach also mentions the imprisonment of Cuthwine's son, by which correct Annal. Ulton a. 730.
[2] Sax. Chron. a. 735. [Ecgberht was celebrated for his love of knowledge, and founded a noble library at York. See his Penitential in Anc. LL. and Inst. Alcuini Epist. W. Malm. lib. i.—T.]
[3] Sax. Chron. aa. 737, 760. Sim. Dunelm. a. 764. H. Hunt. lib. iv.
[4] Sax. Chron. Flor. of Worc. a. 738. Malmesbury calls Ecgberht " fratrem æquivocum."

with Ouengus or Unnust, the hated king of the Picts, successor of Talorgan mac Fergusa, who, in the year 750, had fallen in a battle with the Welsh, he took Alcluyd, the capital city of Strathclyde, and reduced that British kingdom under his subjection.[1] A few days later, however, he lost his life through some mischance, the nature of which is unknown to us.

The Frankish king Pepin sought his friendship, and sent him by his ambassadors costly presents, in which we may discern the respect paid to a powerful prince, and, at the same time recognise the policy of the Franks, to gain friends in the rulers of North-Britain, and, in the event of a war, allies against the more neighbouring southern parts of the country. But Eadberht grew weary of a glorious, though, according to some accounts, not wholly prosperous sway, and, after a reign of twenty-one years, he also renounced his throne and the world.[2] The other kings of Britain

[1] [In App. ad Bedam, a. 740, it is said, "Aruwini et Eadberctus interempti." This obviously clerical error has not been copied by Simeon, and probably did not exist in the MS. used by him: he says (a. 740), "Arwine filius Eadulfi occisus est," without naming Eadberht.—Of this prince Simeon writes (Hist. Dunelm. ii. 3), "Omnibus adversariis vel sibi subjectis vel bello prostratis, reges circumquaque morantes, Anglorum, Pictorum, Britonum, Scottorum, non solum cum eo pacem servabant, sed et honorem illi deferre gaudebant: cujus excellentiæ fama, ac operum virtutis, longe lateque diffusa, etiam ad regem Franciæ Pipinum pervenit, propter quod ei amicitia junctus, multa ei ac diversa dona regalia transmisit."—T.] App. ad Bedam, a. 750. "Eadberctus campum Cyil cum aliis regionibus suo regno addidit." Cf. Annal. Camb. aa. 722, 750, 760. Annal. Ulton. a. 721. Sim. Dunelm. a. 756. Chron. Mailros. Tigernach. aa. 750, 752.

[2] App. ad Bedam, a. 758, assigns his abdication to causes not easily to be reconciled. "Dei amoris causa et cœlestis patriæ, violentia accepta S. Petri tonsuram." H. Hunt. says that, "videns regum prædictorum, Eadelbaldi scil. et Sigeberti, vitam ærumnosam

endeavoured to dissuade him from this step, and, it is said, offered to resign to him portions of territory, if he would continue to bear the sceptre.[1] During the ten remaining years of his life he had ample cause not to regret his resolve, or at least to perceive that the anxieties of his brother-rulers were not groundless. His son Oswulf, to whom he had transferred his crown, was in the following year treacherously murdered by his thanes, when Æthelwald, surnamed Moll, of unknown lineage, was by his faction placed on the throne of Ida,[2] the extinction or neglect of whose race brought the most unhappy consequences to the country. One ealdorman after another seized on the government, and held it till his expelled predecessors returned with a superior force, or popular favour and successful treason had raised up a new competitor. The family connection, which had hitherto been maintained by marriages among the Anglo-Saxon princes, ceased, and the subjects of the usurpers lost not only the friendship and protection of the once allied states, but found in family hatred, thirst for restoration and desire of revenge, new and dangerous enemies. In a battle which lasted three days, at Eadwine's Cliff, or, according to another account, at Eldun near Melrose, the ealdorman Oswine was slain.[3]

---

et finem infaustum, Ceolwlfi vero prædecessoris sui vitam laudabilem et finem gloriosum, meliorem partem elegit," etc. This cannot, however, be strictly correct, as Ceolwulf did not die till nearly thirty years after his abdication (764), or nine years after the retirement of Eadberht. Chr. Mailr., more consistently, " tonsura capitis *pro Deo accepta*, apud Eboracum sub archiepiscopo Egberto factus est canonicus." The Sax. Chron. and Florence place his abdication in 757.—T.

[1] Sim. Dunelm. de Eccl. Dunelm. lib. i.
[2] App. ad Bedam, a. 759. Sim. Dunelm.
[3] Sax. Chron. a. 761. Sim. Dunelm.

This victory, however, afforded but little security to Æthelwald, who, a few years afterwards, by a battle fought at Wincanhealh,[1] lost his kingdom though not his life,[2] and was succeeded by Alhred,[3] a son of Eanwine, who, it is said, traced his descent from Ida. Alhred endeavoured to continue the alliance with the Frankish empire, at the moment when Charles the Great was engaged in the Saxon conquest. He not only sent embassies to the emperor, but was desirous also to use the services of his countryman Lullus for that object, who, after having faithfully followed Boniface in his self-denying calling, had succeeded him in the see of Mayence.[4] It was to this king that the Northumbrian Willehad, a friend of Alcwine, applied for leave to convert the pagan Frisians and Saxons to the Christian faith: whereupon Alhred with all the earnestness and zeal of those who in later ages planned the discovery and conquest of new worlds, summoned his bishops and other ecclesiastics to consult on his request, which after mature deliberation, was granted. The missionary was recommended to the protection of the Almighty, who did not forsake him, but blessed him in the foundation

[1] Pincanhealh?
[2] Fl. of Worc. "regnum remisit." Sim. Dunelm. "regnum amisit in Winchanheale." H. Hunt. "coactus dimisit illud " (sc. regnum). Matt. of Westminst. a. 765, " vita decessit :" whence Turner, vol. i. p. 411, "the tomb received him ;" while Lingard (vol. i. p. 110) has, "he resigned in an assembly of the witan at Finchley."
[3] Sax. Chron. Flor. of Worc. a. 765.
[4] Othloni Vita S. Bonifacii, lib. i. c. 24. For two letters of Alhred to Lullus see Magna Biblioth. Patrum, t. xiii. 108, ep. xc. Alhred and his queen Osgearn write to him: " Nostris quoque, dilectissime frater, legationibus ad dominum nostrum gloriosissimum regem Carl obsecramus consulendo subvenias, ut pax et amicitia, quæ omnibus conveniunt, facias stabiliter inter nos confirmari.' W. Malm. lib. i. " Lullus, et ipse natione Anglus," etc.

ANGLO-SAXON SETTLEMENT, A.D. 446-800. 273

of the bishopric of Bremen, the later archiepiscopal see of Hamburg.¹ After a lapse of some years Alhred, forsaken by his thanes and relations, and driven from York, renounced the throne, and found an asylum with Cyneth, king of the Picts. He was succeeded by Æthelred, a son of Æthelwald Moll,² who in the fifth year of his reign was compelled to abdicate and forsake his country. Two rebel ealdormen, Æthelbald and Heardberht, had slain Ealdwulf, son of Bosa, the chief commander of the royal army at Kingscliff and afterwards his generals Cynewulf and Ecga, in a battle at Hilathirn.³ Alfwold son of Oswulf, and grandson of Eadberht, then obtained the kingdom.⁴ He is praised as a pious and upright king, and adorned with the title of 'friend of God.' But the turbulence of the nobles of his kingdom prevailed over better efforts. The ealdorman Beorn, his chief-justice, was, on account of his rigour, burnt at Silton by the thanes Osbald and Æthelheard, who had assembled a body of forces; and Alfwold himself, after a tumultuous reign of ten years, perished by means of a conspiracy, at the head of which was the ealdorman Siga.⁵

¹ Vita S. Willehadi, c. i., where the king of the Angles is, according to some MSS., called Alachind, in other better ones, Alachrat. In App. ad Bedam, a. 765, he is called Aluchredus. This agreement between the name and race of the king, the native country of the priest (he went in 779 from the Frisians to the Saxons) and the chronology, seems to remove every doubt as to this explanation.
² Sax. Chron. a. 774.   ³ H. Hunt. a. 778. Sim. Dunelm.
⁴ Sax. Chron. Flor. of Worc. a. 778. Sim. Dunelm. a. 779.
⁵ Sax. Chron. Sim. Dunelm. a. 788. [Alfwold, as we learn from Simeon, was buried in the abbey church of St. Andrew at Hexham, built by Wilfrith, which abbey he describes as excelling in beauty all others in the land of the Angles. Its walls were adorned with various colours, and it contained painted histories.—T.]

VOL. I.   T

Osred son of Alhred now ascended the throne once occupied by his father, but so ill defended it, that when Æthelred, son of Æthelwald Moll,[1] returned to the kingdom formerly governed also by his father, Osred, betrayed by his thanes, was declared to have forfeited the crown, was shaven for a monk and put into a monastery, and afterwards obliged to seek safety in exile.[2] Æthelred strove to strengthen himself by violent measures. The ealdorman Eardwulf who had at first governed a part of Northumbria under him, as we learn from existing coins (an abundant source of Anglo-Saxon history), but who afterwards opposed him, was seized and brought to Ripon, where, before the gates of the monastery, he was, by order of Æthelred, to be put to death. Being left for dead, his body was by the friars, singing the Gregorian chant, borne into the church, where in the middle of the night he was found to be yet living, being reserved for still greater vicissitudes. The sons of Alfwold, Ælf and Ælfwine, were less fortunate: for being enticed from their sanctuary in the cathedral of York, they were barbarously murdered at Wonwaldremere.[3] The discontented now again turned their thoughts to the exile Osred, who had withdrawn to the Isle of Man, and bound themselves by oath to restore him to his kingdom; yet scarcely had he landed when, in spite of oaths and fealty, he was seized and put to death by command of Æthelred. His corpse was buried in the church of Tynemouth with marks of honour, which would strike us as the more remarkable, if we had not

---

[1] Sax. Chron. a. 790. Flor. of Worc. has "Æthelredus *frater* Alfwoldi," instead of "*filius*," and, a. 774, Æthelbertum for Æthelredum.
[2] Sax. Chron. Sim. Dunelm. a. 790.
[3] Sim. Dunelm. aa. 790, 791.

seen similar manifestations of respect shown to the remains of other Anglo-Saxon chieftains, who had been branded in life as traitors. But Æthelred sought by other means to strengthen his power, and shortly after he had freed himself from his dangerous rival he repudiated his wife, and married Ælflæd, a daughter of Offa king of Mercia.[1] Events such as are here recorded must have been attended with the saddest effects on the condition of the people; we accordingly meet with no more distinguished individuals among the Northumbrians. Agriculture was neglected; famine and its companion, pestilence, desolated the land. But a more dreadful scourge than these transient evils was at hand. In the year 793 the Northmen first landed on Lindisfarne, plundered the monastery and church, not even sparing the monks, some of whom they slew, some they carried off as slaves, others they sent forth naked, or cast into the sea. In the following year the pirates returned and plundered the monastery at Ecgferthesmynster (Wearmouth? or Jarrow?): but one of their leaders was slain by the inhabitants, their ships were wrecked in a storm, and the survivors who reached the shore perished by the sword of the Northumbrians, so that not one escaped of these "Scaldings," or "Skjoldings," as the Northmen were called by the Anglo-Saxons, perhaps because they knew them as coming from the Scheldt, where they had a settlement.[2] Thus, in accordance with the notions then

---

[1] Sim. Dunelm. a. 792.

[2] Hist. de Cuthberto ap. Sim. Dunelm. p. 69. Here an invasion of the 'Scaldings' after the death of Ecgfrith, and before Ceolwulf's time, i.e. before 729, is supposed, which must be an err r, arising possibly from the inroad of the Picts in 710. Cf. Sim. Dunelm. de Rebus gestis Reg. Angl. aa. 793, 794, who is copied by R. Hoveden

prevailing, did St. Cuthberht, the patron of that cloister, protect Northumbria from the ravages of the Danes, who were, nevertheless, some years after, destined to destroy not only its peace but its independence. The ruin of that holy edifice made a deep impression over all England, which shows that the destructive spirit of the Northmen was not yet universally known.[1]

A few years later Æthelred was murdered by his discontented thanes, among whom the ealdormen Aldred and Wada are especially named as the perpetrators.[2] Many laymen of rank and ecclesiastics now abandoned this realm of internal dissension, which seemed doomed to become the scorn and booty of its neighbours.[3] The ealdorman Osbald, who had been formerly distinguished as the leader of a faction, and had been on terms of close intimacy with Æthelred, was now proclaimed king by his partisans,[4] but the returning

---

—" Pagani . . . princeps eorum ibidem crudeli nece occisus est ab Anglis."

[1] Alcuini Epist. 29, 49, etc. Malmesb. de Pont. lib. iii. 'De Episcopis Lindisfarn.'

[2] Sim. Dunelm, aa. 796, 798. The Sax. Chron. places his murder in 794. Not only does probability speak in favour of the Durham annals, but also the eclipse of the moon on the 28th March, 796, given in both Simeon and the Chronicle as contemporaneous with the accession of Eardwulf. Cf. L'Art de vérifier les Dates, in the calculation of eclipses. [The Chronicle gives the eclipse in 795. In a letter to Offa, Alcwine writes that Charles was so incensed against the Northumbrians, in consequence of the murder of Æthelred, that but for his (Alcwine's) mediation he would have done them all the injury in his power, " gentem illam homicidam dominorum suorum pejorem paganis æstimans." W. Malm. lib. i. In this year (798) London was destroyed by fire, and many of the inhabitants perished. Sim. Dunelm.—T.]   [3] W. Malm. lib. i.

[4] Alcwine (Epist. xxix. Opera, p. 1537) reminds the king Æthelred, the patricius Osbald, and Osbert, " de antiqua amicitia

moon found him a fugitive in the monastery of Lindisfarne, from whence he embarked for the Pictish territory, the usual asylum for Northumbrian exiles. He died about three years afterwards, as an abbot, apparently in his native country,[1] and was buried at York. The Northumbrians now recalled from exile—that school of the Northumbrian kings— the ealdorman Eardwulf, whose life had been so miraculously saved by the monks of Ripon, and with him a better state of things seemed to return. A great synod held under his auspices by the archbishop of York at Pincanhealh[2] bears witness to an earnest desire of good. The turbulent nobles again assumed a threatening attitude, and the ever-increasing number of the descendants or relations of deposed kings necessarily laid greater dangers in the path of every succeeding government. The ealdorman Wada was, however, put to flight and slain at Billingahoh,[3] near Whalley, together with Alric son of Heardberht, and his faction annihilated.[4] Torhtmund, an ealdorman esteemed for his fidelity and valour, revenged the murder of his former

---

. . . de fidei veritate, de pacis concordia, quam habere debetis inter vos; quia amicitia quæ descri potest, nunquam vera fuit." This letter cannot have been written long before the murder of Ethelred, as it makes mention of the destruction of the church of St. Cuthberht by the pagans.

[1] Sim. Dunelm. a. 799.   [2] Sim. Dunelm. a. 798.

[3] Here and in *Billingsgate* we meet with the name of the noble race of the Billings. [In the Scôp's Tale (Cod. Exon. p. 320, and Thorpe's Beowulf, p. 217), we are told that, "Billing (weold) Wernum." *Billing (govern'd) the Warni.*—T.]

[4] Sim. Dunelm. a. 799. Alcuini. Epist. xviii. in Oper. p. 1514. In this letter the archbishop of Canterbury, Torhtmund and others are recommended to the hospitality of the emperor Charles. As Æthelheard went to Rome in 799, we may perhaps assume that Torhtmund left his home immediately after the death of Aldred.

master Æthelred on Aldred, one of the perpetrators. The ealdorman Moll, of the family of Æthelwald, was put to death by order of Eardwulf, as was also Alhmund, a son of Alhred, who, on his clandestine return with other exiles, had been seized by the guards of the king. Yet were his adversaries not disheartened, who, when forced to flee, found an hospitable hearth and protection with Cenwulf king of Mercia. Eardwulf now felt himself strong enough to attack the territory of his treacherous neighbour, the stronghold of the conspirators: the long warfare which ensued was ended, through the intervention of the bishops and nobles of England, by a treaty of peace and friendship between the two kings sworn on the holy evangelists. Five years afterwards Eardwulf was, however, driven by his subjects into exile:[2] his determination not to yield to the rebels, who had once spontaneously sworn fealty to him, and to implore the aid of the mighty Frankish monarch Charles the Great, as well as the intervention of the pope Leo the Third, proves him to have been of a firm and sagacious character. Charles was not ignorant of the affairs of the north of England, which must have been familiar to him through his lately deceased friend Alcwine. Eardwulf sought the emperor at Nimeguen, and, having forwarded his suit there, hastened to the holy father at Rome, by whom the desired mediation was readily undertaken. Accompanied by a papal legate in the person of the deacon Aldulf, and, on the part of the emperor, by the abbots Rotfrid of St. Amand, and Nanther of St. Omer, Eardwulf returned to England,

[1] Sim. Dunelm. a. 801.
[2] Sax. Chron. a. 806. In consequence of an hiatus in Simeon of Durham from a. 803 to 849, we are during that interval nearly without any accounts of the kingdom of Northumbria.

ANGLO-SAXON SETTLEMENT, A D. 446–800. 279

and by the united influence of the pope and emperor was reinstated in his royal dignity.[1] Alfwold, a brother probably of king Æthelred, had, during the two years spent in these negotiations, held the reins of government, but offered no long opposition to the restoration of peace. Eardwulf died in the year following, and was succeeded by his son Eanred, who reigned amid intestine dissensions for thirty-three years,[2] until the occurrence of events, which will enable us to comprise the entire history of England under one head.

[1] Eginh. Annals, a. 808. Enh. Fuldens. eod. That the expulsion of Eardwulf was already known to Leo is evident from his letter to Charles (ap. Bouquet, t. v. p. 602) wherein he says, "quod Eardulphus rex de regno suo ejectus fuisset, jam hoc per Saxones agnoveramus." A messenger from Eanbald, archbishop of York, had not only been sent to Rome but also to the emperor. See the two letters of Leo to Charles in Bouquet, vol. v. p. 601–4. That these letters had reference not only to internal dissensions, but probably to the intention of the king of Mercia not to acknowledge the archbishops and bishops of Rome, seems evident from the words, " Prædictus Cenulfus rex nec suum archiepiscopum (sc. Cantuariensem) pacificum habet, nec istum Eanbaldum item archiepiscopum," etc. p. 602 c.—" Valde pertimescimus, ne ipse populus acquisitionis sanctæ Romanæ ecclesiæ per quamlibet occasionem et certamen prædecessoris mei, D. Gregorii, beatissimi papæ, quod ipsis in partibus posuit, meis temporibus infructuosum existere videatur, nec mihi in judicio eveniat," etc. p. 604 a. See also Palgrave, vol. i. p. 484.

[2] Sim. Dunelm. de Eccl, Dunelm. lib. iii. c. 5. Matt. of Westminst. a. 810.

CHAPTER XIII.

THE EIGHTH CENTURY.

State of Mercia—People warlike, illiterate—Laws of Succession—Penda and his Sons—Æthelbald's Reign—His Successes—Offa—His Expeditions against the Saxons—Charles the Great—Offa's Dyke—London—Archbishopric of Lichfield—Offa's Learning—His Power—His Treachery to young Æthelberht of East-Anglia—Cenwulf—His Successes in Kent and Wales—Disputes with Wulfred his Primate.

MERCIA, towards which we now turn our attention, presents an appearance widely different from that of Northumbria. Long opposition to the introduction of Christianity had been there punished by the absence of the arts and knowledge attending civilization, as well as of institutions conducive to that object. Mercia has not left us the name of an author nor any written law or chronicle. Nowhere was the number of ecclesiastics smaller; and while the other states were divided into dioceses, Mercia proper and Middle Anglia formed together but one bishopric. On the other hand, the energetic measures of Penda had formed valiant soldiers, and created for the posterity of the old sea-heroes a military force alike formidable to the Britons and to the other Germanic states. Placed in the centre of the country, the rulers of Mercia availed themselves of their position to threaten all their neighbours, and obtain a supremacy over them. The advantage of some long reigns promoted both its internal tranquillity

ANGLO-SAXON SETTLEMENT, A.D. 446–800. 281

and the success of its designs against the distracted states around it.

After the death of Wulfhere, his brother Æthelred, who had married Osthryth, a sister of Ecgfrith of Northumbria, succeeded to the throne.[1] In the first year of his reign he made war on Hlothhære (Hlothhæri) king of Kent,[2] and ravaged his kingdom, destroying churches and monasteries, and even the episcopal see of Rochester. A few years afterwards he invaded the dominions of his brother-in-law, king Ecgfrith. In this contest fell Ælfwine, the brother of Ecgfrith, a youth equally beloved by Mercians and Northumbrians, whose ferocity, aggravated by this event, threatened to bring about the direst consequences. At this conjuncture the wholesome influence and judgment of the archbishop Theodore, who, in pursuance of his calling, to mediate between hostile nations, and with the success which more frequently attends mediators, when the passions are at the highest than in earlier stages of the quarrels, prevailed on the Northumbrians to renounce all further vengeance for the death of their prince, in consideration of the payment of the legal wergild, and also to restore to Mercia the province of Lindisse, which had been taken from Wulfhere by Ecgfrith. To the remaining years of Æthelred's long reign no blame seems to be attached. A great misfortune saddened his later days, for the nobles of the northern part of the kingdom, or Southumbria, murdered his consort, an event of so extraordinary a character that we must look eleven centuries onwards into the his-

[1] Beda, iv. 21. Sax. Chron. a. 675. Matt. Westm. a. 696, calls her erroneously, " Egfridi regis filiam."
[2] Beda, iv. 12. Cum Æ lilred . . . adducto maligno exercitu, Cantiam vastaret," eto.

tory of Europe, before we meet with a parallel case.[1] He subsequently gave the government of Southumbria to his nephew Cenred, the son of his brother Wulfhere, to whom at length he resigned the entire kingdom,[2] his own sons being yet in their minority. Hence it would appear that the Mercian law of succession, unlike that of Northumbria, where we have seen a boy of eight years succeed to the throne, required from its king, in addition to right by birth, the qualifications indispensable for the duties of that high office. Among those of mature age, the next by birth seems always to have succeeded, and the right of the elder line at the same time to have been preserved. He who had entered on the government was not, however, compelled to resign it on the maturity of the direct heir, whereby all the dangers and calamities of guardianship were prevented: it is, therefore, merely through an error of a comparatively late writer[3] that Cenred is considered as the guardian of Æthelred's son, since he legally and unconditionally possessed for life the kingly power. The son of Penda entered the monastery of Bardeney, took the tonsure, and for many years, as abbot, directed the peaceful avocations of the monks.[4] So soon had the time passed away, when the sons of Woden knew no greater

[1] Beda, v. 24, "a Merciorum primatibus interempta." Sax. Chron. a. 697. Flor. of Worc. a. 696. Matt. of Westminst. a. 696, "crudeliter necaverunt."

[2] Sax. Chron. aa. 702, 704.

[3] Wallingford (from whom so many errors have found entrance into English history) says (Gale, t. i. p. 527) that Cenred had pledged himself to Æthelred to resign the crown to his (Æthelred's) son on his majority. That the resignation of Cenred took place before the 13th June, 704, appears from the document in Hickes t. iii. p. 262, n. 77.

[4] Sax. Chron. Flor. of Worc. obiit a. 716.

disgrace than to die in a bed! But to the nation the new increasing longing after the cowl was more pernicious than the use of harness.¹ After a few years, passed for the most part in conflicts with the Britons, Cenred also resigned the reins of government to a successor, the young Ceolred, the son of Æthelred and Osthryth, and with Offa of Essex, a prince adorned with all the graces of youth and manners, as well as endowed with every quality befitting a prince, journeyed to Rome, there to take the monastic vow at the hands of pope Constantine, and to fast and pray for the salvation of the souls of their forsaken consorts, their relations and people, to the end of their earthly course.² His successor Ceolred died in the same year as his father.

Ceolred has by later writers, whose accounts are probably derived from the chronicle of some monastery favoured by him, been celebrated, in pompous diction, as the illustrious heir of his father's and his grandfather's virtues; but to us the unfavourable testimony given by the archbishop of Mayence, Boniface, one of his most distinguished contemporaries, appears more worthy of belief.³ He seems to have lacked either the valour or the good fortune of Penda, for in the war between him and Ine, the honour of victory at the battle of Wodnes-beorh was claimed by both parties. His young presumptive successor, the clito ⁴ Æthelbald, son of Alweo, and brother of Penda, who, though remotely, was yet his next relative, he persecuted inexorably.

¹ Vita S. Guthlaci in Actis Sanctorum, App. i. vol. ii. p. 39.
² Beda, v. 19. Sax. Chron. a. 709.
³ Bonifacii Ep. ad Æthelbaldum. Malmesbury has given us a portion of this letter.
⁴ Clito was a title given by the Anglo-Saxons to the members of a royal house, and seems equivalent to ætheling, of which it was probably intended as a translation.

Like Penda he was hostile to the church, and gave himself up to sensual pleasures with a recklessness that made him the prey of death during the riot of a feast; thus supplying an historic interpretation to the monkish tradition, that the evil spirit, while conversing with him, had deprived him of life.[1]

Æthelbald had hitherto found in the marshes of Crowland, where he afterwards founded the celebrated abbey, not only a shelter, but instruction, with the holy hermit St. Guthlac, who, like the royal house of Mercia, was of the noble race of the Icelings. He was acknowledged as king without opposition. He is described as of vast bodily strength, graceful form and great courage; but pride and sensuality were the reproach of his earlier years.[2] While appearing to execute his public duties, providing by strict justice for the internal peace of the country, and making liberal disbursements to the clergy and the poor, he addicted himself to excesses with married women and nuns, and hurried the thanes of Mercia into the same vortex of dissoluteness. The affectionate interest with which Boniface, archbishop of Mayence, ever regarded the fortunes of his native country, the fervour with which he dared to set before the king his transgressions, with a remarkable allusion to the chastity of the Old-Saxons, were not without an effect, which may have been increased by the circumstance, that the scorner of holy wedlock was childless. At a synod held by archbishop Cuthberht, at Clofesho, it was

[1] Sax. Chron. a. 716. Bonifacii Epist. ad Æthelbaldum ap. Malmesb. lib. i.
[2] Ingulph. sub init. See the letter already cited of Boniface. Cf. also Felicis Girwii Vita S. Guthlaci in Actis Sanctor. April. xi. c. 3 et 4.

attempted, through the prelates and monks, to effect a reformation of the laity.[1] Æthelbald's reign of forty-one years was distinguished by many successful conflicts with the Britons. East Anglia, Kent, and Essex, and for a time Wessex also, followed his standard without a struggle, against the common enemy. Taking advantage of a change of government he invaded Northumbria, but was driven back by king Eadberht.[2] Nevertheless the haughty Æthelbald maintained the supremacy in Britain,[3] and was able, either by hostile inroads or by fomenting rebellions, so to weaken his most potent rival, Cuthred of Wessex, that he was reduced to submit to the most humiliating oppressions. But excess of disgrace soon re-assembled the disaffected nobles of his realm around the king of Wessex, who was, moreover, much strengthened by a reconciliation with his brave and

[1] W. Malm. lib. i. c. 4. [The passage relating to the Old-Saxons is worth insertion: "In antiqua Saxonia, ubi nulla est Christi cognitio, si virgo in paterna domo, vel maritata sub conjuge, fuerit adulterata, manu propria strangulatam cremant, et supra fossam sepultæ corruptorem suspendunt; aut, cingulo tenus vestibus abscissis, flagellant eam castæ matronæ et cultellis pungunt, et de villa in villam missæ occurrunt novæ flagellatrices, donec interimant. Insuper et Winedi, quod est foedissimum genus hominum, hunc habent morem, ut mulier viro mortuo se in rogo cremati pariter arsura præcipitet." Malm. l. cit. and De Gestis Pontif. lib. i. c. 4, places the Council of Clofesho in 747. The true date, which is given in the Sax. Chron., is manifest from Æthelbald's charter, beginning "Anno DCCXLII. regni Æthibaldi XXVII. congregatum est magnum concilium apud Clouesho," etc. Cod. Diplom. t. i. p. 105.—T.]

[2] App. ad Bedam, a. 740.

[3] In a charter of 736 he styles himself, "Rex non solum Marcersium, sed et omnium provinciarum quæ generale nomine Sutangli dicuntur:" and signs, "Ego Ætdilbalt, Rex Britanniæ." Cod. Diplom. t. i. p. 96. Smith's Beda, p. 786. Hemingford, t. i. p. 219.

powerful ealdorman Æthelhun,[1] who had unsuccessfully risen in arms against him. The battle at Burford[2] was to the West Saxons a struggle for life and liberty, to the Mercians for the supremacy in Britain. Æthelhun, bearing in his hand the golden dragon, the banner of Wessex, marched in the front of the army, and slew the standard-bearer of the Mercians. The fall of so conspicuous a person struck terror into the enemy, and raised the courage of the West Saxons. A battle of such importance, fought with so much valour and obstinacy, rarely took place between those people. Though none flinched, no one surpassed Æthelhun, whose battle-axe, rapid as lightning, clove both armour and body, and whose path was marked by death. In like manner did the unconquered sword of Æthelbald cut through armour as a garment, and bones as though they had been flesh. Like firebrands in each opposing host these heroes had spread destruction around them, when suddenly they met and stood face to face. A mutual glance, a mutual attack instantly followed, when, strange to relate, yet not without example, strength and courage on a sudden forsook the king, who, while his men were yet bravely fighting, fled at the moment when a single well-aimed stroke might have decided his own and his kingdom's fate. But for both all glory had departed from that day forth. A few years afterwards he fought another battle against Wessex at Secandun,[3] where,

---

[1] The title of Consul is given to him. H. Hunt. a. 750. So Matt. of Westminst. a. 708. "Offerus consul Northamhymbrorum."

[2] Sax. Chron. a. 752. In the account of this battle it will be easy to recognise the pompous diction of Henry of Huntingdon.—T.

Sax. Chron. a. 755. Florence calls the battle-place Segeswald. Seckington in Warwickshire is supposed to be the spot.—T.

disdaining flight, notwithstanding the slaughter of his people, he either fell in the field, or was treacherously murdered by his guards, and buried at Repton.[1] Beornred, who had placed himself at the head of the army and government, was obliged in the following year[2] to yield to the superior power and pretensions of Offa, a descendant of the royal house of Wibba, and to retire from the kingdom of Mercia.

With Offa we seem to be carried back from the safe historic ground on which we have long moved to the insecure realm of myths and fables. His real name is said to have been Winfrith;[3] and his father was an ealdorman called Thingfrith. Though lame, dumb, and blind from his birth, the youth acquired speed of foot, speech, and sight, when the usurper Beornred persecuted his parents and oppressed his native land. Hence he obtained the name of the second Offa, from his resemblance to his ancestor, Offa (Uffo) the son of Wærmund, king of Angeln, who, blind from his birth

[1] Sim. Dunelm. H. Hunt. "non sine miserabili exercituum ruina, fugam dedignans, occisus est," which has been incorrectly copied by Matt. of Westminst. a. 755, " per fugam non declinans ruinam interfectus occubuit."

[2] The Saxon Chronicles are wrong in the year 755, but right in 716, where Æthelbald is said to have reigned forty-one years. Sim. Dunelm. says, a. 757, " Ethelbald . . . interfectus est. Eodem vero anno Merci bellum inter se civile inierunt. Bearnred in fugam verso, Offa rex victor extitit." My more definite account is founded on the acts of the Council of Cealchyth in 789, the thirty-first of the reign of Offa. Hickes, t. i. p. 171. The victory over Beornred took place in the autumn of 757, and the coronation of Offa probably only in 758. That the regnal years are not reckoned from the day of the predecessor's death, but from that of the coronation, appears from many passages, as Sim. Dunelm. aa. 758 and 759.

[3] In the Vita Offæ II. he is called Pinefrid, no doubt a repetition of the usual blunder in the Latin Chronicles of P for the Anglo-Saxon W (ᚹ).—T.

till his seventh year, and dumb till his thirtieth, yet, roused by the impending shame of being excluded from the succession, through a war threatened by the king of the Saxons, suddenly acquired the use of speech and sight.[1]

Such is the account given by the Danish writers, though the author of the Life of Offa II. supposes that

[1] However the several accounts of the genealogies of the Mercian kings may vary with regard to the other names, they all, nevertheless, agree with respect to Wihtlæg, Wermund and Offa. See Nennius, Alfred of Beverley, Saxon Chron. a. 626. This remark holds good also for the same three kings, in the otherwise varying lists of Saxo and that in Eric's Chronicle; though in Svend Aagesen Wiglet (Wihtlæg) is wanting. But in all the three authors, who draw from different sources, we find the same story of Uffo. The Danish or Anglian Uffo, it is true, is not blind, but is the son of the blind Wermund; that he was dumb till his thirtieth year is expressly mentioned by Svend Aagesen. In Beowulf we have Garmund (Wermund), Ongentheow (Angeltheow), belonging to the genealogy of the Mercian kings. See a saga of Offa in Beow. xxvii. [Cod. Exon. p. 320; also Beow. vol. i. p. 258, and vol. ii. p. xxxii. sq. The single combat, in which Uffo revenged the insult offered to his father and himself, took place on an island in the Eyder, where a part of the city of Rensburg, called the Altstadt, now stands. Wermund's adversary is said to have been Sigar, a king of Holstein; the name of his son, slain by Uffo, was Hildebrand. See Saxo, lib. iv., and Sveno Aggonis, ap. Langebek.—T.], also Dahlmann's Forschungen, Th. i. p. 233. The story of the two Offas has been written by a monk of St. Albans, and is printed at the end of Watts's edition of Matt. Paris. The account of the elder Offa agrees for the most part with Svend Aagesen's, not only in the general outline, but also in the first speech of Uffo or Offa. Nor is the agreement of the two sagas in the girding of the youth with the sword by the father, as well as the ensuing combat, to be overlooked. It is, however, remarkable that, besides these 'Vitæ,' the date and author of which are unknown, no other ancient English writer mentions the story of the youth of Offa, not even Bromton himself. [The story of the Danish Uffo is well condensed by Suhm, Historie af Danmark, Bd. i., or in Grüter's translation, Bd. i. p. 117.—T.]

the son of Wærmund reigned in England. In the general outline his story is nearly the same as that given in the Danish chronicles, which are, however, not in perfect accordance with each other. It seems, therefore, not improbable that the monkish biographer derived some parts of his narrative from ancient sources with which we are unacquainted, perhaps the heroic sagas of the Jutes, and that between the two Offas there existed some points of similitude sufficient for a foundation to the parallel.

At the Council of Clofesho and on other occasions, the name of the young patrician Offa appears next in order to that of the king, at least before those of the other laity. Offa himself, in two of his charters, mentions his grandfather Eanwulf, who, in king Æthelbald's time, held land in the territory of the Hwiccas, where, at Bredon, he had founded a church,[1] and who, if we may hazard a conjecture on the alliteration of names, so frequent among the Anglo-Saxons, was either father or brother of the Christian petty kings of that country, Eanfrith and Eanhere. We must, therefore, consider him as the nearest relative of the king, though descending in a collateral line from their common ancestor,[2] and ascribe the bloody wars[3] attending his

[1] See charters in Smith's Beda, pp. 766, 767, and Cod. Diplom. t. i. pp. 169, 176.

[2] "Offa quinto genu Pendæ abnepos." W. Malm. lib. i. But this is incorrect, as he descended from Eawa, son of Wibba, the brother of Penda. Saxon Chron. Fl. of Worc. a. 755, with which Alfred of Beverley agrees, "cujus (sc. Ædilbaldi) patruelis, Enulf nepos Offa." Malmesbury makes a similar mistake with regard to Cenwulf, the second successor of Offa.

[3] App. ad Bedam, a. 757. Alcuinus ap. Malmesb. lib. i. c. 4. "Non arbitror quod nobilissimus juvenis Egfertus propter peccata sua mortuus sit, sed quia pater suus (Offa sc.) pro confirmatione regni ejus multum sanguinem effudit."

accession to the throne to the resistance of Beornred, whom we meet with some years afterwards in Northumbria, where he burnt Catterick, but in the same year perished himself by fire—by the judgment of God—as we are told.[1]

Offa's dominion does not seem to have been firmly established before the death of Beornred; till then we do not find him engaged beyond the limits of his kingdom. His first memorable expedition was against the Hestingas, a people whose locality, like that of many others among the Saxons, is not known with certainty. If they have rightly been sought for about Hastings in Sussex, they may be assumed to have inhabited the district around that town to which they gave their name.[2] Some years after Offa fought a bloody battle against his hated enemies, the men of Kent,[3] at Otford on the Darent, in which the Mercians gained the victory.[4]

In the following year Offa overcame at Bensington in Oxfordshire Cynewulf of Wessex, a prince celebrated for his valour, and took from him the royal town of Bensington.[5] In the wars against the Britons his arms were equally successful. In the early part of his reign he had repulsed them at Hereford,[6] and subsequently

[1] Matt. Westminst. a. 769. Sim. Dunelm., where it is erroneously said, "Earnredo tyranno ... incendio periit, Dei judicio." According to Malmesbury, Beornred was slain by Offa in 757.

[2] Sim. Dunelm. a. 771. To the town of Hastings there belonged, at a later period, a territory of 500 hydes. See Gale, t. i. p. 748. See also Palgrave, vol. ii. p. cclxxix.

[3] W. Malm. lib. i. (speaking of Cenwulf), "Contra Cantuaritas successivum ab Offa suscipiens odium, regionem illam valide afflixit." Sim. Dunelm. a. 798. Mailros. Hoveden h. a., who copies Simeon.

[4] Sax. Chron. a. 774 (one MS. reads 773). Fl. of Worc. a. 774.

[5] Sax. Chron. a. 777 (one MS. reads 775). Fl. of Worc. a. 778. H. Hunt. a. 777.   [6] Annal. Camb. Brut y Tyw. a. 760.

devastated Deheubarth or South Wales.¹ From the king of Powis he took a considerable tract of his territory, and even his residence Pengwern (Shrewsbury). The flat country at the foot of the eastern sides of the mountains, between the Wye and the Severn, he peopled with Anglo-Saxons, no defence being so efficacious as that of free dwellers, and here their settlements may still be traced by their Saxon denominations. To protect the settlers from the sudden inroads and maraudings of the hostile mountaineers, he caused to be constructed a considerable rampart with a ditch,² from the mouth of the Dee to that of the Wye. This work, known by the name of Offa's dyke, traces of which are yet discernible, so well answered its purpose, that it became the boundary between Britons and Mercians, and afterwards between Wales and England. The last Anglo-Saxon king, Harold, ordered that every Briton who should appear armed on the English side of Offa's dyke should have his right hand struck off.³ If the British language and British customs are met with on this side of the barrier,⁴ they are to be attributed to Welshmen, who either were reduced to a state of complete subjection, or who, at a later period, forsook their desert mountain heights for the fertility of the plain.

Nothing would more raise the wars of Offa above de-

¹ Annal. Camb. a. 778. Brut y Tyw. a. 776.
² Asser V. Ælfredi. "Offa . . . qui vallum magnum inter Britanniam atque Merciam de mari usque ad mare facere imperavit." Giraldus de Illaudabilibus.
³ Joh. Salisbur. Polycrat. lib. vi. See a more particular account of Offa's dyke in R. Higden, Polychron. p. 194.
⁴ Asser, x. Camden, edit. Gibson, p. 587. Higden also says, "Sed hodie hinc inde, ultra citraque fossam illam, potissimum in provincia Cestriæ, Salopiæ, Herfordiæ, Wallici cum Anglicis passim sunt permixti."

serving the appellation of battles between the kites and the crows, by which the great epic poet of England has unconsciously eternalized the narrow historic notions of his time,¹ than if it could be granted us to ascertain accurately how far they were influenced by the mighty ruler of the Franks, Charles the Great. If any reliance may be placed on the monkish biographer, the kings of Kent, previously to the invasion of that state by Offa, had applied to Charles for his aid and protection.² The menacing letters of the emperor were unheeded by the Mercian, and in the course of years their mutual success united the lord of the Germanic insular realm with the chief of the Roman continent. Charles sent to Offa— or, as he himself expresses it, the most powerful ruler of the East sent to the most powerful ruler of the West —many costly presents, the catalogue of which has been preserved, though not that of the presents sent in return, which to us would have been of far greater interest. From a charter with its seal still in existence, we know, however, that Offa, king of the Mercians, confirmed certain gifts of land near the port of Lundenwyc,³ made by one of his subjects to the abbey of St. Denis. The same highly favoured cloister received from another of Offa's vassals, the ealdorman Berhtwald of Sussex, with the confirmation of the king, the church of Rotherfield, and his ports of Hastings and Pevensey.⁴ Charles promised not only to pilgrims, but also to merchants

¹ "Such bickerings to recount, met often in these our writers, what more worth is it than to chronicle the wars of kites or crows, flocking and fighting in the air?" Milton, Hist. of England.—T.
² Vita Offæ II.
³ This remarkable charter, dated April 5, 790, together with those of other English kings in favour of St. Denis, exists in the Trésor des Chartes, in the Hôtel Soubise at Paris.
⁴ Charter of 792 ap. Du Chesne. Monast. Angl. t. vi. p. 1077.

ANGLO-SAXON SETTLEMENT, A.D. 446-800. 293

from England, his immediate protection,[1] which last concession may, perhaps, be regarded as an extension of the privilege granted by Dagobert to the Anglo-Saxons attending the fair at St. Denis, and may, therefore, have been the immediate cause of the above-mentioned donations. A dangerous misunderstanding took place, however, between the two monarchs on the following occasion. Charles the Great had demanded for his son Charles the hand of one of Offa's daughters, which the latter would grant only on condition that to his own son Ecgferth (Ecgfrith) should be given in marriage Berhta, the beloved daughter of Charles, who was afterwards secretly married to Angilbert, the learned abbot of St. Riquier, and is celebrated by her contemporaries as the softened resemblance of her father in mind, voice, aspect, and bearing.[2] Gerwold, abbot of St. Wandrille or Fontenelle, of a distinguished family, and formerly chaplain to queen Bertrade, but who had been appointed to the administration of the customs in the northern towns and ports of France, particularly at

[1] See the letter of Charles to Offa in Wilkins, Conc. t. i. p. 158, in Alcuini Oper. t. ii. App. p. 618, and an extract of it in Malmesbury, Leland Collect. t. i. p. 402. Cf. Privilege of Pepin, a. 753, ap. Bouquet, t. v. p. 227. As in this letter he speaks of the death of pope Hadrian I., which took place in Dec. 795, and mentions Æthelred of Northumbria, who died on the following 18th of April, as still living, the date of it is fixed with tolerable accuracy. According to this letter the emperor, besides other presents, sends to Offa a Hunnic sword and belt, and two silken mantles; a circumstance greatly in favour of the genuineness of the letter, as Charles, in the beginning of the year 796, distributed many presents from the treasures taken from the Huns. See Einh. Annal. a. 796. Chron. Moissac. Sim. Dunelm. a. 795. "Karolus . . . Hunorum gentem subegerat . . . sublatis inde xv. plaustris auro argentoque palliisque holosericis preciosis repletis."
[2] See Helperich's or Angilbert's 'Carolus Magnus,' v. 219 sq.

Quentawic, was frequently sent with commissions from the emperor to king Offa, with whom he had become very intimate. He was, nevertheless, unsuccessful in his endeavours to lower the proud pretension of the descendant of Woden, and to induce him to abandon a demand, which had so greatly incensed the invincible emperor of the Franks, that it required all his exertions to prevent the closing of the French sea-ports against the merchants of England.[1] According to other accounts, the decree was already carried into effect, a similar interdict was also issued by Offa in the English ports, and Alcwine, the friend of both princes, was destined to appease a quarrel arising from disappointed ambition.[2] We are made acquainted with the restoration of peace by an earlier document than the before-mentioned letter to Offa, namely, by a letter of intercession in favour of some Mercian exiles, to Æthelheard, archbishop of Canterbury.[3]

The notion of Offa's great influence at this time, entertained by pope Hadrian, was grounded more on the suspicion that the king of Mercia was desirous to instigate the Frankish monarch to cast him from the papal chair[4] than on the splendour attending many victories over his countrymen. That a hostile disposition might have arisen between Offa and the pope is, considering the pretensions raised by the latter at every

[1] Chron. Fontanel. in Monum. Hist. Germ. t. ii. p. 291, according to which this event took place about the year 788.
[2] Epist. Alcuini ad Colcum Lectorem in Scotia. Bouquet, t. v. p. 607; also W. Malm. lib. i. c. 4.
[3] Wilkins, t. i. p. 154. Alcuini Epist. lxi. Æthelheard became archbishop in 791. [These exiles were probably those who had sided with Beornred against Offa. There seems little doubt that they had been harboured by Charles for hostile purposes.—T.]
[4] Hadriani Epist. ap. Bouquet, t. v. p. 589.

ANGLO-SAXON SETTLEMENT, A.D. 446-800.

opportunity, exceedingly probable. While the small kingdom of Kent, which had already been under subjection to his ancestors, possessed the first primacy of the Anglo-Saxon church, and the one next in rank was placed in the rapidly declining state of Northumbria, Offa felt the want, in his own more powerful realm, of a prelate independent of both Canterbury and York. He had long vainly endeavoured to persuade Jaenberht, archbishop of Canterbury, to transfer his see to Lichfield. The archbishop was now accused of having promised aid and shelter in his diocese to the Franks, in the case of their effecting a hostile landing in England;[1] which reason, together with others, such as that Offa was desirous of founding an archiepiscopal see near the spot where he had humbled his enemies, being considered valid, it was resolved, in a synod held at Cealchyth, under the legate of Hadrian, to establish a separate archbishopric for the kingdom of Mercia, which should be conferred on those who were already bishops of Lichfield, and first be held by Aldulf,[2] the successor of Higeberht. This new ecclesiastical arrangement, notwithstanding the ready compliance yielded to the formidable Offa, became a source of heartburning among the neighbouring kingdoms, already in a state of irritation from so many other causes, and the dissatisfaction to which it gave rise was soon manifested in the abolition of the archiepiscopal see of Lichfield.

Offa acquired greater renown to himself and greater power to his state than had ever been possessed by any

[1] W. Malm. lib. i. Vita Offæ II. p. 21.
[2] W. Malm. lib. i. and De Gestis Pont. lib. iv. Vita Offæ. Rad. Dicet. Abbrev. Chron. a. 787, where the limits of the new archbishopric are given. Sim. Dunelm. a. 786.

Anglo-Saxon king or kingdom.[1] His firmness and his valour are incontestable. His delight in reading is also celebrated by his contemporaries.[2] For the better administration of his dominions he provided by the formation or collection of a code of Mercian laws, the loss of which is deeply to be lamented.[3] Yet these estimable qualities, by means of which he had founded his power, were stained with crime which stands in singular contrast to the better part of his character. No deed has excited greater horror than the murder of Æthelberht,[4] the young and accomplished king of the East Angles, of which he is accused. In the hope of obtaining the hand of Æthelthryth, the daughter of Offa, this unfortunate prince had, by the advice of his council, though in opposition to the will of his mother, set out on a journey to the Mercian court. On arriving at the border he sent forward a letter to Offa, together with valuable presents, and in return received an invitation couched in the warmest terms, with an assurance of security. By Offa he was received in the most hospitable and splendid manner; but after he had retired to his apartment for the night, a message was brought to him by an officer of the palace named Wimberht, that Offa was desirous of conferring with him on business of moment. The unsuspecting guest followed the messenger, but when passing through a dark passage he was attacked and basely murdered by assassins posted there for the purpose. By the monk

[1] See charters of 780 in Cod. Diplom. pp. 167, 169. Smith's Beda, p. 767. " Ego Offa, Dei gratia concedente, rex Merciorum simulque nationum in circuitu."
[2] Alcuini Opera, fol. 1554.
[3] See Laws of Alfred in Ancient Laws and Institutes, p. 27, fol. edit.
[4] Sax. Chron. a. 792.

of St. Albans the guilt of this foul murder has been transferred from the head of the founder of his abbey to that of the queen Cynethryth;[1] but, in such a case, privity to the deed is as criminal as the deed itself, especially when, as in the instance of Offa, who soon rendered himself master of the kingless state, the fruits of the perfidy must inevitably fall to the accomplice. Offa affected great sorrow for this atrocious crime, and raised a stately monument over the remains of his victim in the church of Hereford, on which he bestowed rich donations. In the same year Ælflæd, another daughter of Offa, was married to Æthelred king of Northumbria, and it may possibly not be wholly without regard to that untoward event that the marriage was celebrated on Northumbrian ground.

Among those events recorded of Offa's life of which the authenticity is very questionable, is a journey to Rome which he is said to have made towards the latter part of his reign. His munificence to the churches and pious establishments in that city is highly extolled; and though it is difficult to ascribe to Offa other than ambitious motives,[2] yet, if we consider the age in which

[1] So not only the Vita Offæ II., but also Fl. of Worc. a. 793. ["Offæ .... detestanda jussione, suæque conjugis Cynethritho reginæ nefaria persuasione, regno vitaque privatus est capitis abscissione." The Sax. Chron. Ethelwerd, H. Hunt., W. Malm., place the event in 792, and agree as to the decapitation. By R. Wendover we are told that the queen caused her victim to fall into a pit prepared under his couch, where he was smothered by the attendants. See Fl. Hist. t. i. p. 250.—T.]

[2] The monk of St. Albans is perhaps more trustworthy than he has hitherto been considered. The inmate of a monastery founded by Offa, he has, no doubt, placed many actions of the founder in a different light from that in which others have regarded them; yet he may have had the use of documents inaccessible to others. Many of his accounts agree accurately with those of Florence, W.

he lived rather than the individual, a pilgrimage in expiation of the murder of Æthelberht appears by no means improbable. But though Offa himself may not have visited Rome, the accounts of his liberality to the Saxon school there,[1] and of the donation or confirmation of Romescot for the benefit of that foundation, seem not undeserving of credit.

Offa during eight-and-thirty years had toiled indefatigably for the aggrandizement of his dominion, when he was seized by the hand of death [2] only a few years after the murder of Æthelberht, which had called down upon him the execration of Europe. Seldom do we see the hand of the avenging Nemesis so manifest as in the destinies of the house of the perfidious Offa. Cynethryth, of whose ambition and presumption a tangible proof still exists in the coins which she alone of all the Anglo-Saxon queens caused to be stamped with her own image, was, three months after the deed which has branded her, thrown by robbers into her own well; a manner of death which, if void of truth, may, nevertheless, serve to show what her contemporaries wished and thought of her. Tradition will not even acknowledge

---

of Malmesbury and others; if, therefore, he is not older than these, but has made use of them, the circumstance of having availed himself of such sources speaks in favour of his general credibility. He is not therefore to be altogether rejected, but in cases only when, for particular reasons, he is to be regarded with suspicion.

[1] Vita Offæ II. W. Malm. lib. ii. c. ii. Among the traditions concerning Offa a German one may be noticed, viz. that Opho, rex Angliæ, the maternal uncle of St. Willibold, first bishop of Eichstädt, erected the monastery of Schüttern, in the year 703 or 717. See Appendices in Chron. Montis Sereni, ed. Mader, pp. 282, 289.

[2] Sax. Chron. 29 July. Sim. Dunelm. 26 July a. 796. Fl. of Worc. erroneously, 794.

her as an Anglo-Saxon, but represents her as a Frank, who for some atrocious crime had been sent out to sea in an open boat, and having been found by the youthful Offa, had seduced him to conduct her to his home.[1] While the sanctity of the pious Æthelberht was working numerous miracles, the bones of his murderer were washed by the sweeping floods of the Ouse out of their consecrated earth.[2] His son Ecgferth, whom in the year 785 he had caused to be crowned king,[3] died of disease only a few months after the death of his father;[4] in him the male line of Offa was extinguished. Of his daughters, Æthelthryth, the affianced of Æthelberht, ended her days in solitude and sorrow in the abbey of Crowland. Of Eadburh, the abandoned consort of Beorhtric king of Wessex, we shall speak hereafter. The remaining daughter, Ælflæd, lost father, brother and husband in the same year.

The rich inheritance of Offa, dominion, authority,

[1] Vita Offæ. Bromton, a. 752.
[2] Offa was buried in a chapel just without Bedford. R. Wend. t. i. p. 262.—T.
[3] H. Hunt. says king of the province of Kent; but this is not only inconsistent with Malmesbury and other authorities, by whom we are informed that Alric, son of Wihtræd, and the last of the Æscings, reigned in Kent till 794, but is unsupported by the oldest testimonies, which state merely that Offa associated his son with him in the kingdom of Mercia, making no mention whatever of Kent. Sax. Chron. a. 785. "And Ecgferth was consecrated king." Fl. of Worc. "Egferthus rex est consecratus." W. Malm. lib. i. "Egfertum filium, ante mortem suam, in regem inunctum." R. Wendover, t. i. p. 247. "In illo quoque concilio (Cealchyth) Offa rex Merciorum potentissimus in regem fecit solemniter coronari Egfridum, filium suum primogenitum, qui deinceps cum patre . . . usque ad finem vitæ ejus regnavit." See also charters of Offa in Cod. Diplom. Nos. 152, 165, where Ecgferth signs himself 'rex Merciorum.'—T.
[4] Ingulph.

treasures, fell after the short reign of Ecgferth, which was not such as to justify any very sanguine hopes,[1] to Cenwulf, a descendant of Cenwealh, a son of Wibba, and consequently brother of Penda. Cenwulf was endowed with the kingly qualities of Offa, but he knew also how to maintain his power by justice and clemency as well as by valour. So at least proclaims the praise bestowed on him almost unanimously by the ecclesiastical chroniclers of the middle ages, in whose hands were placed the golden keys of earthly immortality and undying renown. The prosperity of his reign, which was followed by no similar one in Mercia, is undeniable. The arts of peace began to be more steadily and, therefore, more successfully cultivated. Almost the only art which has left behind it unquestionable monuments of its time, the coinage, proves that, first under Offa, and subsequently under Cenwulf, it yielded the best impressions which Mercia could produce.

The Æscings who had worn the crown of Kent, though under the supremacy of Mercia, were now extinct, and Cenwulf formed the plan of uniting that kingdom still more closely with his own. He found an opponent in Eadberht, surnamed Præn, who held the sovereignty of Kent for three years. This prince, who seems to have been collaterally connected with the Æscings, and also related to Ecgberht king of Wessex, had formerly been an ecclesiastic.[2] The

[1] So it may be inferred from Alcwine's letter to him (No. xlviii.).
[2] Sax. Chron. a. 794. Fl. of Worc. Thorne, p. 2238. Wallingford, p. 530, confounds Eadberht Præn with the eldest son of Wihtræd, who, according to the Sax. Chron. and Fl. of Worc., died in 748. That he was an ecclesiastic appears from a letter of pope Leo (Anglia Sacra, t. i. p. 460), where it is said, " De illa epistola, quam Æthelhardus (archiep. Cantuar.) nobis transmisit . . . . reddimus respon-

Mercian overcame his rival by the sword, as well as by the equally efficient aid of spiritual weapons. He offered to abolish the archbishopric of Lichfield, an act which could not fail to dispose in his favour all the higher clergy of England, and was especially calculated to gain over to the king of Mercia the archbishop of Canterbury and all whose interests immediately depended on that dignity. The pope, Leo the Third, declared also his willingness to abolish the new archbishopric, and to excommunicate the apostate churchman who had usurped the throne of Kent. Cenwulf, after having laid the Kentish territory waste as far as the marshes, took the king Eadberht prisoner, led him bound into Mercia, having caused the eyes of his captive to be put out and his hands amputated.[1] He did not, however deprive him of life, but, after some time, on the occasion of the consecration of the church founded by him at Winchelcomb, which was conducted with extraordinary pomp, and at which splendid gifts were bestowed both on ecclesiastics and laymen, he restored him to liberty.[2]

---

sum, quia nos de clerico illo apostata, qui ascenderat in regnum, similem illum reputantes Juliano Parabatæ, anathemizantes objicimus," etc. Other particulars concerning him have been preserved only by H. of Huntingdon: "Populos Cantiæ .... rex Egbricht in dominium suscepit, quos prius cognatus suus Pren in-. justo amiserat. Edbriht Pren regnavit III. annis."

[1] Sax. Chron. a. 796. Sim. Dunelm. a. 798. Neither Ethelwerd nor Florence mention the mutilation. "quem vinculis oppressum duxerunt usque ad Merce." Ethelw. a. 796. "ligatum in Merciam secum duxit." Fl. of Worc.—T.

[2] Malmesbury gives a glowing account of Cenwulf's munificence and *clemency* at this ceremony: "Apud Winchelcumbam, ubi ecclesiam Deo exædificaverat, ipsa dedicationis die regem captivum ad altare manumittens, libertate palpavit, memorabile clementiæ suæ spectaculum exhibens [!]. Aderat ibidem regiæ munificentiæ

The arms of Cenwulf were also fortunate against the Welsh. In the first year of his reign the battle of Rhuddlan in the Vale of Clwyd was fought, when they were driven back over Offa's dyke. In another battle Caradoc, king of Gwynedd, perished. In his latter years his army penetrated to Snowdon, and devastated the country adjacent.[1]

The government of Kent was assigned by Cenwulf to his brother Cuthred;[2] but the suppression of the Mercian archbishopric was delayed for some years, until, at a synod held by the primate of Canterbury and his twelve suffragans at Clofesho,[3] it was carried into effect. We read not without surprise in what contemptuous terms the decree of the synod mentions the schemes of Offa, through which the see of the holy Augustine had been prejudiced in its rights, and afterwards learn from the same source that archbishop Æthelheard himself had made a journey to Rome for the purpose of prevailing on the pope to suppress the new archbishopric, and restore to its integrity the foundation of his glorious predecessor Gregory the Great. Pure good-will towards Æthelheard seems to have moved the pope to this remarkable act of com-

---

applausor Cuthredus, quem ille Cantuaritis regem præfecerat. Sonabat basilica plausibus, platea fremebat discursibus, eo quod ibi in conventu tredecim episcoporum, decem ducum, nullus largitatis pateretur repulsam, omnes suffarcinatis marsupiis abirent; nam præter illa xenia quæ magnates susceperant, inæstimabilis scilicet pretii et numeri, in utensilibus, vestibus, equis electissimis, omnibus, qui agros non habebant, libram argenti, presbyteris marcam auri, monachis solidam unum, postremo toti populo multa erogavit."—T.

[1] Annal. Camb. aa. 796, 798, 816, 818. Brut y Tyw. a. 819.
[2] Ob. A.D. 805.
[3] A.D. 803. See Wilkins, Conc. t. i. pp. 163, 167. Smith's Beda p. 787.

pliance in his favour ; the papal court could derive no advantage from it.

Æthelheard died shortly after the completion of his object. Between Cenwulf and Wulfred, the new archbishop, a quarrel soon arose, in which the violence and avarice of the former are bitterly complained of. For six years the king prohibited the primate from exercising the archiepiscopal duties; and, on his return from Rome, where he had obtained a favourable decision of his cause, Cenwulf declared in a council, that, unless he surrendered certain lands, and paid a certain sum of money, he should be expelled from the kingdom, and that no decrees of the pope nor solicitation of the emperor Charles sh.uld ever effect his return. To both demands the archbishop at length yielded, but the promised restoration of its privileges to the church of Canterbury was unfulfilled.[1] The foregoing particulars of the life of Cenwulf seem inconsistent with the praise so liberally bestowed on him by the chroniclers, who, moreover, inform us that, after a reign of twenty-six years, he passed to the reward of his numerous good deeds, and was buried at Winchelcomb.[2]

Cenwulf was succeeded by his son Cenhelm, a child of seven years, who, at the instigation of his sister Cwenthryth, was basely murdered in a wood by Æsceberht, his tutor. Ceolwulf, a brother of Cenwulf, then succeeded to the throne, from which he was driven two years afterwards by the usurper Beornwulf, a Mercian without any pretensions by birth;[3] after which event Mercia rapidly approached its fall.

[1] Evidentiæ Eccles. Cantuar. ap. Twysden, p. 2213.
[2] Sax. Chron. a. 819. [H. Hunt. lib. iv. " Cenwlf regnavit xxvi annis pacifice, et mortuus est communi morte."—T.]
[3] Fl. of Worc. Ingulph.

CHAPTER XIV.

FROM THE SEVENTH TO THE NINTH CENTURY.

The so-called Heptarchy—East Anglia—East Saxons—Kent—Its Rulers—Sussex—The smaller States—Gradual preponderance of Wessex—Its Rulers—The Britons and Armoricans—Ceadwealla; his Baptism, Abdication, and Death.

THE history of the smaller states contributing to form what by later writers has commonly, though erroneously, been called the Heptarchy, is almost wholly lost. Even the genealogies of their kings, which among those people constituted the chief basis of their annals, became, soon after the introduction of Christianity, defective, and soon only the stories or rather legends of a few pious nuns, according to the usual pattern, and in the customary strains of praise, were composed. All that is known beyond this of their kingdoms, consists in accounts of the victories of their more powerful neighbours, and isolated traces of resistance on the part of the weaker.

None of these states excites the curiosity of the historical inquirer so much as that of East Anglia, which, inhabited by Germans probably before the time of Hengest and Horsa, entirely surrounded by German neighbours, and in no contact with the Britons, must necessarily have presented a faithful picture of Teutonic antiquity. Even at the present day in no other part of England do. so many well preserved

German names of places declare who were their ancient lords or founders. Many remarkable traditions, though hitherto not sufficiently investigated and sifted for use as materials of history, are preserved relative to this district. Its position was particularly favourable to an intercourse with the Old-Saxons, and we may regard not only London, in those remote times, but also the East Anglian ports Lynn, Yarmouth and Dunwich, as resorts for Frisic, Saxon and Gallic mariners and members of the several commercial guilds or 'hansen'.

This connection with Germany declares itself in the legends of East Anglia, according to which Eadmund, who reigned there in the ninth century, was a son of Alcmund, a king of Saxony, and born at Nüremberg. The land itself bore for the most part a close resemblance to the opposite marshy coasts of Holland and Friesland, and it was only after the lapse of many ages that the drained fens of Cambridgeshire, or of the so-called isle of Ely, began to yield to the inmates of the several cloisters there the blessing of the land of Goshen. As Offa against the Welsh, so had the first kings of East Anglia raised a vast rampart, defended by a ditch, against Mercia, which bore the name of the Recken-dyke, though known at a later period among the common people as St. Edmund's, sometimes the devil's, and lastly as Cnut's, or Henry the First's.[1] We have already seen that this dyke was no safeguard against the powerful Penda; such artificial defences tending generally to the restraint of intercourse in times of peace, and, in times of danger, to the injury of the people, by a delusive appearance of security. It long continued, however, to define the limit of the

[1] Fl. W. a. 905. "Limes S. Eadmundi." Cf. Sax. Chron. h. a.

authority of the nominal kings of the country, and afterwards of the peaceful jurisdiction of the crosier of Norwich.

After the kings Sigeberht and Ecgric had fallen in battle against Penda, Anna, the son of Æne, a brother of the Bretwalda Rædwald, shared the same fate. He was succeeded by his brother Æthelhere, who, compelled to submit to the formidable conqueror, was in the following year slain with him in the memorable battle against Oswiu of Bernicia.[1] It does not appear that Anna left any male offspring. Of his four daughters, Sexburh, married to Earconberht king of Kent, and Æthelthryth to Ecgfrith of Northumbria, died abbesses of Ely; Æthelburgh was abbess of Faremoustier en Brie, and Wihtburh a nun at Ely.[2] Æthelhere was succeeded by his brother Æthelwald,[3] who was followed by Ealdwulf,[4] a son of his brother Æthelhere, who, after a reign of forty-nine years, was succeeded by his brother Ælfwold.[5] This prince seems to have been the last of the direct line of the Uffings, as after his death we find East Anglia divided between Beonna and Æthelberht or Alberht,[6] who were followed by

[1] Sax. Chr. a. 655. [2] Beda, iii. 8, iv. 19. Fl. W. Gen. [3] A.D. 655.
[4] A.D. 664. Fl. W. and Geneal. Ealdwulf was present at the Synod of Heathfield; his mother was Hereswith, a sister of St. Hild. Beda, iv. 17, 23. He died, according to the Ann. Lauresh., in 713. See Literary Introduction, p. xxxvi. note [3].

[5] A letter of his to archbishop Boniface is extant. See. Max. Bibl. Patrum, t. xiii. ep. lxxvi.

[6] Sim. Dunelm. a. 749. "Elfwald rex Orientalium Anglorum defunctus est, regnumque Hunbeanna et Albert sibi diviserunt." So Chron. Mailr. In the belief, however, that the first-mentioned of these personages never existed, I feel no scruple in eliminating the name from the list of East Anglian kings. Simeon's original was apparently some Saxon chronicle, where two words were joined, as æfter himbeanna feng to rice, *after him Beanna (Beonna) suc-*

Æthelred, the father, by his queen Leofrun, of Æthelberht, the unfortunate victim of Offa and Cynethryth.

The history of no Anglo-Saxon state is so defective as that of the East Saxons. At an early period in subjection to the kings of Kent, they subsequently fell under that of Mercia, or perhaps together with Mercia, under that of Northumbria. Some battles with Wessex in which, about the year 617, their kings Sexred, Sæward and Sigeberht were slain, indicate a short interval of independence. To these succeeded Sigeberht, surnamed the Little, a son of Sæward, who was followed by Sigebert the Good, the son of Sigebald and friend of Oswiu, at whose instance he turned to the Christian faith and received baptism. He was assassinated by two brothers, who, as we are told, hated him for his merciful disposition. He was followed by his brother Swithhelm, also a convert to Christianity.[1] It is probable that the East Saxons were conquered by Penda, though the chroniclers have not condescended to record the event; as if it were a matter of far more importance, they inform us that king Sebbe (Sebbi) assumed the tonsure, and lived till the year 694; and afterwards that the youthful Offa also abdicated the throne and made a pilgrimage to Rome.[2] His suc-

---

ceeded; out of which, misled by the near resemblance in Saxon manuscript of im to un, he formed the name of Hunbeanna. Florence (Geneal.) says, "regnante Offa Beorna regnavit in East Anglia, et post eum Æthelredus," etc. In 'Beorna' the final vowel appears very suspicious, while Beonna (written also Beanna and Bynna) is a common Saxon name. This mistake has undoubtedly arisen from the slight difference in Saxon MS. between n and p.—T.

[1] A.D. 660. Beda, iii. 22. Fl. W. Geneal.

[2] A.D. 709. Beda (v. 19) says of him, "Offa juvenis amantissimæ ætatis et venustatis," but styles him merely "filius Sigheri": hence

cessor was Selred, who was slain, but whether in battle or otherwise we are not informed.¹

Though under subjection to Mercia, the old race of the Uffings continued to rule, whose genealogy, though not altogether clear, yet sufficiently shows the legitimate succession. From the reign of Sleda it seems to have been observed as a family law, during a period of two hundred and fifty years, that the names of their kings should begin with the same letter. To these probably a king Sigebald belonged, who endeavoured to prevail on Boniface to become the spiritual guide of his people.² Even in regard to London itself, the most important place in Essex, we find scarcely anything recorded beyond the names of some ecclesiastics: it must with its environs at an early period have fallen under subjection to Mercia.³

Kent, though probably not the oldest of the Germanic states in Britain, had, through the valour of its first kings and leaders, as well as by its earlier connection with the Frankish realm, and its adherence to the continental church, acquired a certain eminence and even precedence over the other insular kingdoms. Soon,

---

it would seem that he had never assumed the reins of government. The charter in Thorne (ap. Twysden, p. 2219) issued by " Offa rex Anglorum," in the 38th year of his reign, is not of 690, but a century later, and is a charter of Offa of Mercia. [See the document in Cod. Diplom. t. i. p. 191, where it is marked as spurious.—T.]

¹ Sax. Chron. Fl. W. H. Hunt. a. 746. This prince has by some writers, following a blunder of the Chron. Mailros., rather than the authority of Florence, been placed among the rulers of East Anglia, while his name alone would have been sufficient to show the race to which he belonged.—T.

² Bonifacii Epist. xlix.

³ W. Malm. lib. i. " Londonia cum circumjacentibus regionibus Merciorum regibus, quamdiu ipsi imperitaverunt, paruit."

however, after the death of Æthelberht, under his son Eadbald, Kent sank into a condition more commensurate with its physical strength, although the sister of Eadbald was married to the powerful Eadwine of Northumbria, and he himself, reclaimed from his criminal passion for his step-mother, had espoused Emma, a Frankish princess.[1] Eadbald was succeeded by Earconberht,[2] his son by Emma, who guilefully supplanted his elder brother Eormenred, the eldest son of Eadbald. Like his father, Earconberht reigned a round number of twenty-four years. His ecclesiastical regulations are mentioned with praise, and for him was reserved the total destruction of idols. His son Ecgberht succeeded to the throne, on which, as long as his two cousins, Æthelred and Æthelberht, the sons of his father's eldest brother, Eormenred, were alive, he felt no security. A thane named Thunor, either divining the wish or obeying the command of his master, murdered the innocent princes.[3] According to the beautiful legend, to which history itself will not refuse a space, their bodies were buried by the murderer in the king's palace, under the royal seat; but a heavenly light was seen to shine over their resting-place, which led to the detection of the foul misdeed.

[1] For the date of his death (20 June) see the account given by Thorne, p. 1769. We do not, however, find it thus given by the older writers. Emma's name appears in a charter of Eadbald, a. 618. See Smith's Beda, p. 694 [and Cod. Diplom. t. i. p. 8, where it is marked as spurious]. Emma was probably a daughter of the Austrasian king Theudebert II. Langhorne, Chron. Reg. Angl. p. 155. Pagi, a. 640.
[2] Beda, iii. 8. Sax. Chron. a. 640.
[3] Sax. Chron. a. 640. Sim. Dunelm. h. a., whose narrative of the murder is particularly circumstantial and florid. Malmesbury merely alludes to it. See also Thorne, p. 1906.

The guilty king gave to Eormenbeorh,[1] a sister of the murdered princes, a space of land as blood-fine (manbôt); thus making atonement to the secular, as he did afterwards to the ecclesiastical law, by a public supplication and the founding of a monastery in the Isle of Thanet. The course of a hind during a day determined the extent of the land; and the murderer Thunor was swallowed by the gaping earth. Of the daughters of Earconberht, by his wife Sexburh, a daughter of Anna king of the East Angles, we find that Earcongote became abbess of Faremoustier, and that Eormengild was married to Wulfhere of Mercia.

Eadric, the son of Ecgberht,[2] was deprived of his throne by his uncle Hlothhære (Hlothhæri), with whom he seems, however, to have for some time reigned conjointly. With the help of the South Saxons Eadric at length in a battle overcame his faithless kinsman, who died of his wounds.[3] After a reign of about a year and a half, Eadric was carried off by a violent death,[4] when Kent, as we shall presently see, became a prey to invaders, and the seat of a war with Ceadwealla of Wessex, until, at the expiration of nine years, the legitimate succession was restored in the person of Wihtræd son of Ecgberht,[5] with whom, at least in the early part of his reign, a certain Swæbheard or Wæbheard appears to have been associated. After a reign of thirty-three years, Wihtræd was succeeded by his

[1] Called also Domneva. Sim. Dunelm. Fl. W. She was married to Merewald, a son of Penda, king of the West Hecanas.—T.
[2] Ob. A.D. 673.
[3] Beda, iv. 26. Sax. Chron. Fl. W. H. Hunt. a. 685.
[4] Beda, iv. 26. W. Malm. lib. i.
[5] Sax. Chron. a. 694. This date can apply only to his becoming sole possessor of the kingdom, as we find him in 692 already reigning conjointly with Swæbheard. See Beda, v. 8.—T.

sons, Eadberht,[1] Æthelberht II.[2]—six years before whose death the capital suffered by fire—and Alric,[3] in whom, after a reign of thirty-four years, the race of the Æscings became extinct. Eadberht seems to have had a son Eardulf,[4] who for some years reigned with his uncle, but died before him. It was Alric who yielded to the superior power of Offa in the battle of Otford. The state of Kent in the following times is extremely obscure. The small territory was often divided between two or more dependent kings,[5] and served as an appanage for the sons of the Mercian or West Saxon sovereigns. Of Eadberht Præn we have already made

[1] Ob. A.D. 748. A charter of donation to the church of Canterbury (Thorne, p. 2209), purporting to be granted by Eadbrith Eating, is without doubt a forgery of comparatively recent date, by one who confounded Eadberht of Kent with the Northumbrian king Eadberht, the son of Eata.—T.

[2] Ob. A.D. 760. As characteristic of the age may be noticed Æthelberht's request to the venerable archbishop Boniface, that he would send him some hawks. Bonif. Ep. xl. His mother, the consort of Wihtræd, was named Æthelburh (Aedilburg). See facsimile charter of 697 in the Antiquarian Repertory, vol. ii. p. 133, also Cod. Diplom. t. i. p. 50.

[3] Beda, v. 23. Sax. Chron. a. 725.

[4] A charter of Eardulf, dated 762, is extant in the Textus Roffensis (Cod. Diplom. t. i. p. 115) of a donation to the church of St. Andrew at Rochester. The date is evidently a clerical error, which may be corrected by the substitution of v for x, making it cclvii. instead of cclxii. A donation of Eardulf without date is given in Twysden, p. 2220. See also a letter from him to Lullus archbishop of Mainz (Ep. Bonif. xxxvi.) written conjointly with Eardulf bishop of Rochester.

[5] See charter, dated 762, of Sigiræd king of Kent of a donation to Rochester, signed also by "Eadberht rex Cantiæ;" and another of about the same date, signed by "Eanmund rex." Charters of Ecgberht are also extant, dating from 779 to 791, in one of which a "Heahberht rex" appears among the signatures. See Cod. Diplom. t. i.—T.

mention under Cenwulf of Mercia. The see of Canterbury imparted to this little kingdom a greater degree of stability than it could otherwise have enjoyed in its relations with the powerful states of Northumbria, Mercia, and Wessex. To the more universal civilization of Kent it is probably owing, that the earliest Anglo-Saxon laws extant are those enacted under the kings of that country, viz. Æthelberht, Hlothhære and Eadric, and Wihtræd.

Sussex, the kingdom of Ælle, the first Bretwalda of Anglo-Saxon tradition, sank soon after the death of that prince into a state bordering on nonentity. When we consider its small extent in comparison with the neighbouring kingdoms, as well as its position, unfavourable even at the present day to purposes connected with navigation, and too remote from the centre of the country for political influence, we can ascribe the part it acted under the sway of Ælle only to the personal character of that chieftain, and to the valour, displayed also at a later period, of its rugged inhabitants. This virtue of the South Saxons is conspicuous on almost every occasion where their name occurs in history; as in the deadly conflict with Ceolwulf of Wessex, in their wars with his successor Ceadwealla, as well as in instances hereafter to be mentioned. The late conversion of the South Saxons, and the wild state of the country have been already noticed. To these circumstances, and to the consequent lack of literary ecclesiastics, it is probably to be ascribed, that we do not possess even a meagre series of their rulers, much less any circumstantial details concerning them. They were the vassals sometimes of Wessex, sometimes of Mercia. Æthelwealh, the first Christian king of Sussex, received from Wulfhere, king of Mercia, the investiture of the Isle of Wight, and of the mægth[1] or tribe of the Meanwaras in Hampshire; we, nevertheless, regard him, as well as his successors, as the vassal of Wessex, whether under the denomination of heretogas (duces), kings, or under-kings. In the latter days of Æthelwealh occurs the aid, already noticed, afforded by Sussex to Eadric king of Kent. Æthelwealh, we are informed, was succeeded by Eadric, who, like his predecessor, fell in a battle against Ceadwealla of Wessex.[2] At a later period the conquest by Offa of the territory around Hastings is recorded without any mention on the occasion of a king of Sussex.[3] It is the echo of Ælle's name alone to which Sussex is indebted for a place in the Anglo-Saxon Heptarchy; a denomination equally accurate or inaccurate with most similar expressions adopted for the purpose of generalizing the particular facts of history. The expression may possibly be explained by assuming that it refers to a period when Anglo-Saxon Britain was ruled by the descendants of Saxon royal houses, although even then Bernicia is overlooked, perhaps because it belonged for the most part to the Scotland of a later period, or because it had with Deira been united with the kingdom of Northumbria.

But instead of showing that the usually so-called greater kingdoms did not always subsist in a state of

[1] Tribe, territory, so denominated from its inhabitants being all of the same race or tribe.
[2] W. Malm. lib. i.
[3] After the rulers mentioned in the text we meet with the names of Huna, Numa (Nunna), Nothelm, and Wattus, as governing under the supremacy of Ine; and at a later period, Osmund, Æthelberht and Sigeberht are named as kings of the South Saxons. A charter of Nothelm is subscribed by "Cænredus, Rex West Saxonum:" this was, no doubt, the father of Ine. See Palgrave, vol. ii. p. cclxxiv.—T.

independence,[1] it would be more desirable to give some account of the smaller ones, all the traces of which insensibly, and at an early period, almost vanished from the page of history. To these belong: Middel-Seaxe (Middlesex), which owes this appellation both to its position with regard to Essex and to the temporary neighbourhood of the West Saxons, through the conquest of Ceolwulf, but which subsequently passed to the Mercians; Suthrige (Surrey);[2] the Jutish state on the Isle of Wight; Magesetania, or the land of the Magesætas or Hwiccas (Worcestershire) and of the Hecanas (Herefordshire): Middel Engle; Elmet;[3] the Lindisfaras (Lindsey), who were in later times governed by under-kings, and, when that title fell into disuse, by heretogas and ealdormen or gerefas; and without doubt; many others, whose history may yet receive illustration both from local tradition and the use of hitherto neglected records. At present we can only speak with uncertainty of the greater number of these districts, though some others may with confidence be specified, as the extensive territory of the Pecsætas (Peakland in Derbyshire); of the East and West Wilsætas (Wiltshire); the Cilternsætas; Spalda (Spalding);[4] the South and North Gyrwas.[5] We know,

[1] Some of the elder chronicles, omitting Essex and Sussex, speak often of five Anglo-Saxon kingdoms. Chron. Angliæ MS. Hamburg.
[2] Fl. W. a. 823.
[3] Beda (ii. 14) speaks only of the Silva Elmete.
[4] In a charter of 736 mention is made of the Husmeri on the banks of the Stour, Smith's Beda, p. 786.
[5] Considerable information concerning the territorial partition of England before the division into shires might be derived from the ancient notices in Gale, t. i. p. 748, were they not unfortunately too incorrectly written or printed to admit of our founding even a conjecture on the greater part of them: e. g. to the South Saxons, whose territory is estimated by Beda (iv. 13) at 7000 hides, they assign

however, from the accounts transmitted to us relative to the most important of these small states, the Hwiccas, that they were generally held by branches of the greater royal houses in hereditary succession, and were sometimes in the joint possession of two or more brothers. Of this territory the first princes, whose names are recorded, seem to be Eanhere and his brother Eanfrith, whose daughter, as we have already seen, was married to Æthelwealh, king of the South Saxons. These were probably succeeded by Osric [1] (supposed to be a nephew of Æthelred of Mercia) and Oswald,[2] the former ruling over Gloucestershire, the other over Worcestershire. Their follower Oshere [3] was succeeded by his sons Æthelheard, Æthelweard and Æthelric,[4] and these by the brothers Eanberht, Uhtred and Aldred.[5] Under or after these princes, who all bore the title of king, we meet with others styled ealdormen (principes, duces), of whom little more is known than their names.[6]

---

no less than 100,000 hides. See also Ellis's Introd. to Domesday, vol. i. p. 145.

[1] Beda, iv. 23. "provinciam Huicciorum cui rex Osric præfuit." Charter a. 676, in Cod. Diplom. t. i. p. 16, granting 100 manentes to the abbess Bertana for the founding of a convent near Hat Bathu.

[2] Monast. t. i. p. 541.

[3] Charter aa. 680 and 693 ? in Cod. Diplom. t. i. pp. 22, 41.

[4] Charter 704-709, 706, in Cod. Diplom. t. i. pp. 60, 64, 65, 96. Hickes, t. i. pp. 169, 170. Smith's Beda, p. 786.

[5] Chart. from a. 757 to 780 in Cod. Diplom. t. i. Hickes, t. i. p. 170 sq. Smith's Beda, p. 767. This charter is perhaps not spurious, but for v we should read x, making the date 761 instead of 756.

[6] Palgrave, vol. ii. p. cclxxxix. We find a. 800 a dux Merciorum Æthelmund, whose father Ingeld must have borne the same title under Aldred. See charter in Hickes, l. cit. "dux et prefectus regis." Oshere also says (Cod. Diplom. p. 41), "consentiente comite meo Cutberhto." The title of princeps was frequently borne by ealdormen. See Hickes, l. c. 171.

THE ANGLO-SAXON KINGS.

It now remains for us to turn our attention to Wessex, and to consider what were the circumstances which favoured this land more than the other states, and, for some centuries, caused it to be especially regarded as England. A solution of the problem will be found in the circumstance, that when Northumbria was compelled to renounce all thoughts of further aggrandisement, when the hostile neighbours of Mercia were confined within their own limits by Offa's dyke, Wessex, though defended neither by natural barriers nor early success in arms, always found not only a field for warfare, but also land to bestow on the valiant, both on the Severn and in Cornwall, the land of the strangers. Thus martial discipline, legitimate succession, and a tranquil state of possession were rendered so permanent in the country, that it was enabled to adopt many gradual improvements, till, in one of its princes, it found a clear-sighted and energetic man, who united the descendants of the invading hordes into closer connection, and brought them, as far as newly occurring impediments permitted, to a higher degree of political development.

The successor of Ceolwulf, Cynegils (Cynegisl), and latterly conjointly with him his son Cwichelm,[1] conducted the war against the Britons with hereditary success. The boundaries were thus gradually enlarged of this very small state which had hitherto comprised only the districts forming in later times the shires of

[1] Fl. W. aa. 614, 628, 636, 648; also Alfred of Beverley. Malmesbury indeed says (lib. i. 2), 'filii Celrici, Cinegislus et Quicelmus;" though he afterwards calls Cuthred, the son of Cwichelm, the fratruelis of Cenwealh, the son of Cynegils. The cause of the confusion is probably that the son died before the father.

Hampton, Berks, Wilts, Gloucester to the Severn, and a part of Oxfordshire. These kings penetrated far into the territory of the South Britons, who were defeated at Beamdûn (Bampton in Devonshire). Seized with a panic at the sight of their well-appointed foes, of their gleaming battle-axes, and the magnitude of their spears, the Britons took to flight, leaving two thousand and sixty-two of their countrymen dead on the field.[1] The two kings were equally successful against Essex, which lost three kings, the sons of Sæberht, in a bloody battle from which few escaped, flight being impeded by the heaps of slain and torrents of blood.[2] Penda made war on them, though in the battle of Cirencester[3] he did not overcome them. It was only in the contest with Eadwine of Northumbria that they lost a part of their possessions, and the murderous attempt made on the life of that prince, at the instigation of the exasperated Cwichelm, led to a defeat,[4] which does not, however, seem to have been followed up by Eadwine. Cynegils, at the instance of Oswald of Northumbria, became a convert to Christianity, and was baptized by bishop Birinus. Cwichelm also received baptism and died in the year following.[5]

The succeeding years passed on quietly in settling the new ecclesiastical arrangements. Cenwealh, the second son of Cynegils, had married a sister of Penda by which connection a most dangerous enemy or neighbour—the expressions were in those days synonymous —seemed conciliated. Cenwealh, on the death of his

[1] Sax. Chron. Fl. W. H. Hunt. a. 614.
[2] In this and similar descriptions Henry of Huntingdon is easily to be recognized. [3] Sax. Chron. a. 628.
[4] Beda, ii. 9. Sax. Chron. a. 626. W. Malm. lib. i.
[5] Beda, iii. 7. Sax. Chron. Fl. W. H. Hunt. aa. 635, 636.

More dangerous to Cenwealh was the contest which now took place with Wulfhere the king of Mercia, and brother of his first consort; for although, in the beginning of the campaign, the latter sustained an overthrow, and was probably made a prisoner in the territory of Cuthred, at Æscesdûn, where he appears as the assailing party,[1] yet, in the same year, Cenwealh lost two valuable friends in his nephew Cuthred and Cenberht, another under-king. The Mercians too pressed forward, or were successfully supported by their southern friends, in return for the cession by Wulfhere of the Isle of Wight, and of the Meanwara mægth or tribe, a portion of Hampshire, to his ally Æthelwealh, the apparently new king of Sussex.

After a reign of more than thirty years Cenwealh died suddenly[2] without children or lineal descendants. He had, however, provided for the administration of his kingdom by committing it to his queen Sexburh. The talents displayed by this princess, both at the head of the army and of the state, have been extolled in terms which show how great must have been the impression made on her countrymen by a phenomenon so rare as a reigning queen.[3] Nevertheless, within a year the energies of Sexburh proved inadequate to the cares and anxieties of the male dignity, which were not a little aggravated by the illegality of her pretensions. On the death or expulsion of Sexburh,[4] two under-kings of

---

[1] Sax. Chron. a. 661. Ethelw. lib. ii. 7. H. Hunt.
[2] Sax. Chron. a. 672. Bedæ Vita S. Benedicti. "immatura morte prœreptus." [3] W. Malm. lib. i.
[4] W. Malm. lib. i. " plus quam fœmineos animos anhelantem vita destituit, annua vix potestate perfunctam." [R. Wendover, p. 162, however, says that she was expelled, "indignantibus regni magnatibus expulsa est a regno, nolentibus sub sexu fœmineo militare."—T.] So also Matt. Westm. a. 672.

Wessex, Æscwine,[1] a lineal descendant of Ceolwulf, and Centwine, the brother of Cenwealh,—who appears to have been the only rightful heir, and whose exclusion by Sexburh seems inexplicable,—governed the state either in succession or jointly, for several years. The obscurity attending these reigns is further increased by the account, that the immediate successor of Sexburh was Cenfûs, the father of Æscwine.[2] Even Beda, whose early years fell in this period, knew little of the ten years' anarchy in the kingdom of Wessex. The existence of Æscwine himself as king would probably, like that of his father, have been a subject of doubt, had not a great battle which he fought against Wulfhere of Mercia, who had advanced to Bedwin in Wiltshire, gained for him a hero's fame. This bloody conflict was sufficiently important to influence the accounts of it in a manner agreeable to the local feelings of the narrators. While the chronicler of Middle England strives to secure the honours of a hard-earned victory for the king of Mercia, he of Wessex—in whose favour the retreat of the Mercians loudly speaks—entertains no doubt of his defeat.[3] By the death of Æscwine,

[1] Malmesbury says, " Escuinus, regali prosapiæ proximus, quippe qui fuerit Cinegisli ex fratre Cuthgislo abnepos." I follow Fl. of W. a. 674, and Geneal.; also Sax. Chron.

[2] Sax. Chron. Fl. of W. a. 674; but in Geneal. Regum W. Sax. he says, " Deinde Kenfus duobus annis, secundum dicta regis Ælfredi, juxta vero Chronicam Anglicam, filius ejus Æscwinus fero tribus annis regnavit." The latter account only is noticed by Florence in his Chronicle, and on the authority of the 'Anglica Chronica Occidentalium Saxonum.'

[3] Sax. Chron. Fl. of W. a. 675. Late writers follow H. Hunt. —" Rex vero Mercensis, patria et avita virtute usus, aliquantulum præstantior pugna fuit : uterque tamen exercitus terribiliter contritus est," etc.—and overlook W. of Malmesbury, who says, "ille Escuinus) Mercios anxia clade perculit." [The Saxon Chron. and

which followed soon after, Centwine appears as sole ruler of the West Saxons.

The wars of the Anglo-Saxons with each other excited in the Armoricans the hope of recovering the home of their fathers from the hand of the stranger. The absence of the British king Cadwaladyr, who had departed on a pilgrimage to Rome, and left his son Yvor to the care of the king of Armorica, Alan the Second, encouraged the ambitious views of that prince; and a landing effected under the guidance of Yvor and his cousin Inyr led to the conquest of the old British country to the south of the Avon. Centwine led a powerful army against the invaders, but a battle was prevented by an amicable arrangement, according to which Yvor was invested by Centwine with the principality of Dyvnaint and Cernau, and, it is said, obtained the hand of Æthelburh, a niece of the king of Wessex, and, at a subsequent period, his kingdom also.

According to these and other Welsh narratives, Yvor appears completely identical with Ine, the second successor of Centwine; as the story of Yvor's father resembles that of the predecessor of Ine.[1] The part assigned to the king of Armorica in this expedition accords in no respect with the weakness of character ascribed to him in other accounts.[2] It must indeed be confessed that our knowledge of the history of Wessex, derived from Anglo-Saxon sources, is highly unsatisfactory; we must, therefore, have occasional recourse to the Welsh traditions, where, in consequence of the proximity of the two states, much latent history may

---

Florence say nothing of the result of the conflict; the latter's silence seems certainly to be in favour of the W. Saxons.—T.]
[1] Caradoc of Llancarvan, p. 13 sq.   [2] Daru, Hist. de Bretagne.

ANGLO-SAXON SETTLEMENT, A.D. 446-800. 323

reasonably be supposed to exist.[1] If in this respect too little regard has been shown to Geoffrey of Monmouth, on the other hand, care must be taken not to overrate his contemporary Caradoc of Llancarvan, though criticism has hitherto but seldom directed its shafts against the latter, an accumulation of quotations from whom imparts a show of deep research to some modern historic productions. In most instances, however, of such conflicting narratives, it may be assumed that the Welsh historians adopted the policy of purloining from a successful enemy, and skilfully transferring to his British contemporaries, if not to imaginary personages, the successful results of his battles, as well as the permanence of his individuality in history. The case before us leads also to the remark, that a similarity of names sometimes occurs between the West Saxons and the Britons, which is to be accounted for only by the supposition of early alliances between both nations. With regard to the name of Ceadwealla, it may not be unimportant for the genuineness of Anglo-Saxon history, to remark, that this name, as in use among the old Germanic tribes, may be found in Cæsar, and perhaps in Tacitus.[2]

While Centwine maintained or restored the supremacy of Wessex in the south of his kingdom, he extended its

[1] That a war like the above-mentioned was carried on may be inferred from Florence a. 682, where he says, "Centwine, rex West-Saxonum, *occidentales* Britones usque ad mare in ore gladii fugavit." The Sax. Chr. and other authorities state merely that Centwine drove the *Britons* to the sea.

[2] Cæsar (B. G. vi. 31) informs us that a prince of the Eburones, a people near Liege and Aix-la-Chapelle, was called Cativolcus, which is, no doubt, identical with Ceadwealla. The name in Tacitus (Ann. ii. 62), if correctly recorded by him, is rather that of the British Cadwaladyr than of the king of Wessex: "Erat inter Gothones nobilis juvenis nomine Catvalda."—T.

Y 2

influence also over the Britons on the northern side of Gwent, who had endeavoured to cast off the Germanic yoke.[1] But more than by external enemies, the tranquillity of Centwine was disturbed by his nearest relative, Ceadwealla, a bold aspiring youth of the race of Cynric, and son of Cenberht, a sub-king, whose territory is not specified.[2] Ceadwealla had been banished by Centwine, but the flower of the warlike youth gathered round the exile, who found a harbour in the forests of Andredeswald and Chiltene on the boundary of Sussex. With this valiant band he subdued that kingdom which his father had probably ruled, and slew its king Æthelwealh;[3] but Ceadwealla was subsequently expelled by two ealdormen of Sussex, Berhthun and Æthelhun, who through him had lost their former power and influence.[4] At this juncture Centwine, it seems, abdicated the throne. That this sickly and aged prince named Ceadwealla, who had till then been the object of his persecution,[5] his successor, is one of the many improba-

[1] Malmesb. de Pont. t. p. 349. Wharton, Anglia Sacra, t. ii. 14.

[2] In the Sax. Chr. a. 661 he is styled "Cœnbyrht cyning." By Fl. of W. "Cenbriht subregulus." Beda calls Ceadwealla merely "de regio genere Geuissorum." The authorities agree as to his descent, with the exception of Malmesbury, who calls him "Ceaulini ex fratre Cuda pronepos," where the last word shows that, for "fratre," we should read "filio."

[3] A.D. 685. Beda, iv. 15. Care should be taken not to confound Æthelwealh, king of Sussex, with Æthelwald (written in the charters Ecgunld), a vassal king under Ceadwealla. Wendover (t. i. p. 182) erroneously calls the former Athelwoldus.—T.

[4] Fl. of W. a. 685. H. Hunt. lib. iii. "qui prius regnaverunt." [Very probably a mistake for Beda's "qui deinceps regnum provinciæ tenuerunt."—T.] Æthelhun is by Beda called "Audhunus;" in Ælfred's version, "Huue."

[5] Malmesb. de Gestis Pont. lib. v. 1. The Saxon Chronicle a. 685 does not say that Centwine died in that year, but that "Ceadwalla began to contend for the kingdom.": Malmesbury's words

bilities with which the ecclesiastics have sought to embellish the life of their convert. Ceadwealla was the nearest in succession, and had been converted to Christianity by Wilfrith, the banished bishop of York, whom he had attached to himself in Sussex.

The first enterprise of Ceadwealla was to take vengeance on Sussex. Berhthun was slain in battle, also Eadric, the successor of Æthelwealh,[1] and Sussex was partitioned into several small states or kingdoms, under the supremacy of the king of Wessex.

A hard fate befell the Isle of Wight, which, only a few years before, had, by Wulfhere of Mercia, been

---

are, "Kentwinus morbo et senio gravis, Cedwallam regii generis juvenem successorem decreverat." The same writer afterwards adduces a charter dated in August 688, in which the name of Centwine appears: "consilio et confirmatione Kentuuini regis." If, therefore, this document be genuine, Centwine was then not only living, but had retained the kingly title, and had, perhaps, after the resignation of Ceadwalla, been required to give his sanction to a donation. That Centwine abdicated and entered a cloister, having transferred his kingdom to Ceadwealla as the next heir, appears from a disregarded poem of Aldhelm in Alcwine's works (edit. Quercetan. f. 1675 sq.), where, instead of 'Entuuini,' we should no doubt read ' Centwini.'

... " Entuuini filia regis,
Qui primus imperium Saxonum rite regebat.
... rexit regnum plures feliciter annos,
Donec conversus cellam migravit in almam.
Inde petit superas meritis splendentibus arces.
Post hunc successit bello famosus et armis
Rex Ceadualla, potens regni possessor, ut hæres ...
Tertius accepit sceptrum regnator opimum
Quem clamant In incerto cognomine gentes,
Qui nunc imperium Saxonum jure gubernat."

[H. Hunt. a. 686 says, however, Centwino "Occidentalium rege defuncto, Cedwalla post eum regnans."—T.]

[1] A.D. 685. W. Malm. lib. i. 2.

severed from Wessex and ceded to Sussex, though governed by its own prince, Arwald. The twelve hundred families dwelling on the island—the only Anglo-Saxon territory, to our knowledge, which had not yet embraced Christianity — were nearly all slaughtered by the yet unbaptized Ceadwealla, in fulfilment of a vow, that, if he took the island, he would devote to Christ the fourth part both of the land and the spoil. This he performed by assigning it for religious purposes to Wilfrith, who again transferred it to his nephew Bernwine, when the latter, assisted by a priest named Hiddila, effected the conversion of the island. Two young brothers of Arwald fled from the enemy to the adjacent Jutish province, and sought a refuge at Stoneham, where, being betrayed to Ceadwealla, they were condemned to death. On receiving this intelligence, Cyneberht, abbot of Hreutford (Redbridge), besought the king, who had retired to that neighbourhood for the cure of the wounds he had received in the conflict with Arwald, that, if it were absolutely necessary to slay the youths, he might be previously allowed to instil into them the mysteries of the Christian faith. The pious office being fulfilled they readily submitted to their fate,[1] and the anniversary of the young martyrs was celebrated by the church during many centuries.[2] From hence, accompanied by his brother Mul, he proceeded into Kent, which he laid waste, no resistance being offered by the inhabitants, who fled on his approach.[3]

[1] Beda, iv. 16.
[2] The anniversary of the "Fratres Regis Arwaldi MM." was on the 21st of August.—T.
[3] Sax. Chron. Fl. of W. H. Hunt. a. 686. W. Malm. lib. i.

The rapid success which had crowned the enterprises of Ceadwealla, and the internal dissensions which prevailed in Kent, induced him to allow his brother Mul to invade and ravage that kingdom a second time. On this, as on the previous occasion, towns and villages were abandoned by their inhabitants, who retired on the advance of the enemy; when Mul, who is represented as endowed with all the qualities constituting the old Germanic pagan prince and warrior,—formidable strength, elegance of figure, grace of manners, liberality and valour bordering on ferocity,—having with twelve attendants only entered a house for the sake of plunder, was discovered by the country people and burnt to death. A bloody vengeance for the death of his brother was taken by Ceadwealla, whose devastations ceased not while any objects of rapine or slaughter were to be found in the devoted province.[1]

Moved perhaps by the terrible death of his brother, or even by a presentiment of his own approaching end, and mindful of the exhortations addressed to him in his banishment by his revered friend Wilfrith, Ceadwealla, after a successful reign of two years only, resolved to renounce his crown in favour of his cousin Ine (Ini),[2] and to make a pilgrimage to Rome, for the purpose of receiving baptism at the hands of pope Sergius. On his way he was honourably welcomed by Cunibert, king of the Lombards, who had espoused Hermelind, an Anglo-Saxon princess.[3] He was baptized

[1] Sax. Chron. Fl. of W. H. Hunt. a. 687. W. Malm. lib. i.
[2] On the 19th Aug. 688, he issued a charter of donation. Malmesb. de Pont. lib. v. [Cod. Diplom. t. i. p. 32. Kemble questions the authenticity of this document.—T.]
[3] The remarkable connection of this Lombard prince, as well as of his father Bertari, with the insular Saxons, has been already noticed. From the first part of her name we might be induced to

on Easter-day, and assumed the name of Peter in honour of the chief of the apostles; but before he had laid aside the white garb of baptism, he was seized with a malady which terminated in death on the twentieth of April, eight days only after the ceremony, in the thirtieth year of his age. He was interred in the church of St. Peter, where an epitaph, placed by order of the pontiff, recorded, during many ages, the sanctity of this Anglo-Saxon king.[1]

seek for the kindred of Hermelind among the kings of Kent. Cf. Paul. Warnef. lib. vi. c. 15.

[1] Beda, v. 7. The sepulchral inscription on Ceadwealla by S. Benedictus Crispus, archbishop of Milan, was discovered in the 15th century, according to Johannes de Deio 'de Successione S. Barnabæ,' p. 23, but has since disappeared. It is given by Beda l. cit. The Britons make their Cadwaladyr die at Rome on the same day (xii. Kal. Maii) of the year 689. Geof. of Monm. lib. xii. 18. Brut y Tyw. a. 681 also says he died at Rome, but Annal. Camb. a. 682 that he died of pestilence in his own country.

CHAPTER XV.

FROM THE SEVENTH TO THE NINTH CENTURY.

Ine—His Wars against East-Anglia—His Long Reign—His Laws — Boniface — Abdication and Pilgrimage of Ine — Oswald — Æthelheard—Cuthred—War with the Mercian King Æthelbald —Mercians defeated—Wessex freed—Cuthred's Successors— First Landing of Northmen—Queen Eadburh—Her evil Influence—Her Flight and ultimate Fate.

THE early history of Ine is involved in obscurity. The Britons have identified him with their Ivor or Ynor as has been already noticed, and even the English accounts of his descent are inconsistent with each other; still there appears no valid reason for rejecting the testimony of the oldest authorities, which represent him as the son of Cenred, a sub-king, and, like his predecessor, a descendant of Cutha, the son of Ceawlin.[1]

[1] The title "subregulus" is found in Fl. of W. Geneal. Cf. Asseri Vita Ælfredi. Sax. Chron. a. 855. Fl. of W. a. 688. The varying genealogy in Malmesbury, lib. i. 2, "Ina, qui Cinegisli ex fratre Cuthbaldo pronepos," might excite scruples in a modern historian, being similar to that in the Chronicle a. 688, but which is not to be found in all the manuscripts, and is at variance with the other one, a. 855. Cynegils, otherwise known as the son of Ceolric, gets thereby another father, and Cuthwine, the father of Ceolwald or Cuthbald, becomes, instead of a grandson, a son of Ceawlin. In Malmesb. de Pont. lib. ii. Ine's father is named Cissa, and so again in lib. v. (ap. Wharton, t. ii.), though the edition of this work in Gale (t. i. p. 846) gives the name according to the charter there printed, " Cisi, Cenred, pater Inæ." [In the preamble to his laws he says, " I Ine, with the counsel of *Cenred my father*." —T.]

The first years of Ine's reign must have been passed in disquietude, though we are not informed against what foe, foreign or domestic, he had to contend. Thus we find that five years elapsed before he was able to take vengeance on the people of Kent for the murder of his kinsman Mul,[1] when the Kentish king Wihtræd deeming it prudent to avoid an unequal contest, appeased him by the payment of thirty thousand pounds,[2] the wergeld or legal price of the prince, who it was considered had not fallen in open warfare, but had been treacherously murdered.

Impelled by hereditary hatred, Ine is stated to have directed his arms against East Anglia, which he ravaged, having previously expelled the nobility from the country.[3] During the long reign of this ambitious king, hostile collisions with the Britons were inevitable; and among these the most memorable of those known to us is the war against Geraint, king of Cernau, conducted by Ine and his kinsman Nunna, which ended in the flight of the British prince.[4]

A power next to the king's was possessed, from the days of Centwine, in the southern parts of Wessex, by a king or sub-king Baldred, whose influence and importance, though apparent from other sources, is rendered

[1] According to one MS. of the Sax. Chr. and Fl. of. W. a. 694, Mul was a brother of Ine as well as of Ceadwealla. Probably Ine and Mul had the same mother. [R. Wendover, t. i. p. 187, calls him "cognatus;" Ethelwerd, "propinquus" (Inæ).—T.

[2] The Sax. Chron. a. 694 says 30,000 pounds. W. Malm. lib. i. " nundinantur pacem triginta millibus auri mancis." Florence has 3750 pounds (libras), which, reckoning eight mancuses to the pound, agrees with Malmesbury. Ethelwerd's account is, that it was "30,000 solidi, per singulos constanti numero sexdecim nummis."

[3] W. Malm. lib. i. "Nec solum Cantuaritæ, sed et Orientales Angli hæreditarium exceperunt odium, omni nobilitate primo pulsa, post etiam bello fusa." [4] Sax. Chron. Fl. of W. a. 710.

ANGLO-SAXON SETTLEMENT, A.D. 446–800. 331

more manifest by the circumstance, that the Welsh assign to a prince of Devon and Cornwall, living at the time, the Saxon name of Baldrich.[1]

The hardest conflicts were, however, those of the Anglo-Saxons among themselves, in which they engaged with all the ardour and ferocity of their forefathers, to attain martial glory and supremacy in their loosely bound confederation. In the year 715 a battle was fought between the armies of Mercia and Wessex, in which it was unknown on which side the slaughter was most appalling. The scene of this engagement was Wodnesbeorh (Wenborough in Wiltshire), a spot which from its position either natural, or perhaps strengthened by art as a protection to a temple of Woden, had already been strewed with the corpses of the slain in former conflicts.

But not alone for his warlike achievements, which almost exclusively occupy the chronicles of the time, has the name of Ine been celebrated. A collection of the laws of Wessex, made by his command, is, with the exception of those of the Kentish kings, the earliest known to us among the Anglo-Saxons. These laws seventy-six in number, have special reference to theft, murder or manslaughter, feuds, and pecuniary compen-

[1] W. Malm. de Antiq. Glaston. p. 308, a. 681 "Baldred rex . . . Kenwine etiam consentiente dedit," p. 309. "Lanctocay . . . Kenwino etiam et Baldredo consentientibus dedit." Ibid. p. 311. "Privilegium regis Inæ, a. 725. Ina . . . hortatu Balddredi et Athelardi subregulorum."—Baltrec." Ine continues, "a predecessoribus meis Kenewalchio, Kenwino, Cedwalla, Baldredo confirmatum." At the end, "Ego Baldredus rex confirmavi. Ego Adelard frater reginæ consensi." Cuthred also in a charter a. 744 calls Baldred his predecessor, and places him between Centwine and Ceadwealla. In a letter of Aldhelm, written about 701, he is called "patricius Baldredus." Ib. 347. By the Britons, "Baldrich;" see Caradoc, edit. Wynne, p. 17

sations (bôta), with others applicable to the British subjects (Wealas), who were thus placed on a footing nearly equal to that of their Germanic conquerors.

Ine also improved the ecclesiastical administration of his kingdom, by detaching from the diocese of Winchester, after the death of bishop Hedde in 703, a new bishopric, the see of which was established at Sherborne.[1] Among his numerous praiseworthy services in the founding and endowment of monasteries, the rebuilding and enlarged endowment of the old British abbey of Glastonbury for the repose of the soul of his murdered kinsman, Mul, is the most memorable.[2] But we feel more particularly induced to ascribe to the actions and views of Ine a noble character, when we reflect that his friend and counsellor was the excellent bishop Aldhelm (Ealdhelm); a man on whom no brighter lustre would be shed by the royal descent assigned to him by his rank-adoring countrymen, and whose merits we unhesitatingly place on a level with those of the Venerable Beda;[3] for though in comprehensiveness of knowledge he may not, perhaps, have been his equal, yet as a Latin poet he stood higher, while he merited greater praise for the cultivation of his mother-tongue, left him far behind in knowledge of the canon and Roman law, and greatly excelled him in practical activity. For his extensive knowledge of the Greek and Latin tongues he was indebted to the school

[1] Malmesb. de Pont. lib. ii.
[2] Malmesb. de Antiq. Glaston. ap. Gale, t. i.
[3] Aldhelm ob. a. 709. See W. Malm. lib. i. Also the 5th book of Malmesbury, De Gestis Pontificum, published in Savile and Gale, also in Wharton's Anglia Sacra, which is a biography of Aldhelm. An edition of his Latin poems as well as of his work 'De Septenario et de Re Grammatica ac Metrica ad Alfridum regem Northumbrorum' is in Maii Classici Auctores e Vat. Codd. ed. t. v.

of Canterbury, more especially to Hadrian,[1] abbot of the abbey of St. Augustine in that city, who did not come to England till Aldhelm was near thirty years old; though his earlier instruction, particularly in dialectics, he owed to the abbey, founded by a Scot of Maildulfesburh, the modern Malmesbury,[2] a celebrated monk of which—William of Malmesbury—has raised an honourable biographic monument to this most renowned scholar, who was subsequently abbot of his cloister. In enumerating and characterizing the works of Aldhelm, we are struck with the fact that pomp was alike distinctive of this great writer, and of the nation to which he belonged.

There is one man, around whose name a still brighter glory shines than even that around Aldhelm's, and who ought not here be totally passed over in silence, although his noblest efforts scarcely belong to the history of his own country. Winfrith, more generally known under his assumed name of Boniface, was a contemporary of Ine, and, previously to his triumphs over paganism in Germany, had been employed by that prince on a mission to the archbishop of Canterbury, a choice equally illustrative of the discriminating sagacity of the monarch, and honourable to the future apostle of our continental brethren. As the record of the greater and holier acts of Boniface belongs not to our history, we must, though reluctantly, limit our notice of him to this little more than simple mention of his name.[4]

[1] Beda, iv. 1, v. 20. W. Malm. lib. i. See p. 181.
[2] Beda, v. 18, and Smith's note.
[3] Malmesb. de Pont. ap. Gale, p. 342. "Græci involute, Romani splendide, Angli pompatice dictare solent. Quem (Aldhelmum) si perfecte legeris, et ex acumine Græcum putabis, et ex nitore Romanum jurabis, et ex pompa Anglum intelliges."
[4] See Vita S. Bonifacii.

The latter years of Ine's reign were less prosperous than most of the earlier ones. Under the year 721 it is recorded that the ætheling Cynewulf was slain by Ine,[1] the cause of which act can only be sought for in a rebellion raised by the former. The flame once kindled seems, however, not to have been quenched with the blood of Cynewulf. The insurgents had made themselves masters of Tantún (Taunton) in Somersetshire, a town built by Ine; but his warlike queen Æthelburgh wrested it from their hands and razed it to the ground. While Ine was carrying on a successful war against Sussex, and apparently a less decided one against the Britons in Cornwall and Glamorgan, who, under the king of that country, Rodri Malwynog, and Ivor with other chieftains, had taken advantage of the disturbed state of Wessex,[2] Ealdberht, also an ætheling, fled, at the head of the insurgents, from Wessex, after the loss of Taunton, and wandered about in Surrey in all the misery of exile, but afterwards found support in Sussex. He was, however, at length overcome and slain by Ine.[3]

Shortly after these successes, and when he had reigned thirty-seven years, Ine resolved to renounce the sceptre and the world.[4] The wish by which this step

[1] Sax. Chron. Fl. of W. If faith is to be placed in Malmesbury, Ine had no domestic enemy: "Domi gratiam, foris reverentiam mercabatur. Adeo annis duobus de quadraginta potestate functus, sine ullo insidiarum metu securus incanuit, sanctissimus publici amoris lenocinator." [For 'quadraginta,' the reading of five MSS. cited by Mr. Hardy, Savile's text has 'sexaginta.' According to Beda (v. 7), Ine reigned thirty-seven years.—T.]
[2] Annal. Camb. a. 722. Brut y Tyw. a. 721.
[3] Sax. Chron. a. 725.
[4] Sax. Chron. Fl. of W. a 728. This date is unquestionably incorrect. The Chronicle is, moreover, inconsistent with itself,

was preceded must have been occasioned by the cares of royalty and the turbulence of those over whom he had perhaps already reigned too long; but the manner in which it was brought to maturity by the queen Æthelburh is too characteristic to be passed over in silence. A sumptuous entertainment had been given at one of the royal villas. On the following day, after the departure of Ine and his queen, the superintendent, by order of the latter, defiled the palace with the dung of cattle, dust, and other rubbish, and placed in the bed where the royal pair had passed the night, a sow which had recently farrowed. When they had already proceeded more than a mile on their way, Ine, for reasons assigned by his queen, was induced to return to the villa. On arriving there, and seeing the change it had undergone, he turned his inquiring eyes towards his consort, who hereupon took occasion to expatiate on the vanity of human life. The resolve of the deeply affected monarch was no longer delayed; he resigned his crown to the brother of his wife, the under-king Æthelheard, of the race of Cerdic,[1] and went, accompanied by Æthelburh, as a pilgrim to Rome, where, rejecting every vestige of earthly pomp, and declining to lay aside his hair, but clad in a homely garb, he passed the remainder of his years in privacy and devotion. His wife, who had prompted him to this step, was his companion and comfort to the last.[2]

Ine left also another relative in the male line, the ætheling Oswald, to whom he had destined a share of

---

giving to Æthelheard, the successor of Ine, a reign of fourteen years, and placing his death in 741 (some MSS. 740). According to App. ad Bedam he died in 739. [In four MSS. of the Chronicle, Ine's departure is correctly given in 726.—T.]

[1] Fl. of W. a. 728. W. Malm. lib. i.   [2] W. Malm.

his kingdom.[1] The struggle between the two competitors lasted some years, till the death of Oswald, when his party, though powerful, desisted from further opposition to Æthelheard. Attacks from without rendered this union extremely necessary; though the victories which the Britons ascribe to themselves over Adelrad of Wessex, in Wales and Cornwall, by which name Æthelheard seems to be intended, are mentioned as having taken place in the years 720 and 722, consequently during the reign of Ine, and are, therefore, extremely doubtful. At the same time a leader could reckon on no dependents and no renown if he had not been victorious over the refractory Welsh, who it is certain had about this time, that is, after the abdication of Ine, succeeded in great measure in casting off the Saxon yoke;[2] and equally certain it appears that Æthelheard had to answer for this disgrace to his subjects. More formidable, however, for Æthelheard was the preponderance gained over all the Anglo-Saxon states as far as the Humber by the Mercian king Æthelbald, who, having assembled a formidable army, invested Sumertûn (Somerton), the chief town of the Sumersætas, which, the inhabitants being unable to offer any efficient resistance from within, and cut off from external succour, he reduced under his subjection.[3] After a reign of fourteen years Æthelheard died, and was succeeded by his kinsman Cuthred.[4]

It was the lot of Cuthred to pass the greater part of

[1] Beda, v. 7. "ipse, relicto regno ac juvenioribus commendato . . . profectus est." Later writers mention only the final succession of Æthelheard.
[2] Fl. of W. a. 731. "Britones magna ex parte Anglorum servitio mancipati fuere."
[3] Sax. Chron. H. Hunt. a. 733.
[4] Sax. Chron. Fl. of W. a. 741.

ANGLO-SAXON SETTLEMENT, A.D. 446–800. 337

his reign in warfare with Æthelbald of Mercia, which led to no beneficial result for either of the contending parties. The Britons, on the other hand, taking advantage of the discord prevailing among the Anglo-Saxons, had so greatly increased in strength, that both the hostile monarchs united their forces for the purpose of quelling them. In this undertaking, owing to the superior number and the emulation of their men, they were so successful that the honour of victory was indisputably on the side of the Anglo-Saxons.[1] On the occasion of a new quarrel between Cuthred and Æthelbald, the Britons took part with the former, who with their aid is said to have gained a victory over the Mercians near Hereford, but who was, nevertheless, unable to protect his new allies from the vengeance of Æthelbald.[2] In this war the ætheling Cynric, the son of Cuthred, fell. This youth, famed both as an undaunted warrior and a hunter, seems to have perished in a sedition among his followers, who, unable to face the dangers into which he would urge them, saw no other escape than in the murder of their leader.[3]

The supremacy which Mercia had in the course of these contests gained over Wessex became at length so oppressive, that Cuthred resolved to take the field once more against Æthelbald and his ally Oengus or Unnust, king of the Picts,[4] when a dangerous rebellion broke out in his kingdom. At its head was Æthelhun, an ealdorman renowned for his valour, who, with far inferior forces, was yet able for a considerable time to

[1] Sax. Chron. Fl. W. a. 743. H. Hunt. Caradoc also seems to speak of this battle, though, instead of Cuthred, he names Æthelheard.
[2] Caradoc, p. 17.   [3] H. Hunt. Sax. Chron. a. 748.
[4] App. ad Bedam, a. 750. Sim. Dunelm.

VOL. I.   Z

maintain the field against his sovereign; but having received a wound, victory at length declared itself on the side of Cuthred,[1] who used it with generosity, and restored Æthelhun to favour. Two years afterwards a decisive victory, owing chiefly to the valour of Æthelhun, was gained over the Mercians at Burford,[2] which freed Wessex from all further aggression on the part of the other Anglo-Saxon states. From that glorious day the West Saxon dynasty rapidly rose to the supremacy over all the other insular states, which it maintained during a period of three centuries, when it sank under the resistless attacks of a barbarous enemy.

The year following the humiliation of Mercia, Cuthred turned his arms against the Britons, who, weakened apparently by the victories which the Dalriads had obtained over them,[3] and unable to offer effectual resistance, lost great numbers in their flight.[4] Soon after these events Cuthred died childless,[5] and too early to witness the rising prosperity of his nation.

Cuthred was succeeded by his kinsman Sigebyrht, the son of an under-king Sigeric, two names which remind us of the kings of Essex,[6] who were nearly allied to the race of Cerdic. The prosperity of his predecessor had so blinded this prince, that he treated his subjects in the most injurious manner. The exhorta-

[1] Sax. Chr. H. Hunt. a. 750. [2] Sax. Chr. a. 752.
[3] "Congressio Dalriada et Britonum in lapide qui vocatur Minvirce, et Britones devicti sunt." Tigern. a. 717.
[4] Sax. Chron. Fl. W. H. Hunt. a. 753. According to Geffrei Gaimar, v. 1803, Cuthred was beaten by the Welsh:

" Dous anz apres, Gudret li reis   descunfiz fu, mes bien guari,
  se combati contre Gualeis: ne gueres del son ni perdi."

In this he is not, however, copied even by Bromton.
[5] Sax. Chron. Fl. W.
[6] Fl. W. Geneal. Cf. Sax. Chron. a. 823.

ANGLO-SAXON SETTLEMENT, A.D. 446-800. 339

tions of his faithful counsellors, to preserve the laws inviolate and maintain justice, only served to instigate the tyrant to greater acts of violence. At the beginning of the second year of his reign, in an assembly of the nobles and people,[1] Sigebyrht was formally deposed and banished from the kingdom, the government of which was intrusted to Cynewulf, another descendant of Cerdic, Hampshire alone remaining under the authority of Sigebyrht, from whence he was, however, soon compelled to flee, having in his anger murdered the faithful ealdorman Cumbra,[2] who had ventured to give him some wholesome counsel. Like his predecessor Ceadwealla, he fled to Andredeswald, though, unlike him, not again to leave it. A faithful swineherd of Cumbra discovered him, and avenged with his spear the blood of his murdered master.

The long reign[3] of Cynewulf is remarkably barren of events of which any memorial has been preserved. He engaged in several hard-fought though successful conflicts with the Britons, but at what place and in what year we are not informed.[4] One memorial regarding this prince has, however, been preserved in the form of a grant of lands to the church of Wells in expiation of his sins, and of the severities which he

[1] H. Hunt. a. 755. "Congregati sunt proceres et populus totius regni."
[2] "Consul nobilissimus." H. Hunt. In a charter of Cuthred, a. 744 (Cod. Diplom. p. 112), Cumbra signs himself, "præfectus regis."
[3] The Chronicle and other ancient authorities assign to Cynewulf a reign of thirty-one years, while they place his accession in 755, and his murder in 784.—T.
[4] Sax. Chron. H. Hunt. a. 784. In the latter years of this prince, several of the Frisian family of the Fortemanni are said to have served the king of England. See Ocka Scharlensis Chronicke van Frieslandt, fol. 18.

had exercised towards his Cornish enemies.[1] The letter which, in conjunction with his bishops and nobles, he addressed to Lullus, archbishop of Mainz, shows that considerable intercourse existed between the Anglo-Saxon and the German church.[2] A conflict with Offa, the powerful king of Mercia, ended unfortunately for the people of Wessex, who lost Bensington (Benson) in Oxfordshire to the conquerors.[3]

The death of Cynewulf though late was violent. He had ordered into banishment Cyneheard, the younger brother of his predecessor, who, instead of yielding to the mandate, having learned that the king with a slender retinue was gone to visit a female at Merton to whom he was attached, surrounded the house with his followers, when the inmates were wrapt in sleep. On discovering that the place was beset, the king, seizing his weapons, rushed to the door of his apartment and offered a stout resistance to his assailants, when, perceiving the ætheling, he wounded him severely, but was himself immediately overpowered and slain. At this moment the attendants of Cynewulf, who were lodged in the neighbourhood, roused by the cries of the female, hastened, though too late, to their master's succour. Cyneheard's offers of life and rewards they received with scorn, and desperately fighting were all slain with the exception of one, a British hostage, who was sorely wounded.

On the following morning the king's friend, the ealdorman Osric, and Wigferth his faithful thane, with all the thanes who had remained behind, having heard

[1] Charter a. 766 in Monast. Angl. [Also in Cod. Diplom. t. i. p. 141, where its genuineness is questioned.—T.]
[2] Epist. Bonifacii, xcii.
[3] Sax. Chron. a. 775 (777). Fl. W. a. 778.

what had taken place, immediately rode to Merton, where they found the gates closed against them. On their attempting to force an entrance, the ætheling promised them money and lands at their own discretion if they would receive him for their king, at the same time intimating to them, that many of their kindred were with him who would not forsake him. But the faithful band declared unanimously that no kinsman could be dearer to them than their lord, and that they would never follow his murderer. They then called upon their relations who were with Cyneheard to leave him while they were yet safe and unhurt; but these also answered that they had made a similar offer to those who were yesterday with the king, which was not listened to; they could not, therefore, accept that now made to themselves. A conflict then ensued before the gates, which being soon forced, the ætheling and his followers, to the number of eighty-four, were slain, one only, the godson of Osric, escaping with life, although covered with wounds. The corpse of Cynewulf was buried with those of his forefathers at Winchester; that of the ætheling at Axminster.[1]

The next in succession to the vacant throne, as far as our knowledge of the line of Cerdic enables us to judge, was Ealhmund, king of Kent, a great grandson of Ingild, the brother of Ine, whose pretensions, either from disregard to the strict line of succession, provided the individual were of the race of Cerdic, or from some other to us unknown cause, seem to have been passed by, and another member of the royal house, Beorhtric, of whose right it is merely said that he was descended from Cerdic, was chosen by the witan for king, and his election confirmed by the people. Beorhtric justified

[1] Sax. Chron. a. 784. Ethelwerd.

the confidence which had called him to the throne. For the internal security of his realm he provided by the expulsion of Ecgberht, the son of Ealhmund; and against the inroads of foreign foes, whether Britons or other Anglo-Saxons, he also rendered himself secure. The peace of the land was, moreover, not a little confirmed by his alliance with Offa of Mercia, whose daughter Eadburh he had espoused.[1] Ecgberht, who until this event had found shelter among the Mercians, and cherished hopes of one day obtaining the crown of Wessex, now fled to the court of the Frankish emperor.

This reign was remarkable for the first landing of the Northmen in England, which took place on the coast of Dorsetshire from three ships. On being apprised of the event the king's reeve (gerefa), named Beaduheard,[2] who resided at Dorchester, supposing them to be contraband traders rather than pirates, rode hastily to the port and commanded that they should be forcibly conducted to the king's town; whereupon he was assailed by the Northmen and slain with all his retinue.

To the influence of the queen Eadburh, a daughter of that Cynethrith whose memory the murder of the young king of East Anglia has stained with everlasting infamy, may probably be ascribed the indifference with which Beorhtric seems to have regarded the increasing power of Mercia over Kent. Through the fond weakness of her consort, this woman had imperceptibly acquired an absolute dominion in all the internal concerns of the kingdom. Those towards whom Beorhtric evinced an attachment, or who were opposed to her

[1] Sax. Chron. a. 787.
[2] Ethelwerd, lib. iii. Prooem. Fl. W. Sax. Chron. a. 787, where it is said that the Northmen came out of "Hœretha lande."

baneful caprices, she found means to destroy, either by false accusations or, failing in them, by poison. A young ealdorman named Worr, distinguished both on account of his high birth and amiable character, was the favourite of Beorhtric, and consequently an object of hatred to his wife. Accusations against him proving ineffectual, she had recourse to her usual expedient of poison. Her purpose was effected, but her husband also partook of the deadly cup and perished with his friend. In their utter detestation of this abandoned woman, the West Saxons resolved that no future consort of a king should be permitted to occupy a royal throne by the side of her husband, or to bear the title of queen.[1]

After this event, finding that her presence could no longer be tolerated in Wessex, Eadburh fled with her treasures to the court of Charles the Great, who, on her presenting him with various costly gifts, jocosely said to her, " Choose, Eadburh, between me and my son, who stands there in the hall,[2] which you will have." To which she thoughtlessly answered, " If I may be allowed to choose, I will have your son as being the younger." "If you had chosen me," replied Charles laughing, " you should have had my son; but having chosen my son, you shall have neither me nor him." Charles, however, bestowed on her a considerable monastery, in which for a short time she exercised the duties of abbess, but being convicted of criminal intercourse with one of her own countrymen, as well as with others, she was by the emperor's order expelled

[1] Sax. Chron. Fl. W. a. 800. Asser. Sim. Dunelm. W. Malm. From that time the consort of the king usually bore the title of "hlæfdige," *lady*.—T.

[2] "Elige, Eadburgh, quem velis inter me et filium meum, qui mecum in solario isto stat." Asser.—T.

from the convent. Attended by a single slave, the daughter of Offa and wife of Beorhtric, after various wanderings, died a beggar in the city of Pavia.[1]

[1] A.D. 802. "Uno servulo comitata." Asser, a. 856. Sim. Dunelm. a. 802. [Asser informs us that he had the story of Eadburh from Ælfred's own mouth: "a domino meo Ælfredo, Angulsaxonum rege veridico, etiam sæpe mihi referente audivi, quod et ille etiam a veridicis multis referentibus, immo ex parte non modica illud factum commemorantibus, audierat."—T.]

NOTES.

Page 124, note ².—That the Jutes landed in England where they occupied Kent, the Isle of Wight and part of Wessex, is, I believe, generally admitted. That they were under a leader, or (as was usual among the Danes) two leaders, may also be believed, without exposing the believer to the imputation of being over credulous: nor can I found any disbelief or doubt on the circumstance, that the one leader was named Hengest, the other Horsa.

In addition to the testimonies of Nennius, Beda, and the Saxon Chronicle, the following extracts may be adduced in favour of the existence of Hengest, Fin, etc.

1. From the Geographer of Ravenna, who is supposed to have lived in the seventh century.

2. From the Scôp or Scald's Tale. (Cod. Exon. p. 320; Kemble's Beow. vol. i. p. 229.)

. . . . (weold)
Fin Folcwalding
Fresna cynne
. . . . . .
Hnæf Hocingum.

. . . . . .
Fin Folcwalding (rul'd)
the Frisian race
. . . . . .
Hnæf the Hocings.[1]

3. From the Battle of Finnesburh. (Kemble's Beow. vol. i. p. 239.)

Ordlaf and Guðlaf,
and Hengest sylf
hwearf him on laste
. . . . . .
þonne Hnæfe guldon
his hægstealdas.

Ordlaf and Guthlaf,
and Hengest himself
follow'd in his track
. . . . . .
then for Hnæf paid
his followers.

[1] The Hocings are supposed by Zeuss to be identical with the Chauci. See Ettmüller, Scôpes Vidsidh, p. 16, and Cod. Exon. p. 515.

4. **Beowulf.** Hnæf prince of the Hocings, and Hengest the Jute, vassals of the Danish king Healfdene (the Haldanus of Saxo), are sent to invade the Frisian territory, at that time governed by Fin, the son of Folcwalda, and husband of Hildeburh, the daughter of Hoce. A battle is fought, in which Hnæf, together with all the children, brothers, and almost all the thanes of Fin, is slain. During a truce which ensues, the bodies of Hnæf and the rest of the slain are burnt. Hengest remains with Fin, but at the same time meditates vengeance for the death of Hnæf and his followers, which he subsequently wreaks, Fin being slain, and his queen Hildeburh borne off to Denmark. The entire episode is as follows:

XVI.

Ðær wæs sang and sweg	*There was song and sound*
samod ætgædere	*at once together*
fore Healfdenes	*before Healfdene's*
hilde-wísan,	*warlike chiefs,*
gomen-wudu greted,[1]	*the wood of joy was greeted,*
gid oft wrecen,	*the lay oft recited,*
ðonne heal-gamen	*when the joy of hall*
Hroðgares scóp,	*Hrothgar's bard,*
æfter medo-bence,[2]	*after the mead-bench,*
mænan sceolde	*should recount*
be Finnes eaferum,	*concerning Fin's offspring,*
þa hie se fær begeat;	*when them peril o'erwhelm'd;*
hæleð Healfdenes,[3]	*when Healfdene's hero,*
Hnæf Scyldinga,	*the Scyldings' Hnæf,*
in Fres-wæle	*in Frisian slaughter*
feallan sceolde.	*was doom'd to fall.*
Ne huru Hildeburh	*Not Hildeburh at least*
herian þorfte	*had need to praise*
Eotena treowe:	*the faith of the Jutes:*
unsynnum wearð	*she was of her innocent*
beloren leofum	*beloved ones depriv'd*
æt þam lind-plegan,[5]	*at the linden-play,*

[1] i.e. the harp.
[3] MS. Healfdena.
[5] conject Kemble, MS. hild-plegan. So called from the shield being made of the lime, or linden tree.
[2] be, added from conjecture.
[4] unsynnigum?

NOTES.   347

bearnum and broðrum :	*of her children and brothers :*
hie on gebyrd hruron,	*they in succession fell,*
gare wunde.	*by the dart wounded.*
Ðæt wæs geomuru ides :	*That was a mournful woman :*
nalles holinga	*not without cause*
Hoces dohtor	*Hoces daughter*
metodsceaft bemearn,	*the Lord's decree bemourn'd,*
siððan morgen com,	*after morning came,*
þa heo under swegle [1]	*when she under heaven*
geseón meahte	*might see*
morþor-bealo maga,	*the slaughter of her kinsmen,*
þær heo ǽr mæste heold	*where she ere had most possess'd*
worulde wynne.	*of worldly joy.*
Wig ealle fornam	*War destroy'd all*
Finnes þegnas,	*Fin's thanes,*
nemne feaum anum ;	*save a few only ;*
þæt he ne mihte	*so that he might not*
on þam meþel-stede	*on the battle-place*
wið Hengeste [2]	*against Hengest*
wiht gefeohtan,	*at all contend,*
ne þa wea-lafe	*nor the sad remnant*
wige forþringan	*by war protect*
þeodnes þegne ; [3]	*from the king's thane ;*
ac hie him geþingo budon, [4]	*but they to him conditions offer'd,*
þæt hie him oðer flet	*that they to him another dwelling*
eal gerymdon,	*would wholly yield,*
healle and heah-setl ;	*a hall and high seat ;*
þæt hie healfre geweald [5]	*that they half power*
wið Eotena bearn	*with the sons of the Jutes*
agan moston,	*might possess,*
and æt feoh-gyftum	*and at the money-gifts*
Folcwaldan sunu	*Folcwalda's son*
dogra gehwylce	*every day*
Dene weorþode,	*the Danes should honour,*
Hengestes heap	*Hengest's band*
hringum þenede, [6]	*with rings should serve,*
efne swa swiðe	*even as much*
sinc-gestreonum	*with costly treasures*
fættan goldes,	*of rich gold,*

[1] MS. he.   [2] MS. wig.   [3] i.e. Hengest.
[4] hie, *they*, i.e. the Danes and Jutes.
[5] hie, *they*, i.e. the Frisians.   [6] MS. wenede.

swa he Fresna cyn,[1]	*as he the Frisian race,*
on beor-sele	*in the beer-hall*
byldan wolde.[2]	*would adorn.*
Ða hie getruwedon,	*Then they confirm'd,*
on twa healfa,	*on the two sides,*
fæste frioðu-wære,	*a fast peaceful compact,*
Fin Hengeste	*Fin to Hengest*
elne, unflitme,	*earnestly, without dispute,*
áðum benemde,	*by oath enjoin'd,*
þæt he þa wea-lafe,	*that he the sad remnant,*
weotena dome,	*by his witan's doom,*
árum heolde,	*piously should hold,*
þæt ðær ænig mon,	*that there no man,*
wordum ne weorcum,	*by words or works,*
wære ne bræce,	*should break the compact,*
ne þurh inwit-searo	*nor through guileful craft*
æfre gemændon,	*should they ever complain,*
þeah hie hira beag-gyfan[3]	*though they their ring-giver's*
banan folgedon,	*murderer followed,*
þeodenlease,	*lordless,*
þa him swa geþearfod wæs;	*since they were so compel'd ;*
gyf þonne Frysna hwylc,	*but if of the Frisians any one,*
frecnan spræce,	*by audacious speech,*
þæs morþor-hetes	*this deadly feud*
myndgiend wære,	*should call to mind,*
þonne hit sweordes ecg	*then it the edge of sword*
sweðrian sceolde.[4]	*should appease.*
Áð wæs geæfned,	*The oath was completed,*
and icge gold[5]	*and moreover gold*
aháefen of horde.	*rais'd from the hoard.*
Here-Scyldinga	*Of the martial Scyldings*
betst beado-rinca[6]	*the best of warriors*
wæs on bæl gearu :	*on the pile was ready :*
æt þam áde wæs	*at the heap was*
cð-gesyne	*easy to be seen*
swatfah syrce,	*the blood-stain'd tunic,*
swýn eal gylden,	*the swine all golden,*
cofer iren-heard,	*the boar iron-hard,*

[1] he, i.e. Hengest.
[2] gibelde, *ornavit*, inscrip. in Nero. D. 4, MS. Cott.
[3] For þeah I suspect we should read þæt.   [4] MS. syððan.
[5] icge is very questionable.   betst b.-r., i.e. Hnæf.

æþeling mænig	many an ætheling
wundum awyrded,	with wounds afflicted,
sume on wæle crungon.	(some had in the slaughter fall'n).
Het þa Hildeburh,	Bade then Hildeburh,
æt Hnæfes áde,	at Hnæf's pile,
hire selfre suna[1]	her own sons
sweoloðe befæstan,	be to the fire committed,
bán-fatu bærnan,	their carcases be burnt,
and on bæl dón	and on the pile be reduced
earme on axe.[2]	the miserable ones to ashes.
Ides gnornode,	The woman mourn'd,
geomrode giddum;	bewail'd in songs;
guð-rinc astah,[3]	the warrior ascended,
wand to wolcnum,	wended to the clouds,
wœl-fyra mæst	the greatest of death-fires
hlynode for hlawe;	roar'd before the mound;
hafelan multon,[4]	their heads were consum'd,
ben-geato burston;	their wound-gates burst;
ðonne blód æt-sprano	then out sprang the blood
láð-bíte lices:	from the corpse's hostile bite:
lig ealle forswealg,	flame swallow'd all
gæsta gifrost,	(greediest of guests,) [bereft.
þara ðe þær guð fornam.	those whom war had there of life
Bega folca wæs	Of both people was
hira blæd scacen.	their flower departed.

XVII.

Gewiton him ða wigend	The warriors then departed
wica neosian,	their villages to visit,
freondum befeallen,[5]	of their friends deprived,
Frysland gescón,	Friesland to see,
hamas and hea-burh.	its dwellings and high burgh.
Hengest ða-gyt	Hengest yet
wœlfagne winter	the death-hued winter

[1] MS. sunu, i.e. her sons who had been slain.
[2] MS. eaxle.
[3] i.e. *Hnæf ascended* (*in flame and smoke*), like the Ger. (in Feuer und Rauch) aufgehen. So also Homily, MS. Bibl. Pub. Cantab. p. 2ˇ2. MS. þæt ceaf he forbærnð . . . forðan ðe ðæra mánfulra smíc astihð on ecnysse.
[4] So Beow. 4646, bolda selest bryne-wylmum mealt.
[5] *deprived through their having fallen.*

wunode mid Finne,[1]	remain'd with Fin,
unflitme,[2]	without strife,
eard gemunde,	his home remember'd,
þeah þe he ne meahte[3]	although he might not
on mere drifan	on the sea drive
hringed-stefnan.	the ringed prow.
Holm storme weol,	Ocean boil'd with storm,
won wið winde,	war'd against the wind,
winter ybe beleac	winter lock'd the wave
ís-gebinde,	with icy band,
oðþæt oðer com	till that came the second
gear in geardas.	year to the courts.
Swa nu gyt deð	So now yet do
þa ?e singalo[4]	those who constantly
sæle bewitiað,[5]	watch a happy moment,
wuldor-torhtan weder.	gloriously bright weather.
Ða wæs winter scacen,	When winter was departed,
fæger foldan bearm,	earth's bosom fair,
fundode wrecca,	the stranger hasten'd,
gæst of geardum.[6]	the guest from the courts.
He to gyrn-wræce	He on wily vengeance
swiðor þohte[7]	was more intent
þonne to sæ-láde,	than on a sea-voyage,
gif he torn-gemót	if he a conflict
þurhteon mihte;	could bring to pass;
þæs he Eotena bearn[8]	for he the sons of the Jutes
inn-gemunde,	inwardly remember'd,
swa he ne forwyrnde	so he refus'd not
woruldræ lenne,	worldly intercourse,
þonne him Hunlafing,[9]	when he Hunlafing,
hilde leoman,	the flame of war,
billa selest,	the best of falchions,

[1] MS. Finel. [2] MS. unhlitme. [3] ne, added.
[4] MS. singales. [5] MS. sele. [6] MS. gist.
[7] *wily vengeance*, i. e. the fæhð or deadly feud for the death of Hnæf and the others.
[8] *the slain ones.*
[9] Hunlafing is apparently the name of Hengest's sword, which had probably been the property of Hun, king of the Hætweras (Scôps Tale, p. 320, 22). The terminations laf, *a relic, legacy*, and ing are commonly applied to a sword; thus Beow. eald laf, *an ancient sword:* so Tyrfing, Miming, Hrunting, names of celebrated swords. See Kemble's Glossary to Beowulf, v. Laf. Hunlaf occurs, however, as a man's name among the Anglo-Saxons.

NOTES. 351

on bearm dyde;[1]	*in his bosom placed;*
þæs wæron mid Eotenum	*for with the Jutes there were*
ecge cuðe,	*men fam'd for sword-play,*
swylce ferhð-frecan.	*also of spirit bold.*
Fin eft begeat	*Fin afterwards o'erwhelm'd*
sweord-bealo sliðen,	*cruel misery from the sword,*
æt his sylfes hám,	*at his own dwelling,*
siðþan grimne gripe	*when the grim one with gripe*
Guðlaf and Oslaf,[2]	*Guthlaf and Oslaf,*
æfter sǽ-siðe,	*after a sea-journey,*
sorge mændon,[3]	*grievously upbraided,* [*woes:*
ætwiton weana dæl:	*reproach'd for his part in their*
ne meahte wæfre mód	*he might not his wavering soul*
forhabban in hreþre.	*in his breast retain.*
Ða wæs heal broden	*Then was the hall beset*
feonda feorum,	*with foemen,*
swilce Fin slægen,	*also Fin slain,*
cyning on corþre,	*the king amid his people,*
and seo cwen numen.	*and the queen taken.*
Sceotend Scyldinga	*The Scyldings' warriors*
to scypum feredon[4]	*to their ships bore*
eal in-gesteald	*all the house-chattels*
eorð-cyninges,	*of the earth-king,*
swylce hie æt Finnes hám	*such as at Fin's dwelling*
findan meahton,	*they could find,*
sigla, searo-gimma.	*of jewels and curious gems.*
Hie on sǽ-láde	*They on the sea-road*
drihtlice wíf	*the princely woman*
to Denum feredon,	*to the Danes bore,*
læddon to leodum.	*to their people led.*—T.

[1] So Beow. l. 4382: sweord . . . þæt he on Biowulfes bearm alegde; *sword . . . that he in Beowulf's bosom laid.*

[2] 'Ordlaf,' Batt. of Finnesb. perhaps more correct than Oslaf.

[3] mændon. In Homily, MS. Bibl. Pub. Cantab. p. 217, the verse of Luke there quoted (xviii. 15) has 'bemændon' where the editions of the Gospels have 'ciddon,' *rebuked.*

[4] MS. scypon.

(352)

GENEALOGY OF THE SONS OF WODEN.

From the Sax. Chron. a. 855.	From Snorra Edda. edit. Rask.
Noe.	Sif.
Sceaf.	Lorido.
Bedwig.	Henrede.
Hwala.	Vingethor.
Hathra.	Vingener.
Itermon.	Moda.
Heremod.	Magi.
Sceldwa.	Cespheth (Sefsmeg).
Beaw.	Bedvig.
Tætwa.	Atra (*nobis* Anna).
Geat.	Itrmann.
Godwulf.	Heremod.
Finn.	Skialldunn (*nobis* Skiöld).
Frithuwulf.	Biaf (*nobis* Biar and Bavr.)
Frealaf.[1]	Jat.
Frithuwald.	Guthólfr.
	[Finnr.]
Woden.	Fiarlef (Frialafr) (*nobis* Frithleif).
	VOTHINN (*nobis* OTHINN).

Wecta, ancestor of the kings of Kent.	Bældæg. Brond.	Casere, ancestor of the kings of E. Anglia.	Seaxneât, ancestor of the kings of Essex.	Wægdæg, ancestor of the kings of Deira.	Wihtlæg, ancestor of the kings of Mercia.	Wintn, ancestor of the princes of the Lindisfaras.
Frithogar, ancestor of the kings of Wessex.	Beornd (Beonoc), ancestor of the kings of Bernicia.					

[1] Three MSS. for Frealaf give Freawine, and omit the following Frithuwald. In the Bernician list (S. C. a. 547) Frealaf is called Freotholaf.

INDEX TO VOL. I.

Aaron, 63
Aberffraw, 151
Abisa, 88
Acha, 200
Adaling or Ætheling, 119
Adamnan, 265
Adelbert, St., 208 *note*
Adelrad, 326
Adminius, 28
Æbbe, 246
Æcesdûn, 318, 320
Æglesthrep, 93
Ælle, 132–136, 173, 312
Ælf, 274
Ælflæd, 210, 239, 247, 275, 297, 299
Ælfred, 258, 262
Ælfwine, 226 274, 281
Æsc, 94–96, 136
Æscberht, 303
Æscings, 96, 141, 300
Æscwine, 141, 321
Æstii, 9
Æthel, 109
Æthelbald, 269, 273, 283, 285, 336, 337
Æthelberht, 96, 162 *note*, 165, 166, 174, 246, 309, 311
———— ————, conversion of, 175, 182
———— ————, laws of, 182
———— ————, murder of, 296.
Æthelburgh, 247, 306, 334
Æthelburh, 190, 191, 197, 322, 335

Æthelferth, 184, 186, 188
Æthelfrith, 21
Æthelheard, 273, 302, 303, 315, 335
Æthelhere, 210, 211, 306
Æthelhun, 286, 324, 337
Æthelred of Mercia, 235, 236, 281
———— of Northumbria, 273–279, 297
———— of East Anglia, 307
———— of Kent, 309
Æthelric, 315
Æthelthryth, 227, 246, 297, 30 ;
Æthelwald, 208, 210, 211, 271 272, 306
Æthelwealh, 226, 235, 236, 3 2, 320, 324
Æthelweard, 315
Æthelwine, 207
Æthelwulf, 250, 251
Agatho, 234
Agilbert, 213, 215, 218
Agricola, 36–39
Ahlmund, 278
Ahlred, 272, 273
Aidan, 185, 200, 201, 207, 208
Alban, St., 63
Alberht, 306
Albin, 63
Albinus, 52
Albion, 2
Albiones, 9
Alcluyd, 155, 270
Alcmund, 305
Alcwine, 247

INDEX TO VOL. I.

Aldfrith, 237–239, 265, 267
Aldgisl, 229
Aldhelm, 230, 243, 256, 257, 332
Aldred, 276, 315
Aldulf, 278, 295
Alfwold, 273, 274, 279, 306
Allectus, 56
Alphabet, Saxon, 102, 103
Alric, 277, 311
Alweo, 283
Ambrosius Aurelianus, 128
Ancalites, 20
Aneurin, 152
Anderida, 133
Andredes-ceaster, 133
Andredeswald, 339
Andrews, St., see of, 63
Angeln, 114
———, country of, 144
Angilbert, 293
Angles, 113–117, 144
———, laws of, 118, 119
Anglesea, 33, 189
Anglii, 117
Anglo-Saxons, 14
————————, bishops of, 212
————————, history of, 155
————————, language of, 109
————————, laws of, 119–122
Angrivarii, 117
Angul, 114
Anna, 196, 204–210, 227, 306, 318
Anthemius, 130
Antoninus, rampart of, 51
Aquæ Solis, 66
Archbishops, consecration of, 212
Archimedes, 3
Architecture, 224
Arculf, 265
Are river, 211
Aristotle, 2
Armorica, British settlement in, 74
Armoricans, 322
Arthur, 71, 76, 129–131, 138, 149, 151
———, burial-place of, 242
———, coronation of, 168

Arthur, round table of, 154
Arts in England, 224
Arwald, 326
Asclepiodotus, 56
Ashdown, 318
Asser, 243
Atla, King, saga of, 147
Atrebates, 9, 20
Attacotti, 70
Attlebury, 147
Augusta, 45
Augustine, 170, 174, 175, 178, 182, 240
————————, miracles of, 177, 178 *note*
————————'s oak, 177
Augustus, 28
Aurelianus, 93, 128
Aylesbury, 164

BALDHILD, 222
Baldred, 330
Baldrich, 331
Baldwulph, 149
Bamborough, 150, 205
Bampton, battle of, 317
Bangor, 20, 81
———, monastery of, 185
———, school of, 177
——— and St. Asaph, see of, 245
Baptism, 170
Bardeney, 205, 282
Bards, 14
Barking, abbey of, 247
Barrows, 263
Bath, 66, 164
———, see of, 244
Beaduheard, 342
Beamdûn, 317
Beda, 90, 220, 248, 256, 257, 265,
———, writings of, 266
———'s chronology, 233
Bedwin, battle of, 321
Belgæ, 9, 19
Beli mac Elpin, 269
Benedict Biscop, 220, 224, 265, 319

INDEX TO VOL. I. 363

Bensington, 164, 290, 340
Beonna, 306
Beorh, 237
Beorhtric, 341
Beorn, 273
Beornred, 287, 290
Beornwulf, 303
Beowulf, 98
Berhta, 163, 175, 293
Berhtfrith, 267
Berhthun, 324
Berhtwald, 238, 292
Beric, 29
Bernheath, 226
Bernicia, 148, 198
————, kings of, 149, 150
Bernwine, 326
Bertari, 234 *and note*
Bertrade, 293
Bible, British versions of, 81
Bibroci, 20
Bieda, 136
Bignor, Roman villa at, 66
Billingahoh, 277
Binchester, 19
Birinus, 203, 317
Biscop, 220: *see* Benedict.
Bishoprics, Anglo-Saxon, 243
————, early, 168
————, traffic in, 248
Bishops, choice of, 241
————, native, 213
————, revenues of, 246
————, voice of, in legislature, 246
————, work of, 240
Blecca, 194
Bobbio, 231
Boniface, 230, 283, 284, 333
Bonosus, 73
Bosa, 239
Bôta, 332
Boudicea, 34, 35 *and note*
Bradenford, 318
Bradford, 318
Bran ap Llyr, 71
Bread, 16
Brecheiniog, 152

Bredon, 289
Bremen, 273
Bretagne, 74
Bretland, 45
Bretwalda, 134, 159 *et seq.*
Brigantes, 19, 31
Bristol, see of, 246
Britain, early geography of, 4
Britanni, 9
Britannia, prima and secunda, 40
————, superior and inferior, 40
British elements under Romans, 44, 45
———— history, 155
———— States, 150
Briton Morgan, 82
Britons, habits and social condition of, 16-18
———— and Saxons, comparative rights of, 158
Brocmail, 185
Brunhild, 174
Bryneich, 46
Brythones, 9
Buildings, 16
Burford, battle of, 286, 338
Burgh Castle, 67
"By," 116
Byzantium, court of, 145

CADVAN, 185
Cadwaladyr, 322
Cædwalla, 197-199
Cæfi, 192
Cuer, 19
Caer Caradoc, 32
Cære, 267 *note*
Caerlegion, battle of, 185
Caerleon-upon-Usk, 152
————————, Bishop of, 63
————————, see of, 245
Cacrlon, 65
Cæsar, 10, 22, 23
Cæsariensis, Flavia, 40
————, Maxima, 40,
Cæsius Nasica, 33
Cairns, 11

2 B 2

Cairs, 11
Caledonia, 38
Caledonians, 21, 38
Calgacus, 38
Caligula, 28
Calleva, 20
Calpurnius Agricola, 51
Cambria, 151
———, Christianity in, 168,
———, partition of, 153
Cambrians, laws of, 153
Camlan, battle of, 131
Camulodunum, 30, 32, 35
Cangi, 19, 31
Canon law, 253, 255
Canterbury, 175
———, archbishopric of, 241
———, province of, 246
Cantii, 18
Caracalla, 52. 53
Caradoc, 30, 31, 32, 302, 323.
Caractacus, 30
Carausius, 55-57
Carisbrook, 137, 318
Carleol, 154
Carlisle, 19, 238, 246
Cartismandua, 32, 33
Cartmel, 238
Cassi, 20
Cassiterides, 1, 4, 5
Cassivellaunus, 25
Caswallon, 25
Cataractonium, 19
Catgabail, 210, 211
Catholic church, 170
Catholicism, conversion to, 240
Catigern, 89, 93, 94
Catterick, 19, 290
Cattle, 16
Catus, 34
Catuvellani, 19
Ceadda, 223
Ceadwealla, 235, 236, 310, 313, 323-327
Cealchyth, 295
Ceawlin, 139, 162-165
Cedd, 212, 249

Celibacy of clergy, 254
Celts, 7
———, Christianity among, 167
Celts, language of, 46
Cenberht, 320
Cenfûs, 321
Cenhelm, 303
Cenimagni, 9, 19
Conred, 268, 282, 283
Centwine, 321 et seq.
Cenwealh, 204, 209, 213, 317-320
Cenwulf, 278, 300-302
Ceolfrith, 265
Ceollach, 213
Ceolred, 283
Ceolric, 165, 202
Ceolwulf, 202, 268, 303
Cerdic, 135, 138
Cerdices-ford, 137
——— -leah, 138
——— -ora, 135, 137
Ceredigion, 152
Cernau, 151
Charford, 137
Chariots, war, 16, 23
Charles the Great (Charlemagne), 278, 292, 293
Cheese, making of, 16
Chester-le-Street, see of, 244
Chichester, 235
———, see of, 244
———, Roman remains at, 66
Chieftains, 14
Christianity, influence of, on education, 264
———, influence of, on politics, 264
———, Anglo-Saxon, 165, 166
———, introduction of, in Britain, 59-61, 176
———, effects of, 177
Christmas, 263
Chronology, Saxon, 91, 97, 98
Chrotta, 14
Church, abuses in, 248
———, early, 81-83
——— law, 254

INDEX TO VOL. I. 365

Church property, administration of, 249
——, Roman, 172, 179
Church, British, 170, 171 *note*
——, Gallican, 179
Churches, parish, 248
——, Roman and Gallican, disputes between, 215
Chrysanthus, 76
Cilternsætas, 314
Cimbrians, 8
Circles, stone, 11
Cirencester, 164, 209, 317
Cissa, 132, 134
Cities, Roman, 43
Civilis, 74
Clas Merddin, 8
Classicianus, 35
Claudius, 29, 30
Clement, 230
Clergy, Anglo-Saxon, 249.
——, celibacy of, 254
——, drunkenness of, 55
Clerical influence, 227
Clito, 283 *and note*
Clodius, 52
Clofesho, 284, 289, 302
Cloisters, 246, 250
Clothing, 16
Clydesdale, 155
Cnut, 262
Coel, 71
Cœlestinus, 82
Cogidubnus, 30
Coldingham, 227, 246
Colgrim, 149
Colman, bishop, 215
Coloman, 232
Columba, St., 256
Columbanus, 231
Commerce, early, 1-6
Commius, 21, 22, 26
Commodus, 52
Condidan, 164
Conmail, 164
Constans, 77
Constantine, 59, 77
Constantius, 77

Constantius Chlorus, 58
Corbelo, 4
Coritavi, 19
Cornabii, 20
Cornish dialect, 45
Cornwall, 151
Crayford, 94
Creoganford, 94
Crediton, see of, 244
Creoda, or Cridda, 143
Cromlechs, 11
Crowland, 284, 299
Cudda, 219
Cuharan, 147
Cumberland, 8, 154, 238
Cumbria, 154, 339
——, Christianity in, 168
Cumry, 8
Cunedda, 70, 71
Cunibert, 327
Cutha, 164
Cuthberht, St., 249, 276, 284
Cuthburh, 267
Cuthred, 204, 209, 285, 302, 318, 320, 336-338
Cuthwulf, 164
Cwenburh, 190
Cwenthryth, 303
Cwichelm, 190, 203, 316
Cwiram, 147
Cyil, 269
Cymbeline, 26
Cymen, 132
Cymenes-ora, 132
Cymry, language of, 152
Cyndillom, 164
Cyneberht, 326
Cyneburh, 210
Cynegils, 203, 204, 209, 316
Cyneheard, 340
Cynethryth, 297, 298
Cynewulf, 273, 290, 297, 298, 334, 339
Cynobellin, 26
Cynric, 135-139, 337

Dægsanstan, battle of, 185
Dagobert, 197, 229, 233

Dalfinus, 221
Dalrendini, 70
Dalriads, 338
Dalston, 185 *note*
Damianus, 213
Damnonia, 151
Damnonii, 20
Danes, kings of the, 160
Danish traditions, 143, 144
Dates, how fixed, 91
David, St., 169
David's, St., see of, 245
Deffrobany, land of, 8
Dehenbarth, 152, 291
Deira, 147, 148, 150, 198
Deifyr, 46
Denis, St., abbey of, 292
Denmark, missions in, 230
Derham, battle of, 164
Dervan, 61
Derwent, battle of the, 93
Deusdedit, 212, 216
Deva, 66
Devii, 173
Devonshire, 151
Dialects, Anglo-Saxon, 108
Didius, 33
Dimetæ, 19
Dimetia, 151
Dindyrn, 202
Dinevwr, 152
Dinoot, 178
Dioceses of modern England, 246
Diuma, 212, 213
Dobuni, 20
Dol, bishopric of, 149
Domuc, 196, 243
Dorchester, 67, 204, 216 *note*, 243, 244
Doroveruma, 18
Dorsætas, 138
Dover, 45
Druidism, 7, 10–12
Drumnechtan, 238
Drunkenness of clergy, 255
Dubris, 45
Dubritius, 168
Duglas, 149

Dulcitius, 74
Dumbartonshire, **155**
Dumfries, 155
Dunagual, 269
Dunawd, 178
Dunwich, 196, 243, 305
Durham, see of, 244
Durotriges, 20
Dyke, Cnut's, 305
——, Edmund's, 305
——, Henry I.'s, 305
——, Offa's, 291
——, Reckon-, 305
Dyved, 151, 153
Dyvnaint, 151
Dyvnwal Moelmud, 18

EABE, 235
Eadbald, 96, 182, 183, 197
Eadberht, 211, 269, 270, 285, 300, 311
Eadberht Præn, 300, 311
Eadburh, 230, 342
Eadfrith, 197
Eadmund, 305
Eadric, 310–313, 325
Eadwine, 185–197, 246, 317
————'s Cliff, battle of, 271
Eadwulf, 267
Eafha, 211
Ealdberht, 334
Ealdhelm, 332
Ealdorman, 155
Ealdwulf, 273, 306
Ealhflæd, 210
Ealhfrith, 210, 222, 225
Eallmund, 341
Eanberht, 315
Eanflæd, 191
Eanfrith, 198, 289, **315**
Eanhere, 289, 315
Eanred, 279
Eanwulf, 289
Earconberht, 96, 217, 309, **510**
Earcongote, 310
Eardulf, 311
Eardwulf, 274, 277–279
Early inhabitants, 5–7

East Angles, 142
East Anglia, 304, 330
———————, laws of, 119-122
———————, bishoprics of, 228
———————, Christianity in, 195
East Saxons, 307
——— ———, bishops of, 212
Easter, celebration of, 60, 170, 177, 179, 214-216
Eborius, 63
Ebruin, 222, 229
Ebusa, 148
Ecclesiastics, ignorance of, 248
Ecga, 273
Ecgberht, 241, 256, 266, 309, 342
Ecgferth, 299
Ecgferthesmynster, 275
Ecgfrith, 210, 226, 227, 234, 237, 281
Ecgric, 195
Edelfius, 63
Edinburgh, 197
Education, 247, 264
Eldun, battle of, 271
Eleutherius, 62
Elmet, 154, 189, 314
Elmham, see of, 243
Ely, 142
Emma, wife of Eadbald, 309
Engern, 117, 118
English church, growth of, 213, 214
Eomer, 190
Eoppa, 226
Eorconwald, 247
Eormenbeorh, 310
Eormenburh, 228, 235
Eormengild, 310
Eormenred, 309
Eormeuric, 96
Eorpwald, 195
Episcopal sees, choice of, 242
Episford, battle of, 89
Ercenwine, 141
Eremita, 129
Eric, 96
Erigena, 265

Ermin Street 64
Essex, 141
————, Christianity in, 212
————, conversion of, 181-183
Evesham, British church at, 242
Ewald, 267
Exeter, see of, 244
Eynsham, 164

FAGAN, 61
Farinmail, 164
Fel Theis, 8
Felix, bishop, 195
Fethanleah, 164
Finan, 210
Finnesburh, 98
Folkestone, battle of, 89
Fontenelle, 293
Forthere, 191
Forty, the number, 139
Foss, the, 65
Franks, 58, 126, 145, 146, 166
Fridolin, 231
Friesland, 229
Frisians, 124-126, 267, 272
————, bishop of, 230
————, chiefs of, 160
Frithern, battle of, 164
Frontinus, 36
Fullofaudes, 74
Fursæus, 196

GADES, 1
Gai, 211 note
Galba, 30
Gallus, 231
Gavelkind, 48
Geoffrey of Monmouth, 323
Geraint, 130, 136, 330
German cloisters, 233
———— invasions, 143
Germans, 83
Germany, British ecclesiastics in, 232, 233
————, language of, 109
————, legal institutions of, 110
Germain, St., 79

Gerontius, 77
Gertrude of Nivelles, 232
Gerwold, 293
Geta, 30, 52, 53
Gewissas, 138, 202
Gildas, 90, 129, 169
Gilling, 207-209
Glamorganshire, 152
Glarus, 231
Glasgow, see of, 245
Glass, introduction of, 224
Glastonbury, 60, 131, 242, 332
Gleguising, 152
Gloucester, 138 note, 164, 246
Gnoirangon, 88
Godmundham, 194
Gold, 3
Gortimer, 94
Grain, cultivation of, 15, 64
Grampians, 38
Gratian, 77
Greek letters, 14
Gregory, 146, 171, 173, 179, 253
Gregorian chant, 218
Guilds, origin of, 44
Guilglis, 148
Guitolin, 128
Guthlac, 284
Gwent, 152, 153
Gwynedd, 151, 153
Gyrwas, 142, 314

HADELN, 112
Hadrian, 217, 218, 333
———, rampart of, 53
Hadrian, pope, 241
Hallelujah victory, 79 and note
Hamburg, 273
Harold II., 291
Hartlepool, 247
Hastings, 290, 292
———, battle of, 9
Hatfield, 197 note
Havelok the Dane, 147 and note
Heardberht, 273
Hecanas, 314
Hefenfeld, battle of, 199

Helena, 58, 81
Hemwald, 207
Hengest, 87-95, 100 and notes, 132, 148, 149
Henry of Huntingdon, 90
Heptarchy, 160, 304, 313
Hereford, 290
———, bishop of, 143
———, see of, 244
Herefordshire, 314
Hereric, 189
Hermelind, 327
Herodotus, 1
Hestingas, 290
Hexham, 225, 228, 239, 244
Hiddila, 326
Hilathirn, battle of, 273
Hild, 246
Himilco, 2
Historeth, 70
History, 146
Hlothhære, 281, 310, 312
Holstein, churches in, 249
Holy Island, 200, 244
Homilies, 258
Honorius, 77, 78, 195, 197
Horsa, 87-96, 100
Hospitals, 260
Howel Dha, laws of, 153
Hreutford, 326
Hu, 8
Hu Cadarn, 8
Hwiccas, 143, 164, 314, 315
Hwitern, see of, 244

IBERIAN settlers, 5
——— language, 5, 11
Icelings, 234
Iceni, 18, 31, 34
Ictis, 3
Ida, 149
Idle, the battle of, 188
Idolatry, 183
Ierne, 2
Immigration, early, 9
Immin, 211
Ine, 260, 283, 322, 327, 329 et seq.
———, laws of, 331

INDEX TO VOL. I. 369

Inyr, 322
Iona, 167, 244
Ireland, 237
———, church in, 182
———, immigration from, 70
Irin, 70
Irish, 21
Irmin Street, 64
Isca Silurum, 65
Isle of Wight, 137, 139
Ithamar, 212
Ivor, 334

JAENBERHT, 295
Jarrow, 265, 275
Jaruman, 184
Joseph of Arimathea, 60
Judicial combat, 121
Jugantes, 19
Julius, 63
Justinian, 145
Justus, 176, 181-183
Jutes, 122-124, 139, 160, 314, 345

KATYEUCHLANI, 19
Kent, 15, 88, 122-123, 300, 308, 311, 312, 326, 330
———, conversion of, 174
——— White Horse of, 118
Keynor on Selsea, 132
Kilian, 232
Kimmerians, 8
Kings, 15
——— of Mercia, genealogy of, 143
Kingscliff, 273
Kits Coty house, 94
Knights, 14
Kymry, 8

LAITY, rights of, in church property, 249
Lanark, 155
Lancashire, 154
Language, British, 8, 9
———, Anglo-Saxon, 109
Lathes, 123

Laurentius, 176, 182, 183
Law, Church, 254
Laws, Saxon, 156
———, Roman, 256
Leeds, 154
Legal institutions, 110
Leicester, see of, 244
Lenbury, 161
Leo, 301
Leobgyth, 230
Leofrun, 307
Leofwine, 230
Lever Mawr, 61
Lichfield, 236, 244, 301
Lilla, 191
Lincoln, 67, 142
Lindhard, 175
Lindisfaras, 314
Lindisfarne, 200, 219, 224-228, 238, 242, 244, 269, 275, 277
Lindisse, 194, 281
Lindisware, 142
Lindsev, 142, 194, 244, 314
Litus Saxonicum, 57, 142
Llancarvan, 177
Llandaff, 152, 168, 169, 245
Lloegria, 199
Lloegrians, 128
Llocgrwys, 8
Llongborth, battle of, 136
Llydaw, 8
Llywarch Hên, 153
Lollius, 51
London, 18, 35, 45, 56, 141
———, bishopric of, 213
———, diocese of, 243
Longobards, 126
Lucius, 61
Luel, 19
Lugubalia, 154
Lullus, 272, 340
Lundenwyc, 292
Lupus, 83
Luxeuil, 231
Lynn, 305

MÆATÆ, 21
Mægla, 136

Mægth, 313
Magasætania, 314
Magasætus, 143
Magic, 264
Magnentius, 71
Maidulphesburh, 333
Malmesbury, 230, 333
————, William of, 333
Man, Isle of, 46, 189
Mandubratius, 25
Marcus, 77
Marinus, 262
Marriage service, 257
————, degrees of, 255
Marriages, 158
Martin, St., church of, near Canterbury, 175
Martinus, 71
Martyrs, 63
Maserfield, battle of, 204
Massilia, 4
Massilians, 2
Mathern, 202
Mathraval, 152
Matrimony, rite of, 170
Maximus, 74, 75
Meanwaras, tribe of, 313, 320
Mearcredesburne, 133
Medrawd, 131
Melitus, 176, 181-183
Mercia, 142, 280
————, bishopric of, 212, 228, 244, 295
————, civilization of, 280
————, coinage of, 300
————, laws of, 119, 296
Mercian kings, genealogy of, 288 note
Merlin, 76
Merton, 340
Michael's Mount, St., 3
Midacritus, 2
Middel Engle, 314
Middle Angles, 142
Middlesex, 141, 314
Minias, 244
Mining, 5
Minster, 116

Missionaries, 172, 177, 230, 272
Mitre, first use of, 254
Moll, 278
Mollo, 236
Mona, Isle of, 33, 36, 189
Monasteries, 168, 241, 248
Money, 16
Monmouth, Geoffrey of, 129
Monmouthshire, 152
Mourie, 202
Mull, 326, 327
Music, church, 259

Nanther, Ab. of St. Omer, 278
Narbo, 4
Narbonnese, 2
Natanleod, 136, 137
Navigation, 6
Nazaleod, 136
Nechtansmere, 238, 265
Nectaridus, 74
Nith, Synod of the, 239
North, Saxons in the, 149
———-folc, 142
———-men, landing of, 342
Northumbria, 147
————, conversion of, 200
Norwich, see of, 243, 306
Numa, 330
Numerals, Saxon, 103-106
Nynias, 167

Ochta, 88
Octa, 96, 148
Œuba, 234
Oengus, 337
Oestrymnides, 2
Offa, 241, 260, 287-295, 307, 340
————'s dyke, 291
Onengus, 270
Ordination, 170
Ordovicus, 19, 36
Organs, introduction and use of, 258, 259
Osbald, 273, 276
Osfrith, 197
Oshere, 315
Osred, 267, 274

Osric, 198, 268, 315, 340
Osthryth, 205, 235, 281
Ostorius, 30, 31, 33
Oswald, 198-205, 315, 335
Oswin, 207-211, 214-216, 225, 227, 238, 246
Oswine, 207, 208, 271
Oswulf, 271
Otford, battle of, 290, 311
Oxford, see of, 246

PAGANISM, memorials of, 263
Painting, 16
Palestine, pilgrimages to, 81
Palladius, 82
Parish churches, 248, 249
Parisii, 10, 19,
Parret, 310
Patriarchal customs, 15
Patric, St., 167
Paul, church of St., 66, 181
Paulinus, 35, 176, 190, 193, 194, 197
Paulus, 71, 72
Pcada, 210, 211
Peakland, 314
Pecthelm, 245
Pedrede, 319
Peebles, 155
Peght, 69
Pelagians, expulsion of, 83
Pelagius, 82 *note*
Penda, 196, 197, 204-209, 317
Pendragon, 154
Pengwern, 291
Pentateuch, 258
Peonna, 318
Peronne, 232
Pescœtas, 314
Peter's pence, 260
Peterborough, see of, 246
Petilius, 35
Petrus, 176
Pevensey, 292
Phœnicians, 1. 2
Picts, 51, 68, 69, 74, 78, 167, 226
——' wall, 51
Pilgrimages, 81, 259

Pincanhealh, 277
Plautius, 29, 30
Poetry, 146, 264
Polybius, 3
Pomponia Græcina, 59
Poor, secular provision for, 251
Pope, power of, in England, 234
——, supremacy of, 170
Port, 136
Portsmouth, 136
Powis, king of, 291
Powys, 152
Prasutagus, 34
Procopius, 144
Proper names, orthography of, 93
Prydain, 8
Publius Crassus, 4
Pythias, 2

QUENTAWIC, 294.

RACE, diversity of, 127
Radiger, 144
Rœdwald, 162, 184, 188
Ramesbury, 244
Rapes, 135
Recken-dyke, 305
Reculver, 18
Reged, 148, 149, 154
Relics, 262
Renfrew, 155
Repton, 287
Restitutus, 63
Rhuddlan, battle of, 302
Rhutupiæ, 18
Richborough, 18, 67
Ricole, 181
Rings, 16
Ripon, 222, 224
Riquier, St., 293
Risthamus, 130
Roads, 64
Rochester, see of, 181, 212, 243, 281
Rocking Stones, 11
Roderic the Great, 153
Rodri Malwynog, 334
Roman army in Britain, 42

Roman buildings, 65, 66, 67, 242
—— cities, 43
—— civilization, 150, 155, 157, 165
—— government, 40–43
—— invasion, 21–24
—— language, 67
—— law, 256
—— missionaries, 172
—— officials, 40–42
Romans, withdrawal of, 77
Rome, Angles at, 173
——, influence of, 240, 250
——, Saxon school at, 260–262, 298
Rome-feoh, 260
——-scot, 260, 298
Rond, 147
Rotfrid, 278
Rotherfield, 292
Rowena, 88, 92
Rufinianus, 176
Runes, 102

SACRIFICES, human, 13 *and note*
Sæberht, 182, 317
Sæbriht, 181
Sæmil, 148
Sæward, 307
Salisbury, 244
Samson, 166
Sandwich, 39
Sangrael, 76
Sarum, Old, 139, 244
Saxon civilization, 155
—— modes of reckoning, 99
—— numerals, 103–106
—— writing, 102–103
Saxons, ancestral traditions of, 107 *et seq.*
——, arrival of, 97
——, first mention of, 54
——, homes of the, 111–113
——, invasions of, 132
Scaldings, 275
Scandinavian genealogy, 143, 144
Scapula, 30
Sceaf, 144

Scilly Islands, 1
Scipio, 3
Scotch, 21
Scots, 68, 69, 74, 78
——, learning of the, 231
——, religious foundations of the, 231, 232
Scotus, John, 265
Searobyrig, 139
Seaxneot, worship of, 141
Sebbi (Sebbe), King of East Saxons, 184, 307
Secandun, 286
Seckingen, 231
Secular learning, 240
Segontiaci, 20
Selkirk, 155
Selred, 308
Selsea, 235, 244
Seneca, 34
Service, 155
Services, church, 257
Severus, 41, 52, 53
——, wall of, 53
Severus, Bishop, 83
Sexburh, 246, 306, 318, 320
Sexred, 307
Sherborne, 230, 332
Shireburn, 243
Shrewsbury, 291
Sidnacester, see of, 244
Siga, 273
Sigebald, 308
Sigeberht, 195, 196, 212, 246, 307
—— the Good, 183, 307
—— the Little, 307
Sigebyrht, 338
Sigeheri, 184
Silton, 273
Silures, 19, 31, 32, 152
Silver, 3
Sixhyndesmen, 119
Sleda, 141
Sleswig, kings of, 144
Sodor and Man, 245
Somerton, 336
Soul, immortality of the, 12
——, transmigration of the, 12

INDEX TO VOL. I.   373

South Saxons, 134
South Wales, 152
Spalda, 314
Spalding, 314
St. Andrews, see of, 244
St. Columba, 167
St. David's, see of, 152
St. Denis, fair of, 166
St. Gall, 231
St. Germains, see of, 244
St. Petroc, see of, 244
Stilicho, 76
Strabo, 2
Stratford, 19
Strathcluyd, 154
Streoneshealh, 215
Stuf, 137
Succession, laws of, 282
Suetonius Paulinus, 33
Sumertûn, 336
Superstitions, 264
Surrey, 314
Sussex, 135, 312
Suthfolc, 142
Suthrige, 314
Swælbheard, 310
Swithhelme, 307
Synods, 169, 254

TACITUS, 7
Taliesin, 152, 155, 185
Talorgan mac Fergusa, 269
Tartessus, 1
Tate, 190
Tattooing, 16
Taunton, 334
Tendubr, 269
Testaments, Old and New, versions of, 257
Tewdric, 202, 203
Thames, 140
Thanet, Isle of, 87, 174
Thecla, 230
Theodbald, 184
Theodore, Abp., 217, 218, 223, 236, 281
Theodosius, 73
Theodric, 202

Thetford, see of, 243
Theudebert, 145, 174
Theuderic, 174
Thinglrith, 287
Thomas, Bishop, 212
Thor, worship of, 141
Thunor, 309
Tilbury, 249
Tin, traffic in, 6
Tintern, battle of, 202
———— abbey, 203
Tithes, origin of, 250
Titus, 30
Togodumnus, 30
Tondhere, 207
Tonsure, 170
Torhtmund, 277
Tottman, 232
Traditions, British, 7
———— of East Anglia, 147
Trebellius, 36
Trevoux, battle of, 52
Triads, Welsh, 8, 12
Tribes, 15
Tribute, 155
Trinobantes, 18
Tristan, 76
Trumhere, 213
Trumwine, 245
Tûf, 195
Tunberht, 227
Turpilianus, 35
Tyern, 154
Tynemouth, 274

UFFA, 142
Uffings, 142
————, genealogy of, 308
Uhtred, 315
Ulpius Marcellus, 52
Unnust, 270, 337
Urien, 149, 155
Uther, 136

VALENTIA, 40
Valentinus, 73
Vecta, 45
Vellocatus, 33

Venedotia, 151
Veneti, 21
Venta, 19
Venusius, 33, 36
Veranius, 33
Verulam, 19, 35
Vespasian, 30
Vespasiana, 40
Vettius, 36
Victor, 74
Vinovium, 19
Virgilius, 175, 232
Virus Lupus, 52
Vitalian, 217
Volusenus, C., 21
Vortemir, 88
Vortigern, 86 *note*, 88

WADA, 276, 277
Wales, Christianity in, 168, 177
———, dioceses of, 245
———, language of, 7
———, Romans in, 47
———, South, 151 *note*
———, West, 151
Wandrille, St., 293
Wapentake, 115
Ward, 116
Warfare, method of, 17
Warni, 144, 145
Watling Street, 64
Wearmouth, 220, 225, 275
Wednesday, 263
Wells, see of, 244
Welsh history, 153
——— kind, 151
——— traditions, 322. 323
Wenborough, bishop of, 331
Wergild, 119
Wessex, 316
———, bishops of, 213, 236
———, kings of, 316
West Saxons, 138
Westmere, 154
Westminster Abbey, 66
Westmoreland, 154
Whitby, 247
———, synod of, 215

White Horse of Kent, 118
Whitherne, 244
Wibbandun, battle of, 163
Wick, local termination, 110
Wigferth, 340
Wigheard, 217
Wight, Isle of, 3, 6. 30, 45, 226, 236. 313, 314, 320, 325
Whitburh, 306
Wihtgar, 137, 139
Wihtgaresburh, 137
Wihtgeornesburh, 38
Wihtgils, 148
W htrœd, 310. 330
Wilfrith, 215, 219, 224, 228, 229, 233, 235-240, 246, 254, 326
Wilgis, 247
Willebald, 230
Willebrord, 230, 247, 267
Willehad, 249, 272
Wilsætas, 188, 314
Wiltshire, 314
Wimberht, 296
Wimbledon, 163
Wimborne Abbey, 268
Wincanhealh, battle of, 272
Winchelcomb, 301, 303
Winchester, 139, 213, 243, 319
Wine, 213, 248
Winfrith, 230, 287, 333
Winwæd, the battle of, 210
Wipped, 95
Wippedesfleot, battle of, 95
Wives, community of, 17
Wlencing, 132
Woden, genealogy of sons of, 352
———, worship of, 141
Wodnesbeorh, 283, 331
———————, battle of, 115
Women, esteem for, 247
Wonwaldremere, 274
Woodchester, 66
Worcester, 143. 244
Worcestershire, 314
Worr, 343
Writing, Saxon, 102, 103
Wuffa, 142
Wuffings, 142

Wulfhere, 211, 213, 223, 226, 310, 320
Wulfred, 303
Wunibald, 230
Wuschea, 197

YARMOUTH, 305
Yellow plague, 184, 217 *note*

Yffe, 148, 197
York, 59, 148 *note*, 149, 166, 228, 244
——, basilica at, 224
——, school at, 166
Ythancester, 249
Yule feast, 263
Yvor, 322

END OF VOL. L

www.ingramcontent.com/pod-product-compliance
Lightning Source LLC
Chambersburg PA
CBHW020533300426
44111CB00008B/648